James Glaisher

Solutions of the Cambridge Senate-house problems and riders for

the year 1878

James Glaisher

Solutions of the Cambridge Senate-house problems and riders for the year 1878

ISBN/EAN: 9783337151041

Printed in Europe, USA, Canada, Australia, Japan

Cover: Foto ©ninafisch / pixelio.de

More available books at **www.hansebooks.com**

SOLUTIONS

OF THE

CAMBRIDGE SENATE-HOUSE PROBLEMS AND RIDERS

FOR THE YEAR 1878,

BY

J. W. L. GLAISHER, M.A., F.R.S.,
FELLOW AND ASSISTANT TUTOR OF TRINITY COLLEGE, CAMBRIDGE;
SENIOR MODERATOR.

C. H. PRIOR, M.A.,
FELLOW AND LECTURER OF PEMBROKE COLLEGE, CAMBRIDGE;
JUNIOR MODERATOR.

N. M. FERRERS, M.A., F.R.S.,
FELLOW AND TUTOR OF GONVILLE AND CAIUS COLLEGE, CAMBRIDGE;
SENIOR EXAMINER.

A. G. GREENHILL, M.A.,
FELLOW OF EMMANUEL COLLEGE, CAMBRIDGE; PROFESSOR OF MATHEMATICS TO THE
ADVANCED CLASS OF ROYAL ARTILLERY OFFICERS, WOOLWICH;
JUNIOR EXAMINER.

CHARLES NIVEN, M.A.,
LATE FELLOW OF TRINITY COLLEGE, CAMBRIDGE; PROFESSOR OF MATHEMATICS
AT QUEEN'S COLLEGE, CORK;
ADDITIONAL EXAMINER.

EDITED BY

J. W. L. GLAISHER,
SENIOR MODERATOR.

London:
MACMILLAN AND CO.
1879

[The right of translation is reserved.]

Cambridge:
PRINTED BY C. J. CLAY, M.A.
AT THE UNIVERSITY PRESS.

PREFACE.

THE present volume contains the solutions of the problems and riders set in the Mathematical Tripos Examination for 1878; in several cases where it was thought that useful information could be given, additional remarks on the subject of a question have been added. For example, pp. 162—169 may be regarded as a brief general statement of the method of least squares. Although the Moderators and Examiners are collectively responsible for the questions set in the examination, the solutions here given are due to the proposers of the questions individually and have not been submitted to the other examiners; so that each author is alone responsible for the solutions to which his name is attached. I may also state that although my name appears on the title-page as editor, my duties have been confined to the arrangement of the solutions and their passage through the press, &c.: I have not in any way altered the solutions as written or attempted to secure uniformity even in matters of notation.

It may be convenient to state that the examination occupies nine days, the first four days being separated from the last five days by an interval of ten days. The examination began on Monday, December 31, 1877, and ended on Friday, January 18, 1878. The subjects of examination on the first three days (Monday, December 31, 1877, to Wednesday, January 2, 1878) were the following:—

Euclid. Books I. to VI. Book XI. Props. I. to XXI. Book XII. Props. I., II.

Arithmetic; and the elementary parts of Algebra; namely, the rules for the fundamental operations upon algebraical symbols with their proofs, the solution of simple and quadratic equations, ratio and proportion, arithmetical, geometrical and harmonical progression, permutations and combinations, the binomial theorem and logarithms.

The elementary parts of Plane Trigonometry, so far as to include the solution and properties of triangles.

The elementary parts of Conic Sections, treated geometrically, but not excluding the method of orthogonal projections; curvature.

The elementary parts of Statics; namely, the equilibrium of forces acting in one plane and of parallel forces, the centre of gravity, the mechanical powers, friction.

The elementary parts of Dynamics; namely, uniform, uniformly accelerated, and uniform circular motion, falling bodies and projectiles in vacuo, cycloidal oscillations, collisions, work.

The first, second, and third sections of Newton's Principia; the propositions to be proved by Newton's methods.

The elementary parts of Hydrostatics; namely, the pressure of fluids, specific gravities, floating bodies, density of gases as depending on pressure and temperature, the construction and use of the more simple instruments and machines.

The elementary parts of Optics; namely, the reflexion and refraction of light at plane and spherical surfaces, not including aberrations; the eye; construction and use of the more simple instruments.

The elementary parts of Astronomy; so far as they are necessary for the explanation of the more simple phenomena, without the use of spherical trigonometry; astronomical instruments.

The subjects of examination on the fourth day (Thursday, January 3, 1878) and on the last five days (Monday, January 14,

1878 to Friday, January 18, 1878) are contained in the following schedule of the divisions of the subjects.

First Division.

Algebra.
Trigonometry; Plane and Spherical.
Theory of Equations.
Analytical Geometry; Plane and Solid.
Finite Differences.
Differential and Integral Calculus.

Differential Equations.
Statics.
Hydrostatics.
Dynamics of a Particle.
Dynamics of Rigid Bodies.
Optics.
Spherical Astronomy.

Second Division.

Higher parts of Algebra and of the Theory of Equations.
Higher parts of Finite Differences.
Elliptic Functions.
Higher parts of Analytical Geometry.

Higher parts of Differential Equations.
Calculus of Variations.
Theory of Chances, including combination of observations.

Third Division.

Newton's Principia, Book I., Sections IX. and XI.
Lunar and Planetary Theories.
Higher Parts of Dynamics.

Laplace's Coefficients.
Attractions.
Figure of the Earth.
Precession and Nutation.

Fourth Division.

Hydrodynamics.
Theory of Sound.
Physical Optics.
Waves and Tides.

Vibrations of Strings and Bars.
Theory of Elastic Solids treated as continuous.

Fifth Division.

Expression of arbitrary functions by series or integrals involving sines or cosines.

Heat.
Electricity.
Magnetism.

PREFACE.

The Examination was conducted according to the following schedule.

DAYS.	HOURS.	SUBJECTS.	EXAMINERS.
Monday, Dec. 31.	9 to 12. $1\frac{1}{2}$ to 4.	Euclid and Conics. Arith. Alg. and Plane Trig.	Jun. Mod. and Sen. Exam. Sen. Mod. and Jun. Exam.
Tuesday, Jan. 1.	9 to 12. $1\frac{1}{2}$ to 4.	Statics and Dynamics. Hydrostatics and Optics.	Sen. Mod. and Jun. Exam. Jun. Mod. and Sen. Exam.
Wednes. Jan. 2.	9 to 12. $1\frac{1}{2}$ to 4.	Easy Problems in all the three days' Subjects. Newton and Astronomy.	Sen. and Jun. Moderators. Sen. and Jun. Examiners.
Thursday, Jan. 3.	9 to 12. $1\frac{1}{2}$ to 4.	Easy questions from 1st Div. and from Phys. Sub. in other Divisions.	Jun. and Add. Examiners. Sen. and Add. Examiners.
Monday, Jan. 14.	9 to 12. $1\frac{1}{2}$ to 4.	Nat. Philos. from 1st Div. Pure Math. from 1st Div.	Jun. Mod. and Add. Exam. Sen. Mod. and Jun. Exam.
Tuesday, Jan. 15.	9 to 12. $1\frac{1}{2}$ to 4.	Easy Problems. 1st Division.	Senior Moderator. Sen. and Jun. Examiners.
Wednes. Jan. 16.	9 to 12. $1\frac{1}{2}$ to 4.	Easy Problems. 2nd, 4th, 5th Divisions.	Junior Moderator. Jun. and Add. Examiners.
Thursday, Jan. 17.	9 to 12. $1\frac{1}{2}$ to 4.	2nd, 3rd, 4th Divisions. 2nd, 3rd, 5th Divisions.	Sen. Mod. and Sen. Exam. Sen. and Add. Examiners.
Friday, Jan. 18.	9 to 12. $1\frac{1}{2}$ to 4.	2nd, 3rd, 4th, 5th Divisions. 3rd, 4th, 5th Divisions.	Sen., Jun., and Add. Exam. Jun. Mod. and Add. Exam.

J. W. L. GLAISHER.

TRINITY COLLEGE, CAMBRIDGE,
December 20, 1878.

CONTENTS.

		PAGE
Monday, December 31, 1877,	9 to 12	1
,, ,,	1½ to 4	7
Tuesday, January 1, 1878,	9 to 12	15
,, ,,	1½ to 4	22
Wednesday, January 2, 1878,	9 to 12	29
,, ,,	1½ to 4	47
Thursday, January 3, 1878,	9 to 12	52
,, ,,	1½ to 4	60
Monday, January 14, 1878,	9 to 12	68
,, ,,	1½ to 4	83
Tuesday, January 15, 1878,	9 to 12	93
,, ,,	1½ to 4	112
Wednesday, January 16, 1878,	9 to 12	122
,, ,,	1½ to 4	146
Thursday, January 17, 1878,	9 to 12	160
,, ,,	1½ to 4	185
Friday, January 18, 1878,	9 to 12	200
,, ,,	1½ to 4	220

SOLUTIONS OF SENATE-HOUSE PROBLEMS AND RIDERS,

FOR THE

YEAR ONE THOUSAND EIGHT HUNDRED AND SEVENTY-EIGHT.

MONDAY, *December* 31, 1877. 9 to 12.

Mr PRIOR, Arabic numbers.
Mr FERRERS, Roman numbers.

1. PARALLELOGRAMS on the same base, and between the same parallels, are equal to one another.

In a given triangle it is required to inscribe a parallelogram equal to half the triangle, so that one side is in the same straight line with one side of the triangle and has one extremity at a given point of that side.

Let ABC (fig. 1) be the given triangle; D the given point in BC; and let $BD < DC$.

Bisect AB, AC in E, F. Join EF, ED. Draw FG parallel to ED to meet BC in G. $EDGF$ is the required parallelogram.

Join EC, FB. Then $\triangle AEF = \triangle BEF$, these being on equal bases; similarly $\triangle AFE = \triangle CFE$; therefore $\triangle BEF = \triangle CFE$; therefore EF, BC are parallel; therefore, by construction, $EDGF$ is a parallelogram, and

$$= 2 \triangle EBF = \triangle ABF = \tfrac{1}{2} \triangle ABC.$$

2. If a straight line be bisected, and produced to any point, the square on the whole line thus produced, and the square on the part of it produced, are together double of the square on half the line bisected and of the square on the line made up of the half and the part produced.

If a straight line AB be bisected in C and produced to D so that the square on AD is three times the square on CD, and if CB be bisected in E, shew that the square on ED is three times the square on EB.

We have, by the proposition,

sq. on AD + sq. on BD = 2 sq. on AC + 2 sq. on CD;

and by hypothesis,   3 sq. on CD = sq. on AD.

S.-H. P.

Adding these equals to the above equals, and then taking from each sum the sq. on $AD + 2$ sq. on CD, we have

$$\text{sq. on } CD + \text{sq. on } BD = 2 \text{ sq. on } AC$$
$$= 2 \text{ sq. on } CB = 8 \text{ sq. on } CE.$$

But by the proposition,

$$\text{sq. on } CD + \text{sq. on } BD = 2 \text{ sq. on } CE + 2 \text{ sq. on } ED,$$

therefore 2 sq. on $CE + 2$ sq. on $ED = 8$ sq. on CE,
therefore 2 sq. on $ED = 6$ sq. on CE,
therefore sq. on $ED = 3$ sq. on $CE = 3$ sq. on EB.

3. *The opposite angles of any quadrilateral figure inscribed in a circle are together equal to two right angles.*

If a quadrilateral be inscribed in a circle, and the middle points of the arcs subtended by its sides be joined to make another quadrilateral, and so on: shew that these quadrilaterals tend to become squares.

Let $A_1B_1C_1D_1$, $A_2B_2C_2D_2$, $A_3B_3C_3D_3$ be three successive quadrilaterals, made as the question directs, the order of points being given by

$$A_1A_2B_1B_2\ldots\ldots \text{ and } A_2A_3B_2B_3\ldots$$

Then $2 \text{ arc } A_2B_2 = \text{arc } A_1B_1 + \text{arc } B_1C_1,$
$2 \text{ arc } B_2C_2 = \text{arc } B_1C_1 + \text{arc } C_1D_1,$
$\ldots\ldots\ldots\ldots = \ldots\ldots\ldots\ldots\ldots\ldots$

Let A_1B_1 be the greatest; B_1C_1 or C_1D_1 the least of the arcs A_1B_1, B_1C_1, C_1D_1, D_1A_1. Then the above equalities shew that the arc A_2B_2 is less than the greatest and greater than the least of these arcs, and that the same is true for the arcs B_2C_2, C_2D_2, D_2A_2. Hence $A_2B_2C_2D_2$ has no side so great and no side so small as the greatest and least sides of $A_1B_1C_1D_1$ respectively: *i.e.* $A_2B_2C_2D_2$ is more nearly equilateral than $A_1B_1C_1D_1$: and so on. Hence the quadrilaterals tend to become rhombi, but the only rhombus that can be inscribed in a circle is a square, therefore the quadrilaterals tend to become squares.

Or the proof may run thus:

We have

$$2 \text{ arc } A_2B_2 = \text{arc } A_1B_1 + \text{arc } B_1C_1,$$
$$2 \text{ arc } B_2C_2 = \text{arc } B_1C_1 + \text{arc } C_1D_1;$$

therefore $4 \text{ arc } A_2B_2 = 2 \text{ arc } A_1B_1 + 2 \text{ arc } B_1C_1$
$= \text{arc } A_1B_1 + 2 \text{ arc } B_1C_1 + \text{arc } C_1D_1:$

also $2 \text{ arc } D_1A_1 + 2 \text{ arc } B_1C_1 = 2 \text{ arc } A_1B_1 + 2 \text{ arc } C_1D_1:$

therefore, adding these equalities, and taking from each side $2 \text{ arc } B_1C_1$, we have

$$4 \text{ arc } A_2B_2 + 2 \text{ arc } D_1A_1 = 3 \text{ arc } A_1B_1 + 3 \text{ arc } C_1D_1.$$

Similarly $4 \text{ arc } B_2C_2 + 2 \text{ arc } A_1B_1 = 3 \text{ arc } B_1C_1 + 3 \text{ arc } D_1A_1.$

Now $\text{arc } A_1B_1 + \text{arc } D_1A_1 = \text{arc } B_1C_1 + \text{arc } D_1A_1;$

therefore $4 \text{ arc } A_2B_2 + 2 \text{ arc } C_1D_1 = 4 \text{ arc } B_2C_2 + 2 \text{ arc } A_1B_1;$

therefore the difference of the *adjacent* arcs A_1B_1, D_1A_1 = twice the difference of the *adjacent* arcs A_2B_2, B_2C_2;

therefore the quadrilaterals tend to become rhombi; therefore as before, they tend to become squares.

iv. Inscribe a circle in a given triangle.

Prove that four circles may be described, touching the three sides of a triangle, and that the square on the distance between the centres of any two, together with the square on the distance between the centres of the other two, is equal to the square on the diameter of the circle passing through the centres of any three.

It is known that the line joining any two of the centres of these circles is perpendicular to the line joining the other two. Let then O, P, Q, R (fig. 2) be the four centres, and through Q, R draw QE, RE respectively parallel to OR, OQ. Then the angle ERQ is equal to the angle RQO, and therefore is the complement of the angle PRQ. Hence PRE is a right angle. Similarly PQE is a right angle. Therefore the points P, Q, R, E lie on the circumference of a circle, of which PE is a diameter. Again $OREQ$ is a parallelogram, and therefore ER is equal to OQ. Hence the square on OQ and the square on RP are together equal to the square on PE, the diameter of the circle PQR.

v. If the sides of two triangles, about each of their angles, be proportionals, the triangles shall be equiangular to one another, and shall have those angles equal which are opposite to the homologous sides.

The side BC of a triangle ABC is produced to D, so that the triangles ABD, ACD are similar. Prove that AD touches the circle described about the triangle ABC.

Since the triangles ABD, ACD (fig. 3) are similar to one another, and the angle at D is common to both, it follows that the angles ACD, BAD must be equal to one another, and the angles DAC, ABC equal to one another. Hence AD is to CD as BD is to AD, and therefore the square on DA is equal to the rectangle contained by DB, DC. Hence DA touches the circle described about the triangle ABC.

vi. If two straight lines be cut by parallel planes, they shall be cut in the same ratio.

If an equifacial tetrahedron be cut by a plane parallel to two edges which do not meet, the perimeter of the parallelogram in which it is cut shall be double of either edge of the tetrahedron to which it is parallel.

Each edge of an equifacial tetrahedron is equal to the edge opposite to it.

Let A, B, C, D (fig. 4) be the four angular points of the given tetrahedron. Draw a plane, parallel to the edges AB and CD, meeting the edges AC, AD, BC, BD in E, F, G, H respectively. Then, $EFGH$ will be a parallelogram. And EF is to CD as AE is to AC. Also EH is to AB as CE is to AC. Therefore EF and EH together are equal to half AB and CD together. Or the perimeter of the parallelogram $EFGH$ must be equal to the sum of the edges AB and CD.

vii. In the parabola, prove that the distance between the foot of the ordinate of any point and the foot of the normal at that point is equal to half the latus-rectum.

Inscribe a circle in the segment of a parabola cut off by a double ordinate.

Let QV (fig. 5) be half the bounding ordinate of the parabola. From the axis cut off VN equal to QV, draw NP at right angles to the axis, and draw PG the normal at P; G shall be the centre of the required circle.

For
$$PN^2 = 4AS \cdot AN$$
$$= 4AS \cdot AV - 4AS \cdot NV$$
$$= 4AS \cdot AV - 4AS \cdot QV$$
$$= QV^2 - 4AS \cdot QV$$
$$= QV^2 - 2NG \cdot QV;$$

therefore
$$PG^2 = QV^2 - 2NG \cdot QV + NG^2$$
$$= NV^2 - 2NG \cdot NV + NG^2$$
$$= GV^2;$$

therefore $PG = GV$;

and therefore G is the centre of the required circle.

viii. Prove that the tangent, at any point of an ellipse, makes equal angles with the focal distances of that point.

From the foci of an ellipse, perpendiculars are let fall to the tangent at any given point of the curve. With the feet of these perpendiculars as foci, an ellipse is described touching the axis major of the given ellipse. Prove that the point, in which it touches the axis major, will be the foot of the ordinate of the given point, and that the ellipse described will be similar to the given ellipse.

Let SY, HZ (fig. 6) be the perpendiculars from the foci on the tangent. Draw PN perpendicular to the axis major, and join SP, HP, YN, ZN. Then, since SYP and SNP are each right angles, a circle can be described about the quadrilateral $SNPY$, and therefore the angles SNY, SPY are equal to one another. Similarly the angles HNZ, HPZ are equal to one another. Therefore the angles SNY, HNZ are equal to one another, and an ellipse described with Y, Z as foci, and passing through N, will touch SH at N.

Again, SP is the diameter of a circle in which NY subtends the angle NPY, and HP is the diameter of a circle in which NZ subtends the angle NPZ, and these angles are supplementary. Hence NY is to NZ as SP is to HP. And if through Z we draw ZV parallel to SH, meeting SY in V, we see that VZ is the diameter of a circle, in which YZ subtends the angle YVZ, which is supplementary to NPY. Therefore SH is to YZ as SP is to YN, *i.e.* as $SP + HP$ is to $YN + ZN$. Therefore the distance between the foci of the new ellipse is to its axis major as the distance between the foci of the old ellipse is to its axis major; or the ellipses are similar.

ix. Define conjugate diameters of an ellipse; and prove that the sum of the squares on any two conjugate diameters is constant.

A system of parallelograms is inscribed in an ellipse whose sides are parallel to the equi-conjugate diameters; prove that the sum of the squares on the sides is constant.

CP, CD (fig. 7), being the equal conjugate diameters, we have, with the usual notation,

$$PV \cdot VG : QV^2 :: CP^2 : CD^2;$$

therefore $\qquad PV \cdot VG = QV^2$.

But $\qquad PV \cdot VG = CP^2 - CV^2$ (Euc. II. 5),

$$CV^2 + QV^2 = CP^2,$$

or $\qquad QQ'^2 + Qq^2 = 4CP^2;$

therefore the sum of the squares on the sides of the parallelogram is constant.

10. The tangents drawn from any point to a conic subtend equal angles at the focus.

If P be any point of an hyperbola whose foci are S and H, and if the tangent at P meet an asymptote in T, the angle between that asymptote and HP is double the angle STP.

Let HP (fig. 8) meet the asymptote in K. Join SP, and from S draw SL parallel to the asymptote.

Then TP and the asymptote are the tangents from T, and $T\hat{S}L$ is the angle subtended at the focus by the asymptote;

therefore $\qquad P\hat{S}T = T\hat{S}L = S\hat{T}K = S\hat{T}P + K\hat{T}P;$

therefore $\qquad P\hat{S}T + S\hat{T}P = 2S\hat{T}P + K\hat{T}P,$

and $\qquad T\hat{P}S = T\hat{P}K;$

therefore adding, and reversing sides, we have

$$2S\hat{T}P + K\hat{T}P + T\hat{P}K = P\hat{S}T + S\hat{T}P + T\hat{P}S$$
$$= 2 \text{ right angles}$$
$$= P\hat{K}T + K\hat{T}P + T\hat{P}K;$$

therefore $\qquad 2S\hat{T}P = P\hat{K}T.$

11. If two chords of a rectangular hyperbola be at right angles, each of their four extremities is the orthocentre of the triangle formed by the other three.

If four such points and the tangent at one of them be given, find the centre of the hyperbola.

Let A, B, C, P (fig. 9) be four such points, each being the orthocentre of the triangle formed by the other three, and let the tangent at P be given.

(1) The centre of any rectangular hyperbola passing through A, B, C lies on the nine-point circle of $\triangle ABC$. (Besant's *Conics*, Art. 139.)

(2) Let $T'PT$ be the given tangent. Join AP, and produce it to meet BC in L. From L draw LQ parallel to $T'PT$ to meet the nine-point circle in Q. Join QP, and produce it to meet the nine-point circle in O; then O is the required centre.

For, let AP be bisected in V; then V is on the nine-point circle. Join VO. Then $V\hat{O}P = V\hat{L}Q = V\hat{P}T$; therefore (Besant's *Conics*, Art. 136) VO is the diameter conjugate to AP; therefore O is the centre of the hyperbola.

12. The section of a cone by a plane, which is not perpendicular to the axis and does not pass through the vertex, is either an ellipse, a parabola, or an hyperbola.

In a given plane are drawn a series of confocal conics, upon which stand cones with their vertical angles right angles. Shew that the locus of their vertices is given by the intersection of an hyperbola, whose vertices are the foci of the conics, and a circle concentric with the hyperbola and passing through its foci.

Let the given plane intersect at right angles the plane of the paper (fig. 10) in the line $A'HSA$, and let S, H be the given foci. Let V be the vertex of the cone which cuts the plane in the conic whose foci are S, H, and vertices A, A'. Then the circle inscribed in the triangle VAA' will touch AA' at S or H. Let it touch it at S, and let it touch VA, VA' at L, L'.

Then $A'V - AV = A'L' - AL = A'S - AS =$ constant. Hence V is a point on the hyperbola whose foci are A, A' and vertices S, H.

Also, by hypothesis, $A\hat{V}A'$ is a right angle; therefore V lies on the circle of which AA' is a diameter, and this is a circle concentric with the hyperbola, and passing through its foci.

PROBLEMS AND RIDERS.

Monday, *December* 31, 1877. 1½ to 4.

Mr Glaisher, Arabic numbers.
Mr Greenhill, Roman numbers.

1. Obtain the value of π to six places of decimals from the series

$$\pi = \tfrac{24}{5}\left\{1 + \tfrac{2}{3}(\tfrac{1}{50}) + \tfrac{2\cdot 4}{3\cdot 5}(\tfrac{1}{50})^2 + \tfrac{2\cdot 4\cdot 6}{3\cdot 5\cdot 7}(\tfrac{1}{50})^3 + \&c.\right\}$$
$$+ \tfrac{948}{3125}\left\{1 + \tfrac{2}{3}(\tfrac{9}{6250}) + \tfrac{2\cdot 4}{3\cdot 5}(\tfrac{9}{6250})^2 + \tfrac{2\cdot 4\cdot 6}{3\cdot 5\cdot 7}(\tfrac{9}{6250})^3 + \&c.\right\}.$$

If $\dfrac{p}{n}$ and $\dfrac{n-p}{n}$ be converted into circulating decimals, find the relation between the figures in their periods, n being supposed to be prime to 10 and p less than n.

(i) The series are

$$\pi = \tfrac{28}{10}\left\{1 + \tfrac{2}{3}(\tfrac{2}{100}) + \tfrac{2\cdot 4}{3\cdot 5}(\tfrac{2}{100})^2 + \tfrac{2\cdot 4\cdot 6}{3\cdot 5\cdot 7}(\tfrac{2}{100})^3 + \&c.\right\}$$
$$+ \tfrac{30336}{100000}\left\{1 + \tfrac{2}{3}(\tfrac{144}{100000}) + \tfrac{2\cdot 4}{3\cdot 5}(\tfrac{144}{100000})^2 + \&c.\right\}.$$

The work is as follows, every figure that has to be written being printed,

```
   4/300 = 0·013333 33           1
                 16             0·013 333 33
           ───────────              213 33
           213 333 3                  3 66
                 12             ─────────────
           ───────────                    7
         7│255 999             1·013 550 39
           36 57                         28
                               ─────────────
                                8 108 403 12
                               20 271 007  8
                               ─────────────
              First series =   2·8 379 410 92

                                     1
   0·00144      1152            0·000 960 00
         2        96                   1 11
   3│0·00288  ──────            ─────────────
     0·00096   6912.            1·000 961 11
              10368                 30 336
             ───────            ─────────────
             110592             6 005 766 66
                               30 028 833 3
                              300 288 333
                               30 028 833 3
                               ─────────────
                               30 365 156 2
```

$$\begin{aligned}\text{First series} &= 2\cdot 837\ 941\ 092\\ \text{Second ,,} &= 0\cdot 303\ 651\ 562\\ \pi &= \overline{3\cdot 141\ 592\ 654}\end{aligned}$$

Thus, value of π to six places is $3\cdot 141\ 593$. The true value is $3\cdot 141\ 592\ 653\ 589\ldots$, so that the above calculation is correct to the last figure.

(ii) Let
$$\frac{p}{n} = 0.\alpha\beta\gamma\ldots\xi, \quad \frac{n-p}{n} = 0.\alpha'\beta'\gamma'\ldots\xi',$$

then
$$\frac{p}{n} = \frac{\alpha\beta\gamma\ldots\xi}{999\ldots 9}, \quad \frac{n-p}{n} = \frac{\alpha'\beta'\gamma'\ldots\xi'}{999\ldots 9},$$

and, since the sum of the fractions is equal to unity,

$$\alpha\beta\gamma\ldots\xi + \alpha'\beta'\gamma'\ldots\xi' = 999\ldots 9$$

so that, the number of figures in each period being the same,

$$\alpha + \alpha' = \beta + \beta' = \ldots = \xi + \xi' = 9.$$

[The principal rules relating to the conversion of vulgar fractions into decimals are as follows:—Let $\frac{M}{N}$ be a proper fraction in its lowest terms, then (1) if N is of the form $2^m 5^n$, the decimal terminates after r figures from the decimal point, r being the greater of the numbers m and n; (2) if N be prime to 10 the decimal circulates from the figure next to the decimal point (*i.e.* is a pure circulate) and the number of figures in the period is equal either to $\phi(N)$, or to a submultiple of $\phi(N)$, $\phi(N)$ denoting the number of numbers less than N and prime to it; (3) if $N = 2^m 5^n R$, R being prime to 10, there will be r figures between the decimal point and the first figure of the period, r being the greater of the numbers m and n, and the number of figures in the period will be equal to $\phi(R)$, or to a submultiple of $\phi(R)$. It is to be noted that if N be a prime, then $\phi(N) = N - 1$.

If the period of $\frac{1}{N}$ (N prime to 10) contains n figures, then the period of $\frac{M}{N}$ (M any number prime to N) also contains n figures, and the total number of *different* periods obtained by giving all admissible values to M, is $\frac{\phi(N)}{n}$. Thus if the period of $\frac{1}{N}$ contains $N - 1$ figures (in which case N must be a prime, though the converse is not true, viz. if N be a prime the number of figures in the period is either $N - 1$ or a submultiple of $N - 1$), then there is only one distinct period. For example $\frac{1}{7} = \cdot 14285\dot{7}$, $\frac{2}{7} = \cdot 28571\dot{4}$, $\frac{3}{7} = \cdot 42857\dot{1}$, $\frac{4}{7} = \cdot 57142\dot{8}$, $\frac{5}{7} = \cdot 71428\dot{5}$, $\frac{6}{7} = \cdot 85714\dot{2}$, and the periods all contain the same figures in the same order, though beginning with a different figure. Also when the period contains $N - 1$ figures, the second half of the period is *complementary to* 9 to the first half (*i.e.* the two portions when added together $= 999\ldots 9$: take for example the period of $\frac{1}{7}$, here $1 + 8 = 9$, $4 + 5 = 9$, $2 + 7 = 9$).

If $\frac{1}{N}$ has a period of n figures, $\frac{1}{P}$ of p figures, $\frac{1}{Q}$ of q figures…, and if N, P, Q…be primes, then $\frac{1}{NPQ…}$ has a period of a figures, a being the least common multiple of n, p, q…. But the demonstration does not apply to the case of a power of a prime. *Generally* however, $\frac{1}{N^2}$ has a period of nN figures, $\frac{1}{N^3}$ of nN^2 figures, &c., but for an obvious reason this is not true when $N=3$ (a factor of $10-1$), and it is also not true of the number 487, for $\frac{1}{487}$ has a period of 486 figures, and $\frac{1}{487^2}$ has also a period of 486 figures. It is, however, true for all other primes less than 1000*, so that if N, P, Q… be any primes, each less than 1000 (3 and 487 excepted), the period of $\frac{1}{N^a.P^\beta.Q^\gamma…}$ contains a figures, where a is the least common multiple of nN^{a-1}, $pP^{\beta-1}$, $qQ^{\gamma-1}$….]

2. Prove that, if $\phi(x)$ be a rational and integral function of x which vanishes when x is put equal to a, then $x-a$ is a factor of $\phi(x)$.

Shew that
$$b^2(a-b)(c-b)\{(a-b)^2+(c-b)^2\}-ab^3c(a^2+c^2)+b^5(a-b+c)$$
is a complete cube.

By actual development the expression is found to be equal to $\{b(-a+b-c)\}^3$.

3. Explain to what extent the equation $a^m . a^n = a^{m+n}$ admits of being proved. Obtain the values of a^0 and $a^{-\frac{1}{2}}$.

If
$$\phi(x) = \frac{a^x - a^{-x}}{a^x + a^{-x}}, \quad F(x) = \frac{2}{a^x + a^{-x}},$$
shew that
$$\phi(x+y) = \frac{\phi(x)+\phi(y)}{1+\phi(x)\phi(y)},$$
$$F(x+y) = \frac{F(x)F(y)}{1+\phi(x)\phi(y)}.$$

The equations are at once verified by substituting the values of $\phi(x)$, $\phi(y)$, $F(x)$, $F(y)$, in the right-hand members, and performing some slight reductions.

4. Find the sum of the cubes of the first n natural numbers; and shew that every cube is the difference of two squares, such

---

* Desmarest, *Théorie des Nombres* (Paris, 1852), p. 295.

that if the cube contains an uneven factor a^3, each of the squares is divisible by a^3.

Find the sum of the cubes of n consecutive terms of an arithmetical progression; and shew that it is divisible by the sum of the corresponding n terms of the arithmetical progression.

(i) Since $1^3 + 2^3 \ldots + n^3 = \{\tfrac{1}{2}n(n+1)\}^2$ it follows that
$$n^3 = \{\tfrac{1}{2}n(n+1)\}^2 - \{\tfrac{1}{2}n(n-1)\}^2.$$

Let $n = ab$, we have to shew that $\tfrac{1}{2}b(n+1)$ and $\tfrac{1}{2}b(n-1)$ are integers. This is evident, for (1°) suppose n even, then since a is uneven, b is even and $\tfrac{1}{2}b$ is an integer; (2°) suppose n uneven, then $\tfrac{1}{2}(n \pm 1)$ is an integer.

(ii) $a^3 + (a+b)^3 \ldots + \{a+(n-1)b\}^3$
$= na^3 + 3a^2 b \cdot \tfrac{1}{2}n(n-1) + 3ab^2 \cdot \tfrac{1}{6}\{(n-1)n(2n-1)\} + b^3 \cdot \{\tfrac{1}{2}n(n-1)\}^2$
$= \tfrac{1}{2}n\{2a+(n-1)b\}\{a^2 + (n-1)ab + \tfrac{1}{2}n(n-1)b^2\}$.

5. Solve the equations:
$$x^2 - (2a - b - c)x + a^2 + b^2 + c^2 - bc - ca - ab = 0;$$
$$\left.\begin{array}{l} x^2 + 2xy - y^2 = ax + by \\ x^2 - 2xy - y^2 = bx - ay \end{array}\right\}.$$

If $x^2 = px + q$, shew that
$$x^n = \frac{\alpha^n - \beta^n}{\alpha - \beta} x + q \frac{\alpha^{n-1} - \beta^{n-1}}{\alpha - \beta},$$
where $\alpha + \beta = p$, $\alpha\beta = -q$.

If $x^3 = px^2 + qx + r$, express x^n in the form $Ax^2 + Bx + C$.

(i) The roots of the equation are
$$a + b\omega + c\omega^2, \quad a + b\omega^2 + c\omega,$$
where ω is an imaginary cube root of unity.

(ii) Adding and subtracting the equations, we have
$$2(x^2 - y^2) = (a+b)x + (b-a)y, \quad 4xy = (a-b)x + (a+b)y,$$
which may be written
$$\{x - \tfrac{1}{4}(a+b)\}^2 - \{y - \tfrac{1}{4}(a-b)\}^2 = \tfrac{1}{4} ab,$$
$$\{x - \tfrac{1}{4}(a+b)\}\{y - \tfrac{1}{4}(a-b)\} = \tfrac{1}{16}(a^2 - b^2);$$
or, putting $x - \tfrac{1}{4}(a+b) = u$, $y - \tfrac{1}{4}(a-b) = v$, these are $u^2 - v^2 = \tfrac{1}{4}ab$, $uv = \tfrac{1}{16}(a^2 - b^2)$, which give on solution

$$\left.\begin{array}{l} u = -\tfrac{1}{4}(a+b) \\ v = -\tfrac{1}{4}(a-b) \end{array}\right\}, \quad \left.\begin{array}{l} u = \tfrac{1}{4}(a+b) \\ v = \tfrac{1}{4}(a-b) \end{array}\right\}, \quad \left.\begin{array}{l} u = \tfrac{1}{4}i(a-b) \\ v = -\tfrac{1}{4}i(a+b) \end{array}\right\}, \quad \left.\begin{array}{l} u = -\tfrac{1}{4}i(a-b) \\ v = \tfrac{1}{4}i(a+b) \end{array}\right\},$$

(where $i^2 = -1$, as usual), leading to

$$\left.\begin{array}{l}x=0\\y=0\end{array}\right\},\ \left.\begin{array}{l}x=\tfrac{1}{2}(a+b)\\y=\tfrac{1}{2}(a-b)\end{array}\right\},\ \left.\begin{array}{l}x=\tfrac{1}{4}\{(1+i)a+(1-i)b\}\\y=\tfrac{1}{4}\{(1-i)a-(1+i)b\}\end{array}\right\},$$

$$\left.\begin{array}{l}x=\tfrac{1}{4}\{(1-i)a+(1+i)b\}\\y=\tfrac{1}{4}\{(1+i)a-(1-i)b\}\end{array}\right\}.$$

(iii) Let $x^n = Ax + B$, then we have

$$x^n - Ax - B = 0,\ a^n - A\alpha - B = 0,\ \beta^n - A\beta - B = 0,$$

whence, eliminating A and B,

$$x^n(\alpha - \beta) - x(a^n - \beta^n) + \alpha\beta(a^{n-1} - \beta^{n-1}) = 0,$$

which gives at once the required equation.

(iv) The result is obtained by the elimination of A, B, C from the equations

$$x^n = Ax^2 + Bx + C,\ a^n = A\alpha^2 + B\alpha + C,\ \beta^n = A\beta^2 + B\beta + C,\ \gamma^n = A\gamma^2 + B\gamma + C,$$

where α, β, γ are the roots of $x^3 - px^2 - qx - r = 0$. It is of course best expressed as a determinant.

6. Prove that the logarithm of the product of any number of quantities is equal to the sum of the logarithms of the quantities.

Given that $a^2 + b^2 = 1$ and that

$\log 2 = 0\cdot3010300,\ \log(1+a) = 0\cdot1928998,\ \log(1+b) = 0\cdot2622226$,

find $\log(1 + a + b)$.

Since $a^2 + b^2 = 1$, we have,

$$1 + a + b = \sqrt{2(1+a)(1+b)},$$

as is evident by squaring both sides of the equation. Thus

$\log(1 + a + b) = \tfrac{1}{2} \cdot \{0\cdot3010300 + 0\cdot1928998 + 0\cdot2622226\}$
$\qquad\qquad\qquad = 0\cdot3780762$.

[The numbers in the question correspond to $a = \sin 34°$.]

vii. Define the Trigonometrical Ratios of an angle so as to be true for all magnitudes of the angle; and make a table shewing the values of the trigonometrical ratios in terms of any one of them.

Prove that the equation $\tan x = kx$ has an infinite number of real roots.

As x increases from $n\pi - \tfrac{1}{2}\pi$ to $n\pi + \tfrac{1}{2}\pi$, $\tan x$ increases through all real values from $-\infty$ to ∞, and therefore passes through a root of the equation $\tan x = kx$; and to every positive root there is a corresponding negative root.

viii. Prove geometrically

(i) $\sin A + \sin B = 2 \sin \tfrac{1}{2}(A+B) \cos \tfrac{1}{2}(A-B)$,

(ii) $\cos A - \cos B = 2 \sin \tfrac{1}{2}(B+A) \sin \tfrac{1}{2}(B-A)$;

and explain how such formulæ are shewn to be true universally for all magnitudes of the angles A and B.

If
$$\frac{\cos(\alpha+\beta+\theta)}{\sin(\alpha+\beta)\cos^2\gamma} = \frac{\cos(\gamma+\alpha+\theta)}{\sin(\gamma+\alpha)\cos^2\beta},$$
and β and γ are unequal, prove that each member will be equal to
$$\frac{\cos(\beta+\gamma+\theta)}{\sin(\beta+\gamma)\cos^2\alpha},$$
and that
$$\cot\theta = \frac{\sin(\beta+\gamma)\sin(\gamma+\alpha)\sin(\alpha+\beta)}{\cos(\beta+\gamma)\cos(\gamma+\alpha)\cos(\alpha+\beta)+\sin^2(\alpha+\beta+\gamma)}.$$

From the given equation
$$\cot\theta = \frac{\sin(\alpha+\beta)\sin(\gamma+\alpha)\cos^2\beta - \sin(\gamma+\alpha)\sin(\alpha+\beta)\cos^2\gamma}{\cos(\alpha+\beta)\sin(\gamma+\alpha)\cos^2\beta - \cos(\gamma+\alpha)\sin(\alpha+\beta)\cos^2\gamma},$$
of which the numerator
$$= \sin(\beta+\gamma)\sin(\gamma+\alpha)\sin(\alpha+\beta)\sin(\gamma-\beta),$$
and the denominator
$$= \tfrac{1}{2}\{\cos(\alpha+\beta)\sin(\gamma+\alpha) - \cos(\gamma+\alpha)\sin(\alpha+\beta)$$
$$+ \cos(\alpha+\beta)\sin(\gamma+\alpha)\cos 2\beta - \cos(\gamma+\alpha)\sin(\alpha+\beta)\cos 2\beta\}$$
$$= \tfrac{1}{4}\{2\sin(\gamma-\beta) + \sin(2\alpha+\beta+\gamma)(\cos 2\beta - 2\cos 2\gamma)$$
$$+ \sin(\gamma-\beta)(\cos 2\beta + \cos 2\gamma)\} = \tfrac{1}{4}\sin(\gamma-\beta)\{2 + \cos 2\alpha$$
$$+ \cos 2\beta + \cos 2\gamma - \cos(2\alpha+2\beta+2\gamma)\}$$
$$= \tfrac{1}{4}\sin(\gamma-\beta)\{4\sin^2(\alpha+\beta+\gamma) + \cos 2\alpha + \cos 2\beta + \cos 2\gamma$$
$$+ \cos(2\alpha+2\beta+2\gamma)\} = \sin(\gamma-\beta)\cdot\{\sin^2(\alpha+\beta+\gamma)$$
$$+ \cos(\alpha+\beta)\cos(\beta+\gamma)\cos(\gamma+\alpha)\}.$$

Throwing out the factor $\sin(\gamma-\beta)$, which is common to the numerator and denominator, this becomes the expression for $\cot\theta$ in the question, and since it involves α, β, γ symmetrically it follows that each side of the given equation also
$$= \frac{\cos(\beta+\gamma+\theta)}{\sin(\beta+\gamma)\cos^2\alpha}.$$

ix. Find an expression for all angles having a given sine.

If $A+B+C+D = 2\pi$, then
$$\cos\tfrac{1}{2}A\cos\tfrac{1}{2}D\sin\tfrac{1}{2}B\sin\tfrac{1}{2}C - \cos\tfrac{1}{2}B\cos\tfrac{1}{2}C\sin\tfrac{1}{2}A\sin\tfrac{1}{2}D$$
$$= \sin\tfrac{1}{2}(A+B)\sin\tfrac{1}{2}(A+C)\cos\tfrac{1}{2}(A+D).$$

$$\cos\tfrac{1}{2}A\cos\tfrac{1}{2}D\sin\tfrac{1}{2}B\sin\tfrac{1}{2}C - \cos\tfrac{1}{2}B\cos\tfrac{1}{2}C\sin\tfrac{1}{2}A\sin\tfrac{1}{2}D$$
$$= \tfrac{1}{4}\{\cos\tfrac{1}{2}(A-D)+\cos\tfrac{1}{2}(A+D)\}\{\cos\tfrac{1}{2}(B-C)-\cos\tfrac{1}{2}(B+C)\}$$
$$- \tfrac{1}{4}\{\cos\tfrac{1}{2}(A-D)-\cos\tfrac{1}{2}(A+D)\}\{\cos\tfrac{1}{2}(B-C)+\cos\tfrac{1}{2}(B+C)\}$$
$$= \tfrac{1}{2}\cos\tfrac{1}{2}(A+D)\cos\tfrac{1}{2}(B-C) - \tfrac{1}{2}\cos\tfrac{1}{2}(A-D)\cos\tfrac{1}{2}(B+C)$$
$$= \tfrac{1}{2}\{\cos\tfrac{1}{2}(B-C)+\cos\tfrac{1}{2}(A-D)\}\cos\tfrac{1}{2}(A+D)$$
$$= \cos\tfrac{1}{4}(A+B-C-D)\cos\tfrac{1}{4}(A-B+C-D)\cos\tfrac{1}{2}(A+D)$$
$$\sin\tfrac{1}{2}(A+B)\sin\tfrac{1}{2}(A+C)\cos\tfrac{1}{2}(A+D).$$

x. Prove that, in any triangle, $a^2 = b^2 + c^2 - 2bc \cos A$; and hence prove that

$$\frac{a}{\sin A} = \frac{b}{\sin B} = \frac{c}{\sin C}.$$

In a triangle ABC, $AB = AC + \frac{1}{2}BC$, and BC is divided in O so that $BO : OC :: 1 : 3$; prove that the angle ACO is twice the angle AOC.

If h is the perpendicular drawn from the angle A on the side BC, and $c = b + \frac{1}{2}a$, $OC = \frac{3}{4}a$,

$\sin 2AOC = 2 \sin AOC \cos AOC$

$= 2 \dfrac{h}{OA} \dfrac{AO^2 + OC^2 - AC^2}{2AO \cdot OC}$

$= h \dfrac{OC^2 + AC^2 - 2OC \cdot AC \cdot \cos C + OC^2 - AC^2}{(OC^2 + AC^2 - 2OC \cdot AC \cdot \cos C)OC}$

$= h \dfrac{\frac{9}{16}a^2 + b^2 - \frac{3}{2}ab\cos C + \frac{9}{16}a^2 - b^2}{(\frac{9}{16}a^2 + b^2 - \frac{3}{2}ab\cos C)\frac{3}{4}a}$

$= h \dfrac{\frac{9}{8}a^2 - \frac{3}{4}(a^2 + b^2 - c^2)}{\{\frac{9}{16}a^2 + b^2 - \frac{3}{4}(a^2 + b^2 - c^2)\}\frac{3}{4}a}$

$= h \dfrac{\frac{3}{8}a^2 - \frac{3}{4}b^2 + \frac{3}{4}c^2}{(\frac{3}{16}a^2 + \frac{1}{4}b^2 + \frac{3}{4}c^2)\frac{3}{4}a}$

$= h \dfrac{\frac{3}{8}a^2 - \frac{3}{4}b^2 + \frac{3}{4}(b^2 + ab + \frac{1}{4}a^2)}{\{-\frac{3}{16}a^2 + \frac{1}{4}b^2 + \frac{3}{4}(b^2 + ab + \frac{1}{4}a^2)\}\frac{3}{4}a}$

$= h \dfrac{\frac{9}{16}a^2 + \frac{3}{4}ab}{(\frac{3}{4}ab + b^2)\frac{3}{4}a}$

$= \dfrac{h}{b} = \sin C$ and therefore angle $ACO = 2$ angle AOC.

xi. Solve a triangle in which one angle at the base, the opposite side, and the altitude, are given; and explain when the solution is ambiguous or impossible.

If the angle is 36°, the opposite side 4, and the altitude $\sqrt{5}-1$, solve the triangle.

Since $\sin 18° = \dfrac{\sqrt{5}-1}{4}$, there is therefore one triangle satisfying the given conditions, with angles of 18°, 36° and 126°, and sides $4\dfrac{\sin 18°}{\sin 36°}$, 4 and $4\dfrac{\sin 126°}{\sin 36°}$, or $4\dfrac{\sqrt{5}-1}{\sqrt{(10-2\sqrt{5})}}$, 4 and $4\dfrac{\sqrt{5}+1}{\sqrt{(10-2\sqrt{5})}}$.

xii. Find expressions for the radii of the inscribed and circumscribed circles of a triangle.

If the centre of the inscribed circle of a triangle be equidistant from the centre of the circumscribed circle and the orthocentre, prove that one angle of the triangle is 60°.

If O be the centre of the circumscribed circle, I of the inscribed circle, and P the orthocentre,

$$OI^2 = R^2 - 2Rr,$$
$$IP^2 = IA^2 + AP^2 - 2IA \cdot AP \cos IAP.$$

And $\qquad IA = \dfrac{r}{\sin \frac{1}{2} A}, \quad AP = 2R \cos A,$

∴ angle $IAP = \frac{1}{2}\pi - C - \frac{1}{2}A = \frac{1}{2}(B - C).$

Therefore if $\qquad OI^2 = IP^2,$

$$R^2 - 2Rr = \dfrac{r^2}{\sin^2 \frac{1}{2}A} + 4R^2 \cos^2 A - \dfrac{4Rr \cos A}{\sin \frac{1}{2} A} \cos \tfrac{1}{2}(B - C).$$

And $\qquad r = \dfrac{S}{s}, \qquad R = \dfrac{abc}{4S},$

therefore $\qquad \dfrac{R}{r} = \dfrac{4S^2}{abcs} = \dfrac{4(s-a)(s-b)(s-c)}{abc}$

$\qquad\qquad\qquad = 4 \sin \tfrac{1}{2} A \sin \tfrac{1}{2} B \sin \tfrac{1}{2} C.$

Therefore $\qquad 1 - 8 \sin \tfrac{1}{2} A \sin \tfrac{1}{2} B \sin \tfrac{1}{2} C$
$= 16 \sin^2 \tfrac{1}{2} B \sin^2 \tfrac{1}{2} C + 4 \cos^2 A - 16 \sin \tfrac{1}{2} B \sin \tfrac{1}{2} C \cos A \cos \tfrac{1}{2}(B - C),$
or $\qquad 1 - 2 \cos A - 2 \cos B - 2 \cos C + 2$
$= 4 (1 - \cos B)(1 - \cos C) + 4 \cos^2 A - 4 \cos A \sin B \sin C$
$\qquad\qquad\qquad\qquad\qquad\qquad - 16 \cos A \sin^2 \tfrac{1}{2} B \sin^2 \tfrac{1}{2} C$
$= 4 (1 - \cos B)(1 - \cos C) + 4 \cos A (\cos A - \sin B \sin C)$
$\qquad\qquad\qquad\qquad\qquad\qquad - 4 \cos A (1 - \cos B)(1 - \cos C)$
$= 4 (1 - \cos B)(1 - \cos C) - 4 \cos A \cos B \cos C$
$\qquad\qquad\qquad\qquad\qquad\qquad - 4 \cos A (1 - \cos B)(1 - \cos C),$
or $1 - 2 (\cos A + \cos B + \cos C) + 4 (\cos B \cos C + \cos C \cos A + \cos A \cos B)$
$\qquad\qquad - 8 \cos A \cos B \cos C = 0,$
or $\qquad (1 - 2 \cos A)(1 - 2 \cos B)(1 - 2 \cos C) = 0;$
therefore $\qquad \cos A \text{ or } \cos B \text{ or } \cos C = \tfrac{1}{2},$
and therefore A or B or C is 60°.

TUESDAY, *January* 1, 1878.   9 to 12.

Mr GLAISHER, Arabic numbers.
Mr GREENHILL, Roman numbers.

1. Define the resolved part of a force in any given direction.

OA, OB, OC... are any number of fixed straight lines drawn from a point O and spheres are described on OA, OB, OC... as diameters. Any straight line OX is drawn through O and a point P taken in it so that OP is equal to the algebraical sum of the lengths intercepted on OX by the spheres. Find the locus of P.

Let OX make angles θ_1, θ_2, ... with OA, OB, ...; then $OP = OA \cos\theta_1 + OB \cos\theta_2 +$ &c., that is, $OP =$ the resolved part in the direction OX of forces represented by OA, OB, ... If, therefore, OR denote the resultant of the forces OA, OB..., the locus of P is the sphere described upon OR as diameter.

2. If three forces are in equilibrium, they must lie in a plane, and meet in a point or be parallel.

A uniform rod hangs by two strings of lengths l, l', fastened to its ends and to two points in the same horizontal line, distant a apart, the strings crossing one another. Find the position of equilibrium, and shew that if α, α' be the angles that l, l' make with the horizon,

$$\sin(\alpha+\alpha')(l' \cos\alpha' - l \cos\alpha) = a \sin(\alpha-\alpha').$$

In fig. (11) G the centre of gravity of the rod is vertically under O, the point of intersection of the strings, so that the perpendiculars Cm, Dn are equal. Thus $OC \cos\alpha' = OD \cos\alpha$, that is

$$(l' - OB)\cos\alpha' = (l - OA)\cos\alpha.$$

And since

$$\frac{OA}{\sin\alpha'} = \frac{OB}{\sin\alpha} = \frac{a}{\sin(\alpha+\alpha')}$$

this equation becomes

$$\left\{l' - \frac{a \sin\alpha}{\sin(\alpha+\alpha')}\right\} \cos\alpha' = \left\{l - \frac{a \sin\alpha'}{\sin(\alpha+\alpha')}\right\} \cos\alpha,$$

viz. $\sin(\alpha+\alpha')(l' \cos\alpha' - l \cos\alpha) = a \sin(\alpha-\alpha')$ ....(1).

If θ be the inclination of the rod to the horizon, and b be its length,

$b \sin\theta = l' \sin\alpha' - l \sin\alpha$, $b \cos\theta = l \cos\alpha + l' \cos\alpha' - a$,

and these, with (1), give the value of θ in terms of l, l', a, b.

3. Two parallel forces P and Q have a resultant R which lies between them and is distant a and b from them respectively. Find the relations connecting P, Q, R, a, b.

$ABCD$ is a quadrilateral, and two points P, Q are taken in AD, BC such that $AP : PD :: CQ : QB$. From P, Q straight lines PP', QQ' are drawn equal to, parallel to, and in the same directions as BC and DA respectively. Shew that forces represented by AB, CD, PP', QQ' are in equilibrium.

Replace QQ' by parallel forces S_1, S_2 acting at B, C (fig. 12): then S_1, in magnitude, $=\dfrac{CQ}{CB} \cdot QQ' = \dfrac{CQ}{CB} \cdot AD = AP$, since $\dfrac{AP}{AD} = \dfrac{CQ}{CB}$. Similarly S_2 is equal in magnitude to PD. Thus S_1 and AB acting at B have as their resultant PB, and S_2 and CD acting at C have as their resultant CP, so that the four forces AB, CD, PP', QQ' are replaced by PB, CP, PP' which, since $PP' = BC$, are in equilibrium by the triangle of forces.

4. Given the centres of gravity of a body and of any part of it, find the centre of gravity of the remainder.

A body consists of two parts, and one of them is moved into any other position; shew that the line joining the two positions of the centre of gravity of the whole body is parallel, and bears a fixed ratio, to the line joining the two positions of the centre of gravity of the part moved; and apply this theorem to find the position of the centre of gravity of a circular arc.

Let W be the weight of the whole body, and w that of the part moved. Let g (fig. 13) be the centre of gravity of the fixed part, and g_1, g_2, G_1, G_2 the centres of gravity of the moved part and of the whole body in the two positions. Then $gG_1 : gg_1 = w : W$, and $gG_2 : gg_2 = w : W$; so that $G_1 G_2$ is parallel to $g_1 g_2$, and bears to it the ratio of $w : W$.

To apply the theorem to find the centre of gravity of a circular arc AB of radius a subtending an angle 2α at the centre (fig. 14), remove from the end of the arc, A, to the other end of the arc, B, an element subtending at the centre an angle θ. The effect of this is to turn the arc through the small angle θ, and therefore to move the centre of gravity through a distance $x\theta$, x being the distance between the centre and the centre of gravity. The element θ is moved through a distance $2a \sin \alpha$, and the weights are proportional to $a\theta$, and $2a\alpha$, so that, by the theorem,

$$x\theta : 2a \sin \alpha = a\theta : 2a\alpha,$$

and hence
$$x = \dfrac{\sin \alpha}{\alpha} a.$$

5. In the Roman steelyard the distances of the graduations from a certain point are in arithmetical progression, and in the Danish steelyard in harmonical progression.

A brass figure $ABDC$, of uniform thickness, bounded by a circular arc BDC (greater than a semicircle) and two tangents AB, AC inclined at an angle 2α, is used as a letter-weigher as follows. The centre of the circle, O, is a fixed point about which the machine can turn freely, and a weight P is attached to the point A, the weight of the machine itself being w. The letter to be weighed is suspended from a clasp (whose weight may be neglected) at D on the rim of the circle, QD being perpendicular to OA. The circle is graduated and is read by a pointer which hangs vertically from O: when there is no letter attached, the point A is vertically below O and the pointer indicates zero. Obtain a formula for the graduation of the circle, and shew that if $P = \frac{1}{3}w \sin^2 \alpha$, the reading of the machine will be $\frac{1}{3}w$ when OA makes with the vertical an angle equal to

$$\tan^{-1}\left\{\frac{(\pi + 2\alpha)\sin^2\alpha + 2\sin\alpha\cos\alpha}{(\pi + 2\alpha)\sin^2\alpha + 2\cos\alpha}\right\}.$$

Let a be the radius of the circle, and G the centre of gravity of the machine (fig. 15). Taking moments about O,

$$Wa\cos\theta = (w \cdot OG + Pa \operatorname{cosec}\alpha)\sin\theta,$$

W being the weight suspended from D, and θ the angle made by OA with the vertical. Suppose OG determined; then

$$\tan\theta = \frac{Wa}{w \cdot OG + Pa \operatorname{cosec}\alpha} \quad\ldots\ldots\ldots\ldots\ldots(1),$$

and putting for W values corresponding to the weights to be engraved upon the limb of the machine, this formula gives the positions of the graduations.

To find OG, we have (fig. 16) area of sector $BODC = a^2(\frac{1}{2}\pi + \alpha)$, area of triangle $BOC = a^2 \sin\alpha\cos\alpha$, area of triangle $ABC = a^2\cos^2\alpha \operatorname{cosec}\alpha$, and G_1, G_2, G_3 being the centres of gravity of these areas,

$$OG_1 = \tfrac{4}{3}a\frac{\cos\alpha}{\pi + 2\alpha}, \quad OG_2 = \tfrac{2}{3}a\sin\alpha, \quad OG_3 = a\sin\alpha + \tfrac{1}{3}a\cos^2\alpha \operatorname{cosec}\alpha;$$

whence, noticing that OG_1 is negative,

$OG \cdot a^2(\tfrac{1}{2}\pi + \alpha + \cot\alpha) = \tfrac{1}{3}a^3(-2\cos\alpha + 2\cos\alpha\sin^2\alpha + 3\cos^2\alpha + \cos^2\alpha \operatorname{cosec}^2\alpha)$,

$$= \tfrac{1}{3}a^3\cos^3\alpha \operatorname{cosec}^2\alpha;$$

and therefore

$$OG = \tfrac{2}{3}a\frac{\cos^3\alpha}{(\pi + 2\alpha + 2\cot\alpha)\sin^2\alpha}.$$

Substituting this value in (1)

$$\tan\theta = W \cdot \frac{(\pi + 2\alpha)\sin^2\alpha + 2\sin\alpha\cos\alpha}{\tfrac{2}{3}w\cos^3\alpha + P\{(\pi + 2\alpha)\sin\alpha + 2\cos\alpha\}},$$

and the result in the question follows at once on putting

$$W = \tfrac{1}{3}w, \quad P = \tfrac{1}{3}w\sin^2\alpha.$$

6. State the laws of friction; and explain how they may be verified experimentally.

Two rings, each of weight w, slide upon a vertical semicircular wire with the diameter horizontal and convexity upwards. They are connected by a light string of length $2l$ (supposed less than $2a$, the diameter of the semicircle) on which is slipped a ring of weight

W. Shew that when the two rings that slide on the semicircle are as far apart as possible, the angle 2α subtended by them at the centre is given by the equation

$$(W + 2w)^2 \tan^2(\alpha + \epsilon)(l^2 - a^2 \sin^2 \alpha) = W^2 a^2 \sin^2 \alpha,$$

where $\tan \epsilon$ is the coefficient of friction between the rings and the wire.

Let 2θ (fig. 17) denote the angle between the portions of the string, and let T be the tension of the string when the rings are at A, B as far apart as possible. Then $W = 2T \cos \theta$, and the normal pressure on the wire at A is $w \cos \alpha + T \cos(\theta - \alpha)$. Resolving along the tangent at A

$$T \sin(\theta - \alpha) = w \sin \alpha + \tan \epsilon \{w \cos \alpha + T \cos(\theta - \alpha)\},$$

whence
$$T \sin(\theta - \alpha - \epsilon) = w \sin(\alpha + \epsilon),$$

viz.
$$\frac{W}{2 \cos \theta} \sin(\theta - \alpha - \epsilon) = w \sin(\alpha + \epsilon).$$

This gives
$$\tan \theta = \frac{W + 2w}{W} \tan(\alpha + \epsilon).$$

But $l \sin \theta = a \sin \alpha$, so that this becomes

$$\frac{a \sin \alpha}{\sqrt{(l^2 - a^2 \sin^2 \alpha)}} = \frac{W + 2w}{W} \tan(\alpha + \epsilon).$$

vii. State Newton's laws of motion, and explain the bearing of the second law upon the definition of force: prove also that a force may be measured by the kinetic energy generated in the unit of length.

Given that a quadrant of the Earth's surface is 10^9 centimetres, and the mean density of the Earth is 5·67, prove that the unit of force will be the attraction of two spheres each of 3928 grammes, whose centres are a centimetre apart, the acceleration of gravity at the Earth's surface being 981; a centimetre, second, and gramme being the units of length, time, and mass.

The attraction F between m and m' grammes at a distance l centimetres is

$$F = C \frac{mm'}{l^2},$$

where C is a constant.

To determine C, consider a gramme on the earth's surface, attracted by the earth.

Then $F = 981$, $m = 1$, $m' = \frac{32}{3\pi^2} \times 10^{27} \times 5{\cdot}67$, $l = \frac{2}{\pi} \times 10^9$;

and therefore
$$C = \frac{l^2 F}{mm'} = \frac{3 \times 981}{8 \times 10^9 \times 5{\cdot}67}.$$

To find the number of grammes m, which at a distance of 1 centimetre from an equal mass would be attracted with the unit of force, we have
$$1 = Cm^2;$$
and therefore
$$m = \sqrt{\frac{1}{C}} = 3928.$$

(Everett, *The Centimetre-Gramme-Second (C. G. S.) System of Units*, p. 32.)

viii. Describe the theory of Atwood's machine, and explain how it is used to verify the laws of motion.

If the groove in the pulley in which the string runs be cut to that depth at which it is found that the inertia of the pulley may be divided equally between the moving weights, and if Q be the weight required to be added to overcome the friction of the axle of the pulley when equal weights P are hung at the ends of the string, prove that an additional weight R will produce acceleration
$$\frac{R}{2P + 2Q + R + W}g,$$
where W is the weight of the pulley.

All the mass of the pulley may be supposed collected into a ring of certain radius (the radius of gyration), and if the groove in which the string runs be cut down to this depth, the inertia of the pulley may now be allowed for by dividing the mass of the pulley equally between the moving weights.

Suppose now the pulley weightless, and $P + \tfrac{1}{2}W$ the weights suspended from the string: let a be the radius of the groove, b of the axle of the pulley; ϕ the angle of friction of the bearing.

If O be the centre of the pulley, A the point of contact of the axle in the bearing (fig. 18), then when the pulley is in motion or bordering on motion, the inclination of OA to the vertical is ϕ.

If the pulley is bordering on motion when Q is added to one weight, then for equilibrium, taking moments about A,
$$(P + Q + \tfrac{1}{2}W)(a - b\sin\phi) = (P + \tfrac{1}{2}W)(a + b\sin\phi).$$

Suppose f the acceleration when an additional weight R is added, and let T and T' be the tensions of the strings.

Then
$$T(a - b\sin\phi) = T'(a + b\sin\phi),$$
and
$$\frac{f}{g} = \frac{P + Q + R + \tfrac{1}{2}W - T}{P + Q + R + \tfrac{1}{2}W} = \frac{T' - P - \tfrac{1}{2}W}{P + \tfrac{1}{2}W}.$$

Therefore
$$\frac{T}{T'} = \frac{a + b\sin\phi}{a - b\sin\phi} = \frac{P + Q + \tfrac{1}{2}W}{P + \tfrac{1}{2}W}.$$

$$= \frac{(P+Q+R+\tfrac{1}{2}W)\left(1-\tfrac{f}{g}\right)}{(P+\tfrac{1}{2}W)\left(1+\tfrac{f}{g}\right)},$$

or
$$\frac{1-\tfrac{f}{g}}{1+\tfrac{f}{g}} = \frac{P+Q+\tfrac{1}{2}W}{P+Q+R+\tfrac{1}{2}W};$$

therefore
$$\frac{f}{g} = \frac{R}{2P+2Q+R+W}.$$

The same result will be obtained supposing the pulley to retain its weight W; for then taking moments about A when the weight Q is added, and the pulley is bordering on motion,

$$(P+Q)(a-b\sin\phi) = P(a+b\sin\phi) + Wb\sin\phi,$$

or
$$\frac{a+b\sin\phi}{a-b\sin\phi} = \frac{P+Q+\tfrac{1}{2}W}{P+\tfrac{1}{2}W},$$

as before.

And when the weight R is added, and the acceleration of the system is f, if T, T' be the tensions of the strings; for the motion of the pulley, taking moments about O,

$$\frac{f}{g} = \frac{(T-T')a - (T+T'+W)b\sin\phi}{Wa};$$

and for the motion of the weights

$$\frac{f}{g} = \frac{P+Q+R-T}{P+Q+R} = \frac{T'-P}{P}.$$

Therefore
$$T = (P+Q+R)\left(1-\frac{f}{g}\right),$$

$$T' = P\left(1+\frac{f}{g}\right),$$

and
$$\frac{b\sin\phi}{a} = \frac{Q}{2P+Q+W}.$$

Therefore
$$\frac{f}{g} = \frac{R}{2P+2Q+R+W},$$

as before.

ix. If a body, attached at its centre of mass to one end of a string of length r, the other end of which is attached to a fixed point on a smooth horizontal plane, make n revolutions a second, prove that the tension of the string is to the pressure on the plane as $4\pi^2 n^2 r$ to g.

Prove that at the equator a shot fired westward with velocity 8333 or eastward with velocity 7407 metres per second will if unresisted move horizontally round the Earth in one hour and twenty minutes and one hour and a half respectively.

Let r be the radius of the earth, w the angular velocity, and v the velocity with which the shot is fired westward relatively to the earth.

Then since the earth turns round from west to east,

$$\frac{(v-r\omega)^2}{r}=g,$$

or
$$v = r\omega \pm \sqrt{gr}$$
$$= r\omega \left(1 \pm \sqrt{\frac{g}{r\omega^2}}\right)$$
$$= r\omega (1 \pm \sqrt{289})$$
$$= r\omega (1 \pm 17)$$
$$= 18r\omega \text{ or } -16r\omega.$$

The earth's equatorial circumference being 4×10^7 metres, the velocity at the equator due to the rotation

$$r\omega = \frac{4 \times 10^7}{27 \times 60 \times 60};$$

and therefore $18r\omega = 8333$, $16r\omega = 7407$; and the shot will go round the earth in $\frac{1}{18}$th or $\frac{1}{16}$th of day: that is, in one hour and twenty minutes, or one hour and a half.

x. Prove that the path of a projectile if unresisted is a parabola, and that the velocity at any point is due to the level of the directrix.

A shot of m pounds is fired from a gun of M pounds, placed on a smooth horizontal plane and elevated at an angle α. Prove that, if the muzzle velocity of the shot be V, the range will be

$$2\frac{V^2}{g} \frac{\left(1+\frac{m}{M}\right)\tan\alpha}{1+\left(1+\frac{m}{M}\right)^2\tan^2\alpha}.$$

Let u, v be the horizontal and vertical components of the velocity of the shot, U the velocity of recoil of the gun, and β the angle of departure of the shot.

Then $\frac{v}{u}=\tan\beta$; $\frac{v}{u+U}=\tan\alpha$, and $mu=MU$.

Therefore $\tan\beta = \left(1+\frac{m}{M}\right)\tan\alpha.$

The range
$$= 2\frac{V^2}{g}\sin\beta\cos\beta$$
$$= 2\frac{V^2}{g}\frac{\tan\beta}{1+\tan^2\beta}$$
$$= 2\frac{V^2}{g}\frac{\left(1+\frac{m}{M}\right)\tan\alpha}{1+\left(1+\frac{m}{M}\right)^2\tan^2\alpha}.$$

xi. Define an impulse, and explain how it is measured. Find the velocity of a particle of given elasticity after oblique impact at a fixed smooth plane; and prove that, after impact on two planes at right angles, the velocity of the particle is reversed in direction.

If a stream of particles of elasticity e all moving in parallel directions with velocity u impinge successively on two smooth fixed planes at right angles, prove that the average resultant of the pressures on the planes is $Mu(1+e)$, where M is the mass of the particles which strike each plane in one second.

After impact on the two planes, the particles form a stream moving in the opposite direction with velocity eu, and therefore momentum has been communicated, $Mu(1+e)$ per second, to the original incident stream; $Mu(1+e)$ may therefore be taken as the measure of the average resultant of the pressure due to the continued impact of the particles on the planes.

xii. Prove that the kinetic energy of two particles is equal to the kinetic energy of a mass, equal to the sum of their masses moving with the velocity of the centre of mass, together with the kinetic energy due to the motion of the particles relative to their centre of mass; and extend this to the case of any number of particles or a material system.

Of the kinetic energy of a material system in free space, how much is available for conversion into work?

(Maxwell, *Matter and Motion*, Articles LXXIX., LXXX., LXXXI.)

TUESDAY, *January* 1, 1878. 1½ to 4.

Mr PRIOR, Arabic numbers.
Mr FERRERS, Roman numbers.

1. From the behaviour of known fluids under the action of external forces obtain a definition of a perfect fluid; and deduce the characteristic property of the internal forces in such a fluid.

If the linear dimensions of a fluid medium at rest under parallel forces uniformly distributed throughout it be varied uniformly in the ratio $1 : n$, shew that the pressure at any point is varied in the ratio $n^2 : 1$; and that, if A, B, C be three specified elements of the fluid, the moment of the pressure on the plane ABC, about the line AB, is varied in the ratio $1 : n$.

Let A', B', C' denote the elements A, B, C after the variation. Let ϖ be the pressure at C, ϖ' that at C'; and let M be the moment of the pressure on the plane ABC about AB, M' the same for $A'B'C'$ about $A'B'$.

Then since the whole pressure on the area ABC is equal to that on $A'B'C'$, we have in the limit, when ABC is made indefinitely small,

$$\varpi \times \text{area } ABC = \varpi' \times \text{area } A'B'C',$$

therefore $\quad \dfrac{\varpi}{\varpi'} = \dfrac{\text{area } A'B'C'}{\text{area } ABC} = \dfrac{n^2}{1}.$

Again, since the pressures on any area before and after the variation are equal, and when these areas are indefinitely diminished, their distances p, p' from AB before and after the variation are as $1 : n$, we have

$M = \Sigma \{\text{pressure on any small area} \times p\}$

$M' = \Sigma \{\text{pressure on the corresponding area} \times p'\};$

therefore $\quad = n \Sigma \{\text{pressure on the corresponding area} \times p\},$

therefore $\quad \dfrac{M}{M'} = \dfrac{1}{n}.$

2. The difference between the pressures at any two points of a homogeneous liquid at rest under gravity is proportional to the distance between the horizontal planes in which the points lie.

A regular tetrahedron of thin metal, whose weight is equal to the weight of water it would contain, is emptied of water, and cut into two halves by a central section parallel to two opposite edges. If one half be held fast in any position, shew that the force required to draw away the other half from it will be the same, provided the centre of the tetrahedron be always in the same horizontal plane.

Let W be the weight of the half-tetrahedron, Π the pressure at the centre C of its base, a an edge of that base. Let α be the angle which each face of the half-tetrahedron makes with a line CX perpendicular to its base, θ the inclination of CX to the vertical. The pressure on each of the faces is equal to the product of its area into the pressure at its c.g., and has a component along $CX =$ this product $\times \sin \alpha$. Then the component along CX of the pressures on two similar faces is, by symmetry, $= 2 \sin \alpha \times$ the product of the area of each into the pressure due to the depth of the point in which the line joining their centres of gravity cuts CX. Therefore the component of all the pressures $= 4\pi a^2 \{\Pi - g\rho h \cos \theta\}$, where h is the distance from C of some fixed point G on CX, G being the centre of gravity of the surfaces pressed by the water, and ρ being the density of water. Let F be the force required to draw away the half-tetrahedron. Then we have

$$F_\theta = 4\pi a^2 \{\Pi - g\rho h \cos\theta\} + W \cos\theta.$$

But by symmetry, when $\theta = \frac{1}{2}\pi$, since the tetrahedron would be in equilibrium,

$$F_{\frac{\pi}{2}} = 4\pi a^2 \Pi,$$

therefore $\qquad W$ must $= 4\pi a^2 g\rho h,$

therefore $\qquad F_\theta = 4\pi a^2 \Pi.$

Or thus:

Since the weight of the tetrahedron is equal to the weight of water it would contain, suppose it replaced by water which would then be at rest, and the half-tetrahedron of water could be moved by any the slightest force; therefore the force which would move one half-tetrahedron of metal from the other is the force across the plane that separates the half-tetrahedrons of water; which force is constant, because the centre of this plane is always at the same depth.

3. Find the conditions for the equilibrium of a solid body floating in a liquid of greater density than the solid; and shew that, when it is in stable equilibrium, the height of the common centre of gravity of the solid and liquid is a minimum.

If a body be floating in a liquid contained in a cylindrical vessel, and be pressed down through a small distance c, shew that the common centre of gravity of the liquid and body will be raised through a height $\frac{1}{2} \frac{B}{A-B} \frac{c^2}{d}$, where A, B are the areas of the cross-sections of the cylinder and solid in the plane of floatation, and d is the height of this plane above the base of the cylinder.

Let W be the sum of the weights of the liquid and body, which remains unaltered; and let z be the original height of the C.G. of W. Let $\bar{z}$ be the height through which it is raised. The plane of floatation is raised through a height $\frac{A}{A-B} c$, and the weight of liquid raised above the original plane of floatation is $Acg\rho$ where ρ is the density of the liquid. Suppose the change made by lowering the whole system through a depth c, and then raising a weight $Acg\rho$ from below the original base of the cylinder to the top of the liquid. This process gives the equation

$$W(z + \bar{z}) = W(z - c) + Acg\rho \left(d - \frac{c}{2} + \frac{1}{2} \cdot \frac{A}{A-B} c\right),$$

therefore $\qquad \bar{z} = -c + \dfrac{Acg\rho}{W}\left(d + \frac{1}{2} \cdot \dfrac{B}{A-B} c\right).$

But $W = Ag\rho d$, because the weight of the body is equal to the weight of the fluid displaced.

Therefore
$$\dot{z} = -c + \frac{c}{d}\left(d + \tfrac{1}{2} \cdot \frac{B}{A-B} c\right)$$
$$= \tfrac{1}{2} \cdot \frac{B}{A-B} \cdot \frac{c^2}{d}.$$

4. Explain the statement "when gases of different kinds are placed in the same vessel, each acts as if the other were a vacuum": and from it deduce Boyle's Law.

The original pressures of three gases contained in vessels A, B, C of equal volume are α, β, γ. If α_a, β_a, γ_a be their pressures when $\frac{1}{n}$th of the contents of B and C have been transferred to A; α_{ab}, β_{ab}, γ_{ab} their pressures when $\frac{1}{n}$th of the new contents of C and A have been transferred to B; α_{abc}, β_{abc}, γ_{abc} their pressures when $\frac{1}{n}$th of the last-formed contents of A and B have been transferred to C; and if other symbols have similar meanings, shew that

$$\frac{\alpha_{bca} - \alpha_{abc}}{2n-1} = \frac{\alpha_{bca} - \alpha_{cab}}{n} = \frac{\alpha_{cab} - \alpha_{abc}}{n-1} = \frac{\alpha + \beta + \gamma}{n^3}.$$

By the conditions of the question

$$\alpha_a = \alpha + \frac{1}{n}(\beta + \gamma), \quad \beta_a = \frac{n-1}{n}\beta, \quad \gamma_a = \frac{n-1}{n}\gamma;$$

$$\alpha_{ab} = \frac{n-1}{n}\alpha + \frac{n-1}{n^2}(\beta+\gamma), \quad \beta_{ab} = \frac{1}{n}\alpha + \frac{n^2-n+1}{n^2}\beta + \frac{1}{n}\gamma, \quad \gamma_{ab} = \frac{(n-1)^2}{n^2}\gamma;$$

$$\alpha_{abc} = \frac{(n-1)^2}{n^2}\alpha + \frac{(n-1)^2}{n^3}(\beta+\gamma), \quad \beta_{abc} = \frac{n-1}{n^2}\alpha + \frac{n^3-2n^2+2n-1}{n^3}\beta + \frac{n-1}{n^2}\gamma;$$

$$\gamma_{abc} = \alpha + \beta + \gamma - \alpha_{abc} - \beta_{abc} = \frac{1}{n}\alpha + \frac{1}{n}\beta + \frac{n^3-2n^2+3n-1}{n^3}\gamma;$$

therefore by cyclical changes we obtain

$$\alpha_{bca} = \frac{n^3-2n^2+3n-1}{n^3}\alpha + \frac{1}{n}\beta + \frac{1}{n}\gamma,$$

$$\alpha_{cab} = \frac{n^3-2n^2+2n-1}{n^3}\alpha + \frac{n-1}{n^2}\beta + \frac{n-1}{n^2}\gamma;$$

therefore $\alpha_{bca} - \alpha_{abc} = \frac{2n-1}{n^3}(\alpha+\beta+\gamma),$

$$\alpha_{bca} - \alpha_{cab} = \frac{1}{n^3}(\alpha+\beta+\gamma),$$

$$\alpha_{cab} - \alpha_{abc} = \frac{n-1}{n^3}(\alpha+\beta+\gamma).$$

5. Describe Nicholson's Hydrometer; and explain its uses.

An old Nicholson's Hydrometer is found with its stem uniformly coated with rust. Two weights of unknown magnitude are also found with it. The stem has three marks A, B, C upon it which marked the surface of some unknown liquid when the hydrometer (free from rust) floated in it either free, or with one or the other of the two weights in its upper pan. When it is now placed in a liquid, the surface in the three cases is at A', B', C'. Shew that

$$AA'.BC - AC.BB' + AB.CC' = 0.$$

Let w_1, w_2 be the two weights; ρ, ρ' the densities of the two liquids; a, a' the areas of the stem of the hydrometer when free from rust and when rusty respectively. Then, whatever be the weight of the hydrometer, we have

$$w_1 = AB.\rho a \text{ and } = A'B'.\rho'a',$$
$$w_2 = AC.\rho a \text{ and } = A'C'.\rho'a' ;$$

therefore $\qquad \dfrac{AB}{AC} = \dfrac{A'B'}{A'C'}$,

therefore $\quad AB(AC + CC' - AA') = AC(AB + BB' - AA')$,

therefore $\quad AA'(AC - AB) - AC.BB' + AB.CC' = 0$,

therefore $\quad AA'.BC - AC.BB' + AB.CC' = 0$.

6. State clearly the argument which shews that rotating liquid under forces symmetrical with respect to the axis of rotation may be dealt with as if at rest under the given forces and an additional force passing through the axis: and, in the case of heavy homogeneous liquid rotating about a vertical axis, shew that vertical sections of the surfaces of equal pressure are parabolas.

A spherical shell is partly full of water at rest. If the water be made to rotate about the vertical diameter, shew that the greatest depression of the free surface exceeds its greatest elevation.

Let AB (fig. 19) be a vertical great circle of the sphere, CD the intersection of the surface at rest with the plane of the paper, MVN the intersection of the rotating surface with the same plane. Round the sphere describe a cylinder with axis vertical, and suppose the space between it and the sphere filled with water to the height $GCDH$. If this water be made to rotate with the same angular velocity round the axis, its surface will intersect the plane of the paper in MK, NL, being continuations of the parabola MVN.

Now the volume of the paraboloid between KL and $V = \frac{1}{2}$ the volume of the cylinder between these levels; and also, since the mass of water is constant, this volume is equal to the volume of the cylinder between KL and GH; therefore the volume of the cylinder between KL

and GH is $\frac{1}{2}$ its volume between KL and V; therefore V and KL are equidistant from GH; therefore V is depressed below CD more than M, N are raised above CD.

vii. Distinguish between a real and a virtual image; and prove that the image formed by a convex mirror is always virtual, but that that formed by a concave mirror is real or virtual, according as the distance of the object from the centre of the mirror exceeds or falls short of a certain amount. Prove that, in these cases, the image is erect or inverted, according as it is virtual or real.

viii. State the laws of refraction.

A small cylindrical pencil of rays is incident on the curved surface of a solid right cone with a flat base, formed of a refracting substance, the axis of the cone coinciding with the axis of the pencil. Determine the position of the point from which the pencil will diverge, after transmission through the cone.

The pencil, after entering the cone, will diverge from the vertex of the cone, and therefore, after emergence, will diverge from a point on the axis, at a distance from the base $= \mu$ times the height of the cone.

ix. Find the geometrical focus of a small pencil of rays after direct refraction into a medium bounded by a spherical surface.

A luminous point approaches a refracting medium bounded by a spherical surface, the point moving along the axis of the medium. Prove that the point and its geometrical focus always move in the same direction, and that the least distance between them is

$$\frac{\sqrt{\mu}-1}{\sqrt{\mu}+1}r,$$

μ being the refractive index, and r the radius of the surface. Which is then nearer to the surface?

Let u, v, be the respective distances of the luminous point and its image from the surface of the medium. Then, r being the radius of the medium, we have

$$\frac{\mu}{v} - \frac{1}{u} = \frac{\mu-1}{r}.$$

Now, as the luminous point approaches the medium, u diminishes. Hence, $\frac{1}{u}$ increases, therefore $\frac{\mu}{v}$ increases and v diminishes. Or, the luminous point and its image move always in the same direction.

Again, putting $u - v = y$, we have

$$\frac{\mu}{u-y} - \frac{1}{u} = \frac{\mu-1}{r},$$

therefore $\quad \{(\mu - 1) u + y\} r = (\mu - 1)(u - y) u,$

or $\quad u^2 - (r + y) u - \dfrac{ry}{\mu - 1} = 0.$

Hence, that u may be real, we must have

$$(r + y)^2 + \dfrac{4ry}{\mu - 1} = \text{a positive quantity},$$

or $\quad y^2 + 2\dfrac{\mu + 1}{\mu - 1} ry + r^2 = \text{a positive quantity}.$

Thus, y cannot be intermediate in value between the two quantities (both of them negative) which satisfy the equation

$$y^2 + 2\dfrac{\mu + 1}{\mu - 1} ry + r^2.$$

These are $\quad -\dfrac{\sqrt{\mu + 1}}{\sqrt{\mu - 1}} r, \quad -\dfrac{\sqrt{\mu - 1}}{\sqrt{\mu + 1}} r.$

Hence, y is initially infinite, and diminishes till it attains the value $-\dfrac{\sqrt{\mu - 1}}{\sqrt{\mu + 1}} r$. Since this is negative, we infer that u is less than v, and that the luminous point is the nearer to the surface.

x. Define the focal length of a lens; and prove the formula $\dfrac{1}{v} - \dfrac{1}{u} = \dfrac{1}{f}$, the symbols having their usual meanings.

Two lenses of crown-glass and flint-glass are placed with their surfaces in contact and coinciding; determine the relation between their refractive indices and the radii of their surfaces, in order that a pencil of parallel rays may continue parallel, after transmission through the combination.

If f_1, f_2 be the focal lengths of the lenses, V the distance from which the pencil diverges after transmission from the first lens,

$$\dfrac{1}{V} = \dfrac{1}{f}$$

$$-\dfrac{1}{V} = \dfrac{1}{f'}.$$

Hence $f + f' = 0$, or one lens must be convex and the other concave, or the focal lengths of the lenses must be equal and opposite.

And, if μ, μ' be the respective indices, r, r' the radii of the surface of the first lens, v', s of the second,

$$(\mu - 1)\left(\dfrac{1}{r} - \dfrac{1}{r'}\right) + (\mu' - 1)\left(\dfrac{1}{r'} - \dfrac{1}{s}\right) = 0,$$

or $\quad \dfrac{\mu - 1}{r} - \dfrac{\mu' - 1}{s} + \dfrac{\mu' - \mu}{r'} = 0,$

the required relation.

xi. Define the optical centre of a lens; and prove that there are two points which satisfy the definition. When are the two points coincident; and when is one of them infinitely distant?

The centre of a lens is the centre of similitude of its surfaces. Hence there are two such points. They will be coincident when the two surfaces of the lens are portions of concentric spheres; and one of them will be infinitely distant when the radii are equal and opposite.

xii. Describe the Astronomical Telescope; and find its magnifying power and field of view. Where should the eye be placed, to receive the most light?

Trace a pencil, from a distant object near the axis of the telescope, to the retina.

To receive most light, the eye should be placed at the image of the object-glass formed by the eye-glass; or, more strictly, the centre of the pupil should coincide with the image of the centre of the object-glass formed by the eye-glass. For the section of the surface which envelopes all the pencils diverging from the several points of the object-glass will here be smallest.

WEDNESDAY, *January* 2, 1878. 9 to 12.

Mr PRIOR,   Arabic numbers.
Mr GLAISHER,   Roman numbers.

1. ABC is a triangle, and O the centre of its inscribed circle. Shew that AO passes through the centre of the circle described round BOC.

Let D (fig. 20) be the centre of the circle escribed to ABC, which touches BC externally. Then AOD is a straight line, because AD, AO both bisect the interior angle at A. Also since BO, CO bisect the interior angles at B and C; and BD, CD bisect the exterior angles at B and C; therefore OBD, OCD are right angles; therefore AO passes through the centre of the circle described round $BOCD$.

2. Between three towns A, B, C there is a continual migration of families, so that the number of families in each town is unaltered, while the whole number of families migrating at any specified time is always even. Shew that, if by the end of any time an even number of families have left A for B, then by the end of the same time the number of families that have left B for A is also even.

Let A_B be the number of families migrating at any time from A to B, and let similar symbols be employed for the other towns. Then by the given conditions we have

$$A_B + A_C = B_A + C_A,$$
$$B_C + B_A = C_B + A_B,$$
$$C_A + C_B = A_C + B_C,$$

and $\quad A_B + A_C + B_C + B_A + C_A + C_B = $ an even quantity $= 2n$ say.

Now, adding the two first of these equations, we obtain
$$A_C + B_C = C_A + C_B;$$
and substituting this result in the last of the equations, we have
$$A_B + B_A + 2C_A + 2C_B = 2n.$$
If then A_B be an even number, so is B_A.

iii. If
$$a = \tfrac{1}{3}\left\{\left(\frac{23+\sqrt{513}}{4}\right)^{\tfrac{1}{3}} + \left(\frac{23-\sqrt{513}}{4}\right)^{\tfrac{1}{3}} - 1\right\},$$
$$b = \tfrac{2}{81}\left\{\left(\frac{23+\sqrt{513}}{4}\right)^{\tfrac{1}{3}} + \left(\frac{23-\sqrt{513}}{4}\right)^{\tfrac{1}{3}} - 1\right\}^{4},$$
shew that the difference of a and b, the quotient of b divided by a, and the sum of the squares of a and b are all equal.

It has to be shewn that
$$a - b = \frac{b}{a} = a^2 + b^2,$$
and the values of a and b are such that $b = 2a^4$. The first equation therefore becomes $2a^8 + 2a^2 = 1$, and the second $4a^9 - 2a = -1$. The latter is deducible from the former, for squaring
$$4a^8 = (1 - 2a^2)^2 = 1 - 4a^2 + 4a^4,$$
$$= 1 - 4a^2 + 2a(1 - 2a^2),$$
$$= 1 - 4a^2 + 2a - 2(1 - 2a^2),$$
$$= -1 + 2a.$$

It remains therefore only to prove that $2a^8 + 2a^2 = 1$: and this readily appears, for writing the first equation in the question in the form
$$3a + 1 = (a+\beta)^{\tfrac{1}{3}} + (a-\beta)^{\tfrac{1}{3}},$$
we have $\quad (3a+1)^3 = 2a + 3(a^2 - \beta^2)^{\tfrac{1}{3}}(3a+1),$
that is $\quad 27a^3 + 27a^2 + 9a + 1 = \tfrac{99}{2} + 3(3a+1),$
viz. $\quad a^3 + a^2 = \tfrac{1}{2}.$

4. If $x + y + z = 0$, shew that
$$\left\{\frac{y-z}{x} + \frac{z-x}{y} + \frac{x-y}{z}\right\}\left\{\frac{x}{y-z} + \frac{y}{z-x} + \frac{z}{x-y}\right\} = 9.$$

We have $\left\{\dfrac{y-z}{x} + \dfrac{z-x}{y} + \dfrac{x-y}{z}\right\}\dfrac{x}{y-z} = 1 + \dfrac{x}{y}\cdot\dfrac{z-x}{y-z} + \dfrac{x}{z}\cdot\dfrac{x-y}{y-z}$

$$= 1 + \frac{xz(z-x) + xy(x-y)}{yz(y-z)}$$

$$= 1 + \frac{x(z^2 - zx + xy - y^2)}{yz(y-z)}$$

$$= 1 + \frac{x}{yz}(x - y - z)$$

$$= 1 + \frac{2x^2}{yz} \text{ (for } y + z = -x\text{),}$$

therefore
$$\left\{\frac{y-z}{x}+\frac{z-x}{y}+\frac{x-y}{z}\right\}\left\{\frac{x}{y-z}+\frac{y}{z-x}+\frac{z}{x-y}\right\}$$
$$=3+2\frac{x^3+y^3+z^3}{xyz}=3+6=9,$$

for, since $x+y+z=0$, $x^3+y^3+z^3-3xyz=0$.

5. Find the real roots of the equations:
$$x^2+z'^2+y'^2=a^2, \qquad y'z'+x'(y+z)=bc,$$
$$z'^2+y^2+x'^2=b^2, \qquad z'x'+y'(z+x)=ca,$$
$$y'^2+x'^2+z^2=c^2, \qquad x'y'+z'(x+y)=ab.$$

We have
$$b^2c^2=\{z'^2+y^2+x'^2\}\{y'^2+x'^2+z^2\} \text{ and } =\{y'z'+x'(y+z)\}^2,$$
therefore $\quad 0=(z'x'-yy')^2+(z'z-x'y')^2+(yz-x'^2)^2.$

Since then all the quantities are real, we must have
$$yz=x'^2, \text{ and similarly } zx=y'^2, xy=z'^2.$$

Hence, substituting in the three first equations, we have
$$x^2+xy+xz=a^2, \quad xy+y^2+yz=b^2, \quad xz+yz+z^2=c^2,$$
therefore $\quad \dfrac{x}{a^2}=\dfrac{y}{b^2}=\dfrac{z}{c^2}=\dfrac{1}{x+y+z} \text{ and }=\dfrac{x+y+z}{a^2+b^2+c^2},$

therefore $\quad x+y+z=\sqrt{a^2+b^2+c^2},$
$$x=\frac{a^2}{\sqrt{a^2+b^2+c^2}}, \quad y=\frac{b^2}{\sqrt{a^2+b^2+c^2}}, \quad z=\frac{c^2}{\sqrt{a^2+b^2+c^2}},$$
$$x'=\frac{bc}{\sqrt{a^2+b^2+c^2}}, \quad y'=\frac{ca}{\sqrt{a^2+b^2+c^2}}, \quad z'=\frac{ab}{\sqrt{a^2+b^2+c^2}},$$
which satisfy all the equations.

vi. If a and b be positive quantities, and if $a_1=\frac{1}{2}(a+b)$, $b_1=(a_1b)^{\frac{1}{2}}$, $a_2=\frac{1}{2}(a_1+b_1)$, $b_2=(a_2b_1)^{\frac{1}{2}}$ and so on, shew that
$$a_\infty=b_\infty=\frac{(b^2-a^2)^{\frac{1}{2}}}{\cos^{-1}\dfrac{a}{b}}.$$

Shew that the value of π may be calculated by means of this theorem.

Let $a=b\cos\phi$, then $a_1=b\cos^2\frac{1}{2}\phi$, $b_1=b\cos\frac{1}{2}\phi$, $a_2=b\cos\frac{1}{2}\phi\cos^2\frac{1}{4}\phi$, $b_2=b\cos\frac{1}{2}\phi\cos\frac{1}{4}\phi$, $a_3=b\cos\frac{1}{2}\phi\cos\frac{1}{4}\phi\cos^2\frac{1}{8}\phi$, $b_3=b\cos\frac{1}{2}\phi\cos\frac{1}{4}\phi\cos\frac{1}{8}\phi$, &c.

Thus
$$a_\infty = b_\infty = b\cos\tfrac{1}{2}\phi\cos\tfrac{1}{4}\phi\cos\tfrac{1}{8}\phi\ldots$$
$$= b\frac{\sin\phi}{\phi} = \frac{(b^2-a^2)^{\frac{1}{2}}}{\cos^{-1}\dfrac{a}{b}}.$$

To calculate the value of π it is only necessary to give a and b such values that $\dfrac{a}{b}$ shall be the cosine of $\tfrac{1}{2}\pi$ or $\tfrac{1}{3}\pi$ or $\tfrac{1}{4}\pi$, &c.

The simplest case is that of $a=0$, $b=1$, when we have
$$a_\infty = b_\infty = \frac{2}{\pi}.$$

[The result in the question is, in fact, Euler's product under a slightly different form: for Euler's product, viz.
$$\frac{\sin\phi}{\phi} = \cos\tfrac{1}{2}\phi\cos\tfrac{1}{4}\phi\cos\tfrac{1}{8}\phi\ldots$$
may be written
$$\frac{(1-p^2)^{\frac{1}{2}}}{\cos^{-1}p} = \{\tfrac{1}{2}(1+p)\}^{\frac{1}{2}}\{\tfrac{1}{2}(1+p_1)\}^{\frac{1}{4}}\{\tfrac{1}{2}(1+p_2)\}^{\frac{1}{8}}\ldots$$
where p_1 denotes the previous factor $\{\tfrac{1}{2}(1+p)\}^{\frac{1}{2}}$, p_2 denotes the previous factor $\{\tfrac{1}{2}(1+p_1)\}^{\frac{1}{2}}$, &c.

Now let $p=\dfrac{a}{b}$, $p_1=\dfrac{a_1}{b_1}$, &c., then
$$\frac{a_1}{b_1} = \left\{\tfrac{1}{2}\left(1+\frac{a}{b}\right)\right\}^{\frac{1}{2}} = \frac{\tfrac{1}{2}(a+b)}{\{\tfrac{1}{2}(a+b)b\}^{\frac{1}{2}}},$$
so that we may take $a_1 = \tfrac{1}{2}(a+b)$, $b_1 = (a_1 b)^{\frac{1}{2}}$, &c., as in the question.

The quantities $a_1, b_1, a_2, b_2\ldots$ converge to the value of π very slowly. I have calculated the values for the case of $a=0$, $b=1$, which are as follows:

$a\;\;\;= 0\cdot 0000000,\qquad b\;\;\;= 1\cdot 0000000,$
$a_1 = 0\cdot 5000000,\qquad b_1 = 0\cdot 7071068,$
$a_2 = 0\cdot 6035534,\qquad b_2 = 0\cdot 6532813,$
$a_3 = 0\cdot 6284173,\qquad b_3 = 0\cdot 6407287,$
$a_4 = 0\cdot 6345730,\qquad b_4 = 0\cdot 6376435,$
$a_5 = 0\cdot 6361083,\qquad b_5 = 0\cdot 6368754,$
$a_6 = 0\cdot 6364919,\qquad b_6 = 0\cdot 6366837,$
$a_7 = 0\cdot 6365878,\qquad b_7 = 0\cdot 6366357,$
$a_8 = 0\cdot 6366117,\qquad b_8 = 0\cdot 6366238,$
$a_9 = 0\cdot 6366178,\qquad b_9 = 0\cdot 6366207,$
$a_{10} = 0\cdot 6366193,\qquad b_{10} = 0\cdot 6366200,$
$a_{11} = 0\cdot 6366197,\qquad b_{11} = 0\cdot 6366199,$
$a_{12} = 0\cdot 6366198,\qquad b_{12} = 0\cdot 6366198.$

In this case the formula gives

$$a_\infty = b_\infty = \frac{2}{\pi},$$

and the value of $\frac{2}{\pi}$ is $0\cdot 63661977\ldots$

The method, regarded as a means of obtaining the value of π, is in fact only the method of polygons in a not very convenient form, for if $\phi = \frac{\pi}{m}$, then

$$b_n = b \cos\frac{\pi}{2m} \cos\frac{\pi}{2^2 m} \ldots \cos\frac{\pi}{2^n m},$$

$$= b \sin\frac{\pi}{m} \div 2^n \sin\frac{\pi}{2^n m},$$

so that the value of the circumference obtained from b_n is equal to the perimeter of an inscribed regular polygon of $2^n m$ sides. The formula used above (viz. for the case $a = 0$, $b = 1$) is in fact

$$\frac{2}{\pi} = \frac{\sqrt{2}}{2} \cdot \frac{\sqrt{(2+\sqrt{2})}}{2} \cdot \frac{\sqrt{(2+\sqrt{(2+\sqrt{2})})}}{2} \ldots \ldots (1),$$

and was given in a form equivalent to this by Vieta; but it does not appear to have been actually employed in the calculation of π. The formulæ that were employed were equivalent to

$$2^n m \sin\frac{\pi}{2^n m} \text{ and } 2^n m \tan\frac{\pi}{2^n m}$$

for the inscribed and circumscribed polygons, *i.e.* Van Ceulen would have calculated

$$\frac{\sqrt{(2 - \sqrt{(2 + \sqrt{(2 + \sqrt{(2 \ldots + \sqrt{2})})})})}}{2},$$

$\left(\text{involving } n-1 \text{ square root signs, and which} = \sin\frac{\pi}{2^n}\right)$, in preference to the first $n-1$ factors of (1), which $= \cos\frac{1}{4}\pi \cos\frac{1}{8}\pi \ldots \cos\frac{\pi}{2^n}$.]

vii. In the sides BC, CA, AB of a triangle three points A', B', C' are taken such that
$BA' : A'C = p_1 : q_1$, $CB' : B'A = p_2 : q_2$, $AC' : C'B = p_3 : q_3$;
shew that if BB' and CC', CC' and AA', AA' and BB' intersect in A'', B'', C''; then the area of the triangle $A''B''C''$ is to the area of the triangle ABC as
$(p_1 p_2 p_3 - q_1 q_2 q_3)^2 : (p_2 p_3 + q_2 q_3 + p_2 q_3)(p_3 p_1 + q_3 q_1 + p_3 q_1)$
$(p_1 p_2 + q_1 q_2 + p_1 q_2)$.

Since CC' (fig. 21) is a transversal of the triangle ABB',

$$BA'' \cdot B'C \cdot AC' = BC' \cdot AC \cdot B'A'',$$

whence
$$\frac{BA''}{B'A''} = \frac{AC}{B'C} \cdot \frac{BC'}{AC'} = \frac{p_2 + q_2}{p_2} \cdot \frac{q_3}{p_3}.$$

Thus
$$\frac{\triangle BA''C}{\triangle BB'C} = \frac{BA''}{BB'} = \frac{(p_2+q_2)q_3}{p_2p_3+q_2q_3+p_2q_3},$$

and
$$\frac{\triangle BB'C}{\triangle BAC} = \frac{B'C}{AC} = \frac{p_2}{p_2+q_2},$$

so that
$$\frac{\triangle BA''C}{\triangle BAC} = \frac{p_2q_3}{p_2p_3+q_2q_3+p_2q_3}.$$

Now $\triangle A''B''C'' = \triangle ABC - \triangle BA''C - \triangle CB''A - \triangle AC''B$,

so that
$$\frac{\triangle A''B''C''}{\triangle ABC} = 1 - \frac{p_2q_3}{p_2p_3+q_2q_3+p_2q_3} - \frac{p_3q_1}{p_3p_1+q_3q_1+p_3q_1}$$
$$- \frac{p_1q_2}{p_1p_2+q_1q_2+p_1q_2},$$

which, after some reduction,
$$= \frac{(p_1p_2p_3 - q_1q_2q_3)^2}{(p_2p_3+q_2q_3+p_2q_3)(p_3p_1+q_3q_1+p_3q_1)(p_1p_2+q_1q_2+p_1q_2)}.$$

viii. If PQ be a focal chord of a parabola, and R any point on the diameter through Q; shew that the focal chord parallel to $PR = \dfrac{PR^2}{PQ}$.

Let pq, pr (fig. 22) be the tangents parallel to PQ, PR, and let F denote the focal chord parallel to PR.

Let rp meet the diameter through q in t. Then $pt = pr$.

Hence, and by similar triangles,
$$PQ^2 : PR^2 = pq^2 : pt^2 = pq^2 : pr^2,$$
$$= PQ : F.$$

Therefore $F = \dfrac{PR^2}{PQ}$.

ix. If OP, OQ are two tangents to an ellipse, and CP', CQ' the parallel semidiameters, shew that
$$OP \cdot OQ + CP' \cdot CQ' = OS \cdot OH,$$
S, H being the foci.

Since by orthogonal projection the triangle $CP'Q'$ (fig. 23) is equal to CPQ, the angles between any two diameters of a circle being equal to those between their conjugates; and since the triangles SPQ, CPQ, HPQ on the same base PQ have their altitudes, and consequently their areas, in arithmetical progression; therefore
$$\triangle CP'Q' = \tfrac{1}{2} \triangle SPQ + \tfrac{1}{2} \triangle HPQ.$$

Hence $\triangle OPQ + \triangle CP'Q' = \tfrac{1}{2} OPSQ + \tfrac{1}{2} OPHQ = \tfrac{1}{2} p . AA'$,

where AA' is the major axis, and p the common magnitude of the four perpendiculars from O to the focal distances SP, SQ, HP, HQ.

Let HP produced to S' be equal to AA'.

Then, from above, $\triangle OPQ + \triangle CP'Q' = \triangle OS'H$;

and, the angles at O and C in the three triangles being equal, and the length OS' being equal to OS, therefore

$$OP . OQ + CP' . CQ' = OS . OH.$$

This proof is due to Mr C. Taylor, of St John's College.

10. A rhombus is formed of four rods of length a, hinged together. Two opposite rods are supported in a vertical plane by two smooth pegs, which are separated by an horizontal distance h and vertical distance k. Shew that the product of the horizontal distances of either peg from the ends of the nearer unsupported rod is $\tfrac{1}{4}(k^2 - 2ah + h^2)$, and that there is no bending moment round a point in either supported rod, whose distance from its supporting peg is three times the shorter of the distances of that peg from an unsupported rod.

Let $ABCD$ (fig. 24) be the rhombus; P, Q the pegs; and let the reactions at the hinges be denoted by the letters in the figure, the weight of each rod being W. Let $AP = x$, $CQ = x'$, $A\hat{D}C = \theta$.

Resolving horizontally, we see that

$$X_1 = X_2 = X_3 = X_4, = X \text{ say.}$$

Resolving vertically for the unsupported rods, we have

$$Y_1 + W = Y_4, \quad Y_2 + W = Y_3, \text{ therefore } Y_1 - Y_2 + Y_3 - Y_4 = 0;$$

and taking moments round the centres of these rods, we have

$$(Y_1 + Y_4) \cos\theta + 2X \sin\theta = 0,$$
$$(Y_2 + Y_3) \cos\theta - 2X \sin\theta = 0,$$

therefore $Y_1 + Y_2 + Y_3 + Y_4 = 0$;

and since $Y_1 - Y_2 + Y_3 - Y_4 = 0,$

we have $Y_3 = -Y_1, \quad Y_4 = -Y_2.$

Now, taking moments about P and Q for the supported rods, and using previous results, we have

$$Y_1 x - Y_2 (a-x) + W(\tfrac{1}{2}a - x) = 0,$$
$$Y_1 x' - Y_2 (a-x') + W(\tfrac{1}{2}a - x') = 0,$$

therefore $x = x'.$

Hence, if PN be drawn perpendicular to DC,

$$DN = a - x - h \text{ and also } = a\cos\theta + x,$$

therefore $\quad 2x = a(1 - \cos\theta) - h,$

therefore $\quad x = \tfrac{1}{2} a(1 - \cos\theta) - \tfrac{1}{2} h,$

$$a - x - h = \tfrac{1}{2} a(1 + \cos\theta) - \tfrac{1}{2} h,$$

therefore $\quad AP \cdot DN = x(a - x - h) = \left(\dfrac{a-h}{2}\right)^2 - \dfrac{a^2}{4}\cos^2\theta,$

$$= \tfrac{1}{4}\{a^2 \sin^2\theta - 2ah + h^2\},$$
$$= \tfrac{1}{4}\{k^2 - 2ah + h^2\}.$$

Next let R be a point in AB such that $PR = 3x$; then the bending moment round R is

$$Y_2(a - 4x) - \dfrac{a - 4x}{a} W \cdot \dfrac{a - 4x}{2} = (a - 4x)\left\{Y_2 - W\dfrac{a - 4x}{2a}\right\}.$$

Now, we have

$$Y_1 = -Y_2 - W,$$

and $\quad Y_1 x - Y_2(a - x) + W(\tfrac{1}{2} a - x) = 0,$

therefore $\quad Y_2 a - W(\tfrac{1}{2} a - 2x) = 0,$

therefore $\quad Y_2 - W\dfrac{a - 4x}{2a} = 0,$

therefore there is no bending moment round R.

xi. An elliptic lamina of eccentricity e rests upon a perfectly rough equal and similar lamina, the two bodies being symmetrically situated with respect to their common tangent at the point of contact. If a be the inclination of the major axis of the fixed ellipse to the horizon, and θ be the inclination, measured in the same direction, of the major axis of the moving ellipse in a position of equilibrium, then

$$\sin\tfrac{1}{2}(\theta + a) = e^2 \sin\theta \cos\tfrac{1}{2}(\theta - a).$$

In fig. 25 OM is horizontal, PG' is the normal, C' the centre, and PN' perpendicular to $A'C'$. In the position of equilibrium $C'P$ is vertical, so that the angle $PC'O = \tfrac{1}{2}\pi - \theta$, and since OP bisects the angle $C'OC$, the angle $C'OP = \tfrac{1}{2}(\theta - a)$.

Now $C'G' = e^2 C'N'$, and

$$C'G' : C'P :: \sin\tfrac{1}{2}(\theta + a) : \cos\tfrac{1}{2}(\theta - a).$$

Also $C'N' = C'P \sin\theta$,

whence $\dfrac{\sin\frac{1}{2}(\theta+a)}{\cos\frac{1}{2}(\theta-a)} C'P = e^2 C'P \sin\theta$,

giving the equation in the question at once.

[Or, otherwise, since PO is parallel to the diameter conjugate to $C'P$,

$$\tan POC' \tan OC'P = \frac{b^2}{a^2}; \text{ that is,}$$

$$\tan\tfrac{1}{2}(\theta-a)\cot\theta = \frac{b^2}{a^2}, \text{ viz. } 1-\tan\tfrac{1}{2}(\theta-a)\cot\theta = e^2.]$$

12. A cube with two faces horizontal is pressed against a rough vertical wall by two strings in vertical planes perpendicular to the wall which are attached to the ends of a rod which forms the upper edge of the face furthest from the wall, and passing over pullies in the same horizontal line in the wall support equal weights. If the coefficient of friction be $\tan\beta\,(\beta > \tfrac{1}{4}\pi)$, where $\tan 3\beta + \tan\beta = 2$, and if the ratio of the weight of the cube to each of the supporting weights be $4\sin\beta$, shew that, in the two limiting positions of equilibrium, the directions of the slant portions of the strings are inclined to each other at an angle $4\beta - \pi$.

In any position of equilibrium, let the pressure between the cube and the wall be R and let the vertical force due to friction be F.

If the upper horizontal face of the cube be above the pullies as in fig. 26, where $ABDC$ is one vertical face of the cube and E is one pulley, let $\angle ACE = \theta$. If on the other hand it be below the pullies, as in fig. 27, let $\angle ACE = \phi$; and let this difference of notation distinguish the two cases.

Let W be each supporting weight, and $2a$ an edge of the cube. Firstly, so far as turning round the edge B is concerned, there will be equilibrium if

$$2W\cos\theta \cdot 2a > 2W\sin\theta \cdot 2a + 4W\sin\beta \cdot a,$$

or $\qquad \cos\theta - \sin\theta > \sin\beta$.

But $\qquad \tan 3\beta + \tan\beta = 2$, therefore $\sin 4\beta = 2\cos 3\beta \cos\beta$,

therefore $\qquad 4\cos 2\beta \sin\beta \cos\beta = 2\cos 3\beta \cos\beta$,

therefore $\qquad 2\cos 2\beta \sin\beta = \cos 3\beta$,

therefore $\qquad \sin 3\beta - \sin\beta = \cos 3\beta$, therefore $\sin 3\beta - \cos 3\beta = \sin\beta$.

Hence there will be equilibrium, while

$$\cos\theta - \sin\theta > \sin 3\beta - \cos 3\beta,$$

i.e. while $\qquad \cos\theta - \sin\theta > \cos(3\beta-\pi) - \sin(3\beta-\pi)$,

i.e. while $\qquad \cos\theta - \cos(3\beta-\pi) > \sin\theta - \sin(3\beta-\pi)$,

i.e. while $\sin\dfrac{3\beta-\pi-\theta}{2}\sin\dfrac{3\beta-\pi+\theta}{2} > -\sin\dfrac{3\beta-\pi-\theta}{2}\cos\dfrac{3\beta-\pi+\theta}{2}$, i.e. while $\sin \dfrac{3\beta - \pi - \theta}{2}$ is $+$, for $\sin \dfrac{3\beta - \pi + \theta}{2} > -\cos \dfrac{3\beta - \pi + \theta}{2}$

i.e. while $\theta < 3\beta - \pi$.

Secondly, so far as turning round the same edge is concerned, there will be equilibrium, if
$$2W \sin \phi . 2a + 2W \cos \phi . 2a > 4 W \sin \beta . a,$$
or $\qquad \sin \phi + \cos \phi > \sin \beta,$
$\qquad\qquad\qquad\qquad > \cos (3\beta - \pi) - \sin (3\beta - \pi),$
or $\qquad \sin \phi + \sin (3\beta - \pi) > \cos (3\beta - \pi) - \cos \phi,$
or $\qquad \sin \dfrac{\phi + 3\beta - \pi}{2} \cos \dfrac{\phi - 3\beta + \pi}{2} > \sin \dfrac{\phi + 3\beta - \pi}{2} \sin \dfrac{\phi - 3\beta + \pi}{2},$
or $\qquad \tan \dfrac{\phi - 3\beta + \pi}{2} < 1,$
or $\qquad \dfrac{\phi - 3\beta + \pi}{2} < \dfrac{\pi}{4},$ or $\phi < 3\beta - \dfrac{\pi}{2}.$

Thirdly, so far as turning round the edge A is concerned, there will be equilibrium, if
$$2W \sin \phi . 2a < 4 W \sin \beta . a,$$
or $\qquad \sin \phi < \sin \beta,$ or $\phi < \beta.$

Now $\beta < 3\beta - \dfrac{\pi}{2}$; hence the cube will not be in equilibrium, unless $\phi < \beta$.

As far then as turning is concerned, the limiting positions of equilibrium are given by $\theta = 3\beta - \pi$, and $\phi = \beta$, where we notice that
$$\theta + \phi = 4\beta - \pi.$$

It only remains then to shew that for positions of the cube between these it has no tendency to slip.

If $\theta < 3\beta - \pi$, we have $R = 2W \cos \theta$, $F = 2W \sin \theta + 4W \sin \beta$,
therefore $\qquad R \tan \beta - F = 2W (\cos \theta \tan \beta - \sin \theta - 2 \sin \beta)$
$\qquad\qquad\qquad = 2W \sec \beta \{\sin (\beta - \theta) - \sin 2\beta\}$
$\qquad\qquad\qquad = - 4W \sec \beta \sin \dfrac{\beta + \theta}{2} \cos \dfrac{3\beta - \theta}{2};$

therefore $\qquad F < R \tan \beta,$ if $\cos \dfrac{3\beta - \theta}{2}$ be negative,

i.e. if $3\beta - \theta > \pi,$
i.e. if $\qquad \theta < 3\beta - \pi.$

Again, if $\phi < \beta$, we have $R = 2W \cos \phi$, $F = 4W \sin \beta - 2W \sin \phi$,
therefore $\qquad R \tan \beta - F = 2W (\cos \phi \tan \beta + \sin \phi - 2 \sin \beta)$
$\qquad\qquad\qquad = 2W \sec \beta \{\sin (\beta + \phi) - \sin 2\beta\};$

therefore $\quad F < R \tan \beta$, if $\sin(\beta + \phi) > \sin 2\beta$,

if $\beta + \phi < 2\beta$ or $> \pi - 2\beta$,

if $\phi < \beta$ or $> \pi - 3\beta$, which is negative.

Therefore, between the limiting positions of equilibrium given by $\theta = 3\beta - \pi$ and $\phi = \beta$, $F < R \tan \beta$, i.e. the cube will not slip.

These are therefore the true limiting positions of equilibrium.

13. A particle is projected from a platform with velocity V and elevation β. On the platform is a telescope, fixed at elevation α. The platform moves horizontally in the plane of the particle's motion, so as to keep the particle always in the centre of the field of view of the telescope. Shew that the original velocity of the platform must be $V \dfrac{\sin(\alpha - \beta)}{\sin \alpha}$, and its acceleration $g \cot \alpha$.

Let A (fig. 28) be the point of projection; BC the position of the telescope, P that of the particle at the time t.

Then
$$AB = AM - BM$$
$$= V(\cos\beta \cdot t - (V\sin\beta \cdot t - \tfrac{1}{2}gt^2)\cot\alpha$$
$$= V(\cos\beta - \sin\beta \cot\alpha)t + \tfrac{1}{2}g\cot\alpha\, t^2$$
$$= V \frac{\sin(\alpha - \beta)}{\sin\alpha} t + \tfrac{1}{2}g\cot\alpha\, t^2.$$

Since this is true for all values of t, we learn that the original velocity of the platform must be $V \dfrac{\sin(\alpha - \beta)}{\sin\alpha}$ and its acceleration $g\cot\alpha$.

XIV. Two bodies are projected from the point A in the same direction with velocities v_1 and v_2. P and Q are any two points on their respective trajectories, and PM, QN the perpendiculars upon the horizontal plane through A. If AM, AN, be denoted by a_1, a_2, and the angles PAM, QAN by α_1, α_2, then

$$gv_1^4 a_2^2 \frac{\cos\alpha_2}{\cos\alpha_1} + gv_2^4 a_1^2 \frac{\cos\alpha_1}{\cos\alpha_2}$$
$$= 2v_1^2 v_2^2 \{ga_1 a_2 \cos(\alpha_2 - \alpha_1) + (v_2^2 a_1 - v_1^2 a_2)\sin(\alpha_2 - \alpha_1)\}.$$

Let i be the angle the direction of projection makes with the horizon, and let t be the time of flight of the first body from A to P (fig. 29): then

$$a_1 \tan\alpha_1 = v_1 \sin i \cdot t - \tfrac{1}{2}gt^2, \quad a_1 = v_1 \cos i \cdot t,$$

whence $\quad a_1 \tan\alpha_1 = a_1 \tan i - \tfrac{1}{2}\dfrac{ga_1^2}{v_1^2}\sec^2 i,$

viz. $\quad ga_1 \tan^2 i - 2v_1^2 \tan i + 2v_1^2 \tan\alpha_1 + ga_1 = 0.$

Similarly $\quad ga_2 \tan^2 i - 2v_2^2 \tan i + 2v_2^2 \tan\alpha_2 + ga_2 = 0.$

Eliminating tan i from these two quadratic equations,

$$(2ga_1v_2{}^2 - 2ga_2v_1{}^2)\{2v_1{}^2(2v_2{}^2\tan a_2 + ga_2) - 2v_2{}^2(2v_1{}^2\tan a_1 + ga_1)\}$$
$$= \{ga_1(2v_2{}^2\tan a_2 + ga_2) - ga_2(2v_1{}^2\tan a_1 + ga_1)\}^2,$$

which, on reduction, at once assumes the form given in the question.

15. Two buckets P, Q hang at the ends of a light string which passes over a smooth fixed pulley. Above each bucket is a fixed point from which hangs a light string supporting very small balls of mass m at equal intervals a. Initially, the lowest ball of the string above P is just touching the base of P, while a number of balls of the string above Q are coiled upon the base of Q, so that Q descends and at the first instant of the motion one ball is lifted from its base. Find the acceleration of the system after r balls have been lifted off Q.

Shew that when the square of the mean velocity throughout a complete interval from ball to ball is to ga as the difference between the total descending and total ascending masses in that interval is to m, the velocity at the end of the interval is approximately the same as it was at the beginning.

Let P, Q be the masses of the buckets, m the mass of each ball, N the mass of balls initially on the base of Q. The geometrical conditions of the problem shew that the number of balls in motion is always the same; therefore the moving mass is always $P + Q + N$.

At the time t let r balls have been lifted off Q. Let u_r be the velocity just after the impact last before t; v_r that just before, u_{r+1} that just after, the next impact.

During the interval in which t lies, the weight on Q's side is $(Q + N - mr)g$, and on P's side $(P + mr)g$; therefore during this interval the acceleration is

$$\frac{(Q + N - mr) - (P + mr)}{P + Q + N}g = \frac{Q + N - P - 2mr}{P + Q + N}g.$$

And at the ensuing impact, since the velocity of one ball is destroyed by the string above Q, we have

$$(P + Q + N)u_{r+1} = (P + Q + N - m)v_r.$$

Now the space throughout which the system has the above acceleration is a,

therefore $(P + Q + N)\{v_r{}^2 - u_r{}^2\} = 2(Q + N - P - 2mr)ga,$

and $$v_r = \frac{P + Q + N}{P + Q + N - m}u_{r+1},$$

therefore $(P + Q + N)^2 u_{r+1}{}^2 - (P + Q + N - m)^2 u_r{}^2$

$$= 2ga\frac{(Q + N - P - 2mr)(P + Q + N - m)^2}{P + Q + N}.$$

If then $u_{r+1} = u_r$ approximately, we have

$$\{(P+Q+N)^2 - (P+Q+N-m)^2\} u_r^2 = 2ga \frac{(Q+N-P-2mr)(P+Q+N-m)^2}{P+Q+N};$$

or, approximately,

$$2m(P+Q+N) u_r^2 = 2ga \frac{(Q+N-P-2mr)(P+Q+N-m)^2}{P+Q+N};$$

therefore $\quad \left\{ \dfrac{P+Q+N}{P+Q+N-m} u_r \right\}^2 = \dfrac{ga}{m} \{Q+N-P-2mr\} \ldots\ldots(1)$.

But, if τ be the time in which the complete interval is described, the indefinitely small time of one impact being included, we have

$$v_r = u_r + \frac{Q+N-P-2mr}{P+Q+N} g\tau,$$

and $\quad v_r = \dfrac{P+Q+N}{P+Q+N-m} u_{r+1} = \dfrac{P+Q+N}{P+Q+N-m} u_r$, for this interval,

therefore $\quad m \left\{ \dfrac{P+Q+N}{P+Q+N-m} u_r \right\} = (Q+N-P-2mr) g\tau,$

therefore $\quad \left\{ \dfrac{P+Q+N}{P+Q+N-m} u_r \right\}^2 = \dfrac{g^2\tau^2}{m^2} \{Q+N-P-2mr\}^2 \ldots\ldots(2)$.

From (1) and (2) we obtain

$$a = \frac{g\tau^2}{m} \{Q+N-P-2mr\}.$$

Now, if w be the mean velocity, $w\tau = a$; therefore $\tau^2 = \dfrac{a^2}{w^2}$;
hence,

$$mw^2 = \{Q+N-P-2mr\} ga,$$

or $\quad w^2 : ga :: \{(Q+N-mr) - (P+mr)\} : m.$

xvi. Prove that the periodic time of a body describing an elliptic orbit under an attraction to a fixed point O within the ellipse is $\dfrac{2\pi\rho_0^{\frac{3}{2}}}{\sqrt{\mu}}$, where p_0 is the perpendicular from the centre of the ellipse on the polar of O; assuming the acceleration of the body at distance r from O to be $\dfrac{\mu r}{p^3}$, where p is the perpendicular from the body on the polar of O.

In Newton, Section II., Prop. VII., Cor. 3, it is shewn that the force under the action of which a body P revolves in any orbit about a centre of force C is to the force under the action of which it can revolve in the same orbit in the same periodic time about any other centre of force O, as $OP^2 \cdot CP$ to CG^3, CG being drawn parallel to OP, and cutting the tangent at P in G.

Now let C be the centre, so that the law of force is μr and the periodic time $\frac{2\pi}{\sqrt{\mu}}$: then (fig. 30)

$$\frac{\text{force to } O}{\text{force to } C} = \frac{CG^3}{OP^2 \cdot CP},$$

therefore
$$\text{force to } O = \mu \left(\frac{CG}{OP}\right)^3 OP = \mu \left(\frac{CY}{OZ}\right)^3 OP,$$

CY and OZ being perpendicular to the tangent at P.

Now if UV be the polar of O and CY', PZ' are perpendiculars let fall upon it

$$\frac{CY}{OZ} = \frac{CY'}{PZ'} \quad \ldots\ldots\ldots\ldots\ldots\ldots\ldots\ldots(1),$$

so that
$$\text{force to } O = \mu \left(\frac{CY'}{PZ'}\right)^3 OP = \mu \left(\frac{p_0}{p}\right)^3 r,$$

and the periodic time is $\frac{2\pi}{\sqrt{\mu}}$: so that if the law of force be, as supposed in the question, $\frac{\mu r}{p^3}$, the periodic time will be $2\pi \frac{p_0^{\,3}}{\sqrt{\mu}}$.

The proposition (1), the truth of which is suggested by the wording of the question in which the law of force $\frac{\mu r}{p^3}$ is given, may be readily proved as follows. We have (fig. 31)

$$\frac{\text{perpendicular from } O \text{ on tangent at } P}{\text{perpendicular from } C \text{ on tangent at } P} = \frac{OR}{CR},$$

and
$$\frac{\text{perpendicular from } P \text{ on polar of } O}{\text{perpendicular from } C \text{ on polar of } O} = \frac{LN}{CN},$$

PL being parallel to the polar of O. It remains therefore only to shew that $\frac{OR}{CR} = \frac{LN}{CN}$, and this is readily seen to be true for

$$CO \cdot CN = CV^2 = CL \cdot CR, \text{ whence } \frac{CO}{CR} = \frac{CL}{CN},$$

and therefore $\frac{CR - CO}{CR} = \frac{CN - CL}{CN}$, that is $\frac{OR}{CR} = \frac{LN}{CN}$.

[This is only a particular case of a more general proposition, in which P and the tangent at P may be replaced by any point P and its polar: see Salmon's *Conics*, 5th edition, Art. 101, where the proposition is proved for circles. The simplest proof is analytical, viz. let the coordinates of O and P be h, k and h', k', then

$$\frac{\text{perpendicular from } P \text{ on polar of } O}{\text{perpendicular from centre on polar of } O} = \frac{hh'}{a^2} + \frac{kk'}{b^2} - 1$$

$$= \frac{\text{perpendicular from } O \text{ on polar of } P}{\text{perpendicular from centre on polar of } P}.$$

The proposition that an elliptic orbit might be described about any point O under the action of a force $\frac{\mu r}{p^3}$ is due to Sir W. R. Hamilton; but the formula for the periodic time is, I believe, new. If O coincide with the centre, then the polar is at infinity, so that $\frac{\mu}{p^3} = \frac{\mu}{p_0^3} = \text{const} = \mu'$ suppose; thus the force is $\mu' r$, and the periodic time is $\frac{2\pi}{\sqrt{\mu'}}$. If O coincide with the focus S, the polar is the directrix, so that $p = \frac{r}{e}$: thus the force is $\frac{\mu e^3}{r^3}$, and the periodic time is $\frac{2\pi}{\sqrt{\mu}} \cdot \left(\frac{a}{e}\right)^{\frac{3}{2}}$, that is the force is $\frac{\mu'}{r^3}$, and the periodic time $\frac{2\pi a^{\frac{3}{2}}}{\sqrt{\mu'}}$. It can be deduced from the law $\frac{\mu r}{p^3}$, that the most general laws of force such that, whatever be the circumstances of projection in the plane xy, the body will always describe a conic, are

$$\frac{\mu r}{(ax + by + c)^3} \text{ and } \frac{\mu r}{(ax^2 + bxy + cy^2)^{\frac{3}{2}}}.$$

Independent proofs that a body subject to the action of either of these laws of force will describe a conic about the origin as centre of force, and that these are the most general laws for which this is true, are given by MM. Darboux and Halphen, *Comptes Rendus*, t. 84, pp. 760—762 and 936—941 (1877).]

xvii. A semicircle is immersed vertically in liquid with the diameter in the surface; shew how to divide it into any number of sectors, such that the pressure on each is the same.

Consider the pressure upon the sector BOP (fig. 32), AOB being the surface of the water. The pressure is equal to the area of the sector × pressure at the centre of gravity $= \frac{1}{2} a^2 \theta \cdot \rho \frac{2}{3} \frac{\sin \frac{1}{2}\theta}{\frac{1}{2}\theta} \sin \frac{1}{2}\theta$, a being the radius, and θ the angle BOP. Thus the pressure $\propto 1 - \cos \theta$, that is, $\propto$ the versed sine BN.

The construction therefore is: divide the diameter AB (fig. 33) into n equal parts in $N_1, N_2, N_3 \ldots$ and draw vertical lines $N_1 M_1, N_2 M_2, N_3 M_3, \ldots$ then the pressures upon the n sectors $OBM_1, OM_1 M_2, OM_2 M_3, \ldots$ are equal.

18. A fixed vertical circular tube full of air has within it two diaphragms of weight w_1, w_2 which fit the tube closely, and are originally in contact with one another. They are separated by water being forced into the tube through a small hole which is closed when the weight of water forced in is w_3. Shew that in the position of stable equilibrium the line joining the weight w_1 to the

centre of the tube is inclined to the horizon at the angle

$$\tan^{-1} \frac{w_1 \gamma + w_2 \gamma \cos \gamma + w_3 \sin \gamma}{w_3 (1 - \cos \gamma) + w_2 \gamma \sin \gamma},$$

where γ is the angle subtended at the centre of the tube by the water.

Let θ_1 be the angle required, θ_2 the corresponding angle for w_2, being positive when below the horizontal. Let ϖ be the pressure of the water at the lowest point of the tube, p the pressure of the air. Let a be the radius of the tube. Let the area of a cross section be unity, and let ρ be the density of the water.

At the diaphragms the pressures of the water are $\varpi - g\rho a (1 - \sin \theta_1)$ and $\varpi - g\rho a (1 - \sin \theta_2)$ respectively, where $\theta_1 + \gamma + \theta_2 = \pi$.

Hence, resolving along the tube at w_1, w_2, we must have, in equilibrium,

$$p + w_1 \cos \theta_1 = \varpi - g\rho a (1 - \sin \theta_1),$$
$$p + w_2 \cos \theta_2 = \varpi - g\rho a (1 - \sin \theta_2);$$

therefore $\quad w_1 \cos \theta_1 - w_2 \cos \theta_2 = g\rho a (\sin \theta_1 - \sin \theta_2).$

Now $\quad g\rho a \gamma = w_3$ and $\theta_2 = \pi - \theta_1 - \gamma,$

therefore $w_1 \gamma \cos \theta_1 + w_2 \gamma \cos (\theta_1 + \gamma) = w_3 \{\sin \theta_1 - \sin (\theta_1 + \gamma)\},$

therefore

$$\{w_1 \gamma + w_2 \gamma \cos \gamma + w_3 \sin \gamma\} \cos \theta_1 = \{w_3 (1 - \cos \gamma) + w_2 \gamma \sin \gamma\} \sin \theta_1,$$

therefore $\quad \tan \theta_1 = \dfrac{w_1 \gamma + w_2 \gamma \cos \gamma + w_3 \sin \gamma}{w_3 (1 - \cos \gamma) + w_2 \gamma \sin \gamma}.$

xix. In order to determine the vapour-density of a liquid, a small quantity of the liquid is sealed up in a thin bulb of glass and weighed. The bulb and its contents are then placed in a glass tube full of mercury, which is inverted in a bath of mercury. The tube is graduated so as to shew the volume measured from the closed end. The upper end of the tube is now warmed so that the bulb bursts, and the whole of the liquid is evaporated, and becomes vapour above the mercury. Obtain a formula for the vapour-density of the liquid in terms of m, the weight of the evaporated liquid, v the volume of the vapour, t the temperature of the vapour, b the height of the barometer in the room, h the height of the mercury, over which the vapour is, above that in the bath, and e the pressure of the vapour of mercury for the temperature t.

If m be measured in grammes, v in cubic centimetres, b, h, e in millimetres, and if t be the temperature centigrade, then the formula for the vapour density is

$$\frac{m}{v} \frac{1 + 0.003665\, t}{0.001293} \frac{760}{b - h - e}.$$

(See *Kohlrausch's Physical Measurements*, London, 1873, p. 50.)

xx. Any two parallel rays are incident upon the surface of a reflecting parabola. Give a geometrical construction for finding the point of intersection of the reflected rays; and employ the result to find the point in which any reflected ray cuts the caustic by reflexion of a parabola, the incident rays being all inclined to the axis at a given angle.

Let TP (fig. 34) be one of the rays, cutting the axis at an angle a, let PT' be the reflected ray and PG the normal. Then $\angle SPT' = \angle SPG + \angle GPT' = \angle SGP + \angle TPG = a$. Therefore $\angle SPT'$ is constant for parallel rays. Hence if P, P' be the points of incidence of two parallel rays, describe the circle circumscribing SPP', and it will cut either of the reflected rays in the point required.

Hence, to find the point on the caustic corresponding to the ray TP, draw SQ perpendicular to SP and QR perpendicular to the reflected ray: R will be the point on the caustic.

21. A and B are fixed points, A being a luminous point and B the nearest point of a glass sphere with refractive index μ. C a point on BA produced is the image of A as seen by an eye on AB produced beyond the sphere. Shew that AC is least when the radius of the sphere is $\dfrac{3\mu - 2}{2 - \mu} AB$.

Let the radius of the sphere be r, $BA = u$, $AC = x$; and let O be the centre of the sphere, and D the image of A after refraction into the sphere.

Then we have the equations:

$$\frac{\mu}{OA} - \frac{1}{OD} = \frac{\mu - 1}{r},$$

$$\frac{1}{OD} - \frac{\mu}{OC} = \frac{\mu - 1}{r};$$

therefore
$$\frac{\mu}{OA} - \frac{\mu}{OC} = 2\frac{\mu - 1}{r},$$

or
$$\frac{\mu}{r+u} - \frac{\mu}{r+u+x} = 2\frac{\mu - 1}{r};$$

therefore
$$\frac{x}{(r+u)(r+u+x)} = \frac{2(\mu - 1)}{\mu r},$$

therefore
$$x\left\{\frac{\mu}{2(\mu - 1)}r - r - u\right\} = (r+u)^2,$$

therefore
$$x = \frac{(r+u)^2}{\lambda r - u}, \quad \text{if } \lambda = \frac{2-\mu}{2(\mu - 1)}.$$

The least value of x will be found by solving this equation as a quadratic in r.

The equation is
$$r^2 + r(2u - \lambda x) + u^2 + ux = 0;$$
which has real roots if
$$(2u - \lambda x)^2 > 4(u^2 + ux),$$
or
$$\lambda^2 x > 4u(1+\lambda).$$

Thus the least value of x is $\dfrac{4(1+\lambda)}{\lambda^2} u$, and the corresponding value of r is $\tfrac{1}{2}(\lambda x - 2u) = \left(\dfrac{2(1+\lambda)}{\lambda} - 1\right) u = \dfrac{2+\lambda}{\lambda} u = \dfrac{3\mu - 2}{2-\mu} u.$

22. If the Earth be supposed at rest, shew that Venus will have the same apparent brightness at both points of her orbit which have the elongation
$$\cos^{-1} \frac{v + \sqrt{2e^2 - v^2}}{2e},$$
where e, v are the distances of the Earth and Venus respectively from the Sun.

Hence shew that there are positions of Venus in her orbit besides inferior and superior conjunction at which her apparent brightness is a maximum or minimum.

Let S, E, V (fig. 35) represent the Sun, Earth and Venus respectively, and $EC_1 SC_2$ the line of conjunctions.

Let $SE = e$, $SV = v$, $EV = x$, $SEV = \theta$, $VSC_2 = \phi$.

The projection on a plane perpendicular to EV of the illuminated area is proportional to $1 + \cos(\phi - \theta)$, and its distance from E is x.

Then the apparent brightness I is proportional to
$$\frac{1 + \cos(\phi - \theta)}{x^2}, \text{ or } \frac{1}{x^2}\left\{1 + \frac{x^2 + v^2 - e^2}{2xv}\right\},$$
therefore $I = \mu \dfrac{(x+v)^2 - e^2}{x^3}$, where μ is a constant.

The two values of x (x_1, x_2), which correspond to one value of θ, are given by the roots of the equation,
$$\cos\theta = \frac{x^2 + e^2 - v^2}{2xe}, \text{ or } x^2 - 2xe\cos\theta + e^2 - v^2 = 0,$$
therefore
$$x_1 x_2 = e^2 - v^2 = c^2 \text{ say.}$$

It is required to find two points P_1, P_2 in Venus' orbit with the same elongation θ, for which $I_{P_1} = I_{P_2}$. When these are equal, we have
$$\frac{(x_1 + v)^2 - e^2}{x_1^3} = \frac{(x_2 + v)^2 - e^2}{x_2^3},$$
or
$$x_1^2 x_2^2 (x_2 - x_1) + 2vx_1 x_2 (x_2^2 - x_1^2) - c^2(x_2^3 - x_1^3) = 0;$$

therefore $\quad c^4 + 2vc^2(x_2 + x_1) - c^2\{(x_2 + x_1)^2 - c^2\} = 0$,

therefore $\quad (x_2 + x_1)^2 - 2v(x_2 + x_1) + v^2 = v^2 + 2c^2 = 2e^2 - v^2$,

therefore $\quad x_2 + x_1 = v \pm \sqrt{2e^2 - v^2}$;

and since $e > v$, $\sqrt{2e^2 - v^2} > v$, so that we must take the upper sign.

Now $\quad \cos\theta = \dfrac{x^2 + e^2 - v^2}{2xe} = \dfrac{x_1^2 + x_1 x_2}{2x_1 e} = \dfrac{x_1 + x_2}{2e}$

$\quad\quad\quad\quad = \dfrac{v + \sqrt{2e^2 - v^2}}{2e}$.

Thus for this value of θ, $I_{P_1} = I_{P_2} = \mu \dfrac{\sqrt{2e^2 - v^2} - v}{e^2 - v^2}$.

Hence between P_1 and P_2 there must be some point at which I is a maximum or minimum.

WEDNESDAY, *January* 2, 1878. 1½ to 4.

Mr FERRERS, Arabic Numbers.
Mr GREENHILL; Roman Numbers.

1. ENUNCIATE and prove Newton's first lemma.

A point P moves in such a manner that its distance from a given point S varies inversely as PN, the perpendicular let fall from it on a given straight line. Prove that, if the tangent to the path of P meet the straight line in Q and the line SR, drawn at right angles to SP, in R, PR is equal to PQ.

Let P' (fig. 36) be a point on the locus of P, join SP', and draw $P'N'$ perpendicular to the given straight line. From SP' cut off SV equal to SP, then when P' is indefinitely close to P, PV is perpendicular to SP. Draw PU perpendicular to PN.

Now $\quad\quad\quad SP \cdot P'N' = SP \cdot PN$;

therefore $\quad (SV + VP')(PN - PU) = SP \cdot PN$,

whence, since $SV = SP$,

$\quad\quad\quad VP' \cdot PN - SP \cdot PU = VP' \cdot PU$.

But VP', PU are each indefinitely small, as compared with PN or SP.

Hence $\quad\quad PN \cdot \dfrac{PP'}{PU} = SP \dfrac{PP'}{VP'}$;

therefore $\quad PN \sec NPP' = SP \sec SPP'$;

therefore $\quad\quad PQ = PR$.

2. Find the radius of curvature at any point of an ellipse.

If the centre of curvature, corresponding to a point on an ellipse, fall on the conjugate diameter, the area of the corresponding circle of curvature is equal to that of the ellipse.

This gives, with the usual notation,

radius of curvature $= CD$,

or
$$\frac{CD^3}{AC \cdot BC} = CD;$$

therefore $CD^2 = AC \cdot BC$,

whence the result follows at once.

3. Given the velocities at three points of a central orbit, determine the position of the centre.

If the velocities be proportional in magnitude to the sides of the triangle formed by their directions, the centre of force coincides with the centre of gravity of the triangle.

Let ABC be the triangle, S the centre, SP, SQ, SR the perpendiculars on BC, CA, AB respectively. Then, SP, SQ, SR are to one another inversely as BC, CA, AB, or $SP \cdot BC = SQ \cdot CA = SR \cdot AB$. Thus the areas of the three triangles, SBC, SCA, SAB, are equal, or S is the centre of gravity of the triangle.

iv. Prove that a body, attracted to a fixed centre, will describe areas about the centre proportional to the times of describing them.

Define the hodograph of an orbit; and prove that, if the velocity in the hodograph is proportional to the angular velocity of the corresponding point in the orbit about the centre of attraction, the orbit will be an ellipse described about the focus.

The velocity in the hodograph being proportional to the acceleration in the orbit, the acceleration is therefore proportional to the angular velocity about the centre of attraction.

But the angular velocity about the centre of attraction in a central orbit is inversely proportional to the square of the distance, by the principle of the equable description of areas.

Therefore the acceleration is inversely proportional to the square of the distance, and the orbit is therefore a conic section described about a focus.

v. Find the law of attraction under which a body will describe an ellipse about a focus.

Prove that, when the distance between the centres of the Sun and the Earth is r, the attraction between them is

$$\frac{4\pi^2}{T^2} \frac{SE}{S+E} \frac{a^3}{r^2},$$

where T is the periodic time, S the mass of the Sun, E of the Earth in astronomical units, and a is the mean distance between their centres.

(Maxwell, *Matter and Motion*, Article CXXXIV.)

vi. State Kepler's laws; and give Newton's dynamical interpretation of them.

Prove that, neglecting the disturbances produced by the planets on each other's orbits, the statement of Kepler's third law should be amended to "The cubes of the mean distances of the planets from the Sun are as the squares of the periodic times multiplied into the sum of the masses of the Sun and the planet."

(Maxwell, *Matter and Motion*, Articles CXXXVI, CXXXVII.)

vii. Explain the different methods used in Astronomy for defining the positions of terrestrial and celestial objects.

Describe the shortest course of a steamer which is to go from one point to another without going beyond a certain latitude, supposing the great circle course to cross that latitude.

If a string be stretched between the two points on a terrestrial globe, wrapping it on the parallel of latitude, the string will represent the shortest course, which therefore consists of two great circle arcs, touching the parallel of latitude, and the intercepted arc of the small circle of latitude.

viii. Give the arguments in favour of and the proofs of the Earth's rotation.

If, at any instant, the plane of vibration of a Foucault's pendulum pass through a star near the horizon, prove that the plane will continue to pass through the star so long as it is near the horizon.

The angular velocity of the vertical plane through the pendulum is equal to the resolved part of the apparent angular velocity of the celestial sphere about the vertical, and consequently the plane of vibration of the pendulum will follow a star near the horizon. (Maxwell, *Matter and Motion*, Article CVI.)

ix. Describe the transit-circle, and the residual errors of adjustment to be allowed for in the reduction of an observation.

If a north and south collimator be made to collimate with each other, and if α be the micrometer reading for the coincidence of the moveable wire of the transit with the cross wires of the north collimator, β the reading for the south collimator, and γ for coincidence with its image when pointed downwards at a trough of mercury, prove that the level error is $\gamma - \frac{1}{2}(\alpha + \beta)$.

The line of collimation is the line drawn from the centre of the object-glass through and perpendicular to the line of the pivots.

S.-H. P.

Therefore if c be the micrometer reading for the line of collimation, $c = \frac{1}{2}(\alpha + \beta)$.

If l be the level error, then $l = \gamma - c$;

and therefore $l = \gamma - \frac{1}{2}(\alpha + \beta)$.

10. Describe and explain the phases of the Moon.

Mars rotates on his axis in 24 hours, and the periods of sidereal revolution of his two satellites around him are $7\frac{1}{2}$ hours and 30 hours respectively. Find the length of the lunar day for each; and describe and explain the appearances respectively presented by them, between two successive transits over any meridian of Mars. In what directions do they respectively appear to move across the sky?

If L_1, L_2 be the number of hours in the lunar day for the first and second satellites respectively,

$$\frac{1}{L_1} = \frac{1}{7\frac{1}{2}} - \frac{1}{24} = \frac{11}{120}, \text{ therefore } L_1 = 10\tfrac{10}{11};$$

$$\frac{1}{L_2} = \frac{1}{24} - \frac{1}{30} = \frac{1}{120}, \text{ therefore } L_2 = 120.$$

Hence the lengths of the respective lunar days are $10\tfrac{10}{11}$ hours, and 120 hours, respectively.

Since the time of the sidereal revolution of each satellite is very small as compared with that of Mars, the length of a lunation will be sensibly the same as that of a sidereal revolution. The first satellite will therefore go through its phases about $1\frac{1}{2}$ times between two successive culminations, and the second about four times. The first satellite, since it revolves round Mars in less time than that in which Mars rotates on its axis, will rise in the West and set in the East. The second will rise in the East and set in the West.

11. Define a True Solar, and a Mean Solar, Day. From what two causes does the difference between them arise? Define the Equation of Time; and prove that it vanishes four times a year.

Assuming that, if the orbit of the Earth were a circle with the Sun in its centre, the Sun's right ascension (a) and its longitude (l) would be connected by the equation $\tan a = \tan l \cos \omega$, where ω is the obliquity of the ecliptic, prove that the equation of time will have its greatest value when $\tan a = \sqrt{\cos \omega}$, and that, if θ be then the difference between the Sun's longitude and right ascension, $\tan \theta = \dfrac{(\sin \frac{1}{2}\omega)^2}{\sqrt{\cos \omega}}$.

The Equation of Time, in the case supposed, would arise only from the obliquity, and will therefore have its greatest magnitude when the difference between a and l is greatest. Now

$$\tan(l-a) = \tan l \frac{1-\cos\omega}{1+\tan^2 l \cos\omega}$$

$$= \tan l \frac{\sec\omega - 1}{\sec\omega + \tan^2 l}.$$

Hence $$\tan^2 l + \sec\omega = \frac{\sec\omega - 1}{\tan(l-a)} \tan l\,;$$

therefore $$\tan^2 l - \frac{\sec\omega - 1}{\tan(l-a)} \tan l + \sec\omega = 0.$$

Hence, in order that $\tan l$ must be real, we must have

$$\left\{\frac{\sec\omega - 1}{\tan(l-a)}\right\}^2 - 4\sec\omega \text{ not negative.}$$

If θ be the value of $l-a$, when this quantity $=0$, we have

$$(\tan\theta)^2 = \frac{(\sec\omega - 1)^2}{4\sec\omega} = \frac{(1-\cos\omega)^2}{4\cos\omega} = \frac{(\sin\tfrac{1}{2}\omega)^4}{\cos\omega};$$

therefore $$\tan\theta = \frac{(\sin\tfrac{1}{2}\omega)^2}{\sqrt{\cos\omega}}.$$

Hence, this is the greatest value of $\tan(l-a)$.

12. Explain the cause of Eclipses. Why are the intervals between the Solar ecliptic limits larger than between the Lunar?

Having given that the line of nodes of the Moon's orbit makes a complete revolution, in a retrograde direction, in 6799·5 days, and that the length of a lunation is 29·53 days, prove that eclipses will recur, in an invariable order, after 223 lunations.

If S be the number of days in a synodic revolution of the Sun and the line of nodes, then, since the nodes move in a retrograde direction,

$$\frac{1}{S} = \frac{1}{365\cdot25} + \frac{1}{6799\cdot53}$$

$$= \frac{7164\cdot78}{2483528\cdot3325}$$

$$= \frac{1}{346\cdot630089} \text{ nearly.}$$

Hence, 19 synodic revolutions of the Sun and the line of nodes $= 6585\cdot97169$ days nearly.

And 223 lunations $= 6585\cdot19$ days.

It thus appears that 223 lunations are very nearly equal to 19 synodic revolutions of the Sun and the line of nodes, and therefore that, at the end of this period, the Sun, the Moon and the line of nodes will be nearly in the same relative positions as at the beginning of it. Hence, eclipses will recur after the lapse of this period in an invariable order.

THURSDAY, *January* 3, 1878. 9 to 12.

Mr GREENHILL, Arabic numbers.
Mr NIVEN, Roman numbers.

1. SHEW how to find the convergents to a continued fraction. Prove that the ascending continued fraction

$$\frac{b_1}{a_1} + \frac{b_2}{a_2} + \frac{b_3}{a_3} \ldots + \frac{b_n}{a_n} = \frac{b_1}{a_1} + \frac{b_2}{a_1 a_2} + \frac{b_3}{a_1 a_2 a_3} + \ldots + \frac{b_n}{a_1 a_2 a_3 \ldots a_n}.$$

The logarithm of the radical

$$R = \sqrt[a_1]{\beta_1 \sqrt[a_2]{\beta_2 \sqrt[a_3]{\beta_3 \ldots \sqrt[a_n]{\beta_n}}}}$$

leads to the expression

$$\log R = \frac{\log \beta_1}{a_1} + \frac{\log \beta_2}{a_2} + \frac{\log \beta_3}{a_3} \ldots + \frac{\log \beta_n}{a_n}.$$

But, by reduction,

$$R = \sqrt[a_1 a_2 \ldots a_n]{\beta_1^{a_2 a_3 \ldots a_n} \beta_2^{a_3 a_4 \ldots a_n} \ldots \beta_{n-1}^{a_n} \beta_n},$$

and therefore

$$\log R = \frac{\log \beta_1}{a_1} + \frac{\log \beta_2}{a_1 a_2} + \frac{\log \beta_3}{a_1 a_2 a_3} + \ldots + \frac{\log \beta_n}{a_1 a_2 a_3 \ldots a_n}.$$

Putting $\log \beta_1 = b_1$, $\log \beta_2 = b_2$, ... $\log \beta_n = b_n$, we obtained the required equality.

2. Prove that in a spherical triangle,

$$\cos a = \cos b \cos c + \sin b \sin c \cos A,$$

and hence prove that

$$\tan^2 \tfrac{1}{2} a = \frac{\tan^2 \tfrac{1}{2} b - 2 \tan \tfrac{1}{2} b \tan \tfrac{1}{2} c \cos A + \tan^2 \tfrac{1}{2} c}{1 + 2 \tan \tfrac{1}{2} b \tan \tfrac{1}{2} c \cos A + \tan^2 \tfrac{1}{2} b \tan^2 \tfrac{1}{2} c}.$$

If $A_1, A_2, A_3, \ldots A_n$ be n equidistant points on a small circle of a sphere of which the pole is O, and if P be any other point on the sphere, prove that

$$\tan^2 \tfrac{1}{2} PA_1 \tan^2 \tfrac{1}{2} PA_2 \ldots \tan^2 \tfrac{1}{2} PA_n$$

$$= \frac{\tan^{2n} \tfrac{1}{2} OA - 2 \tan^n \tfrac{1}{2} OA \tan^n \tfrac{1}{2} OP \cos nPOA + \tan^{2n} \tfrac{1}{2} OP}{1 + 2 \tan^n \tfrac{1}{2} OA \tan^n \tfrac{1}{2} OP \cos nPOA + \tan^{2n} \tfrac{1}{2} OA \tan^{2n} \tfrac{1}{2} OP}.$$

Denoting the angle POA_1 by θ,

$$\tan^2 \tfrac{1}{2} PA_1 \tan^2 \tfrac{1}{2} PA_2 \ldots \tan^2 \tfrac{1}{2} PA_n$$

$$= \prod_{r=0}^{r=n-1} \frac{\tan^2 \tfrac{1}{2} OA - 2\tan \tfrac{1}{2} OA \tan \tfrac{1}{2} OP \cos\left(\dfrac{2\pi r}{n}+\theta\right) + \tan^2 \tfrac{1}{2} OP}{1 + 2\tan \tfrac{1}{2} OA \tan \tfrac{1}{2} OP \cos\left(\dfrac{2\pi r}{n}+\theta\right) + \tan^2 \tfrac{1}{2} OA \tan^2 \tfrac{1}{2} OP},$$

which is equal to the required result, by De Moivre's property of the circle.

3. Find the length and the equations of the shortest line joining the straight lines whose equations are

$$\frac{x-a}{\cos\alpha} = \frac{y-b}{\cos\beta} = \frac{z-c}{\cos\gamma},$$

and

$$\frac{x-a'}{\cos\alpha'} = \frac{y-b'}{\cos\beta'} = \frac{z-c'}{\cos\gamma'}.$$

Prove that the volume of the tetrahedron of which a pair of opposite edges is formed by lengths r, r' on these straight lines is

$$\tfrac{1}{6} rr' \begin{vmatrix} a-a', & b-b', & c-c' \\ \cos\alpha, & \cos\beta, & \cos\gamma \\ \cos\alpha', & \cos\beta', & \cos\gamma' \end{vmatrix}.$$

If d be the shortest distance and θ the angle between the opposite edges, then the determinant is equal to $d\sin\theta$ (Frost, *Solid Geometry*, § 60); and the volume of the tetrahedron formed by the given opposite edges, being $\tfrac{1}{6} rr' d \sin\theta$, is equal to the given result.

4. Prove the theorem for the differentiation of a product any number of times; and deduce the theorem

$$\phi\left(\frac{d}{dx}\right) e^{ax} y = e^{ax} \phi\left(a + \frac{d}{dx}\right) y.$$

Prove that

$$\left(\frac{d}{dx}\right)^n \left(x\frac{d}{dx} - n\right)^r y = \left(x\frac{d}{dx}\right)^r \frac{d^n y}{dx^n}.$$

Putting $x = e^\theta$, and using the theorem

$$x^n \frac{d^n y}{dx^n} = \left(\frac{d}{d\theta} - 1\right)\left(\frac{d}{d\theta} - 2\right)\ldots\left(\frac{d}{d\theta} - n + 1\right) y,$$

we have

$$\left(\frac{d}{dx}\right)^n \left(x\frac{d}{dx} - n\right)^r y$$

$$= e^{-n\theta} \left(\frac{d}{d\theta} - 1\right)\left(\frac{d}{d\theta} - 2\right) \ldots \left(\frac{d}{d\theta} - n + 1\right)\left(\frac{d}{d\theta} - n\right)^r y$$

$$= e^{-n\theta}\left(\frac{d}{d\theta} - n\right)^r \left(\frac{d}{d\theta} - 1\right)\left(\frac{d}{d\theta} - 2\right)\cdots\left(\frac{d}{d\theta} - n + 1\right)y$$

$$= \left(\frac{d}{d\theta}\right)^r e^{-n\theta}\left(\frac{d}{d\theta} - 1\right)\left(\frac{d}{d\theta} - 2\right)\cdots\left(\frac{d}{d\theta} - n + 1\right)y$$

$$= \left(x\frac{d}{dx}\right)^r \frac{d^n y}{dx^n}.$$

5. Form the general equations of equilibrium of an inextensible string under given forces; and prove that the form of the chains of a suspension bridge with uniform horizontal load is a parabola.

If an endless chain be placed round a rough circular cylinder, and pulled at a point in it parallel to the axis, prove that, if the chain be on the point of slipping, the curve formed by it on the cylinder when developed will be a parabola; and find the length of the chain when this takes place.

The chain being on the point of slipping, the friction at every point is parallel to the generating lines of the cylinder, and therefore the resolved part of the tension of the chain perpendicular to the generating lines of the cylinder is constant.

Therefore the pressure and consequently the friction at any point per unit length of the chain is proportional to the cosine of the angle between the tangent line to the chain and the generating line.

The chain is therefore in equilibrium under forces, similar to those on a chain with uniform horizontal load, wrapped round a smooth vertical cylinder, and therefore the curve formed by the chain when developed will be a parabola.

Analytically, if x be the abscissa of any point in the developed curve, and ψ the inclination of the tangent to the axis of x,

$$T \cos \psi = T_0,$$

$$R = \frac{T_0}{a} \cos \psi,$$

$$\frac{d}{ds}(T \sin \psi) = \mu R.$$

Therefore
$$\frac{d}{ds}(\tan \psi) = \frac{\mu}{a} \cos \psi,$$

or
$$\frac{d^2 y}{dx^2} = \frac{\mu}{a},$$

the differential equation of a parabola of latus rectum $\dfrac{2a}{\mu}$.

The required length of the chain, when on the point of slipping, is therefore the length of the arc of a parabola of latus rectum $\dfrac{2a}{\mu}$, comprised between the ordinates $-\pi a$ and πa.

vi. Shew that two similar curves, if similarly placed, have always one centre of similitude; and that, if not similarly placed, they have always one pair of homographic points coincident.

A triangle, the magnitudes of whose angles are given, moves with its vertices on three given right lines, shew that corresponding points of the triangle always lie on right lines, except one point which is fixed.

Two similar and similarly situated figures may always be brought by a movement of pure translation to have any assigned pair of homographic points coincident; and, starting from this position, any movement of pure translation given to one of them will bring one pair of homographic points into coincidence; those, namely, which lie in the direction along which the translation takes place, and whose distance is equal to the given translation. In the original position, therefore, one pair of homographic points coincide and form a centre of similitude.

Any relative position of two similar figures in a plane may be attained by moving one through a given angle. After turning through a given angle a, a pair of homographic points will come into coincidence in P, where $APA' = a$, and $AP : A'P =$ ratio of similitude of the two figures. P is therefore found as the intersection of two circular arcs.

Let the three fixed lines form a triangle ABC (fig. 37), and let $\alpha\beta\gamma$ be the triangle of given form. If circles be described round the triangles $A\beta\gamma$, $B\gamma\alpha$, $C\alpha\beta$, they will intersect in a point P, at which the sides of the triangle $\alpha\beta\gamma$ will subtend constant angles, it is therefore one of the homographic points of the triangle, and may be shewn to be fixed, for $\angle BPa = \angle \beta\gamma a$, and $CPa = C\beta a$, and therefore

$$\angle BPC = 2\pi - (\beta + \gamma) - (\pi - A) = \pi + A - (\beta + \gamma),$$

a constant angle. Similarly APB and APC are constant angles; P is therefore fixed. It may also be proved that any homographic point δ of the triangle describes a straight line; for describe circles round $\alpha P\delta$, $\gamma P\delta$, to cut BC, BA in $C'A'$.

The angles $P\delta C' + P\delta A' =$ two right angles, for they are respectively equal to PaB, and $P\gamma B$, which are together equal to two right angles. Hence $A'\delta C'$ is a straight line. Further, the angle $PC''B =$ angle $P\delta a$, and is therefore fixed. Hence C', and similarly A', are fixed points.

[The theorem, as well as the above elegant demonstration of it, are due to Mr McFarlane Gray, of the Board of Trade.]

It may also be proved analytically; for, if $x_1 y_1$ be the co-ordinates of α, $x_2 y_2$ those of β, $x_3 y_3$ those of γ, we have

$$(x_3 - x_1) \sin \gamma = (x_2 - x_1) \sin \beta \cos a - (y_2 - y_1) \sin \beta \sin a,$$
$$(y_3 - y_1) \sin \gamma = (y_2 - y_1) \sin \beta \cos a + (x_2 - x_1) \sin \beta \sin a.$$

The co-ordinates of any fourth homographic point are given by

$$(l + m + n) x_4 = lx_1 + mx_2 + nx_3,$$
$$(l + m + n) y_4 = ly_1 + my_2 + ny_3,$$

where $l : m : n$ are given ratios. These equations being all linear, it follows that, if x_1y_1, x_2y_2, x_3y_3 satisfy linear relations, we can express x_4y_4 in the form

$$(l + m + n)\, x_4 = A_1 x_1 + B_1,$$
$$(l + m + n)\, y_4 = C_1 x_1 + D_1,$$

where A_1, B_1, C_1, D_1 are linear functions of l, m, n; the locus of the fourth point will thence be a straight line, except for the particular values of $l : m : n$ which make $A_1 = 0$, $C_1 = 0$; in which case the fourth point is fixed.

vii. In the moon's motion there occurs an inequality whose argument is $(2 - 2m)pt - 2\beta$; investigate the magnitude of the corresponding term in the expression for the longitude, and explain the physical meaning of the term.

viii. Define the specific heat of saturated vapour; and shew that, if h be the specific heat of the vapour, c that of the liquid from which it is derived, at the same pressure and temperature, L the latent heat, then

$$h = c + \frac{dL}{dt} - \frac{L}{t}.$$

What conclusion can be drawn from a knowledge that h is positive for some substance?

Trace the entropy of a pound of water from the solid into the gaseous state.

The following brief sketch of the fundamental formulæ in Thermodynamics may perhaps help the student. We shall suppose that we are dealing with a fluid body, so that the variations of the thermodynamic quantities due to changes of the state of strain may be neglected, and that therefore, of the three magnitudes pressure p, volume v, temperature θ, one is a function of the other two. We shall also suppose the heat expressed in mechanical units, and suppose that we are dealing with unit of mass of the body. To change the state of the body from v, θ to $v + dv$, $\theta + d\theta$, δH units of heat must be added, where

$$\delta H = M dv + K_v d\theta \quad \text{............................(1)},$$

increase of energy contained in it

$$dE = \delta H - p dv \quad \text{..............................(2)};$$

and the First Law is equivalent to assuming that dE is an exact differential with regard to v, θ.

For a reversible cycle, the Second Law gives $\int \frac{\delta H}{\theta} = 0$, so that if

$$d\phi = \frac{\delta H}{\theta} \quad \text{..................................(3)},$$

$d\phi$ is an exact differential; in other words, between any two states, $E - E_0$ and $\phi - \phi_0$ are independent of the mode in which the passage between them has been effected.

We may write equation (2) in the form
$$dE = \theta d\phi - p dv \quad\quad\quad (4),$$
and from this equation flow at once a variety of elementary results. We may choose any two of the five magnitudes v, θ, p, ϕ, E as the two independent variables, and imagine the other three expressed in terms of them by means of three relations which are proper to the substance itself, and do not depend on the manner in which its changes of state take place.

We shall here content ourselves with considering the ordinary case, in which v and θ are chosen as variables. In this case
$$d(E - \theta\phi) = -\phi d\theta - p dv,$$
and the condition, that the right-hand member may be an exact differential, is that
$$\frac{d\phi}{dv} = \frac{dp}{d\theta}.$$

This result is equivalent to Carnot's theorem, for since
$$\theta d\phi = M dv + K_v d\theta,$$
$$M = \theta \frac{d\phi}{dv} = \theta \frac{dp}{d\theta}.$$

To this may be added the other result $K_v = \theta \dfrac{d\phi}{d\theta}$.

The most important case of this theorem is when the body passes from the liquid to the gaseous state. For let ϕ_1 and ϕ_2 be the values of the entropy just before and just after the transformation has been effected; then, θ being constant,
$$\phi_2 - \phi_1 = \int \frac{dH}{\theta} = \frac{L}{\theta},$$
where L is the latent heat; and therefore, if h and c be the specific heats of the body as saturated gas and as liquid on the point of boiling,
$$h - c = \theta \frac{d}{d\theta}(\phi_2 - \phi_1) = \frac{dL}{d\theta} - \frac{L}{\theta}.$$

When h is positive, as in the case of ether, $h d\theta$ is the quantity of heat which must be given to a pound of saturated ether to raise its temperature $d\theta$, it being still kept saturated. If, therefore, it were kept in a non-conducting vessel and the pressure were suddenly increased, the temperature could not at the same time rise to the corresponding saturation temperature, unless heat were added; therefore, if no heat were added, the ether would be partially condensed. The reverse takes place with steam.

To trace the entropy of a pound of water from ice to steam.

To avoid considering the strains in ice let us suppose it just on the point of liquefaction at state θ_0, r_0, p_0, and let θ_1, r_1, p_1 be the corresponding values when it becomes gaseous, and $\theta v p$ the final values in the state of perfect gas.

In liquifying ϕ receives the change $\phi_0' - \phi_0 = \dfrac{L_0}{\theta_0}$.

In the state of water, ϕ changes to ϕ_1, where

$$\phi_1 - \phi_0' = \int\left(\frac{dp}{d\theta}\,dv + \frac{K_\bullet}{\theta}\,d\theta\right),$$

where $K_\bullet$ is the capacity of water for heat; and if we suppose that it is sensibly incompressible, the change of ϕ will be $\displaystyle\int_{\theta_0}^{\theta_1} \frac{K_\bullet}{\theta}\,d\theta$.

In evaporating, the change of ϕ is $\phi_1' - \phi_1 = \dfrac{L_1}{\theta_1}$.

In passing from state $v_1\theta_1$ to $v\theta$ as a perfect gas, ϕ receives a change

$$\phi - \phi_1' = \int\left(\frac{dp}{d\theta}\,dv + \frac{c}{\theta}\,d\theta\right),$$

where c is the specific heat of dry steam under constant volume: if k be its specific heat under constant pressure,

$$pv = (k-c)\,\theta;$$

$$\therefore\ \phi - \phi_1' = (k-c)\log\left(\frac{v}{v_1}\right) + c\log\frac{\theta}{\theta_1}.$$

Adding all these changes together, we find

$$\phi - \phi_0 = \frac{L_0}{\theta_0} + \int_{\theta_0}^{\theta_1}\frac{K_\bullet}{\theta}\,d\theta + \frac{L_1}{\theta_1} + (k-c)\log\left(\frac{v}{v_1}\right) + c\log\frac{\theta}{\theta_1}.$$

The value of ϕ, so found, is evidently independent of the temperature and pressure at which the evaporation takes place.

ix. State the laws of the magnetic action of a current, and investigate the magnetic strength of the field inside a long solenoid.

An electro-magnet is constructed by winding a wire uniformly round n long coaxal circular cylinders of soft iron of equal thickness and length, enclosing each other; the number of layers of wire between two adjacent cylinders being always the same and equal to the number of layers outside the last cylinder; shew how to find the magnetic moment of the combination.

Solve fully the case where $n = 2$.

In this problem we suppose the force inside a solenoid to be uniform, and thus neglect the disturbing effect of the ends; and the iron cylinders will be magnetized uniformly, if we neglect in addition their mutual induction which would thus depend only on their ends.

The force on the outside will thus be, to the same approximation, sensibly zero.

The solenoids being all of equal thickness and similarly wound, the force on unit pole inside any one of them will be uniform and equal to $4\pi mi$, where i is the strength of the current, and m the number of turns per unit length. This magnitude we shall denote by F.

If A_1, A_2, ... be the areas of the sections enclosed by the coils, beginning with the outside one, B_1, B_2, ... those of the cores, K the coefficient of induction for soft iron; the strengths of the poles of the iron cores will be

$$KFB_1, \quad 2KFB_2, \quad 3KFB_3 \ldots$$

Thus the total number of lines of force from the electro-magnet will be

$$F \cdot \Sigma_{j=1}^{j=n}(A_j + 4\pi K j B_j),$$

and its magnetic moment will be

$$lmi \, \Sigma_{j=1}^{j=n}(A_j + 4\pi K j B_j),$$

l being the length of the electro-magnet.

x. Define the electric capacity of a conductor, and the coefficient of electric induction between two conductors; and shew that the latter is negative, and numerically less than the former which is positive.

If the capacities of two bodies are A, a when they are each at an infinite distance from any other body, shew that when they are at a distance R, great compared with their dimensions, their capacities are increased in the ratio $R^2 : R^2 - Aa$.

Call the two conductors (A), (a), and let (A) be charged with a quantity E of electricity; the potential at (a) is $\dfrac{E}{R}$; and, if (a) be uninsulated, there will be induced on it a charge $-\dfrac{aE}{R}$. The potential due to this charge at (A) is $-\dfrac{a}{R^2} \cdot E$, which being sensibly constant over this conductor, will not alter the distribution of its electrification. The total potential at (A) will therefore be $\left(\dfrac{1}{A} - \dfrac{a}{R^2}\right) E$. But, if (a) were at an infinite distance, the potential at (A) would be $\dfrac{E}{A}$. The capacity of (A) is therefore changed in the ratio $R^2 : R^2 - Aa$. The same result is evidently true of (a).

THURSDAY, *January* 3, 1878. 1½ to 4.

Mr FERRERS, Arabic numbers.
Mr NIVEN, Roman numbers.

1. IF the equation $f(x) = 0$ have two equal roots, one root of the equation $f'(x) = 0$ will be equal to either of them.

If the equation $ax^3 + 3bx^2 + 3cx + d = 0$ have two equal roots, they are each equal to $\frac{1}{2}\dfrac{bc - ad}{ac - b^2}$.

If the equation $ax^3 + 3bx^2 + 3cx + d = 0$ have two equal roots, they must be equal to one of the roots of the derived equation

$$ax^2 + 2bx + c = 0.$$

Hence the expressions $ax^3 + 3bx^2 + 3cx + d$, $ax^2 + 2bx + c$, must have a common factor, or the equations

$$ax^2 + 2bx + c = 0,$$
$$bx^2 + 2cx + d = 0,$$

must have a common root, to which the two equal roots of the given equation must be equal. Hence the value of this root is given by the equations

$$\frac{x^2}{bd - c^2} = \frac{2x}{bc - ad} = \frac{1}{ac - b^2}.$$

Hence the equal roots are each equal to $\frac{1}{2}\dfrac{bc - ad}{ac - b^2}$, or to $2\dfrac{bd - c^2}{bc - ad}$, which two expressions are equal to each other, when the given equation has two equal roots.

2. Sum the series

$$m \cos \theta - \tfrac{1}{3} m^3 \cos 3\theta + \tfrac{1}{5} m^5 \cos 5\theta - \ldots \text{ ad infinitum,}$$

m being less than unity; and prove that it has always the same sign as $m \cos \theta$.

Trace the curve

$$r = a (\cos \alpha \cos \theta - \tfrac{1}{3} \cos 3\alpha \cos 3\theta + \tfrac{1}{5} \cos 5\alpha \cos 2\theta - \ldots).$$

Express the doubly infinite series

$$\sum_{m=1}^{m=\infty} \sum_{n=1}^{n=\infty} (-1)^{m+n} \frac{\cos mx \cos ny}{mn(m^2 + n^2)}$$

in the form of a singly infinite series of cosines of multiples of y.

(a) If C denote the sum of the series

$$m \cos \theta - \tfrac{1}{3} m^3 \cos 3\theta + \tfrac{1}{5} m^5 \cos 5\theta - \ldots \text{ ad inf.,}$$

we have

$$2C = m\epsilon^{\sqrt{-1}\theta} - \tfrac{1}{3} m^3 \epsilon^{3\sqrt{-1}\theta} + \tfrac{1}{5} m^5 \epsilon^{5\sqrt{-1}\theta} - \ldots$$
$$+ m\epsilon^{-\sqrt{-1}\theta} - \tfrac{1}{3} m^3 \epsilon^{-3\sqrt{-1}\theta} + \tfrac{1}{5} m^5 \epsilon^{-5\sqrt{-1}\theta} - \ldots$$
$$= \tan^{-1} m\epsilon^{\sqrt{-1}\theta} + \tan^{-1} m\epsilon^{-\sqrt{-1}\theta}$$
$$= \tan^{-1} \frac{2m \cos \theta}{1 - m^2},$$

therefore $\quad C = \tfrac{1}{2} \tan^{-1} \dfrac{2m \cos \theta}{1 - m^2}.$

This result holds for all values of θ, since m is less than unity, and since $1 - m^2$ is positive, C has always the same sign as $m \cos \theta$.

(β) We have

$$\frac{2r}{a} = \cos(\theta - a) - \tfrac{1}{3} \cos 3(\theta - a) + \tfrac{1}{5} \cos 5(\theta - a) \ldots$$
$$+ \cos(\theta + a) - \tfrac{1}{3} \cos 3(\theta + a) + \tfrac{1}{5} \cos 5(\theta - a) \ldots$$

Now it is known that the upper line of the right-hand member of this equation is equal to $\tfrac{1}{4}\pi$ from $\theta = -(\tfrac{1}{2}\pi - a)$ to $\theta = \tfrac{1}{2}\pi + a$, and to $-\tfrac{1}{4}\pi$ from $\theta = \tfrac{1}{2}\pi + a$ to $\theta = \tfrac{3}{2}\pi + a$.

And that the lower line is equal to $\tfrac{1}{4}\pi$ from $\theta = -(\tfrac{1}{2}\pi + a)$ to $\theta = \tfrac{1}{2}\pi - a$, and to $-\tfrac{1}{4}\pi$ from $\theta = \tfrac{1}{2}\pi - a$ to $\theta = \tfrac{3}{2}\pi - a$.

Hence the whole expression is equal to 0 from $\theta = -(\tfrac{1}{2}\pi + a)$ to $\theta = -(\tfrac{1}{2}\pi - a)$, to $\tfrac{1}{2}\pi$ from $\theta = -(\tfrac{1}{2}\pi - a)$ to $\theta = \tfrac{1}{2}\pi - a$, to 0 from $\theta = \tfrac{1}{2}\pi - a$ to $\theta = \tfrac{1}{2}\pi + a$, and to $-\tfrac{1}{2}\pi$ from $\theta = \tfrac{1}{2}\pi + a$ to $\theta = \tfrac{3}{2}\pi - a$.

Therefore the curve represented by the above equation will be an arc of a circle, radius $\tfrac{1}{4}\pi a$, subtending an angle $\pi - 2a$ at the centre; and also (corresponding to zero values of r) the centre itself.

(γ) It will be sufficient, for this purpose, to sum the coefficient of $(-1)^n \dfrac{\cos ny}{n}$ viz. the series

$$-\frac{\cos x}{1^2 + n^2} + \frac{\cos 2x}{2(2^2 + n^2)} - \ldots + (-1)^m \frac{\cos mx}{m(m^2 + n^2)} + \ldots$$

Call the sum of this series u, then

$$\frac{d^2 u}{dx^2} - n^2 u = \cos x - \frac{\cos 2x}{2} + \frac{\cos 3x}{3} - \ldots$$
$$= \tfrac{1}{2} \{\log(1 + \epsilon^{\sqrt{-1}x}) + \log(1 + \epsilon^{-\sqrt{-1}x})\}$$
$$= \tfrac{1}{2} \log(2 + 2 \cos x) = \log 2 + \log \cos \tfrac{1}{2} x.$$

This holds from $x = -\pi$ to $x = \pi$,

therefore
$$u = A\epsilon^{nx} + B\epsilon^{-nx}$$
$$-\frac{1}{n^2}\log 2 + \epsilon^{-nx}\int_0^x \epsilon^{nx}\log\cos\frac{x}{2}\,dx + \epsilon^{nx}\int_0^x \epsilon^{-nx}\log\cos\frac{x}{2}\,dx,$$

A and B being arbitrary constants.

To determine A and B we observe, first, that the value of u is unchanged by a change in the sign of n. Hence $A = B$. And putting $x = 0$, and denoting
$$-\frac{1}{1^2+n^2} + \frac{1}{2(2^2+n^2)} - \ldots \text{ by } \phi(n)$$
$$\phi(n) = 2A - \frac{1}{n^2}\log 2,$$

therefore
$$A = \tfrac{1}{2}\phi(n) + \frac{1}{2n^2}\log 2.$$

3. If ω be the angle between the positive directions of the axes of x and y, prove that the axes of the curve
$$ax^2 + 2hxy + by^2 = 1$$
are represented by the equation
$$(a\cos\omega - h)x^2 + (a-b)xy + (h - b\cos\omega)y^2 = 0.$$

If x, y be the rectangular co-ordinates of a point, and
$$\xi = x + \sqrt{-1}\,y, \quad \eta = x - \sqrt{-1}\,y,$$
and α, β be the values of ξ, η at a focus of the curve
$$a\xi^2 + 2h\xi\eta + b\eta^2 = 1,$$

prove that
$$\alpha^2 = \frac{b}{ab - h^2}, \quad \beta^2 = \frac{a}{ab - h^2}.$$

We may determine the foci of the curve
$$a\xi^2 + 2h\xi\eta + b\eta^2 = 1$$
by the consideration that the two tangents drawn from either focus satisfy the analytical condition of representing a circle.

Now, these tangents are given by the equation
$$(a\alpha^2 + 2h\alpha\beta + b\beta^2 - 1)(a\xi^2 + 2h\xi\eta + b\eta^2 - 1) = \{(a\alpha + h\beta)\xi + (h\alpha + b\beta)\eta - 1\}^2.$$

Hence, since for a circle the coefficients of ξ^2 and η^2 are each zero
$$a(a\alpha^2 + 2h\alpha\beta + b\beta^2 - 1) - (a\alpha + h\beta)^2 = 0$$
$$b(a\alpha^2 + 2h\alpha\beta + b\beta^2 - 1) - (h\alpha + b\beta)^2 = 0,$$

therefore
$$(ab - h^2)\beta^2 - a = 0$$
$$(ab - h^2)\alpha^2 - b = 0,$$

therefore
$$\alpha^2 = \frac{b}{ab - h^2}, \quad \beta^2 = \frac{a}{ab - h^2}.$$

4. Shew how the values of $\int \cos^n x\, dx$ and $\int \sin^n x\, dx$ may be made to depend on those of $\int \cos^{n-2} x\, dx$ and $\int \sin^{n-2} x\, dx$; and prove that

$$\int_0^{\frac{\pi}{4}} \sin^{2n} x\, dx = -\frac{1}{2^{n+1}}\left\{\frac{1}{n} + \frac{(2n-1)}{n(n-1)} + \frac{(2n-1)(2n-3)}{n(n-1)(n-2)} + \cdots\right\}$$
$$+ \frac{(2n-1)(2n-3)\ldots 3}{2n(2n-2)\ldots 4 \cdot 2} \frac{\pi}{4}.$$

We have $(\sin x)^{2n} = (\sin x)^{2n-2}(1 - \cos^2 x)$.

And $\int (\sin x)^{2n-2}(\cos x)^2\, dx = \frac{(\sin x)^{2n-1} \cos x}{2n-1} + \frac{1}{2n-1}\int (\sin x)^{2n}\, dx$,

therefore

$$\int (\sin x)^{2n}\, dx = \int (\sin x)^{2n-2}\, dx - \frac{(\sin x)^{2n-1}\cos x}{2n-1} - \frac{1}{2n-1}\int (\sin x)^{2n}\, dx$$

$$= \frac{2n-1}{2n}\int (\sin x)^{2n-2}\, dx - \frac{(\sin x)^{2n-1}\cos x}{2n}.$$

Hence, writing u_n for $\int_0^{\frac{\pi}{4}} (\sin x)^{2n}\, dx$,

$$u_n = \frac{2n-1}{2n} u_{n-1} - \frac{1}{2^{n+1} n}.$$

Similarly $\quad u_{n-1} = \frac{2n-3}{2n-2} u_{n-2} - \frac{1}{2^n \cdot (n-1)}$,

$\ldots\ldots = \ldots\ldots$

and $\quad u_1 = \int_0^{\frac{\pi}{4}} \sin^2 x\, dx = \int_0^{\frac{\pi}{4}} \frac{1-\cos 2x}{2}\, dx = \frac{\pi}{8}.$

Hence $\quad u_n = -\frac{1}{2^{n+1}}\left\{\frac{1}{n} + \frac{2n-1}{n(n-1)} + \frac{(2n-1)(2n-3)}{n(n-1)(n-2)}\cdots\right\}$
$$+ \frac{(2n-1)(2n-3)\ldots 3}{2n(2n-2)\ldots 4 \cdot 2}\frac{\pi}{4}.$$

5. Prove that the Action, through any arc of the path of a projectile, is proportional to the area subtended by that arc at the focus; and express it in terms of the chord joining the ends of the arc, and the sum of the focal distances of those ends.

The action, in general, $= \int v\, ds$, and in the case of a projectile $v = \left(\frac{g}{a}\right)^{\frac{1}{2}} p$, $4a$ being the latus rectum of the parabola, and p the perpendicular on the tangent.

Hence the action $= 2\left(\dfrac{g}{a}\right)^{\frac{1}{2}} A$, A being the area subtended by the arc at the focus.

And this may be expressed in terms of the quantities mentioned in the question, by Lambert's Theorem.

vi. Investigate the "equation of continuity" in fluid motion; and explain clearly what its physical signification is. What form does it assume in the case of an incompressible fluid moving irrotationally?

A stream of uniform depth and of uniform width $2a$ flows slowly through a bridge consisting of two equal arches resting on a rectangular pier of width $2b$, the bridge being so broad that under it the fluid moves uniformly with velocity U. Shew that, after the stream has passed through the bridge, the velocity potential of the motion is

$$\frac{a-b}{a} Ux + \frac{2aU}{\pi^2} \sum_1^\infty \frac{1}{i^2} \sin\frac{i\pi b}{a} \cos\frac{i\pi y}{a} e^{-\frac{i\pi x}{a}},$$

the axis of x being in the forward direction of the stream and the origin at the middle point of the pier.

Find the equation of the path of any particle of the water.

The water is supposed to issue from the bridge with uniform velocity U, and the motion will be evidently irrotational, if we neglect friction.

The velocity potential satisfies the following conditions:

$$\frac{d^2\phi}{dx^2} + \frac{d^2\phi}{dy^2} = 0,$$

$$\phi = \frac{a-b}{a}\cdot Ux, \quad x = \infty,$$

$\dfrac{d\phi}{dx} = U$ when $x = 0$, except from $y = -b$ to $x = +b$, when it $= 0$;

$\dfrac{d\phi}{dy} = 0$ at the banks, or when $y = -a$ and $y = +a$.

These conditions are evidently satisfied by the function

$$\phi = \frac{a-b}{a}\cdot Ux + \Sigma_1^\infty A_i \cos\frac{i\pi y}{a} e^{-\frac{i\pi x}{a}},$$

provided

$$\frac{a-b}{a}\cdot U - \frac{\pi}{a}\Sigma_1^\infty iA_i \cos\frac{i\pi y}{a} = 0 \text{ from } y = 0 \text{ to } y = b,$$

$$= U \text{ from } y = b \text{ to } y = a.$$

A_i is easily found by Fourier's theorem; we have

$$\frac{a-b}{a} \cdot U \int_0^a \cos \frac{i\pi y}{a} dy - \frac{\pi i A_i}{a} \int_0^a \cos^2 \frac{i\pi y}{a} dy = U \int_b^a \cos \frac{i\pi y}{a} dy.$$

The first of these integrals vanishes, and the integration of the two others furnishes

$$A_i = \frac{2aU}{\pi^2} \cdot \frac{1}{i^2} \sin \frac{i\pi b}{a},$$

whence

$$\phi = \frac{a-b}{a} \cdot Ux + \frac{2aU}{\pi^2} \cdot \Sigma_1^\infty \frac{1}{i^2} \sin \frac{i\pi b}{a} \cos \frac{i\pi y}{a} e^{-\frac{i\pi x}{a}}.$$

The stream lines, which in this case coincide with the lines of flow of the individual particles, are given by

$$\frac{d\psi}{dy} = \frac{d\phi}{dx}, \quad \frac{d\psi}{dx} = -\frac{d\phi}{dy},$$

hence

$$\psi = \int \left(\frac{d\phi}{dx} \cdot dy - \frac{d\phi}{dy} \cdot dx \right)$$

$$= \frac{a-b}{a} \cdot U \cdot y - \frac{2aU}{\pi^2} \Sigma_1^\infty \frac{1}{i^2} \sin \frac{i\pi b}{a} \sin \frac{i\pi y}{a} e^{-\frac{i\pi x}{a}}.$$

vii. Investigate the phenomena observed when a star is viewed through a telescope, and the object-glass is limited by a small rectangular opening.

When the opening is a parallelogram of any shape, shew that the bars of the same order form parallelograms similar to it, but turned through a right angle.

We have to consider the image formed on the focal plane of the telescope. When the parallelogram is rectangular, we find from Airy's tract on the Undulatory Theory (Prop. 20), that the displacement at any point (p, q) of the focal plane is

$$\int dx \int dy \sin \frac{2\pi}{\lambda} \left(vt - B + \frac{px + qy}{b} \right),$$

b being the focal length of the object glass, $dxdy$ any element of area of the rectangle, and the origin of co-ordinates being the projection of the centre of the rectangle on the focal plane.

The total intensity of light at p, q, is also found to be the square of

$$4ef \left(\frac{b\lambda}{2\pi pe} \sin \frac{2\pi pe}{b\lambda} \right) \left(\frac{b\lambda}{2\pi qf} \sin \frac{2\pi qf}{b\lambda} \right);$$

$2e, 2f$ are the sides of the rectangle in the direction of the axes of x and y.

If the parallelogram be oblique, the angle between two sides being ω, and we choose axes parallel to its sides, we must substitute $dxdy \sin \omega$ for $dxdy$. If ϖ, κ be the contra-ordinates of the point on the focal plane considered, the function $px + qy$ for rectangular axes becomes, for oblique axes, $\varpi x + \kappa y$. The contra-ordinates of a point referred to oblique axes are the intercepts cut off by perpendiculars on the axes of x and y; in fact $\varpi = p + q \cos \omega$, $\kappa = q + p \cos \omega$.

The edges of the parallelogram being again $2e$, $2f$, the intensity of illumination for any given colour is, at any point, the square of

$$4ef \sin \omega \left(\frac{b\lambda}{2\pi \varpi e} \sin \frac{2\pi \varpi e}{b\lambda}\right)\left(\frac{b\lambda}{2\pi \kappa f} \sin \frac{2\pi \kappa f}{b\lambda}\right).$$

The bright or dark bands of any colour are given by

$$\varpi e = \frac{b\lambda}{2\pi} \cdot J, \quad \kappa f = \frac{b\lambda}{2\pi} \cdot J,$$

where J is a pure number.

They are therefore lines at right angles to the axes; and, since $\varpi : \kappa :: f : e$, they therefore evidently form figures similar to the opening, but turned through a right angle.

viii. Investigate the velocity of transmission of sound through a uniform gas; stating the correction to Newton's result introduced by Laplace, and explaining how the magnitude so introduced may be found by experiment.

A gas is formed by mixing a number of simple gases in the proportions by mass of $m_1 : m_2 : m_3 \ldots$ The specific heats of these gases at constant volume and pressure are, respectively, $c_1, k_1; c_2, k_2; \ldots$, and the velocities of sound in them are $u_1, u_2, u_3 \ldots$; shew that the velocity of sound in the mixture is given by

$$U^2 = \frac{\Sigma (mk)}{\Sigma (mc)} \cdot \frac{\Sigma \left(\frac{mcu^2}{k}\right)}{\Sigma (m)}.$$

If the simple gases be such that $\frac{k}{c}$ is the same for all, what will this result become?

The velocity of sound in a gas is given by $u^2 = \frac{p_0 v_0}{\theta_0} \cdot \theta \cdot \gamma$, where v_0 is the volume of a pound of gas at pressure p_0 and temperature θ_0, θ is the temperature of the gas under consideration, and $\gamma = k : c$.

Let there be a mass of gas $m_1 + m_2 + \ldots$ consisting of the given gases in the proportions $m_1 : m_2 : m_3 \ldots$, and let it be kept in a vessel of given volume, and let heat be applied to raise the temperature of the whole $\delta\theta$ degrees; then the quantities of heat absorbed are $m_1 c_1 \delta\theta$, $m_2 c_2 \delta\theta$, ... while, if C be the specific heat of the whole mixture under constant volume, the total heat absorbed $= (m_1 + m_2 + \ldots) C \delta\theta$;

therefore $(m_1 + m_2 + m_3 + \ldots) C = m_1 c_1 + m_2 c_2 + \ldots$.

In a precisely similar manner
$$K\Sigma(m) = \Sigma(mk).$$

Now, if V_0 be the volume of 1 lb. of the mixture at p_0, θ_0,
$$V_0 \Sigma(m) = \Sigma(mv_0).$$

We see from the equations written down above that
$$\Sigma \frac{mc}{k} u^2 = \frac{p_0}{\theta_0} \Sigma(mv_0) \cdot \theta,$$

hence we have
$$U^2 = \frac{p_0 V_0}{\theta_0} \cdot \theta \cdot \frac{K}{C}$$

$$= \frac{\Sigma(mk)}{\Sigma(mc)} \cdot \frac{\Sigma\left(\frac{mc}{k} u^2\right)}{\Sigma(m)}.$$

If $\dfrac{k}{c}$ were the same for each of the component gases
$$U^2 = \frac{\Sigma(mu^2)}{\Sigma(m)}.$$

ix. Give the theory of Wheatstone's Bridge; and explain how it can be applied to determine the position of a fault in a telegraph wire.

If A and B be the ends of a wire with one fault, and R, S the resistances to a current sent from A when B is insulated and to earth respectively; and if R', S' be the corresponding resistances to a current sent from B, prove that $R : S :: R' : S'$.

Prove also that the same result will be true if there are two faults.

In Cumming's Electricity, Art. 192, it is proved that, if the fault be at C, and the resistances of AC, CB, and of the fault be, respectively, xyz, then, for a current sent from A,
$$R = x + z, \quad S = x + \frac{yz}{y+z};$$
similarly, for a current sent from B,
$$R' = y + z, \quad S'' = y + \frac{xz}{x+z}.$$

A comparison of these expressions at once shows that
$$R : S :: R' : S'.$$

We may similarly solve the case where there are two faults, one at C, and another at D.

Let $AC = x$, $CD = y$, $DB = z$,

and let the resistances of the faults at C, D be u, v.

First, let the current go from A to B, and let B be to earth, and let the potentials at A, C, D (fig. 38), be V, V_1, V_2, and let the currents in AC, CD, DB be i_1, i_2, i_3, and those through the faults be j_1, j_2.

$$V - V_1 = xi_1, \quad V_1 - V_2 = yi_2, \quad V_2 = zi_3,$$
$$V_1 = uj_1, \quad V_2 = vj_2;$$

also $\quad i_1 = i_2 + j_1$, and $i_2 = i_3 + j_2$.

If we eliminate from these equations all the currents and potentials except i_1 and V, we obtain

$$V\left\{\frac{1}{uy} + \frac{1}{uz} + \frac{1}{uv} + \frac{1}{yz} + \frac{1}{yv}\right\}$$
$$= i_1 x\left\{\frac{1}{xy} + \frac{1}{xz} + \frac{1}{xv} + \frac{1}{uv} + \frac{1}{uy} + \frac{1}{uz} + \frac{1}{yz} + \frac{1}{yv}\right\}.$$

But since $V = Ri_1$, we find

$$R\left\{\frac{1}{uy} + \frac{1}{vy} + \frac{1}{uv} + \frac{1}{uz} + \frac{1}{yz}\right\}$$
$$= x\left\{\frac{1}{xy} + \frac{1}{yz} + \frac{1}{uy} + \frac{1}{vy} + \frac{1}{uv} + \frac{1}{xv} + \frac{1}{uz} + \frac{1}{xz}\right\}.$$

To find S we may suppose the resistance in DB to be infinitely great, that is $z = \infty$.

This gives us

$$S\left(\frac{1}{uy} + \frac{1}{vy} + \frac{1}{uv}\right) = x\left(\frac{1}{xy} + \frac{1}{uy} + \frac{1}{uv} + \frac{1}{vy} + \frac{1}{xv}\right).$$

The corresponding expressions for R' and S' are found by interchanging x, z and u, v; but the symmetry of the expression for $\dfrac{R}{S}$ shews that it will be not be altered by this change; that is to say,

$$R : S :: R' : S'.$$

MONDAY, *January* 14, 1878. 9 to 12.

Mr PRIOR,   Arabic numbers.
Mr NIVEN,   Roman numbers.

1. A BODY being subject to any given forces, find the conditions of equilibrium.

A gipsy's tripod consists of three uniform straight sticks freely hinged together at one end. From this common end hangs the kettle. The other ends of the sticks rest on a smooth horizontal plane, and are prevented from slipping by a smooth circular hoop which encloses them and is fixed to the plane. Shew that there cannot be equilibrium unless the sticks be of equal length; and if the weights of the sticks be given (equal or unequal) the bending moment of each will be greatest at its middle point, will be independent of its length, and will not be increased on increasing the weight of the kettle.

Let DA, DB, DC be the sticks; ABC the hoop, D the common end from which hangs the kettle. Let w_1, w_2, w_3 be the weights of the sticks, W that of the kettle.

Firstly, the forces on DA are its weight, the reaction at D and that at A. Hence, taking moments about a vertical through D, we see that unless the horizontal reaction at A meets this vertical it will produce an unbalanced couple round it, and there will not be equilibrium.

Thus the reactions at A, B, C must all meet in the vertical through D; also being normal to the hoop they meet in its centre; therefore the vertical through D passes through the centre of the hoop; therefore the sticks are of equal length. Similarly we learn that the reactions at D on DA are in the vertical plane through DA.

Secondly, let the inclination of each stick to the horizon be θ and its length $2l$. Then if X_1, Y_1 be the horizontal and vertical components of the reaction at D on DA, we have, taking moments about A,
$$X_1 \, 2l \sin \theta = Y_1 \, 2l \cos \theta + W_1 \, l \cos \theta,$$
therefore $\qquad 2X_1 \tan \theta = 2Y_1 + w_1.$

Similarly if X_2, Y_2, X_3, Y_3 be the reactions at D on DB, DC, we have
$$2X_2 \tan \theta = 2Y_2 + w_2,$$
$$2X_3 \tan \theta = 2Y_3 + w_3,$$
therefore $2 (X_1 + X_2 + X_3) \tan \theta = 2 (Y_1 + Y_2 + Y_3) + w_1 + w_2 + w_3.$

Also, since the hinge at D is in equilibrium, we have
$$Y_1 + Y_2 + Y_3 = W,$$
$$\frac{X_1}{\sin 2A} = \frac{X_2}{\sin 2B} = \frac{X_3}{\sin 2C}.$$

From the four last equations we obtain
$$X_1 = \frac{\sin 2A \cdot \cot \theta}{\sin 2A + \sin 2B + \sin 2C} \left\{ W + \frac{w_1 + w_2 + w_3}{2} \right\},$$
$$Y_1 = \frac{\sin 2A}{\sin 2A + \sin 2B + \sin 2C} \left\{ W + \frac{w_1 + w_2 + w_3}{2} \right\} - \frac{w_1}{2}.$$

The bending moment about a point P of DA, at a distance z from D, is
$$\frac{w_1 z}{2l} \cdot \frac{z}{2} \cos\theta + Y_1 z \cos\theta - X_1 z \sin\theta,$$
and is therefore greatest when
$$\frac{w_1 z \cos\theta}{2l} + Y_1 \cos\theta - X_1 \sin\theta = 0,$$
i. e. when
$$z = \frac{2l}{w_1}(X_1 \tan\theta - Y_1)$$
$$= \frac{2l}{w_1}\left(\frac{w_1}{2}\right) = l \, ;$$
therefore the bending moment is greatest at the middle point of each rod.

The bending moment about the middle point of DA is
$$l \cos\theta \cdot \left\{\frac{w_1}{4} + Y_1 - X_1 \tan\theta\right\}$$
$$= l \cos\theta \left\{\frac{w_1}{4} - \frac{w_1}{2}\right\}$$
$$= -\frac{l \cos\theta \, w_1}{4} = -\frac{a w_1}{8},$$
where a is the radius of the hoop: therefore the bending moment about the middle point of DA is independent of l and W.

2. Find the intrinsic and Cartesian equations of the common catenary.

A string of length $2l$ hangs over two smooth pegs which are in the same horizontal plane and at a distance $2a$ apart. The two ends of the string are free and its central portion hangs in a catenary. Shew that equilibrium is impossible unless l be at least equal to ae; and that, if $l > ae$, the catenary in the position of stable equilibrium for symmetrical displacements will be defined by that root of $ce^{\frac{a}{c}} = l$ which is greater than a.

In any position of equilibrium let $2s$ be the length of the catenary. Then we have
$$s = \frac{c}{2}\left(e^{\frac{a}{c}} - e^{-\frac{a}{c}}\right);$$
and, by equating the tensions on each side of a peg, we have
$$l - s = \frac{c}{2}\left(e^{\frac{a}{c}} + e^{-\frac{a}{c}}\right),$$
therefore
$$l = ce^{\frac{a}{c}},$$
an equation which gives c when l is given.

It is plain that we may increase the value of l indefinitely. The least possible value of l is given by
$$0 = e^{\frac{a}{c}} - ce^{\frac{a}{c}} \cdot \frac{a}{c^2},$$
or $\qquad c = a,$
and then $\qquad l = ae.$

The roots of the equation $ce^{\frac{a}{c}} = l$ are separated by those of its first derived equation
$$e^{\frac{a}{c}} - \frac{c}{a} e^{\frac{a}{c}} = 0,$$
which has only one root, $c = a$.

Therefore $ce^{\frac{a}{c}} = l$ has only two roots, one less and one greater than a.

It would appear from general reasoning that the root less than a corresponds to unstable equilibrium; for if l be very large, this root will give a catenary consisting approximately of two vertical portions which will clearly rise or fall, if a portion of string be pulled over each peg. The following is a more formal proof.

Suppose s slightly increased by pulling over a length δs of each straight portion. Then the tension T_1 on the catenary side of the peg is $w(y + \delta y)$ and that T_2 on the other side $w(l - s - \delta s)$, where w is the weight of an unit length of string, y is the height of the peg above the directrix of the original catenary, $y + \delta y$ its height above the new directrix.

Now $\qquad y = \frac{c}{2}(e^{\frac{a}{c}} + e^{-\frac{a}{c}}), \quad s = \frac{c}{2}(e^{\frac{a}{c}} - e^{-\frac{a}{c}}),$

therefore $\qquad \delta y = \delta c \left\{ \frac{y}{c} - \frac{as}{c^2} \right\};$

$\qquad \delta s = \delta c \left\{ \frac{s}{c} - \frac{ay}{c^2} \right\};$

therefore $\quad T_1 - T_2 = w \left\{ y + \delta c \frac{cy - as}{c^2} - l + s + \delta c \frac{cs - ay}{c^2} \right\}.$

But $\qquad y + s = ce^{\frac{a}{c}} = l,$

therefore $\quad T_1 - T_2 = \frac{w\delta c}{c^2}(c - a)l.$

Again, $cs - ay = \frac{c}{2}\left\{ (c-a)e^{\frac{a}{c}} - (c+a)e^{-\frac{a}{c}} \right\}$

$\qquad = \frac{c}{2} e^{-\frac{a}{c}} \left\{ (c-a)e^{\frac{2a}{c}} - (c+a) \right\}$

$\qquad = \frac{c}{2} e^{-\frac{a}{c}} \left\{ (c-a)\left(1 + \frac{2a}{c} + \frac{2a^2}{c^2} + \frac{4a^3}{3c^3} + \frac{2a^3}{3} + \ldots \right) - (c+a) \right\},$

where we observe that the successive numerical coefficients in the expansion of $e^{\frac{2a}{c}}$ diminish.

Therefore $(cs - ay) = \dfrac{c}{2} e^{-\frac{a}{c}} \left\{ (\tfrac{4}{3} - 2)\dfrac{a^3}{c^3} + (\tfrac{2}{3} - \tfrac{4}{3})\dfrac{a^4}{c^3} + \ldots \right\}$,

and is therefore negative.

Now $\qquad \delta s = \delta c \left\{ \dfrac{cs - ay}{c^2} \right\}$,

therefore δs and δc are of opposite signs.

If then δs be positive, δc is negative, and $T_1 - T_2$ has the same sign as $a - c$; i.e. if $c > a$, the equilibrium is stable for this displacement; and, if δs be negative, the result is clearly the same.

The problem may also be readily solved by finding the depth of the centre of gravity of the whole string beneath the horizontal plane through the pegs and forming the condition that this should be a maximum.

iii. Determine the conditions of stability, for small displacements, of a body floating in water.

A vessel, which may be treated as a cylinder symmetrical about a plane parallel to its length, floats in apparently neutral equilibrium: prove that the equilibrium will really be stable for small displacements if $a\kappa < \sin \alpha$, where $2a$ is the breadth of a transverse section at the water-mark, α the inclination to the horizon, and κ the curvature of the side at that point.

If the vessel be displaced through a small angle, discuss the nature of the motion which takes place in righting.

Let G be the centre of gravity of the vessel (fig. 39),

H that of fluid originally displaced,

AB original plane of floatation,

$A'B'$ the new plane after the vessel has turned through an angle β.

Let AB and CD cut in O, and let $OC = c$.

Let the equation of section referred to Cx and GCz be

$$x^2 = a^2 + 2bz + (\epsilon - 1) z^2 \ldots\ldots\ldots\ldots\ldots\ldots(1),$$

higher powers than z^2 being neglected.

When the origin is transferred to O, the equation will be

$$(x + c)^2 = a^2 + 2bz + (\epsilon - 1) z^2.$$

If we put $\qquad x = r \cos \theta, \; z = r \sin \theta,$

$$r^2 (1 - \epsilon \sin^2 \theta) - 2r (b \sin \theta - c \cos \theta) + c^2 - a^2 = 0 \ldots\ldots(2).$$

We shall now approximate on the supposition that β is small; it is clear that c is a small quantity of the order β, as the calculation itself verifies. With this understanding, it is clear that in (2)

$$r_1 + r_2 = 2(b\theta - c),$$
$$r_1 r_2 = c^2 - a^2 - \epsilon\theta^2 a^2,$$
$$(r_1 - r_2)^2 = 4a^2(1 + \vartheta), \text{ where } \vartheta = \epsilon\theta^2 + \frac{(b\theta - c)^2}{a^2} - \frac{c^2}{a^2},$$

and therefore $\qquad r_1 - r_2 = 2a(1 + \tfrac{1}{2}\vartheta)$.

Since the volume of the fluid displaced is always the same,

$$\int_0^\beta (r_1^2 - r_2^2)\, d\theta = 0, \quad \text{therefore} \quad b\beta^2 - 2c\beta = 0 \text{ or } c = \tfrac{1}{2}b\beta.$$

The turning moment consists, partly of the weight of the fluid originally displaced acting through H, and partly of a couple, being the weights of the two wedges on opposite sides of O; the latter, reckoned as a righting couple,

$$= \tfrac{1}{3}\int_0^\beta (r_1^3 - r_2^3)\, d\theta \cdot \cos\theta.$$

But $\quad r_1^3 - r_2^3 = (r_1 - r_2) \cdot \dfrac{3(r_1 + r_2)^2 + (r_1 - r_2)^2}{4}$

$$= 2a^3 + 6a(b\theta - c)^2 + 3a^3\vartheta,$$

therefore righting moment

$$= \frac{2a^3}{3}\sin\beta + a\int_0^\beta \{\epsilon\theta^2 a^2 + 3(b\theta - c)^2 - c^2\}\, d\theta,$$
$$= \frac{2a^3}{3}\sin\beta + \frac{a^3\epsilon\beta^3}{3}.$$

The equation of motion of the vessel is

$$MK^2 \frac{d^2\beta}{dt^2} = V \cdot GH \sin\beta - \frac{2a^3}{3}\sin\beta - \frac{a^3\epsilon}{3}\beta^3.$$

Since the equilibrium is neutral, $V \cdot GH = \dfrac{2a^3}{3}$,

therefore $\qquad \dfrac{d^2\beta}{dt^2} = -\dfrac{a^3\epsilon}{3MK^2} \cdot \beta^3 \quad\dotfill\quad (3).$

The equilibrium will be stable if ϵ be positive.

Now, from (1),

$$\epsilon = 1 + \tfrac{1}{2}\frac{d^2x^2}{dz^2} = 1 + \left(\frac{dx}{dz}\right)^2 + x\frac{d^2z}{dx^2}, \text{ when } z = 0.$$

But $\quad \dfrac{dx}{dz} = \cot a, \quad \dfrac{d^2x}{dz^2} = -\operatorname{cosec}^2 a \cdot \dfrac{da}{ds} \cdot \dfrac{ds}{dx} = -\operatorname{cosec}^3 a \cdot \kappa,$

hence $\qquad \epsilon = \operatorname{cosec}^3 a\,(\sin a - a\kappa) \dotfill (4).$

The equilibrium will therefore be stable if $a\kappa < \sin a$.

The equation of motion (3) shows that the righting oscillations are not harmonic; β may be expressed in terms of t by means of elliptic functions.

If β_0 be the extreme angle through which the vessel swings, the period of a complete oscillation is

$$T = 4\sqrt{\frac{6MK^2}{a^3\epsilon}} \int_0^{\beta_0} \frac{d\beta}{\sqrt{\beta_0^4 - \beta^4}}.$$

iv. A particle moves in a plane curve; state the expressions for the accelerations along and perpendicular to the radius vector from a fixed point, and investigate the differential equation of the path when the forces acting on the particle pass through the fixed point.

A particle describes a parabola under two forces, one constant and parallel to the axis, and the other passing through the focus; prove that the latter force varies inversely as the square of the distance from the focus.

Shew also that, if the force through the focus be repulsive and numerically equal, at the vertex, to the constant force, the particle will come to rest at the vertex; and find the time occupied in describing any arc of the curve.

Let the force along the focal radius vector be P, and the constant force f, then the equations of motion are (fig. 40),

$$\frac{v^2}{2} = fx - \int P\,dr + \text{const.} \quad\ldots\ldots\ldots\ldots\ldots (1),$$

$$\frac{v^2}{\rho} = (f + P)\frac{p}{r} \quad\ldots\ldots\ldots\ldots\ldots\ldots\ldots\ldots (2).$$

But, in a parabola, $p^2 = ar$, therefore $\dfrac{1}{\rho} = \dfrac{p}{2r^2}$,

therefore $v^2 = 2r(f + P)$;

also (1) may be written $v^2 = 2fr - 2\int P\,dr + \text{const.}$;

therefore, substituting, we obtain $2\int P\,dr + 2Pr = \text{const.}$,

$$2P\,dr + r\,dP = 0,$$

$$Pr^2 = \text{const. or } P \propto \frac{1}{r^2}.$$

If P be repulsive, and $= \dfrac{\mu}{r^2}$ where $\dfrac{\mu}{a^2} = f$,

$$v^2 = 2f\left(r - \frac{a^2}{r}\right).$$

This vanishes when $r = a$: the particle, therefore, comes to rest at the vertex.

To find the time in any arc of the curve,
$$\left(\frac{dr}{dt}\right)^2 = \left(\frac{dr}{ds}\right)^2 \cdot \left(\frac{ds}{dt}\right)^2 = \frac{2f}{r}(r^2 - a^2)\left(1 - \frac{a}{r}\right),$$

therefore
$$\sqrt{2f} \cdot dt = \frac{r}{(r-a)\sqrt{r+a}} \cdot dr.$$

Let
$$r + a = au^2,$$

$$dt\sqrt{2f} = 2\sqrt{a}\frac{u^2 du}{u^2 - 2} = \sqrt{a}\left\{2 + \sqrt{2}\left(\frac{1}{u - \sqrt{2}} - \frac{1}{u + \sqrt{2}}\right)\right\}du$$

$$\sqrt{2f} \cdot t = 2\sqrt{a}(u_1 - u_2) + \sqrt{2a}\log_e\frac{(u_1 - \sqrt{2})(u_2 + \sqrt{2})}{(u_1 + \sqrt{2})(u_2 - \sqrt{2})},$$

where
$$u_1 = \sqrt{\frac{r_1 + a}{a}}, \quad u_2 = \sqrt{\frac{r_2 + a}{a}};$$

and r_1, r_2 are the focal distances of the extremities of the arc.

v. A particle moves on a smooth plane curve under given forces; shew how to determine the motion and to find the pressure on the curve.

The force between two small masses attracting according to the law of the inverse square of the distance is equal, at distance a, to a very small fraction $\frac{1}{n}$ of the weight of either. They are suspended by two strings of length l from points a apart in a horizontal plane, and set to perform small vibrations in the same vertical plane; prove that the motion of each will be compounded of two harmonic motions whose periods are very nearly as $1 : 1 + \frac{2l}{na}$.

Let the strings at any instant make angles θ, ϕ with vertical: and let m be the mass of each particle (see fig. 41).

In finding the small oscillations of the system we may neglect squares and products of θ, ϕ.

The horizontal distance between the masses
$$= a + l(\sin\phi - \sin\theta)$$
$$= a + l(\phi - \theta);$$

the vertical distance between them
$$= l(\cos\phi - \cos\theta) = 0,$$

and therefore the distance between them $= a + l(\phi - \theta)$, to the same degree of approximation.

The equations of motion, remembering that the force between them at unit distance $= \dfrac{ga^2}{n}$, are

$$a\ddot{\theta} = -g\theta + \dfrac{1}{n}\dfrac{ga^2}{\{a+l(\phi-\theta)\}^2} = \dfrac{g}{n} - g\theta - \dfrac{2gl}{na}(\phi-\theta),$$

$$a\ddot{\phi} = \qquad\qquad\qquad\qquad \dfrac{g}{n} - g\phi + \dfrac{2gl}{na}(\phi-\theta).$$

From these equations we derive the following by addition and subtraction,

$$a(\ddot{\theta}+\ddot{\phi}) = \dfrac{2g}{n} - g(\theta+\phi),$$

$$a(\ddot{\theta}-\ddot{\phi}) = -g\left(1 - \dfrac{4l}{na}\right)(\theta-\phi),$$

the solutions of which are

$$\theta + \phi = \dfrac{2g}{na} + A\sin(pt+a)$$

$$\theta - \phi = B\sin(p't+a'),$$

where $\quad p^2 = \dfrac{g}{a}, \text{ and } p'^2 = \dfrac{g}{a}\left(1 - \dfrac{4l}{na}\right).$

When n is very great, $p : p' :: 1 + \dfrac{2l}{na} : 1$ nearly.

6. State D'Alembert's principle; and explain its relations to the principles of Conservation of Energy and Momentum.

Two particles A, B are moving always with equal velocities starting from rest at the same time. A is of constant, B of variable mass. Shew that at any instant when the mass of B is equal to that of A, twice the kinetic energy of B has the same rate of change as the sum of the amounts of work done by the actual forces producing the motion of A and B.

Let v be the velocity of each particle at time t, and suppose them to be moving in lines parallel to the axis of x, X_1, X_2 being the forces then acting upon them.

Their equations of motion are

$$A\dfrac{dv}{dt} = X_1, \quad \dfrac{d}{dt}(Bv) = X_2.$$

Now, the kinetic energy of $B = \tfrac{1}{2}Bv^2$;

and $\quad \dfrac{d}{dt}(Bv^2) = \dfrac{d}{dt}\cdot(Bv\cdot v) = Bv\dfrac{dv}{dt} + v\dfrac{d}{dt}(Bv)$

$$= Av\dfrac{dv}{dt} + v\dfrac{d}{dt}(Bv) \text{ (at the instant when } B=A\text{)}$$

$$= (X_1 + X_2)v$$
$$= (X_1 + X_2)\frac{dx}{dt},$$
or
$$\delta(Bv^2) = (X_1 + X_2)\delta x;$$
which is the theorem as stated.

7. When a rigid body is moving in two dimensions, shew that at every instant there is an instantaneous axis of rotation; and that, if the moment of the effective forces about this axis be equated to the moment of the impressed forces about it, the time of small oscillations may thus be found.

Two circular rings, each of radius a, are firmly jointed together at one point so that their planes make an angle 2α with one another, and are placed on a perfectly rough horizontal plane. Shew that the length of the simple equivalent pendulum is

$$a \frac{(1 + 3\cos^2\alpha)\cos\alpha}{2\sin^2\alpha}.$$

If m be the mass of each ring, their moment of inertia about an axis through their centres is

$$2ma^2\cos^2\alpha + ma^2\sin^2\alpha = ma^2(1 + \cos^2\alpha).$$

The motion of the rings may be made clear by considering that of the horizontal cylinder passing through them. A cross section of this cylinder will be an ellipse whose semi-axes are a and $a\cos\alpha$, the latter being vertical in the position of equilibrium. As this ellipse rolls on the plane in small oscillations, the normal at the point of contact always passes through the centre of curvature at the extremity of its minor axis; therefore both the pressures on the rings pass through an horizontal axis at height $a\sec\alpha$ above the plane. Let their sum be R. Then, taking moments about the lowest generator of the cylinder, which is the instantaneous axis of rotation, and denoting the angle turned through by θ, we have

$$m\{a^2(1 + \cos^2\alpha) + 2a^2\cos^2\alpha\}\frac{d^2\theta}{dt^2} = \{2mga\cos\alpha - Ra\sec\alpha\}\theta.$$

Now the centre of gravity of the system has no vertical velocity in the oscillations; therefore

$$R = 2mg;$$

therefore the above equation becomes

$$m\{a^2(1 + \cos^2\alpha) + 2a^2\cos^2\alpha\}\frac{d^2\theta}{dt^2} = 2mga(\cos\alpha - \sec\alpha)\theta;$$

therefore the length of the simple equivalent pendulum is

$$a\frac{1 + \cos^2\alpha + 2\cos^2\alpha}{2(\sec\alpha - \cos\alpha)} = a\frac{(1 + 3\cos^2\alpha)\cos\alpha}{2\sin^2\alpha}.$$

viii. Determine the initial motion of a rigid body which receives a given impulse; and find the screw round which it will begin to twist.

A perfectly rough inelastic heavy ring rolls, with its plane vertical, down an inclined plane, on which lie a series of pointed obstacles which are equal and at equal distances from each other, and which are sufficiently high to prevent the ring from touching the plane. If the ring start from rest from a position in which it is in contact with two obstacles, prove that its angular velocity as it leaves the $(n+1)^{\text{th}}$ obstacle is given by

$$\omega^2 = \frac{2g}{a} \sin i \sin \gamma \cos^4 \gamma \cdot \frac{1 - \cos^{4n} \gamma}{1 - \cos^4 \gamma},$$

where a is the radius of the ring, i the inclination of the plane to the horizon, and 2γ is the angle which two adjacent obstacles subtend at the centre of the ring when it is in contact with both.

The motion is supposed quite regular; that is to say, it is not supposed to have become so great that, in turning round one of the obstacles, its centrifugal force is sufficient to carry it away.

The moment of inertia of the ring about an axis through its centre perpendicular to its plane is Ma^2, and about an axis through a point on its circumference perpendicular to its plane $2Ma^2$; therefore if ω_n be its angular velocity as it leaves the $(n+1)^{\text{th}}$ obstacle, and ω' just before it meets the $(n+2)^{\text{th}}$, its increase of kinetic energy

$$\tfrac{1}{2} \cdot 2Ma^2 (\omega'^2 - \omega_n^2) = Mgh,$$

where h is the space through which the centre has fallen in passing between the two obstacles.

But, by the geometry of the figure (see fig. 42), $h = \sin i \cdot 2a \sin \gamma$,

therefore
$$\omega'^2 - \omega_n^2 = \frac{2g}{a} \sin i \sin \gamma.$$

We have now to consider the impact at the $(n+2)^{\text{th}}$ obstacle B. If C be the centre of the ring, the impulsive forces will consist of two, R along BC, and the other T through B at right angles to BC. There will be no impulse at A, because all force at that point is instantly relaxed at the moment that the ring comes in contact with B and begins to turn round it.

Before impact the velocity of C at right angles to CB is $a\omega' \cos 2\gamma$, and after it $a\omega_{n+1}$,

hence
$$Ma (\omega_{n+1} - \omega' \cos 2\gamma) = T.$$

Also, taking moments about the centre of the ring,

$$Ma^2 (\omega_{n+1} - \omega') = - Ta.$$

By combining these equations, $\omega_{n+1} = \omega' \cos^2 \gamma$, hence substituting in above equation,

$$\omega^2_{n+1} \sec^4 \gamma - \omega_n^2 = \frac{2g}{a} \sin i \sin \gamma.$$

To solve this put $\omega_n^2 = A + B \cos^{4n} \gamma$,

where
$$A = \frac{2g}{a} \frac{\sin i \sin \gamma \cdot \cos^4 \gamma}{1 - \cos^4 \gamma}.$$

To find B we observe that when $n = 0$ the motion is just commencing, and therefore $A + B = 0$;

hence
$$\omega_n^2 = \frac{2g}{a} \sin i \sin \gamma \cos^4 \gamma \cdot \frac{1 - \cos^{4n} \gamma}{1 - \cos^4 \gamma}.$$

The greatest possible value of Ω is given by

$$\Omega^2 = \frac{2g}{a} \cdot \frac{\sin i \sin \gamma \cos^4 \gamma}{1 - \cos^4 \gamma};$$

but it might happen that, before this is attained, the regular motion we have supposed breaks up by the centrifugal force round an obstacle overbalancing the effect of gravity in keeping the ring on the point.

Let us find the condition that this may take place in turning round the $(n + 2)^{th}$ obstacle, and let the radius be then inclined at an angle θ to the vertical.

The angular velocity is given by $\omega^2 = \omega_n^2 + \frac{g}{a} \{\cos(\gamma - i) - \cos \theta\}$, and the component of gravity along CB is $g \cos \theta$; the value of θ for which the normal reaction against the obstacle vanishes is given by

$$\frac{a \omega_n^2}{g} + \cos(\gamma - i) = 2 \cos \theta.$$

If, therefore, $\dfrac{2 \sin i \sin \gamma \cos^4 \gamma}{1 - \cos^4 \gamma} + \cos(\gamma - i) < 2$, there will be some period of the motion at which the ring will bound off from the obstacles, and the foregoing investigation will not hold beyond this period.

ix. If a system of rays of light emanate from a point, shew that, however they may be reflected or refracted, they will always be normal to some surface; and apply this result to shew that a small pencil of rays always passes through two focal lines at right angles to each other.

A pencil of rays diverging from a point P, whose position is variable, is incident on a refracting sphere at a given point in a given direction; if Q be the corresponding primary focus after refraction through the sphere, G the position of Q when the incident pencil consists of parallel rays, F that of P when Q is at an infinite distance, prove that

$$PF \cdot QG = \frac{a^2}{16} \frac{\sin^2 2i \cos^2 r}{\sin^2(i-r)},$$

where a is the radius of the sphere, i the angle of incidence on the sphere, and r the angle of refraction.

Shew how to find the corresponding theorem for a pencil refracted through any number of spheres, the axis of the pencil lying always in one plane.

Let the axis of the ray pass through the sphere in the direction $PABQ$ (fig. 43), and let $AP = u$, $Aq_1 = u_1$, and let the corresponding quantities for B be $BQ = v$, $-Bq_1 = v_1$, q_1 being the primary focus after refraction into the sphere at A.

The equation which gives u_1 is

$$\frac{\mu \cos^2 r}{u_1} - \frac{\cos^2 i}{u} = -\frac{\mu \cos r - \cos i}{a},$$

and $\mu = \dfrac{\sin i}{\sin r}$, and a the radius of the sphere.

In the same way we find

$$\frac{\mu \cos^2 r}{v_1} - \frac{\cos^2 i}{v} = -\frac{\mu \cos r - \cos i}{a};$$

we have to combine these with $-v_1 = u_1 + 2a \cos r$.

I observe, first of all, that

$$u_1 = \frac{\lambda}{\dfrac{1}{u} - \dfrac{1}{c}}, \quad v_1 = \frac{\lambda}{\dfrac{1}{v} - \dfrac{1}{c}},$$

where
$$\lambda = \frac{\sin i \cos^2 r}{\sin r \cos^2 i}, \quad \frac{1}{c} = \frac{\sin(i-r)}{a \cos^2 i \sin r}.$$

We have then

$$\frac{2a \cos r}{\lambda c} = \frac{u}{u-c} + \frac{v}{v-c}.$$

If the left-hand be written $\dfrac{1}{a}$, we get, on multiplying up,

$$uv - c(u+v) + c^2 = a\{2uv - c(u+v)\},$$
$$uv(1-2a) - c(u+v)(1-a) + c^2 = 0,$$
$$uv - c \cdot \frac{1-a}{1-2a}(u+v) + \left\{\frac{c(1-a)}{1-2a}\right\}^2 = \frac{c^2(1-a)^2}{(1-2a)^2} - \frac{c^2}{(1-2a)}$$

$$= \frac{c^2}{(1-2a)^2}\{1 + a^2 - 2a - (1-2a)\} = \left(\frac{ac}{1-2a}\right)^2,$$

or
$$(u-f)(v-f) = \left(\frac{ac}{1-2a}\right)^2 \quad \dots\dots\dots\dots(A).$$

But
$$a = \frac{\lambda c}{2a \cos r} = \frac{\sin i \cos^2 r}{\sin (i-r)} \cdot \frac{1}{2\cos r} = \frac{\sin i \cos r}{2 \sin (i-r)},$$

$$\frac{a}{1-2a} = \frac{\sin i \cos r}{2 \sin (i-r) - 2 \sin i \cos r} = \frac{\sin i \cos r}{2 \cos i \sin r},$$

and
$$c = \frac{a \cos^2 i \sin r}{\sin (i-r)},$$

therefore the right-hand member of equation (A) may be written
$$\left(\frac{a \sin 2i \cos r}{4 \sin (i-r)}\right)^2 = K^2.$$

If we put the above equation in the form
$$(u - f)(v - f) = K^2,$$
we see that when $u = \infty$, $v = f$, and when $v = \infty$, $u = f$; $u - f$ is therefore what has been denoted by PF and $v - f$ by QG.

We obtain therefore $\quad PF \cdot QG = K^2,$

where
$$K = \frac{a \sin 2i \cos r}{4 \sin (i-r)}.$$

To extend the theorem, we observe that the distances of one pair of conjugate foci P, Q from another pair P_0, Q_0 are connected by a very simple relation; for if $P_0 P = x$, $Q_0 Q = y$, both being measured in the same direction along the axis of the pencil, and if $P_0 F = u_0$, $Q_0 G = v_0$, we have
$$u_0 v_0 = K^2,$$
$$(u_0 - x)(v_0 + y) = K^2.$$

It results from these that
$$\frac{u_0}{x} - \frac{v_0}{y} = 1.$$

If we trace the foci corresponding to these foci through the system of spheres, and suppose p, q are their last positions, then, if $pq = X$, we have an equation of the form
$$\frac{A}{X} + \frac{B}{x} = 1.$$

This result is evidently of the same form as the theorem in the first part of the question.

10. Give a formula for finding the parallax of Mars by two observations made out of the plane of the meridian.

Shew that a small error in the place of the zero-point on the graduated scale of the altazimuth will have no effect upon the accuracy of this formula, if
$$\left(\frac{\sin z_1}{\sin h_1} - \frac{\sin z_2}{\sin h_2}\right) \div \left(\frac{\sin z_1}{\tan h_1} - \frac{\sin z_2}{\tan h_2}\right) = \frac{h_1 - h_2 - c}{\sin h_1 - \sin h_2},$$

where z_1, z_2, h_1, h_2 are the observed zenith-distances and hour-angles of the planet at the two times of observation, and c is the real decrement of its hour-angle during the interval between them.

Hymers's formula (Art. 260) is

$$P \text{ (parallax)} = \tfrac{1}{2} \frac{(h_1 - h_2 - c) \cos \delta}{\sin \tfrac{1}{2}(h_1 - h_2) \cos \tfrac{1}{2}(h_1 + h_2) \cos l},$$

where δ, l are the declination of the star and latitude of the place of observation respectively.

Then an error in the zero-point from which the zenith-distances are measured will not affect the accuracy of this formula if $\delta \log P = 0$; *i.e.* if

$$\frac{\delta h_1 - \delta h_2}{h_1 - h_2 - c} - \frac{\delta h_1 - \delta h_2}{2 \tan \tfrac{1}{2}(h_1 - h_2)} + \frac{\delta h_1 + \delta h_2}{2 \cot \tfrac{1}{2}(h_1 + h_2)} = 0.$$

Now $\qquad \cos z_1 = \sin \delta \sin l + \cos \delta \cos l \cos h_1,$

therefore $\qquad \sin z_1 \, \delta z_1 = \cos \delta \cos l \sin h_1 \, \delta h_1.$

Similarly $\qquad \sin z_2 \, \delta z_2 = \cos \delta \cos l \sin h_2 \, \delta h_2;$

and, since the error is in the zero-point of z_1, z_2, $\delta z_1 = \delta z_2.$

Hence the above equation becomes

$$\frac{\dfrac{\sin z_1}{\sin h_1} - \dfrac{\sin z_2}{\sin h_2}}{h_1 - h_2 - c} - \frac{\dfrac{\sin z_1}{\sin h_1} - \dfrac{\sin z_2}{\sin h_2}}{2 \tan \tfrac{1}{2}(h_1 - h_2)} + \frac{\dfrac{\sin z_1}{\sin h_1} + \dfrac{\sin z_2}{\sin h_2}}{2 \cot \tfrac{1}{2}(h_1 + h_2)} = 0,$$

therefore $\qquad \dfrac{\dfrac{\sin z_1}{\sin h_1} - \dfrac{\sin z_2}{\sin h_2}}{h_1 - h_2 - c} = \dfrac{\sin z_1}{2 \sin h_1} \{\cot \tfrac{1}{2}(h_1 - h_2) - \tan \tfrac{1}{2}(h_1 + h_2)\}$

$- \dfrac{\sin z_2}{2 \sin h_2} \{\cot \tfrac{1}{2}(h_1 - h_2) + \tan \tfrac{1}{2}(h_1 + h_2)\}$

$= \dfrac{\sin z_1}{2 \sin h_1} \cdot \dfrac{\cos h_1}{\sin \tfrac{1}{2}(h_1 - h_2) \cos \tfrac{1}{2}(h_1 + h_2)} - \dfrac{\sin z_2}{2 \sin h_2} \cdot \dfrac{\cos h_2}{\sin \tfrac{1}{2}(h_1 - h_2) \cos \tfrac{1}{2}(h_1 + h_2)}$

$= \left\{ \dfrac{\sin z_1}{\tan h_1} - \dfrac{\sin z_2}{\tan h_2} \right\} \dfrac{1}{\sin h_1 - \sin h_2};$

therefore $\qquad \left\{ \dfrac{\sin z_1}{\sin h_1} - \dfrac{\sin z_2}{\sin h_2} \right\} \div \left\{ \dfrac{\sin z_1}{\tan h_1} - \dfrac{\sin z_2}{\tan h_2} \right\} = \dfrac{h_1 - h_2 - c}{\sin h_1 - \sin h_2}.$

MONDAY, *January* 14, 1878. 1½ to 4.

Mr GLAISHER, Arabic numbers.
Mr GREENHILL, Roman numbers.

1. IF the series $a_0 + a_1x + a_2x^2 + $ &c. and $b_0 + b_1x + b_2x^2 + $ &c. be convergent, and equal to one another, for all values of x, give the ordinary proof that $a_0 = b_0$, $a_1 = b_1$, $a_2 = b_2$, &c.; and point out the difficulties in it.

Prove that, if $a < 1$,

$$(1+ax)(1+a^3x)(1+a^5x)\ldots$$
$$= 1 + \frac{ax}{1-a^2} + \frac{a^4x^2}{(1-a^2)(1-a^4)} + \frac{a^9x^3}{(1-a^2)(1-a^4)(1-a^6)} + \&c.$$

(i) In order to make the ordinary proof complete it has to be shewn (1) that we are entitled to put $x = 0$, and so obtain $a_0 = b_0$ (see De Morgan's *Algebra*, chapter VIII.). We then have left

$$a_1x + a_2x^2 + \&c. = b_1x + b_2x^2 + \&c., \text{ viz. } x(a_1 + a_2x + \&c.) = 0,$$

or say $xS = 0$. This implies either that $x = 0$ or that $S = 0$, and it might be contended that for x finite, S was equal to zero, but that when x was infinitesimal or zero, xS was zero in virtue of the factor x. It has therefore to be shewn (2) that S must be zero for all values of x, and the difficulty is to establish this without introducing conceptions with regard to vanishing quantities that really belong to the differential calculus.

(ii) Let
$$(1+ax)(1+a^3x)(1+a^5x)\ldots = 1 + A_1x + A_2x^2 + \&c.$$

Put a^2x for x, and this becomes
$$(1+a^3x)(1+a^5x)\ldots = 1 + A_1a^2x + A_2a^4x^2 + \&c.$$

Therefore
$$(1+ax)(1 + A_1a^2x + A_2a^4x^2 + \&c.) = 1 + A_1x + A_2x^2 + \&c.$$

Equating coefficients
$$a + A_1a^2 = A_1, \quad A_1a^3 + A_2a^4 = A_2, \quad A_2a^5 + A_3a^6 = A_3, \&c.,$$

whence
$$A_1 = \frac{a}{1-a^2}, \quad A_2 = \frac{a^3}{1-a^4}A_1, \quad A_3 = \frac{a^5}{1-a^6}A_2, \&c.,$$

and the theorem follows at once.

2. Obtain from Demoivre's theorem the exponential value of $\cos x$, and thence, or otherwise, find the expansion of $\cos x$ in ascending powers of x.

Prove that
$$\tan^{-1}\left(\frac{\tan 2\theta + \tanh 2\phi}{\tan 2\theta - \tanh 2\phi}\right) + \tan^{-1}\left(\frac{\tan\theta - \tanh\phi}{\tan\theta + \tanh\phi}\right) = \tan^{-1}(\cot\theta\coth\phi),$$
where tanh and coth are defined by the equations
$$\tanh x = \frac{e^x - e^{-x}}{e^x + e^{-x}}, \quad \coth x = \frac{e^x + e^{-x}}{e^x - e^{-x}}.$$

(i) By Demoivre's theorem
$$\cos\theta + i\sin\theta = (\cos 1 + i\sin 1)^\theta = k^\theta \text{ say,}$$
therefore $\cos\theta - i\sin\theta = k^{-\theta}$, and $2\cos\theta = k^\theta + k^{-\theta}$, $2i\sin\theta = k^\theta - k^{-\theta}$.

Expanding the right-hand side of the second equation,
$$2i\sin\theta = 2\left(\theta\log k + \frac{(\theta\log k)^3}{1.2.3} + \&c.\right),$$
whence $i\dfrac{\sin\theta}{\theta} = \log k + $ powers of θ^2 (a convergent series).

Proceeding to the limit $\theta = 0$, this becomes $i = \log k$, whence $k = e^i$, and therefore $2\cos\theta = e^{i\theta} + e^{-i\theta}$, $2i\sin\theta = e^{i\theta} - e^{-i\theta}$.

(ii) We have
$$\tan 2x = \frac{2\tan x}{1-\tan^2 x} = \frac{2}{t^{-1}-t}, \text{ if } t \text{ denotes } \tan\theta,$$
$$\tanh 2x = \frac{2\tanh x}{1+\tanh^2 x} = \frac{2}{T^{-1}+T}, \text{ if } T \text{ denotes } \tanh\phi,$$
and
$$\tan^{-1}\left(\frac{1}{iT}\right) - \tan^{-1}\left(\frac{t-T}{t+T}\right) = \tan^{-1}\left(\frac{\dfrac{1}{iT} - \dfrac{t-T}{t+T}}{1 + \dfrac{1}{iT}\dfrac{t-T}{t+T}}\right)$$
$$= \tan^{-1}\left(\frac{(t+T) - iT(t-T)}{iT(t+T) + t - T}\right) = \tan^{-1}\left(\frac{T^{-1} + t^{-1} - t + T}{t + T + T^{-1} - t^{-1}}\right)$$
$$= \tan^{-1}\left(\frac{(t^{-1}-t)^{-1} + (T^{-1}+T)^{-1}}{(t^{-1}-t)^{-1} - (T^{-1}+T)^{-1}}\right) = \tan^{-1}\left(\frac{\tan 2\theta + \tanh 2\phi}{\tan 2\theta - \tanh 2\phi}\right).$$

3. Shew how to obtain the sum of the mth powers of the roots of an equation in terms of the coefficients.

If s_m denote the sum of the mth powers of the roots of the equation
$$x^n + a_1 x^{n-1} + a_2 x^{n-2} \ldots + a_n = 0,$$
prove that a_m is equal to the coefficient of h^m in the expansion of
$$e^{-s_1 h} \cdot e^{-\frac{1}{2}s_2 h^2} \cdot e^{-\frac{1}{3}s_3 h^3} \ldots$$

Let $a_1, a_2, \ldots a_n$ denote the roots: then
$$x^n + a_1 x^{n-1} + a_2 x^{n-2} \ldots + a_n = (x - a_1)(x - a_2) \ldots (x - a_n),$$
whence, dividing by x^n and putting $x^{-1} = h$,
$$1 + a_1 h + a_2 h^2 \ldots + a_n h^n = (1 - a_1 h)(1 - a_2 h) \ldots (1 - a_n h)$$
$$= e^{\log(1-a_1 h) + \log(1-a_2 h) + \ldots + \log(1-a_n h)},$$
$$= e^{-s_1 h - \frac{1}{2} s_2 h^2 - \frac{1}{3} s_3 h^3 - \ldots},$$
$$= e^{-s_1 h} \cdot e^{-\frac{1}{2} s_2 h^2} \cdot e^{-\frac{1}{3} s_3 h^3} \ldots$$

and the theorem follows by equating coefficients of h^m.

4. Find the sine of the angle between the two straight lines represented by the equation
$$Ax^2 + 2Hxy + By^2 = 0.$$

Prove that the equation of the locus of the points of intersection of pairs of tangents to the ellipse
$$\frac{x^2}{a^2} + \frac{y^2}{b^2} = 1$$
inclined to one another at a given angle α is
$$(x^2 + y^2 - a^2 - b^2)^2 = 4 \cot^2 \alpha \, (a^2 y^2 + b^2 x^2 - a^2 b^2).$$

If α be the angle between these straight lines,
$$\tan \alpha = \frac{2\sqrt{(H^2 - AB)}}{A + B}, \quad \sin \alpha = \frac{2\sqrt{(H^2 - AB)}}{4H^2 + (A - B)^2}.$$

The former equation is $(A + B)^2 - 4 \cot^2 \alpha (H^2 - AB) = 0$, and the equation of the pair of tangents drawn from the point h, k to the ellipse being $(a^2 k^2 + b^2 h^2 - a^2 b^2)(a^2 y^2 + b^2 x^2 - a^2 b^2) - (a^2 ky + b^2 hx - a^2 b^2)^2 = 0$, we have $A = a^2 b^2 (k^2 - b^2)$, $H = -a^2 b^2 hk$, $B = a^2 b^2 (h^2 - a^2)$, and the result in the question follows at once by substituting these values.

5. If $ABCD$ be a spherical quadrilateral inscribed in a small circle, prove that $A + C = B + D$.

If a, b, c, d be the sides in order of a spherical quadrilateral inscribed in a small circle, and α be the diagonal joining the intersections of a, b and c, d, prove that $\cos^2 \tfrac{1}{2} \alpha =$

$$\frac{\sin \tfrac{1}{2} b \sin \tfrac{1}{2} c \cos \tfrac{1}{2}(a+d) \cos \tfrac{1}{2}(a-d) + \sin \tfrac{1}{2} a \sin \tfrac{1}{2} d \cos \tfrac{1}{2}(b+c) \cos \tfrac{1}{2}(b-c)}{\sin \tfrac{1}{2} b \sin \tfrac{1}{2} c + \sin \tfrac{1}{2} a \sin \tfrac{1}{2} d}.$$

(i) Let O (fig. 44) be the centre of the small circle circumscribing $ABCD$; then, since OA, OB, OC, OD are all equal, therefore $\angle OAB = \angle OBA$, $\angle OAD = \angle ODA$, $\angle OCB = \angle OBC$, $\angle OCD = \angle ODC$, whence, adding these four equations, $A + C = B + D$.

(ii) Draw the chords AB, BC, CD, DA, BD; then chord $AB = 2\sin\frac{1}{2}a$, chord $BC = 2\sin\frac{1}{2}b$, &c. We thus have a *plane* quadrilateral whose sides $AB, \ldots DA$ are $2\sin\frac{1}{2}a, \ldots 2\sin\frac{1}{2}d$ and diagonal BD is $2\sin\frac{1}{2}a$. Now in the plane quadrilateral $ABCD$, whose sides AB, BC, CA, AD are a', b', c', d', by a well-known theorem,

$$BD^2 = \frac{(a'b' + c'd')(a'c' + b'd')}{b'c' + a'd'},$$

whence

$$\sin^2\tfrac{1}{2}a = \frac{(\sin\tfrac{1}{2}a\sin\tfrac{1}{2}b + \sin\tfrac{1}{2}c\sin\tfrac{1}{2}d)(\sin\tfrac{1}{2}a\sin\tfrac{1}{2}c + \sin\tfrac{1}{2}b\sin\tfrac{1}{2}d)}{\sin\tfrac{1}{2}b\sin\tfrac{1}{2}c + \sin\tfrac{1}{2}a\sin\tfrac{1}{2}d}.$$

Therefore

$$\cos^2\tfrac{1}{2}a = \frac{\sin\tfrac{1}{2}b\sin\tfrac{1}{2}c(\cos^2\tfrac{1}{2}a + \cos^2\tfrac{1}{2}d - 1) + \sin\tfrac{1}{2}a\sin\tfrac{1}{2}d(\cos^2\tfrac{1}{2}b + \cos^2\tfrac{1}{2}c - 1)}{\sin\tfrac{1}{2}b\sin\tfrac{1}{2}c + \sin\tfrac{1}{2}a\sin\tfrac{1}{2}d}$$

and $\cos^2\tfrac{1}{2}a + \cos^2\tfrac{1}{2}d - 1 = \tfrac{1}{2}(\cos a + \cos d) = \cos\tfrac{1}{2}(a+d)\cos\tfrac{1}{2}(a-d)$: similarly $\cos^2\tfrac{1}{2}b + \cos^2\tfrac{1}{2}c - 1 = \cos\tfrac{1}{2}(b+c)\cos\tfrac{1}{2}(b-c)$,
whence we have the formula in the question for $\cos^2\tfrac{1}{2}a$.

vi. Prove that the equations of the generating lines through the point

$$x = a\frac{\cos\tfrac{1}{2}(\theta+\phi)}{\cos\tfrac{1}{2}(\theta-\phi)}, \quad y = b\frac{\sin\tfrac{1}{2}(\theta+\phi)}{\cos\tfrac{1}{2}(\theta-\phi)}, \quad z = c\frac{\sin\tfrac{1}{2}(\theta-\phi)}{\cos\tfrac{1}{2}(\theta-\phi)},$$

on the hyperboloid of one sheet

$$\frac{x^2}{a^2} + \frac{y^2}{b^2} - \frac{z^2}{c^2} = 1,$$

are

$$\frac{x}{a} = \frac{z}{c}\sin\theta + \cos\theta, \quad \frac{y}{b} = -\frac{z}{c}\cos\theta + \sin\theta;$$

and

$$\frac{x}{a} = -\frac{z}{c}\sin\phi + \cos\phi, \quad \frac{y}{b} = \frac{z}{c}\cos\phi + \sin\phi.$$

Prove that, if a model of a hyperboloid of one sheet be constructed of rods representing the generating lines, jointed at the points of crossing; then if the model be deformed it will assume the form of a confocal hyperboloid, and prove that the trajectory of a point on the model will be orthogonal to the system of confocal hyperboloids.

The equations of a generating line may be written

$$\frac{x - a\cos\theta}{a\sin\theta} = \frac{y - b\sin\theta}{-b\cos\theta} = \frac{z}{c} = \frac{r}{\sqrt{\{(a^2+c^2)\sin^2\theta + (b^2+c^2)\cos^2\theta\}}},$$

where r is the distance of the point xyz from the plane of xy measured along the generating line.

When the model is deformed, r, θ, $\dfrac{x}{a}$, $\dfrac{y}{b}$, $\dfrac{z}{c}$ will remain unchanged, provided $a^2 + c^2$ and $b^2 + c^2$ remain unchanged.

Hence when the model is deformed it assumes the shape of a confocal hyperboloid, and the trajectory of a point on the model is a series of corresponding points, which is therefore orthogonal to the system of confocals.

[Another solution is given by Prof. Cayley in the *Messenger of Mathematics*, Vol. vii. pp. 51, 52 (August, 1878).]

vii. Find expressions for the co-ordinates of the centre of curvature and the radius of curvature at any point of a plane or tortuous curve, taking the arc of the curve as the independent variable.

Prove that, at corresponding points of a plane curve traced on a cylinder and its development when the surface of a cylinder is developed into a plane, the ordinates drawn to corresponding axes which are perpendicular to the generating lines of the cylinder are in a constant ratio: prove also that the product of the radius of curvature and the normal intercepted by the axis is the same at corresponding points of the curve and its development.

Let AP (fig. 45) be a plane section of a cylinder, and BN a transverse section, the planes of AP and BN intersecting in the axis OM; and when the cylinder is developed into a plane, let the curve AP be developed into the curve AP' and the curve BN into the axis BN', corresponding to the axis OM.

Then $PN = P'N'$ and the arc $AP = $ arc AP'.

Hence if $MP = y$, $N'P' = y'$, and if a is the angle between the planes of AP and BN,
$$y' = y \sin a\,;$$
and therefore if $y = f(s)$ in the curve AP, then $y' = \cos a\, f(s)$ in the curve AP', s denoting the arc AP or the arc AP'.

If ρ denote the radius of curvature at the point P of the curve AP, and if the normal PQ be denoted by n and the angle MPQ by ψ, then
$$\frac{dy}{ds} = \sin \psi = f'(s),$$
and
$$\cos \psi \frac{d\psi}{ds} = f''(s),$$
or
$$\rho = \frac{\cos \psi}{f''(s)}.$$
Also
$$n = y \sec \psi = \sec \psi\, f(s),$$
therefore
$$\rho n = \frac{f(s)}{f''(s)}.$$

If ρ', n', ψ' denote the corresponding quantities at the corresponding point P' of the curve AP',

$$\frac{dy'}{ds} = \sin \psi' = \sin a f'(s),$$

$$\cos \psi' \frac{d\psi'}{ds} = \sin a f''(s),$$

or
$$\rho' = \frac{\cos \psi'}{\sin a f''(s)},$$

and
$$n' = y' \sec \psi' = \sec \psi' \sin a f(s);$$

therefore
$$\rho' n' = \frac{f(s)}{f''(s)} = \rho n.$$

[As an example, suppose the cylinder a right circular cylinder; then the curve AP is an ellipse of eccentricity $\cos a$, and the curve AP' is the curve of sines; and thus it is evident that the surface generated by the revolution of the ellipse AP about the axis OM is applicable on the surface generated by the revolution of the curve of sines AP' about the axis BN', that is, if the part of the surface, generated by the revolution of an ellipse of eccentricity e about any axis parallel to its minor axis, between two meridian planes inclined at an angle $2\pi e$ be taken and the ends joined, the meridian curve will become the curve of sines; a problem due to Mr Droop, and set in the Senate House in 1860.]

viii. Integrate:

$$\frac{1}{(a+x)^2(c+x)^{\frac{1}{2}}}, \quad \frac{1}{(a+x)(c+x)^{\frac{3}{2}}}, \quad \text{and} \quad \frac{1}{(x^2-a^2)(x^2-c^2)^{\frac{1}{2}}}.$$

Prove, by means of the substitution

$$\frac{a-x}{x-b} = \frac{a-d}{b-c} \frac{c-y}{y-d},$$

that, if m be any positive quantity, and $a > b > c > d$,

$$\int_b^a \frac{\{(a-x)(x-c)\}^{m-1}}{\left\{\frac{(a-x)(x-d)}{a-d} + \frac{(x-b)(x-c)}{b-c}\right\}^m} dx$$

$$= \int_d^c \frac{\{(a-x)(c-x)\}^{m-1}}{\left\{\frac{(a-x)(x-d)}{a-d} + \frac{(b-x)(c-x)}{b-c}\right\}^m} dx.$$

(i) $\displaystyle\int \frac{dx}{(a+x)^2 (c+x)^{\frac{1}{2}}}$ and $\displaystyle\int \frac{dx}{(a+x)(c+x)^{\frac{3}{2}}}$

are found by differentiating with respect to a and c respectively $\int \dfrac{dx}{(a+x)(c+x)^{\frac{1}{2}}}$, and this, when $a > c$, is equal to

$$\dfrac{2}{\sqrt{a-c}} \tan^{-1} \sqrt{\dfrac{c+x}{a-c}},$$

when $a < c$ is equal to

$$\dfrac{1}{\sqrt{c-a}} \log \dfrac{\sqrt{c+x}-\sqrt{c-a}}{\sqrt{c+x}+\sqrt{c-a}}.$$

(ii)
$$\int \dfrac{dx}{(x^2-a^2)(x^2-c^2)^{\frac{1}{2}}}$$

$$= \int \dfrac{\cos\phi \, d\phi}{a^2 \sin^2\phi + c^2 - a^2} \text{ if } x = c \sec\phi,$$

$$(a>c) = \dfrac{1}{2a\sqrt{a^2-c^2}} \log \dfrac{a \sin\phi - \sqrt{a^2-c^2}}{a \sin\phi + \sqrt{a^2-c^2}}$$

$$= \dfrac{1}{2a\sqrt{a^2-c^2}} \log \dfrac{a\sqrt{x^2-c^2}-x\sqrt{a^2-c^2}}{a\sqrt{x^2-c^2}+x\sqrt{a^2-c^2}};$$

$$(a<c) = \dfrac{1}{a\sqrt{c^2-a^2}} \tan^{-1} \dfrac{a \sin\phi}{\sqrt{c^2-a^2}}$$

$$= \dfrac{1}{a\sqrt{c^2-a^2}} \tan^{-1} \dfrac{a}{x} \sqrt{\left(\dfrac{x^2-c^2}{c^2-a^2}\right)}.$$

(iii) If
$$\dfrac{a-x}{x-b} = \dfrac{a-d}{b-c} \dfrac{c-y}{y-d},$$

then
$$\dfrac{dx}{a-x} + \dfrac{dx}{x-b} = \dfrac{dy}{c-y} + \dfrac{dy}{y-d},$$

or
$$\dfrac{a-b}{a-x \cdot x-b} dx = \dfrac{c-d}{c-y \cdot y-d} dy.$$

Also
$$x = b \cdot a-d \cdot c-y + a \cdot b-c \cdot y-d \div D,$$
$$a-x = a-b \cdot a-d \cdot c-y \div D,$$
$$x-b = a-b \cdot b-c \cdot y-d \div D,$$
$$x-c = b-c \cdot c-d \cdot a-y \div D,$$
$$x-d = a-d \cdot c-d \cdot b-y \div D,$$

where
$$D = a-d \cdot c-y + b-c \cdot y-d.$$

Therefore $\dfrac{a-x \cdot x-d}{a-d} + \dfrac{x-b \cdot x-c}{b-c}$

$= a-b \cdot a-d \cdot c - d \cdot b - y \cdot c - y + a - b \cdot b - c \cdot c - d \cdot a - y \cdot y - d \div D^2$,

$= a-b \cdot a-d \cdot b-c \cdot c - d \left(\dfrac{a-y \cdot y-d}{a-d} + \dfrac{b-y \cdot c-y}{b-c} \right) \div D^2$.

Therefore $\displaystyle\int_b^a \dfrac{(a-x \cdot x-c)^{m-1}}{\left(\dfrac{a-x \cdot x-d}{a-d} + \dfrac{x-b \cdot x-c}{b-c} \right)^m} dx$

$= \displaystyle\int_d^c \dfrac{\left(\dfrac{a-b \cdot a-d \cdot b-c \cdot c-d \cdot a-y \cdot c-y}{D^2} \right)^{m-1} \dfrac{c-d \cdot a-b \cdot a-d \cdot b-c}{D^2}}{\left\{ \dfrac{a-b \cdot a-d \cdot b-c \cdot c-d}{D^2} \left(\dfrac{a-y \cdot y-d}{a-d} + \dfrac{b-y \cdot c-y}{b-c} \right) \right\}^m} dy,$

$= \displaystyle\int_d^c \dfrac{(a-y \cdot c-y)^{m-1}}{\left(\dfrac{a-y \cdot y-d}{a-d} + \dfrac{b-y \cdot c-y}{b-c} \right)^m} dy.$

ix. Shew how to integrate the differential equation
$$xf(p) + yF(p) = \phi(p).$$
Obtain the complete primitive of the differential equation
$$2y = xp + \dfrac{a}{p};$$
and shew that exactly the same equation is obtained by expressing the condition that p should have equal roots in the differential equation as by expressing the condition that c (the arbitrary constant) should have equal roots in the complete primitive; and determine the geometrical meaning of this equation. Is it a singular solution?

If $\qquad 2y = xp + \dfrac{a}{p},$

differentiating

$$2p = p + x\dfrac{dp}{dx} - \dfrac{a}{p^2} \dfrac{dp}{dx},$$

or $\qquad p\dfrac{dx}{dp} - x = -\dfrac{a}{p^2},$

or $\qquad \dfrac{p\dfrac{dx}{dp} - x}{p^2} = -\dfrac{a}{p^4},$

or $\qquad \dfrac{d}{dp}\left(\dfrac{x}{p}\right) = -\dfrac{a}{p^4};$

and therefore
$$\frac{x}{p} = c + \frac{a}{3p^3}.$$

We have therefore to eliminate p between

$$xp^2 - 2yp + a = 0 \dots\dots\dots\dots\dots\dots(1),$$

and
$$cp^3 - xp^2 + \frac{a}{3} = 0 \dots\dots\dots\dots\dots\dots(2).$$

The condition that (1) should have equal roots is $y^2 - ax = 0$.

The condition that the equation in c obtained by eliminating p from (1) and (2) should have equal roots reduces to $(y^2 - ax)^3 = 0$.

The equation $y^2 - ax = 0$ is *not* a singular solution, for it does not satisfy the differential equation; since it is obtained both by giving equal roots to p and to c, we infer that it is not a tac-locus, and that it is therefore a locus of singular points. It is in fact a cusp-locus.

x. Solve the difference equation $au_{n+1}u_n + bu_{n+1} + cu_n + d = 0$.

Prove that the solution of the equations

$$v_n = \frac{b^2}{c - u_n}, \text{ and } u_{n+1} = \frac{a^2}{c - v_n},$$

subject to the condition that $u_0 = 0$, is

$$u_n = a \frac{\sin nC}{\sin (nC - B)}, \quad v_n = -b \frac{\sin (nC - B)}{\sin (n+1)C},$$

where A, B, C are the angles of the triangle whose sides are a, b, c.

$$u_{n+1} = \frac{a^2}{c - v_n} = \frac{a^2}{c - \dfrac{b^2}{c - u_n}} = \frac{a^2(c - u_n)}{c^2 - b^2 - cu_n},$$

or
$$cu_{n+1}u_n + (b^2 - c^2)u_{n+1} - a^2 u_n + a^2 c = 0.$$

To solve this equation (similar to the equation of the book-work) put

$$u_n = \frac{w_{n+1}}{w_n} - \frac{b^2 - c^2}{c};$$

therefore
$$u_{n+1} = \frac{w_{n+2}}{w_{n+1}} - \frac{b^2 - c^2}{c};$$

and the equation becomes

$$\left(\frac{w_{n+2}}{w_{n+1}} - \frac{b^2 - c^2}{c}\right)\left(\frac{w_{n+1}}{w_n} - \frac{b^2 - c^2}{c}\right)$$
$$+ \frac{b^2 - c^2}{c}\left(\frac{w_{n+2}}{w_{n+1}} - \frac{b^2 - c^2}{c}\right) - \frac{a^2}{c}\left(\frac{w_{n+1}}{w_n} - \frac{b^2 - c^2}{c}\right) + a^2 = 0,$$

or
$$w_{n+2} - \frac{a^2 + b^2 - c^2}{c} w_{n+1} + \frac{a^2 b^2}{c^2} w_n = 0,$$

or
$$w_{n+2} - 2\frac{ab}{c}\cos C w_{n+1} + \frac{a^2 b^2}{c^2} w_n = 0.$$

The auxiliary equation is
$$m^2 - 2\frac{ab}{c}\cos Cm + \frac{a^2 b^2}{c^2} = 0,$$

and therefore
$$m = \frac{ab}{c}(\cos C \pm \sqrt{-1}\sin C),$$

and
$$w_n = P\left(\frac{ab}{c}\right)^n \sin(nC - a);$$

therefore
$$u_n = \frac{ab}{c}\frac{\sin(nC + C - a)}{\sin(nC - a)} - \frac{b^2 - c^2}{c}$$

$$= a\frac{\sin B}{\sin C}\frac{\sin(nC + C - a)}{\sin(nC - a)} - a\frac{\sin^2 B - \sin^2 C}{\sin A \sin C}$$

$$= a\frac{\sin B \sin(nC + C - a) - \sin(B - C)\sin(nC - a)}{\sin C \sin(nC - a)}$$

$$= a\frac{\sin(nC + B - a)}{\sin(nC - a)}.$$

Also since $u_0 = 0$, therefore $a = B$, and therefore
$$u_n = a\frac{\sin nC}{\sin(nC - B)}.$$

$$\frac{v_n}{b} = \frac{b}{c - u_n}$$

$$= \frac{\sin B}{\sin C - \dfrac{\sin A \sin nC}{\sin(nC - B)}}$$

$$= \frac{\sin B \sin(nC - B)}{\sin C \sin(nC - B) - \sin A \sin C}$$

$$= -\frac{\sin(nC - B)}{\sin(n + 1)C}.$$

[A solution of this question is contained in Prof. Cayley's paper "Note on the function $\Im x = a^2(c \div x) \div \{c(c - x) - b^2\}$" *Quarterly Journal of Mathematics*, vol. xv. pp. 338—348 (1878).]

TUESDAY, *January* 15, 1878.   9 to 12.

Mr GLAISHER.

1. THE sides BC, CA, AB of a triangle cut a straight line in D, E, F; through D, E, F three straight lines $DLOG$, $EHOM$, $FKON$ having the common point O are drawn, cutting the sides CA, AB in L, G; AB, BC in M, H; BC, CA in N, K. Prove that

$$\frac{AK.BG.CH}{AM.BN.CL} = \frac{AG.BH.CK}{AL.BM.CN} = \frac{GD.HE.KF}{LD.ME.NF} = \frac{HD.KE.GF}{ND.LE.MF}.$$

Regarding GL (fig. 46) as a transversal of the triangle ABC,

$$AL.BG.CD = AG.BD.CL,$$

and BC as a transversal to the triangle AGL,

$$AC.GB.LD = AB.GD.LC,$$

whence

$$\frac{BG}{CL} = \frac{AG.BD}{AL.CD} = \frac{AB.GD}{AC.LD} \quad\ldots\ldots\ldots\ldots\ldots (1).$$

Similarly, regarding HM, CA as respectively transversals of the triangles ABC, BHM,

$$\frac{CH}{AM} = \frac{BH.CE}{BM.AE} = \frac{BC.HE}{BA.ME} \quad\ldots\ldots\ldots\ldots\ldots (2),$$

and KN, AB as respectively transversals to the triangles ABC, CNK,

$$\frac{AK}{BN} = \frac{CK.AF}{CN.BF} = \frac{CA.KF}{CB.NF} \quad\ldots\ldots\ldots\ldots\ldots (3),$$

whence, multiplying together (1), (2), (3), and reducing in the second product by the relation $AE.BF.CD = AF.BD.CE$ (obtained by regarding DEF as a transversal of the triangle ABC), we prove the equality of the first three ratios in the question. To prove that they are equal to the fourth ratio, regard DEF as a transversal of the triangles AGL, BHM, CKN; whence

$$AE.GF.LD = AF.GD.LE,$$
$$BF.HD.ME = BD.HE.MF,$$
$$CD.KE.NF = CE.KF.ND,$$

multiplying and using $AE.BF.CD = AF.BD.CE$, we find

$$\frac{GD.HE.KF}{LD.ME.NF} = \frac{HD.KE.GF}{ND.LE.MF}.$$

94   SOLUTIONS OF SENATE-HOUSE   [TUESDAY,

This equation may also be obtained by regarding DEF as a transversal of the triangles OGM, OHN, OKL; whence

$$OD \cdot GF \cdot ME = OE \cdot GD \cdot MF,$$
$$OE \cdot HD \cdot NF = OF \cdot HE \cdot ND,$$
$$OF \cdot KE \cdot LD = OD \cdot KF \cdot LE,$$

and the equation follows at once by multiplication.

2. Prove that, if x be less than unity,

$$\frac{x}{(1-x)(1-x^{2n+1})} + \frac{x^3}{(1-x^3)(1-x^{2n+3})} + \frac{x^5}{(1-x^5)(1-x^{2n+5})} + \&c. \, ad \, inf.$$
$$= \frac{1}{1-x^{2n}}\left(\frac{x}{1-x} + \frac{x^3}{1-x^3} \cdots + \frac{x^{2n-1}}{1-x^{2n-1}}\right).$$

We have

$$\frac{x - x^{2n+1}}{(1-x)(1-x^{2n+1})} = \frac{x}{1-x} - \frac{x^{2n+1}}{1-x^{2n+1}},$$

$$\frac{x^3 - x^{2n+3}}{(1-x^3)(1-x^{2n+3})} = \frac{x^3}{1-x^3} - \frac{x^{2n+3}}{1-x^{2n+3}},$$

$$\&c. \quad = \quad \&c.$$

whence

$$\frac{x}{(1-x)(1-x^{2n+1})} + \frac{x^3}{(1-x^3)(1-x^{2n+3})} + \frac{x^5}{(1-x^5)(1-x^{2n+5})} + \&c. \, ad \, inf.$$

$$= \frac{1}{1-x^{2n}}\left\{\frac{x}{1-x} + \frac{x^3}{1-x^3} + \frac{x^5}{1-x^5} + \&c. \, ad \, inf.\right.$$

$$\left. - \frac{x^{2n+1}}{1-x^{2n+1}} - \frac{x^{2n+3}}{1-x^{2n+3}} - \&c. \, ad \, inf.\right\} \dots\dots\dots (1),$$

$$= \frac{1}{1-x^{2n}}\left\{\frac{x}{1-x} + \frac{x^3}{1-x^3} \cdots + \frac{x^{2n-1}}{1-x^{2n-1}}\right\} \dots\dots\dots (2),$$

since, x being less than unity, the terms in each of the two infinite series in (1) continually tend to zero.

[If x be greater than unity, then using the formulæ

$$\frac{x - x^{2n+1}}{(1-x)(1-x^{2n+1})} = \frac{1}{1-x} - \frac{1}{1-x^{2n+1}},$$

$$\frac{x^3 - x^{2n+3}}{(1-x^3)(1-x^{2n+3})} = \frac{1}{1-x^3} - \frac{1}{1-x^{2n+3}},$$

$$\&c. \quad = \quad \&c.$$

the series

$$= \frac{1}{1-x^{2n}}\left\{\frac{1}{1-x} + \frac{1}{1-x^3} + \frac{1}{1-x^5} + \&c.\ ad\ inf.\right.$$

$$\left. - \frac{1}{1-x^{2n+1}} - \frac{1}{1-x^{2n+3}} - \&c.\ ad\ inf.\right\}$$

$$= \frac{1}{1-x^{2n}}\left\{\frac{1}{1-x} + \frac{1}{1-x^3} \cdots + \frac{1}{1-x^{2n-1}}\right\} \dots\dots\dots(3),$$

since, x being greater than unity, the terms in the two series continually decrease.

Thus, if $x < 1$, the given series $= (2)$, and if > 1, it $= (3)$. The two forms are readily deducible the one from the other; for in (1), since the number of terms in each series is the same, there are n terms left over in the second series each $= \frac{x^q}{1-x^q}$ (q infinite) $= -1$ when $x > 1$, and thus we must add to (2), if x be > 1, the term

$$\frac{n}{1-x^{2n}},$$

and this is easily seen to be the difference between (2) and (3), for

$$\frac{x}{1-x} + 1 = \frac{1}{1-x},\quad \frac{x^3}{1-x^3} + 1 = \frac{1}{1-x^3},\ \&c.$$

We therefore have the given series $= (2)$ if $x < 1$ and $= (2) + \frac{n}{1-x^{2n}}$ if $x > 1$, and the change of form is deserving of notice.]

3. If
$$F(x) = f(x) + \tfrac{1}{2}f(x^2) + \tfrac{1}{3}f(x^3) + \tfrac{1}{4}f(x^4) + \tfrac{1}{5}f(x^5) + \&c.$$
prove that
$$f(x) = F(x) - \tfrac{1}{2}F(x^2) - \tfrac{1}{3}F(x^3) - \tfrac{1}{5}F(x^5) + \tfrac{1}{6}F(x^6) - \tfrac{1}{7}F(x^7) + \tfrac{1}{10}F(x^{10}) - \&c.$$

where only terms involving numbers that contain no square factor appear in the second series, and the sign is positive or negative according as the number of prime factors of the number is even or uneven.

Let E_a be a symbol of operation such that when operating upon a function of x it converts it into $\left(\dfrac{1}{a}\right)^{\text{th}}$ of the same function of x^a, so that

$$E_a \phi(x) = \frac{1}{a}\phi(x^a),\quad E_a \phi(x^2) = \frac{1}{a}\phi(x^{2a}),\ \&c.$$

Then $E_a E_b \phi(x) = E_b E_a \phi(x) = E_{ab} \phi(x) = E_{ba} \phi(x) = \dfrac{1}{ab} \phi(x^{ab})$,
so that, in the question,

$$F(x) = (1 + E_2 + E_3 + E_4 + E_5 + \&c.) f(x)$$

$$= \dfrac{1}{(1 - E_2)(1 - E_3)(1 - E_5) \dots} f(x),$$

2, 3, 5 ... being the prime numbers.

Therefore $f(x) = (1 - E_2)(1 - E_3)(1 - E_5) \dots F(x)$

$\qquad\qquad = (1 - E_2 - E_3 - E_5 + E_6 - \&c.) F(x)$

$\qquad\qquad = F(x) - \tfrac{1}{2} F(x^2) - \tfrac{1}{3} F(x^3) - \tfrac{1}{5} F(x^5) + \&c.,$

the law of the terms being as stated in the question.

Or otherwise, thus. Substitute for $F(x)$, $F(x^2)$, $F(x^3)$, ... their values in terms of $f(x), f(x^2), f(x^3), \dots$ given by the first series; we thus have

$x = x + \tfrac{1}{2} x^2 + \tfrac{1}{3} x^3 + \tfrac{1}{4} x^4 + \tfrac{1}{5} x^5 + \tfrac{1}{6} x^6 + \tfrac{1}{7} x^7 + \tfrac{1}{8} x^8 + \tfrac{1}{9} x^9 + \tfrac{1}{10} x^{10} + \&c.$
$\qquad - \tfrac{1}{2} \qquad\quad - \tfrac{1}{4} \qquad\quad - \tfrac{1}{6} \qquad\quad - \tfrac{1}{8} \qquad\quad - \tfrac{1}{10}$
$\qquad\qquad - \tfrac{1}{3} \qquad\qquad\quad - \tfrac{1}{6} \qquad\qquad\quad - \tfrac{1}{9}$
$\qquad\qquad\qquad - \tfrac{1}{5} \qquad\qquad\qquad\qquad\qquad - \tfrac{1}{10}$
$\qquad\qquad\qquad\quad + \tfrac{1}{6}$
$\qquad\qquad\qquad\qquad\qquad - \tfrac{1}{7}$
$\qquad\qquad\qquad\qquad\qquad\qquad\qquad\qquad\qquad + \tfrac{1}{10}$

in which x, x^2, x^3, ... are written for $f(x), f(x^2), f(x^3), \dots$ to save space, and the second line contains the value of $-\tfrac{1}{2} F(x^2)$, the third line of $-\tfrac{1}{3} F(x^3)$, &c. It is evident that every coefficient that appears in the $f(x^m)$ column will be $\dfrac{1}{m}$, so that we need consider only coefficients of $\dfrac{1}{m} f(x^m)$, such coefficients being always $+1$ or -1. Now in the case of $m = 6$, we have a coefficient $+1$ from $F(x)$, -1 from $-\tfrac{1}{2} F(x^2)$, -1 from $-\tfrac{1}{3} F(x^3)$, $+1$ from $\tfrac{1}{6} F(x^6)$; and generally for $m = a_1 a_2 \dots a_n$, where $a_1, a_2, \dots a_n$ are primes, there will be a coefficient $+1$ corresponding to the factor 1, i.e. from $F(x)$, a coefficient -1 corresponding to each of the factors $a_1, a_2, \dots a_n$, $+1$ corresponding to each product of two factors, $a_1 a_2, a_1 a_3, \dots,$ -1 corresponding to each product of three factors, $a_1 a_2 a_3$, and so on. Thus the whole coefficient

$$= 1 - n + \dfrac{n(n-1)}{1 \cdot 2} - \dots (-)^n 1 = (1 - 1)^n = 0.$$

Now consider the term for which $m = a_1{}^\alpha a_2{}^\beta \dots a_n{}^\nu$: the $+1$'s and -1's will occur exactly as for the term for which $m = a_1 a_2 \dots a_n$. This is readily seen to be the case, for we only obtain a term from each prime factor, or product of different prime factors in m; and these are the same for $a_1{}^\alpha a_2{}^\beta \dots a_n{}^\nu$ as for $a_1 a_2 \dots a_n$.

[It is evident that the theorem is still true if $\frac{1}{m}f(x^m)$ and $\frac{1}{m}F(x^m)$ be replaced by $m^p f(x^m)$ and $m^p F(x^m)$; p being any quantity, positive or negative, or zero, viz. if

$$F(x) = f(x) + 2^p f(x^2) + 3^p f(x^3) + 4^p f(x^4) + \&c.$$

then $\qquad f(x) = F(x) - 2^p F(x^2) - 3^p F(x^3) - 5^p F(x^5) + \&c.$

In order to apply the first method of proof to the general theorem, it is only necessary to define E_a by the equation $E_a \phi(x) = a^p \phi(x^a)$. The theorem itself is due to Möbius. *Crelle*, t. IX. p. 105—123.]

4. If a spherical triangle ABC be taken as the fundamental triangle, and α, β, γ be the spherical trilinear co-ordinates of a point P on the sphere, and p, q, r the spherical tangential co-ordinates of any great circle passing through P, then

$$\sin a \sin \alpha \sin p + \sin b \sin \beta \sin q + \sin c \sin \gamma \sin r = 0.$$

Let $XZPY$ be any great circle passing through P (fig. 47), and making angles θ, ϕ, ψ with BC, CA, AB. Then $\sin \alpha = \sin PX \sin \theta$,

$$\sin p = \sin AZ \sin \psi = \frac{\sin YZ \sin \phi}{\sin A} \sin \psi,$$

therefore $\quad \sin A \sin \alpha \sin p = \sin \theta \sin \phi \sin \psi . \sin PX \sin YZ,$

and (observing that in the figure p is negative) it has to be shewn that

$$- \sin PX \sin YZ + \sin PY \sin ZX + \sin PZ \sin XY = 0,$$

and, putting $PX = x, PY = y, PZ = z$, this expression on the left-hand side

$$= - \sin x \sin (y + z) + \sin y \sin (x - z) + \sin z \sin (x + y)$$
$$= \tfrac{1}{2} \{- \cos (y + z - x) + \cos (x + y + z) + \cos (y + z - x) - \cos (x + y - z)$$
$$+ \cos (x + y - z) - \cos (x + y + z)\} = 0.$$

Or, otherwise, thus:

$$\sin \alpha = \sin BP \sin PBC, \quad \sin p = \sin AP \sin APY,$$

$$\sin a = \sin CP \frac{\sin BPC}{\sin PBC},$$

therefore $\sin a \sin \alpha \sin p = \sin AP \sin BP \sin CP . \sin APY \sin BPC.$

The equation to be proved is therefore

$$- \sin APY \sin BPC + \sin BPX \sin CPA + \sin CPY \sin APB = 0,$$

viz. putting $\qquad \angle APY = x, \quad \angle BPY = y, \quad \angle CPZ = z,$

this is $\quad - \sin x \sin (y - z) + \sin y \sin (x + z) - \sin z \sin (x + y) = 0,$

which is at once seen to be true as above.

[The equation in the question, which is due to Mr H. Hart, becomes, when the radius of the sphere is made infinite, $aap + b\beta q + c\gamma r = 0$, which is the well-known relation between the tangential co-ordinates of a line *in plano*.]

5. An ellipse, centre C, turns in its plane about one focus S as a fixed point, and intersects a fixed straight line SX in P; along the normal to the ellipse at P a distance PT is taken equal to CD, the semi-diameter conjugate to CP; prove that the locus of T, in the plane, is one or other of two circles, according as the normals are drawn inwards or outwards.

First, suppose PT is measured inwards. In fig. 48 let $SP = x$, $ST = r$, $\angle XST = \theta$, then

$$ST^2 = SP^2 + PT^2 - 2SP \cdot PT \cos SPT \text{ and } \cos SPT = \frac{b}{PT},$$

therefore, since $PT^2 = x(2a - x)$,

$$r^2 = x^2 + 2ax - x^2 - 2bx = 2(a-b)x \quad \ldots\ldots\ldots\ldots(1).$$

Also $\quad \cos\theta = \dfrac{SP^2 + ST^2 - PT^2}{2SP \cdot ST} = \dfrac{x^2 + r^2 - 2ax + x^2}{2xr} = \dfrac{x-b}{r} \quad \ldots\ldots(2),$

on substituting for r^2 the value just found. Whence from (1) and (2),

$$r \cos\theta = \frac{r^2}{2(a-b)} - b,$$

viz. $\quad\quad r^2 - 2(a-b)r\cos\theta - 2b(a-b) = 0.$

The locus of T is therefore a circle of radius ae, and having its centre at M where $SM = a - b$.

Similarly, if PT' be measured outwards, it can be shewn in exactly the same manner that the equation of the locus of T' is

$$r^2 - 2(a+b)r\cos\theta + 2b(a+b) = 0.$$

The locus of T' is therefore an equal circle having its centre at M' where $SM' = a + b$.

[We have $CT^2 = CP^2 + PT^2 - 2CP \cdot PT \cos CPT = a^2 + b^2 - 2ab$, whence $CT = a - b$, and similarly $CT' = a + b$; so that $SM = CT = a - b$ and $SM' = CT' = a + b$; also $CS = TM = T'M' = ae$. Thus $SMTC$ and $SM'T'C$ are contra-parallelograms. For an account of the linkages with which these contra-parallelograms are connected see Mr Hart's paper "On some Cases of Parallel Motion," *Proceedings of the London Mathematical Society*, Vol. VIII. pp. 286—289 (1877).]

6. Prove that

$$\left(\frac{d}{dx}\right)^m x^{m+r} \left(\frac{d}{dx}\right)^r x^{-m} \left(\frac{d}{dx}\right)^{n-r} \phi(x) = x^r \left(\frac{d}{dx}\right)^{m+n} \phi(x).$$

We have
$$x^{-m}\left(\frac{d}{dx}\right)^{n-r} x^a = a(a-1)\ldots(a-n+r+1)x^{a-n+r-m}.$$

Differentiating r times and multiplying by x^{m+r}, this becomes
$$= a(a-1)\ldots(a-n+r+1).(a-n+r-m)(a-n+r-m-1)\ldots$$
$$(a-n-m+1)x^{a-n+r},$$

which, differentiated m times,
$$= a(a-1)\ldots(a-n+r+1).(a-n+r-m)(a-n+r-m-1)\ldots(a-n-m+1)$$
$$.(a-n+r)(a-n+r-1)\ldots(a-n+r-m+1)x^{a-n+r-m}$$
$$= a(a-1)\ldots(a-m-n+1)x^{a-m-n+r} = x^r\left(\frac{d}{dx}\right)^{m+n} x^a.$$

Thus the theorem is true when the quantity operated upon is x^a, and therefore it is true for $\phi(x)$, where $\phi(x) = Ax^a + Bx^b + Cx^c + \&c.$, that is, when $\phi(x)$ is any function of x expressible in ascending or descending powers of x. The theorem must therefore be true when $\phi(x)$ is unrestricted, for it merely asserts an identical relation between the differential coefficients of $\phi(x)$, and the truth of such a relation cannot be affected by the fact of whether $\phi(x)$ is or is not expressible in any particular form.

[The above method of proof is of general application to formulæ involving differentiations and multiplications as in the previous question; and, in order to obtain such identical relations, it is only necessary to start with x^a and so arrange the differentiations and multiplications that the factors thus introduced may be the same for both sides of the equation. Thus, for example, $\left(\frac{d}{dx}\right)^{n+1} x^a = a(a-1)\ldots(a-n)x^{a-n-1}$, and multiplying by $x^{n+\frac{1}{2}}$ and differentiating n times, we have
$$\left(\frac{d}{dx}\right)^n x^{n+\frac{1}{2}} \left(\frac{d}{dx}\right)^{n+1} x^a = a(a-1)\ldots(a-n).(a-\tfrac{1}{2})(a-\tfrac{3}{2})\ldots(a-n+\tfrac{1}{2})x^{a-n-\frac{1}{2}}$$
$$= \frac{2a(2a-1)(2a-2)\ldots(2a-2n)}{2^{2n+1}}(x^{\frac{1}{2}})^{2a-2n-1}$$
$$= \frac{1}{2^{2n+1}}\left(\frac{d}{dx^{\frac{1}{2}}}\right)^{2n+1}(x^{\frac{1}{2}})^{2a} = \frac{1}{2^{2n+1}}\left(\frac{d}{dx^{\frac{1}{2}}}\right)^{2n+1} x^a,$$
whence
$$\left(\frac{d}{dx}\right)^n x^{n+\frac{1}{2}}\left(\frac{d}{dx}\right)^{n+1} \phi(x^{\frac{1}{2}}) = \frac{1}{2^{2n+1}} \phi^{(2n+1)}(x^{\frac{1}{2}}).$$

The general principle upon which all such theorems depend is that since
$$x^{1-m}\frac{d}{dx} x^m . x^a = (a+m)x^a,$$

the operation $x^{1-m}\dfrac{d}{dx} x^m$ is equivalent to multiplication by $a+m$, and therefore any number of operators $x^{1-m}\dfrac{d}{dx}x^m$, $x^{1-n}\dfrac{d}{dx}x^n$, ... are convertible in regard to order[1].

In reference to the extension from the case when the operand is x^s to the general case when the operand is $\phi(x)$, it is to be observed that the theorem asserts an identical relation between the derivatives of $\phi(x)$, viz. $\phi(x)$, $\phi'(x)$, $\phi''(x)$ ..., and that this is proved to hold good when $\phi(x)$ is of the form $Ax^a + Bx^b + Cx^c + \&c$. It must therefore hold good for all forms of $\phi(x)$ since the process of differentiation cannot distinguish between whether $\phi(x)$ is expansible in powers of x or not;

i.e. the developed expression for $\left(\dfrac{d}{dx}\right)^n x^m \phi^{(r)}(x)$ is

$$x^m \phi^{(r+n)}(x) + nmx^{m-1} \phi^{(r+n-1)}(x) + \&c.,$$

whatever form $\phi(x)$ may have, and since the theorem merely expresses the identity of the results obtained by applications of this formula, it follows that, if we know that this identity holds good for all functions, subject only to a restriction, which restriction could not influence the direct proof, then we may assert the general truth of the theorem. It is generally interesting in theorems obtained by an extension of this kind to actually work out, by performing the differentiations, a particular case obtained by giving numerical values to the letters m, n, r .... The present is a good instance of a restriction, necessary in order that a particular proof of a theorem may apply, and yet such that the theorem itself shews obviously that it may be removed.]

Or, otherwise, thus. Put $\left(\dfrac{d}{dx}\right)^{n-r}\phi(x) = \psi(x)$ and the equation becomes

$$x^m \left(\dfrac{d}{dx}\right)^m \cdot x^m \cdot x^r \left(\dfrac{d}{dx}\right)^r \cdot x^{-m} \psi(x) = x^{m+r}\left(\dfrac{d}{dx}\right)^{m+r}\psi(x).$$

If ϑ denote the operation $x\dfrac{d}{dx}$, then the left-hand side

$$= \vartheta(\vartheta-1)\ldots(\vartheta-m+1)\,x^m\,\vartheta(\vartheta-1)\ldots(\vartheta-r+1)\,x^{-m}\psi(x)$$

$$= \vartheta(\vartheta-1)\ldots(\vartheta-m+1)(\vartheta-m)\ldots(\vartheta-m-r+1)\psi(x) = x^{m+r}\left(\dfrac{d}{dx}\right)^{m+r}\psi(x).$$

[Boole, in his *Differential Equations*, does not consider the operative symbol $x\dfrac{d}{dx}$, but puts $x = e^\theta$ so that $x\dfrac{d}{dx}$ is replaced by $\dfrac{d}{d\theta}$ and x^s by $e^{s\theta}$. It is however generally preferable not to make this transformation, but to retain the symbol $x\dfrac{d}{dx}$, or, say ϑ, the fundamental properties of which are
    (1) $\vartheta^n x^s = s^n x^s$,

    (2) $x^n\left(\dfrac{d}{dx}\right)^n u = \vartheta(\vartheta-1)\ldots(\vartheta-n+1)u$,

    (3) $\phi(\vartheta)x^n u = x^n \phi(\vartheta+n)u$.]

[1] See *Proceedings of the London Mathematical Society*, Vol. VIII. pp. 47—51.

7. If
$$u = e^{-\int \phi(x)\,dx} \int e^{\int \phi(x)\,dx}(c_0 + c_1 x + c_2 x^2 \ldots + c_n x^n) f(x)\,dx + C e^{-\int \phi(x)\,dx},$$
where $c_0, c_1, \ldots c_n, C$ are $(n+2)$ arbitrary constants, and
$$\frac{\phi(x)}{f(x)} = a_0 + a_1 x + a_2 x^2 \ldots + a_m x^m,$$
where $a_0, a_1, \ldots a_m$ are m given constants, shew that if m be not greater than n, $\dfrac{du}{dx}$, obtained by the direct differentiation of u with regard to x, contains only $n+1$ arbitrary constants.

By differentiating the expression for u,
$$\frac{du}{dx} = (c_0 + c_1 x \ldots + c_n x^n) f(x)$$
$$- \phi(x) e^{-\int \phi(x)\,dx} \int e^{\int \phi(x)\,dx} (c_0 + c_1 x \ldots + c_n x^n) f(x) - C\phi(x) e^{-\int \phi(x)\,dx},$$
whence
$$\frac{1}{\phi(x)} e^{\int \phi(x)\,dx} \frac{du}{dx} = (c_0 + c_1 x \ldots + c_n x^n) \frac{f(x)}{\phi(x)} e^{\int \phi(x)\,dx}$$
$$- \int e^{\int \phi(x)\,dx}(c_0 + c_1 x \ldots + c_n x^n) f(x)\,dx - C$$
$$= c_0 \left(\frac{f(x)}{\phi(x)} e^{\int \phi(x)\,dx} - \int e^{\int \phi(x)\,dx} f(x)\,dx \right)$$
$$+ c_1 \left(\frac{x f(x)}{\phi(x)} e^{\int \phi(x)\,dx} - \int e^{\int \phi(x)\,dx} x f(x)\,dx \right),$$
$$\ldots\ldots\ldots\ldots\ldots\ldots\ldots\ldots\ldots\ldots\ldots\ldots\ldots\ldots\ldots$$
$$+ c_n \left(\frac{x^n f(x)}{\phi(x)} e^{\int \phi(x)\,dx} - \int e^{\int \phi(x)\,dx} x^n f(x)\,dx \right) - C$$
$$= c_0 B_0 + c_1 B_1 \ldots + c_n B_n - C.$$
Now $\quad \dfrac{dB_0}{dx} = e^{\int \phi(x)\,dx} \dfrac{d}{dx}\left(\dfrac{f(x)}{\phi(x)}\right), \quad \dfrac{dB_1}{dx} = e^{\int \phi(x)\,dx} \dfrac{d}{dx}\left(\dfrac{x f(x)}{\phi(x)}\right),$
$$\ldots, \quad \frac{dB_m}{dx} = e^{\int \phi(x)\,dx} \frac{d}{dx}\left(\frac{x^m f(x)}{\phi(x)}\right),$$
whence, multiplying by $a_0, a_1, \ldots a_m$ and adding,
$$\frac{d}{dx}(a_0 B_0 + a_1 B_1 \ldots + a_m B_m) = e^{\int \phi(x)\,dx} \frac{d}{dx}\left\{(a_0 + a_1 x \ldots + a_m x^m)\frac{f(x)}{\phi(x)}\right\}$$
$$= 0,$$
therefore $\quad a_0 B_0 + a_1 B_1 \ldots + a_m B_m = B$ (a constant);

and, substituting for B_0,

$$\frac{1}{\phi(x)} e^{\int \phi(x)dx} \frac{du}{dx} = \frac{1}{a_0} \{(c_0 B - a_0 C) + (a_0 c_1 - a_1 c_0) B_1 \ldots + (a_0 c_m - a_m c_0) B_m\}$$
$$+ c_{m+1} B_{m+1} \ldots + c_n B_n,$$

which only contains $n+1$ arbitrary constants.

Or, otherwise, thus. We have

$$u e^{\int \phi(x)dx} = \int e^{\int \phi(x)dx} (c_0 + c_1 x \ldots + c_n x^n) f(x) \, dx + C,$$

whence $\quad \dfrac{du}{dx} + \phi(x) u = (c_0 + c_1 x \ldots + c_n x^n) f(x),$

viz. $\quad \dfrac{1}{f(x)} \dfrac{du}{dx} + (a_0 + a_1 x \ldots + a_m x^m) u = c_0 + c_1 x \ldots + c_n x^n.$

Differentiate this equation $m+1$ times, and we obtain an equation of the form

$$\frac{1}{f(x)} \frac{d^{m+2}u}{dx^{m+2}} \ldots + N \frac{du}{dx} = c'_{m+1} + c'_{m+2} x \ldots + c'_n x^{n-m-1},$$

the coefficient of u vanishing. This is a differential equation of the $(m+1)^{\text{th}}$ order in $\dfrac{du}{dx}$ and therefore $\dfrac{du}{dx}$ involves $m+1$ constants in addition to the $n-m$ constants $c'_{m+1}, c'_{m+2}, \ldots c'_n$, that is, $\dfrac{du}{dx}$ in $n+1$ arbitrary constants.

[The above theorem is true whatever function $f(x)$ may be of x; but if $\dfrac{1}{f(x)} = b_0 + b_1 x \ldots + b_r x^r$, it can be shewn in the same manner by continuing the differentiations, that if $r \gtreqless n+1$ and $m \gtreqless n$, then each differentiation of u reduces the number of independent constants by one until we come to $\dfrac{d^{n-p+1}u}{dx^{n-p+1}}$ which only involves $p+1$ constants, p being the greater of the quantities m, $r-1$.]

8. Prove that

$$\int_0^1 v^{rx} dv = 1 - \frac{x}{2^2} + \frac{x^2}{3^3} - \frac{x^3}{4^4} + \frac{x^4}{5^5} - \&c.$$

The coefficient of x^n in v^{rx}, that is in $e^{rx\log v}$, $= \dfrac{v^n (\log v)^n}{1 \cdot 2 \cdot 3 \ldots n}$, and, integrating by parts,

$$\int_0^1 v^n (\log v)^n dv = \frac{1}{n+1} \left[v^{n+1} (\log v)^n \right]_0^1 - \frac{n}{n+1} \int_0^1 v^n (\log v)^{n-1} dv$$

$$= (-)^n \frac{n}{n+1} \cdot \frac{n-1}{n+1} \cdot \frac{n-2}{n+1} \ldots \frac{1}{n+1} \int_0^1 v^n dv,$$

whence the coefficient of $x^n = (-)^n \dfrac{1}{(n+1)^{n+1}}$.

9. Two equal circular discs of radius a with their planes parallel are fastened at their centres to a bar, the discs being inclined to the bar at an angle α. The two wheels thus formed being rolled along a plane, prove that the intrinsic equation to the track of either wheel on the plane is

$$\sin \psi = \cos \alpha \sin \frac{s}{a}.$$

The track of each wheel will be the trace of a circular section of an elliptic cylinder when the cylinder is rolled on the plane.

If AP (fig. 49) be one circular disc, BN a transverse elliptic section of the cylinder; and if $A'P'$, $B'N'$ be the traces of AP, BN on the plane; then the elliptic arc BN = the abscissa $B'N'$; the circular arc AP = the arc $A'P'$, and the ordinates AB, NP = the ordinates $A'B'$, $N'P'$ respectively.

Therefore if the arc AP or $A'P'$ be denoted by s, and NP or $N'P'$ by y, we have $y = c - a \cos \alpha \cos \frac{s}{a}$, where c denotes the distance between the centres of the sections AP, BN; therefore $\sin \psi = \frac{dy}{ds} = \cos \alpha \sin \frac{s}{a}$.

[The curve $\sin \psi = \cos \alpha \sin \frac{s}{a}$ possesses the property that the product of the radius of curvature and normal at any point $= a^2$, the normal being terminated by the axis of the curve, *i.e.* the straight line which divides it symmetrically. This is at once seen to be true, for the radius of curvature $= \frac{ds}{d\psi}$, and the normal $= y \sec \psi$, where $y = a \cos \alpha \cos \frac{s}{a}$.]

10. Prove that

$$\left\{ \frac{1 - k^2 \dfrac{\operatorname{cn}^2(u+v) \operatorname{cn}^2(u-v)}{\operatorname{dn}^2(u+v) \operatorname{dn}^2(u-v)}}{1 - k^2 \operatorname{sn}^2(u+v) \operatorname{sn}^2(u-v)} \right\}^{\frac{1}{2}} = k' \frac{1 - k^2 \operatorname{sn}^2 u \operatorname{sn}^2 v}{1 - k^2 \operatorname{sn}^2 u - k^2 \operatorname{sn}^2 v + k^2 \operatorname{sn}^2 u \operatorname{sn}^2 v}.$$

Writing x, y for $\operatorname{sn} u$, $\operatorname{sn} v$, then (Cayley's *Elliptic Functions*, 1876, p. 63),

$$\operatorname{sn}(u+v) \operatorname{sn}(u-v) = (x^2 - y^2) \div (1 - k^2 x^2 y^2),$$
$$\operatorname{cn}(u+v) \operatorname{cn}(u-v) = (1 - x^2 - y^2 + k^2 x^2 y^2) \div (1 - k^2 x^2 y^2),$$
$$\operatorname{dn}(u+v) \operatorname{dn}(u-v) = (1 - k^2 x^2 - k^2 y^2 + k^2 x^2 y^2) \div (1 - k^2 x^2 y^2),$$

whence

$$\left\{ 1 - k^2 \frac{\operatorname{cn}^2(u+v) \operatorname{cn}^2(u-v)}{\operatorname{dn}^2(u+v) \operatorname{dn}^2(u-v)} \right\} \div \left\{ 1 - k^2 \operatorname{sn}^2(u+v) \operatorname{sn}^2(u-v) \right\}$$

$$= \frac{(1 - k^2 x^2 - k^2 y^2 + k^2 x^2 y^2)^2 - k^2 (1 - x^2 - y^2 + k^2 x^2 y^2)^2}{(1 - k^2 x^2 y^2)^2 - k^2 (x^2 - y^2)^2} \cdot \frac{(1 - k^2 x^2 y^2)^2}{(1 - k^2 x^2 - k^2 y^2 + k^2 x^2 y^2)^2}.$$

The first fraction reduces to k'^2, for, working out the numerator and denominator, the former $= k'^2 (1 - k^2 x^4 - k^2 y^4 + k^4 x^4 y^4)$, and the latter

$$= 1 - k^2 x^4 - k^2 y^4 + k^4 x^4 y^4;$$ whence the result in the question follows at once.

Or, otherwise, thus. In the known equation

$$1 - k^2 \operatorname{sn}^2(u+v) \operatorname{sn}^2(u-v) = \frac{(1 - k^2 \operatorname{sn}^4 u)(1 - k^2 \operatorname{sn}^4 v)}{(1 - k^2 \operatorname{sn}^2 u \operatorname{sn}^2 v)^2} \quad \ldots (1),$$

put $K + u$ for u and we have

$$1 - k^2 \frac{\operatorname{cn}^2(u+v)\operatorname{cn}^2(u-v)}{\operatorname{dn}^2(u+v)\operatorname{dn}^2(u-v)} = \frac{(\operatorname{dn}^4 u - k^2 \operatorname{cn}^4 u)(1 - k^2 \operatorname{sn}^4 v)}{(\operatorname{dn}^2 u - k^2 \operatorname{cn}^2 u \operatorname{sn}^2 v)^2} \quad \ldots (2),$$

and the result follows at once by dividing (2) by (1) and observing that

$$\operatorname{dn}^4 u - k^2 \operatorname{cn}^4 u = k'^2 (1 - k^2 \operatorname{sn}^4 u)$$

$$\operatorname{dn}^2 u - k^2 \operatorname{cn}^2 u \operatorname{sn}^2 v = 1 - k^2 \operatorname{sn}^2 u - k^2 \operatorname{sn}^2 v + k^2 \operatorname{sn}^2 u \operatorname{sn}^2 v.$$

11. If 1, 2, 3, 4 denote the foci (lying in order on the circumference of a circle) of a bicircular quartic, whose equation is

$$l\rho_1 + m\rho_2 + n\rho_3 = 0,$$

ρ_1, ρ_2, ρ_3 being the distances of any point on the curve from the three foci 1, 2, 3; prove that

$$l^2 \overline{12} \cdot \overline{13} \cdot \overline{14} - m^2 \overline{23} \cdot \overline{24} \cdot \overline{21} + n^2 \overline{34} \cdot \overline{31} \cdot \overline{32} = 0,$$

where $\overline{12}$ means the distance between the foci 1, 2.

Produce 12, 34 to meet in O. Then, by a known theorem, the curve is its own inverse in respect to O. Let $O1 = a$, $O2 = b$, $O3 = c$, $O4 = d$, $OP = \rho$, $\angle PO1 = \theta$, $\angle 104 = \alpha$ (fig. 50).

Then

$$\rho_1^2 = \rho^2 - 2a\rho\cos\theta + a^2, \quad \rho_2^2 = \rho^2 - 2b\rho\cos\theta + b^2, \quad \rho_3^2 = \rho^2 - 2c\rho\cos(\theta + \alpha) + c^2,$$

substituting in the equation $l\rho_1 + m\rho_2 + n\rho_3 = 0$, and clearing of radicals, the equation becomes

$$l^4\{\rho^2 - 2a\rho\cos\theta + a^2\}^2 + m^4\{\rho^2 - 2b\rho\cos\theta + b^2\}^2 + n^4\{\rho^2 - 2c\rho\cos(\theta+\alpha) + c^2\}^2$$
$$- 2l^2m^2\{\rho^2 - 2a\rho\cos\theta + a^2\}\{\rho^2 - 2b\rho\cos\theta + b^2\}$$
$$- 2l^2n^2\{\rho^2 - 2a\rho\cos\theta + a^2\}\{\rho^2 - 2c\rho\cos(\theta+\alpha) + c^2\}$$
$$- 2m^2n^2\{\rho^2 - 2b\rho\cos\theta + b^2\}\{\rho^2 - 2c\rho\cos(\theta+\alpha) + c^2\} = 0,$$

or, say,
$$\alpha\rho^4 + \beta\rho^3 + \gamma\rho^2 + \delta\rho + \epsilon = 0 \ldots\ldots\ldots\ldots\ldots\ldots(1).$$

Now the curve is its own inverse in respect to O, the modulus being $ab, = cd$, therefore (1) is not altered by substituting $\dfrac{ab}{\rho}$ for ρ, so that

$$\alpha a^4 b^4 + \beta a^3 b^3 \rho + \gamma a^2 b^2 \rho^2 + \delta ab\rho^3 + \epsilon\rho^4 = 0$$

is identical with (1). Thus

$$\frac{aa^4b^4}{\epsilon} = \frac{\beta a^3b^3}{\delta} = \frac{\gamma a^2b^2}{\gamma} = \frac{\delta ab}{\beta} = \frac{\epsilon}{a},$$

whence $ab\beta = \delta$. Putting for β and δ their values, this gives

$$ab\left\{A\cos\theta + c\left(n^4 - l^2n^2 - m^2n^2\right)\sin\theta\sin a\right\}$$
$$= B\cos\theta + c\left(c^2n^4 - a^2l^2n^2 - b^2m^2n^2\right)\sin\theta\sin a,$$

which is true for all values of θ, so that $abA = B$ and

$$abc\,n^2\left(n^2 - l^2 - m^2\right) = cn^2\left(c^2n^2 - a^2l^2 - b^2m^2\right),$$

viz. $\qquad (ab - c^2)\,n^2 + (a^2 - ab)\,l^2 - (ab - b^2)\,m^2 = 0,$

viz. $\qquad a\,(a-b)\,l^2 - b\,(a-b)\,m^2 + c\,(d-c)\,n^2 = 0,$ since $ab = cd$.

Also $a - b = \overline{12}$, $d - c = \overline{34}$, and by similar triangles $a : c = \overline{14} : \overline{23}$ and $b : c = \overline{24} : \overline{13}$, whence the equation becomes

$$l^2.\,\overline{12}.\,\overline{13}.\,\overline{14} - m^2\,\overline{23}.\,\overline{24}.\,\overline{21} + n^2\,\overline{34}.\,\overline{31}.\,\overline{32} = 0.$$

(It may be noted that the term corresponding to the middle one of the three foci considered has the negative sign.)

12. Shew that the focal length of a lens equivalent to n given lenses of powers $\kappa_1, \kappa_2, \kappa_3, \ldots \kappa_n$, placed on the same axis at distances $a_1, a_2, a_3, \ldots a_{n-1}$ apart, is given by the formula

$$\frac{1}{F_n} = - \begin{vmatrix} -\kappa_n, & -1, & 0, & 0, & 0,\ldots & 0, & 0 \\ 1, & -a_{n-1}, & -1, & 0, & 0,\ldots & 0, & 0 \\ 0, & 1, & -\kappa_{n-1}, & -1, & 0,\ldots & 0, & 0 \\ 0, & 0, & 1, & -a_{n-2}, & -1,\ldots & 0, & 0 \\ \multicolumn{7}{c}{\dotfill} \\ 0, & 0, & 0, & 0, & 0,\ldots & -a_1, & -1 \\ 0, & 0, & 0, & 0, & 0,\ldots & 1, & -\kappa_1 \end{vmatrix} \;(2n-1\text{ rows}),$$

the incident ray being supposed parallel to the axis.

A lens is equivalent to a system of n lenses on the same axis, if, being placed in the position of the first lens, it produces the same deviation on a given ray as the system of lenses. A ray passing through a lens at a distance y from the axis suffers a deviation $\dfrac{y}{f}$ from the axis. Suppose a ray parallel to the axis to be incident on the first lens of the system at a distance y_1 from the axis: let δ_1 be the deviation after passing through the first lens, y_2 the distance from the axis at which the ray cuts the second lens, δ_2 its deviation after the second refraction and so on. Then putting $\kappa_1, \kappa_2, \ldots \kappa_n$ for $f_1^{-1}, f_2^{-1}, \ldots f_n^{-1}$, we have the equations

$$\delta_1 = \kappa_1 y_1, \quad y_2 = a_1\delta_1 + y_1, \quad \delta_2 = \kappa_2 y_2 + \delta_1, \ldots y_n = a_{n-1}\delta_{n-1} + y_{n-1}, \quad \delta_n = \kappa_n y_n + \delta_{n-1}.$$

Writing these in the reverse order,

$$\delta_n - \kappa_n y_n - \delta_{n-1} = 0$$
$$y_n - a_{n-1}\delta_{n-1} - y_{n-1} = 0$$
$$\cdots\cdots\cdots$$
$$y_2 - a_1\delta_1 = y_1$$
$$\delta_1 = \kappa_1 y_1,$$

whence

$$\delta_n = y_1 \begin{vmatrix} 0, & -\kappa_n, & -1, & 0, \ldots & 0 \\ 0, & 1, & -a_{n-1}, & -1, \ldots & 0 \\ \cdots\cdots\cdots\cdots\cdots\cdots\cdots\cdots \\ 1, & 0, & 0, & 0, \ldots & -a_1 \\ \kappa_1, & 0, & 0, & 0, \ldots & 1 \end{vmatrix},$$

and since $\delta_n = \dfrac{y_1}{F}$, this at once gives the result in the question, by moving the first column so that it becomes the last.

[The equations also show that $\dfrac{1}{F}$ is equal to the numerator of the last convergent to the continued fraction

$$\frac{1}{1+}\frac{1}{\kappa_1+}\frac{1}{a_1+}\frac{1}{\kappa_2+}\ldots\frac{1}{\kappa_n};$$

see Mr Pendlebury's note "On equivalent lenses," *Messenger of Mathematics*, Vol. VII. pp. 129—131 (1878)].

13. Three equal uniform bars, formed of such material that any particle repels any other with intensity proportional to the product of their masses and directly as the distance between them, are loosely jointed at their ends so as to form an equilateral triangle. If one of these connexions at the angles be severed, find the motion of the system.

Prove that the angular velocity of either of the outer bars when all three are in a straight line is $\sqrt{8\cdot4}$ times their angular velocity when they are at right angles to the middle bar.

Suppose the three rods placed in a straight line and a small impulse given to the middle rod through its centre and perpendicular to its length, find the time of the small oscillations.

Let m be the mass and $2a$ the length of any one of the bars, then if x be the distance of the centre of the middle bar from the centre of gravity of the system and θ the exterior angle between either of the outer bars and the middle bar, the kinetic energy of the system will be

$$\tfrac{1}{2}m\{\dot{x}^2 + 2(\dot{x} - a\cos\theta\dot{\theta})^2 + 2a^2\sin^2\theta\dot{\theta}^2 + \tfrac{2}{3}a^2\dot{\theta}^2\}.$$

The quantity $\dot{x}$ can be eliminated from this expression by means of the equation

$$\dot{x} + 2(\dot{x} - a\sin\theta) = 0,$$

viz.
$$3\dot{x} = 2a\sin\theta\,\dot{\theta}\ldots\ldots\ldots\ldots\ldots\ldots\ldots(1),$$

which expresses the obvious fact that the centre of gravity of the system remains a fixed point during the motion. The kinetic energy then becomes
$$\tfrac{2}{5} m (1 + \sin^2 \theta)\, a^2\, \dot\theta^2 \quad\ldots\ldots\ldots\ldots\ldots\ldots\ldots\ldots (2).$$

Now let μ be the repulsion between two units of mass placed at unit distance apart, then the force upon any one of the bars will be $3m^2\mu r$, where r is the distance of the centre of the bar considered from the centre of gravity of the system. The work done by this force from the commencement of the motion is clearly
$$\tfrac{3}{2} m^2 \mu (r^2 - r_0^2),$$
where r_0 is the initial value of r. The work done on the system by its mutual repulsions is thus
$$3m^2\mu \{\tfrac{1}{2} x^2 + (x - a\sin\theta)^2 + (a + a\cos\theta)^2 - \tfrac{1}{2} a^2\}.$$

By eliminating x we reduce this to
$$3m^2\mu a^2 \{\tfrac{1}{3} \sin^2\theta + (1 + \cos\theta)^2 - \tfrac{1}{2}\} \quad\ldots\ldots\ldots\ldots\ldots (3).$$

The expressions (2) and (3) are equal, and being equated lead easily to the result in the question.

The second part of the question is easily solved by an application of Lagrange's equations. We may however solve it otherwise as follows: Let the middle bar be brought to rest by applying to the system a reversed acceleration equal to $\ddot x$. The equation of moments about the fixed end of either of the outer bars is then
$$m \cdot \tfrac{4}{3} a^2 \ddot\theta = - m^2 \cdot 5a\mu \cdot a\theta + m\ddot x a,$$
whence by means of (1) we have
$$\tfrac{2}{3} \ddot\theta = - 5m\mu\theta.$$
viz.
$$\ddot\theta = - \frac{15m\mu}{2}\, \theta.$$

The time required is therefore $2\pi \sqrt{\dfrac{2}{15m\mu}}$.

14. Prove that, when the angular velocity of a vertical cylindrical shaft of radius a, revolving in two bearings at a distance l apart, exceeds $\tfrac{1}{2} \dfrac{m^2 a}{l^2} \sqrt{\dfrac{E}{\rho}}$, where m is the least root of the equation $\cos m \cosh m = 1$, the shaft will tend to bend laterally under the influence of the rotation; and find the curve assumed by the axis when the deflection is small; E being the modulus of elasticity, and ρ the density of the shaft.

Let the shaft turn in fixed bearings at O and B (fig. 51), and let $OPAB$ be the curve assumed by the axis of the shaft when the deflection due to the rotation is small.

Take O as the origin and OB as the axis of x; and let G be the bending moment at O due to the constraint of the bearing.

Then, if ω denote the angular velocity, the bending moment at P will be equal to
$$G + \pi a^2 \rho \omega^2 \int_0^x (x - x') y'\, dx';$$
and, since the curvature at P is approximately $\dfrac{d^2y}{dx^2}$, therefore
$$EI \frac{d^2y}{dx^2} = G + \pi a^2 \rho \omega^2 \int_0^x (x - x')\, y'\, dx',$$
I being the moment of inertia of the circular section about a diameter, and therefore EI the flexural rigidity of the shaft.

Differentiating twice,
$$EI \frac{d^3y}{dx^3} = \pi a^2 \rho \omega^2 \int_0^x y'\, dx',$$
$$EI \frac{d^4y}{dx^4} = \pi a^2 \rho \omega^2 y,$$

viz.
$$\frac{d^4y}{dx^4} = \frac{\pi a^2 \rho \omega^2}{EI} y = \frac{4\rho \omega^2}{Ea^2} y,$$

the differential equation of the axis of the shaft, when the deflection is small.

The problem therefore becomes the same as the determination of the lateral vibrations of a bar clamped at both ends (see Lord Rayleigh's *Theory of Sound*, § 172).

We must therefore have m the least root of the equation
$$\cos m \cosh m = 1,$$

where $\quad \dfrac{m^4}{l^4} = \dfrac{4\rho \omega^2}{Ea^2}, \quad$ viz. $\omega = \tfrac{1}{2} \dfrac{m^2 a}{l^2} \sqrt{\dfrac{E}{\rho}}.$

When the angular velocity exceeds this value, the shaft will tend to bend laterally more and more as the angular velocity is increased under the influence of the rotation.

(The shaft is supposed vertical in order that gravity may have no influence upon the result).

15. Find an expression for the average energy transmitted across a fixed vertical plane parallel to the fronts of an infinite train of irrotational harmonic waves, of given small elevation, moving on water of uniform depth.

Let H be the maximum elevation of a train of waves of wave-length λ, moving parallel to the axis of x. Then, if $\kappa = 2\pi \lambda^{-1}$, $n = 2\pi V \lambda^{-1}$, where V is the velocity of propagation, the elevation at any point x at any time t may be taken to be
$$h = H \cos(nt - \kappa x).$$

By the known theorem the velocity of propagation is connected with the wave-length and the depth of the water l by the equation

$$V^2 = \frac{g}{\kappa} \frac{e^{\kappa l} - e^{-\kappa l}}{e^{\kappa l} + e^{-\kappa l}},$$

and the corresponding velocity-potential ϕ is given by

$$\phi = -VH \frac{e^{\kappa(z-l)} + e^{-\kappa(z-l)}}{e^{\kappa l} - e^{-\kappa l}} \sin(nt - \kappa x),$$

z being measured downwards from the surface. In fact, ϕ satisfies $\nabla^2 \phi = 0$, and gives a value for $\dfrac{d\phi}{dz}$ equal to zero when $z = l$, and equal to $-\dfrac{dh}{dt}$ when $z = 0$.

By the equations of hydrodynamics the part of the pressure due to the motion is

$$\delta p = -\rho \frac{d\phi}{dt} - \tfrac{1}{2}\rho \left\{ \left(\frac{d\phi}{dx}\right)^2 + \left(\frac{d\phi}{dz}\right)^2 \right\};$$

whence, if the square of the motion be neglected,

$$\delta p = -\rho \frac{d\phi}{dt},$$

$$= \rho n V H \frac{e^{\kappa(z-l)} + e^{-\kappa(z-l)}}{e^{\kappa l} - e^{-\kappa l}} \cos(nt - \kappa x).$$

The rate of transmission of work at any moment is found by integrating $\delta p \dfrac{d\phi}{dx} dz$ from $z = 0$ to $z = l$. Thus

$$\frac{dW}{dt} = n\kappa V^2 H^2 \rho \frac{\cos^2(nt - \kappa x)}{(e^{\kappa l} - e^{-\kappa l})^2} \int_0^l \{e^{\kappa(z-l)} + e^{-\kappa(z-l)}\}^2 dz,$$

in which

$$\int_0^l \{e^{\kappa(z-l)} + e^{-\kappa(z-l)}\}^2 dz = \frac{4\kappa l + e^{2\kappa l} - e^{-2\kappa l}}{2\kappa}.$$

Introducing the value of V we get

$$\frac{dW}{dt} = \tfrac{1}{2} g\rho H^2 V \cos^2(nt - \kappa x) \left[1 + \frac{4\kappa l}{e^{2\kappa l} - e^{-2\kappa l}} \right],$$

or, on integration over a long range of time,

$$W = \tfrac{1}{4} g\rho H^2 \cdot Vt \cdot \left[1 + \frac{4\kappa l}{e^{2\kappa l} - e^{-2\kappa l}} \right].$$

16. An ellipsoidal conductor is placed in a uniform field of electric force, the potential of which is $Ax + By + Cz$, the axes $(2a, 2b, 2c)$ of the ellipsoid being taken for co-ordinate axes. Prove

that the density of the induced electricity at a point (x, y, z) on the surface of the conductor is

$$\frac{1}{4\pi abc \sqrt{\frac{x^2}{a^4} + \frac{y^2}{b^4} + \frac{z^2}{c^4}}} \left(\frac{Ax}{a^2 \frac{d\phi}{da^2}} + \frac{By}{b^2 \frac{d\phi}{db^2}} + \frac{Cz}{c^2 \frac{d\phi}{dc^2}} \right),$$

where

$$\phi = \int_0^\infty \frac{d\lambda}{\sqrt{(a^2 + \lambda)(b^2 + \lambda)(c^2 + \lambda)}}.$$

This problem is easily solved by the use of ellipsoidal co-ordinates, for an explanation of which see Mr Ferrers's *Treatise on Spherical Harmonics*, Chap. VI. The following solution, which is of general application in the case of the sphere, does not apply readily to ellipsoids, except in the one case stated in the question, viz. when the potential is a linear function of x, y, z.

Let U be the potential at any outside point due to a solid ellipsoid of uniform density, then $l \frac{dU}{dx} + m \frac{dU}{dy} + n \frac{dU}{dz}$ is the potential at an outside point due to an ellipsoidal shell of the first degree, viz. a shell formed by the coexistence of two solid ellipsoids, of equal uniform densities, one attracting and the other repelling, whose centres are infinitely near and on the line whose direction cosines are l, m, n. If we suppose the matter composing this shell to be an electrical distribution, then the potential at any outside point due to the outside field and to the supposed distribution is

$$Ax + By + Cz + l \frac{dU}{dx} + m \frac{dU}{dy} + n \frac{dU}{dz},$$

that is,

$$Ax + By + Cz + \tfrac{3}{2} M \left(l \frac{d\phi_\epsilon}{da^2} x + m \frac{d\phi_\epsilon}{db^2} y + n \frac{d\phi_\epsilon}{dc^2} z \right).$$

(See Thomson and Tait's *Natural Philosophy*, § 522.)

Inside the shell the potential will be zero at every point, provided the following relations hold good, viz.

$$A + \tfrac{3}{2} Ml \frac{d\phi}{da^2} = 0,$$

$$B + \tfrac{3}{2} Mm \frac{d\phi}{db^2} = 0,$$

$$C + \tfrac{3}{2} Mm \frac{d\phi}{dc^2} = 0,$$

where ϕ is the value of ϕ_ϵ when ϵ has the value zero, viz. at the surface of the ellipsoid. If then l, m, n, M are thus determined, the supposed distribution is in reality the distribution induced on the ellipsoid by the outside field.

The potential due to the induced electricity is therefore given, inside the conductor, by
$$V = -(Ax + By + Cz),$$
and, outside, by
$$V' = -\left(A\frac{\dfrac{d\phi_\epsilon}{da^2}}{\dfrac{d\phi}{da^2}}x + B\frac{\dfrac{d\phi_\epsilon}{db^2}}{\dfrac{d\phi}{db^2}}y + C\frac{\dfrac{d\phi_\epsilon}{dc^2}}{\dfrac{d\phi}{dc^2}}z\right).$$

To find the density we have
$$4\pi\rho = \frac{dV}{dn} - \frac{dV'}{dn}.$$

Now
$$p^2 = a^2\alpha^2 + b^2\beta^2 + c^2\gamma^2 + \epsilon,$$
therefore
$$2p\, dn = d\epsilon,$$
whence
$$\frac{dV'}{dn} = 2p\frac{dV'}{d\epsilon}.$$

In the expression for $4\pi\rho$ it is clear that $\dfrac{dV}{dn}$ will cancel those parts of $\dfrac{dV'}{dn}$ which depend on differentiating x, y, z, and therefore the only part which is left is that which depends on differentiating $\dfrac{d\phi_\epsilon}{da^2}$, &c., and then putting $\epsilon = 0$. We finally obtain the result
$$4\pi\rho = -\frac{p}{abc}\left(\frac{Ax}{a^2\dfrac{d\phi}{da^2}} + \frac{By}{b^2\dfrac{d\phi}{db^2}} + \frac{Cz}{c^2\dfrac{d\phi}{dc^2}}\right).$$

[By putting
$$\lambda = \frac{a^2\cos^2\theta - c^2}{\sin^2\theta}$$
and transforming the integral for ϕ, we have
$$\phi = \frac{2}{\sqrt{(a^2-c^2)}}\int_0^{\cos^{-1}\frac{c}{a}} \frac{d\theta}{\sqrt{(1-k^2\sin^2\theta)}}, \text{ where } k^2 = \frac{a^2-b^2}{a^2-c^2}$$
$$= \frac{2}{\sqrt{(a^2-c^2)}} F\left\{\cos^{-1}\frac{c}{a},\ \sqrt{\left(\frac{a^2-b^2}{a^2-c^2}\right)}\right\}.]$$

17. A copper wire in the form of a complete circle is suspended so that it can turn without friction about a diameter which is perpendicular to the direction of the earth's magnetic force; it is set in rotation and then left free, determine its subsequent motion, neglecting the self-induction of the wire.

The energy of the wire consists of two parts:

1. Its energy of motion $\frac{1}{2} M k^2 \dot{\theta}^2$, where $M k^2$ is the moment of inertia about the axis of rotation, and θ is the angle between the normal to the circle and the direction of the magnetic force.

2. The kinetic energy of the current $\frac{1}{2} \gamma \dot{\phi}^2$, where γ is a constant representing the self-induction of the wire, and which will be presently put equal to zero, and ϕ is the current at time t.

Let A be the area of the circle, R the resistance of the wire, and E the electromotive force round the wire at time t. Then

$$E = \frac{dA \cos \theta}{dt} = -A \sin \theta \cdot \dot{\theta} \, ;$$

also the heat generated in the circuit in time dt measured as equivalent work $= R\phi^2 dt$; this, added to the increment of energy of the wire, must be zero; viz.

$$R\phi^2 + Mk^2 \dot{\theta}\ddot{\theta} + \gamma \dot{\phi}\ddot{\phi} = 0.$$

We have also

$$\gamma \ddot{\phi} = E - R\phi = -A \sin \theta \cdot \dot{\theta} - R\phi.$$

Introducing now the assumption that the self-induction may be neglected, and eliminating ϕ, we have

$$\frac{A^2 \sin^2 \theta \cdot \dot{\theta}}{R} + Mk^2 \ddot{\theta} = 0,$$

$$\frac{A^2 (\theta - \frac{1}{2} \sin 2\theta)}{2R} + Mk^2 (\dot{\theta} - \omega) = 0,$$

ω being the angular velocity when $\theta = 0$;

whence

$$t = \int_0^\theta \frac{Mk^2 \, d\theta}{Mk^2 \omega - \frac{A^2}{2R} (\theta - \sin \theta \cos \theta)}.$$

TUESDAY, *January* 15, 1878. 1½ to 4.

Mr GREENHILL, Arabic numbers.
Mr FERRERS, Roman numbers.

1. FIND the equations of the tangent and normal at any point of a hyperbola.

Prove that the part of the tangent at any point intercepted between the point of contact and the transverse axis is a harmonic mean between the lengths of the perpendiculars drawn from the foci on the normal at the same point.

Let the tangent and normal at a point P of the hyperbola $\dfrac{x^2}{a^2} - \dfrac{y^2}{b^2} = 1$ (fig. 52) meet the transverse axis in T and G, and let SZ, $S'Z'$ be the perpendiculars from the foci on the normal at P.

If (xy) be the co-ordinates of P, then the equation of the tangent at P is $\dfrac{x'x}{a^2} - \dfrac{y'y}{b^2} = 1$, and therefore $OT = \dfrac{a^2}{x}$.

The equation of the normal at P is

$$a^2 \frac{x'}{x} + b^2 \frac{y'}{y} = a^2 + b^2,$$

and therefore $\qquad OG = \dfrac{a^2 + b^2}{a^2} x = e^2 x.$

Therefore $\qquad TG = e^2 x - \dfrac{a^2}{x} = \dfrac{e^2 x^2 - a^2}{x},$

$\qquad\qquad SG = e^2 x - ae,$

$\qquad\qquad S'G = e^2 x + ae;$

and therefore

$$\frac{1}{SG} + \frac{1}{S'G} = \frac{1}{e^2 x - ae} + \frac{1}{e^2 x + ae} = \frac{2x}{e^2 x^2 - a^2} = \frac{2}{TG}.$$

Or, immediately, since PT, PG are the internal and external bisectors of the angle SPS', therefore $GSTS''$ is a harmonic range.

Therefore, by similar triangles,

$$\frac{1}{ZG} + \frac{1}{Z'G} = \frac{2}{PG},$$

and therefore PG is a harmonic mean between ZG and $Z'G$.

ii. The three principal planes of the surface

$$(a, b, c, a', b', c' \mathbin{\rlap{)}\,(} x, y, z)^2 = 1$$

are represented by the equation

$$\begin{vmatrix} ax + c'y + b'z, & c'x + by + a'z, & b'x + a'y + cz \\ Ax + C'y + B'z, & C'x + By + A'z, & B'x + A'y + Cz \\ x, & y, & z \end{vmatrix} = 0,$$

where A, B, C, A', B', C' are the several minors of the determinant

$$\begin{vmatrix} a, & c', & b' \\ c', & b, & a' \\ b', & a', & c \end{vmatrix}.$$

114   SOLUTIONS OF SENATE-HOUSE   [TUESDAY,

Consider the surface $ax^2 + by^2 + cz^2 = 1$, its polar reciprocal $Ax^2 + By^2 + Cz^2 = 1$, and the sphere $x^2 + y^2 + z^2 = r^2$.

Take any point on one of the co-ordinate planes, which are the principal planes of the first two surfaces. Let its co-ordinates be $0, g, h$. Its polar planes with respect to the three surfaces are

$$bgy + chz = 1, \quad Bgy + Chz = 1, \quad gy + hz = r^2,$$

which are all parallel to the axis of x.

Hence, a principal plane of a given surface may be regarded as the locus of a point whose polar planes with respect to the given surface, to its polar reciprocal, and to a concentric sphere, are parallel to the same straight line.

Now, the reciprocal of the surface mentioned in the question is $(A, B, C, A', B', C' \mathbin{\rlap{\,)}} x, y, z)^2 = 1$. Hence the result follows.

iii. (α) Integrate

$$\frac{dx}{(5x^3 - 3x)^{\frac{2}{3}}(x^2 - 1)}.$$

(β) Prove that

$$\int_0^\pi (1 - \sin\alpha\cos\theta)^n \, d\theta = (\cos\alpha)^{2n+1} \int_0^\pi \frac{d\theta}{(1 - \sin\alpha\cos\theta)^{n+1}}.$$

(β) Let O (fig. 53) be the centre of a circle, Q any point within it, PQP' any chord through Q, $OP = a$, $OQ = b$, $QOP = \theta$, $QOP' = \theta'$.

Then $(a^2 + b^2 - 2ab\cos\theta)^{\frac{1}{2}} (a^2 + b^2 - 2ab\cos\theta')^{\frac{1}{2}} = (a^2 - b^2)^2$......(1).

Again, if the chord PQP' turn through a small angle, so that P comes to p, P' to p',

$$d\theta = \frac{Pp}{OP}, \quad d\theta' = -\frac{P'p'}{OP'},$$

and

$$\frac{Pp}{PQ} = \frac{P'p'}{P'Q},$$

therefore

$$\frac{d\theta}{(a^2 + b^2 - 2\cos b\cos\theta)^{\frac{1}{2}}} = -\frac{d\theta'}{(a^2 + b^2 - 2ab\cos\theta')^{\frac{1}{2}}}.$$

Hence

$$(a^2 + b^2 - 2ab\cos\theta)^n \, d\theta = -(a^2 + b^2 - 2ab\cos\theta)^n \left(\frac{a^2 + b^2 - 2ab\cos\theta}{a^2 + b^2 - 2ab\cos\theta'}\right)^{\frac{1}{2}} d\theta'$$

$$= -\frac{(a^2 - b^2)^{2n}}{(a^2 + b^2 - 2ab\cos\theta')^n} \frac{a^2 - b^2}{a^2 + b^2 - 2ab\cos\theta'} d\theta'$$

$$= -\frac{(a^2 - b^2)^{2n+1}}{(a^2 + b^2 - 2ab\cos\theta')^{n+1}} d\theta'.$$

Put $a = c \cos \tfrac{1}{2}a$, $b = c \sin \tfrac{1}{2}a$, and we get

$$(1 - \sin a \cos \theta)^n \, d\theta = - \frac{(\cos a)^{2n+1}}{(1 - \sin a \cos \theta')^{n+1}} \, d\theta'.$$

Integrate this between the limits 0 and π of θ, which respectively correspond to the limits π and 0 of θ', and we get (writing θ for θ')

$$\int_0^\pi (1 - \sin a \cos \theta)^n \, d\theta = (\cos a)^{2n+1} \int_0^\pi \frac{d\theta}{(1 - \sin a \cos \theta)^{n+1}}.$$

This result may also be obtained by considering $\sin a$ as the eccentricity of an ellipse, θ as the eccentric angle of any point, θ' as its vectorial angle, taking a focus as origin, and the positive direction of the prime radius passing through the further extremity of the axis major.

iv. Shew how to integrate a linear differential equation with constant coefficients.

Integrate the following differential equations:

(a) $\quad \dfrac{d^4y}{dx^4} + (m^2 + n^2)\dfrac{d^2y}{dx^2} + m^2n^2 y = \cos \tfrac{1}{2}(m+n)x \cos \tfrac{1}{2}(m-n)x$;

(β) $\quad \dfrac{dx}{dt} = ax + hy + c, \quad \dfrac{dy}{dt} = hx + by + e,$

and determine the arbitrary constants in the latter system, having given that when $t = 0$, $x = a$, $y = \beta$.

(a) The given equation may be written in the form

$$\frac{d^4y}{dx^4} + (m^2 + n^2)\frac{d^2y}{dx^2} + m^2n^2 y = \tfrac{1}{2}(\cos mx + \cos nx).$$

Consider the equation

$$\frac{d^4y}{dx^4} + (m^2 + n^2)\frac{d^2y}{dx^2} + m^2n^2 y = \tfrac{1}{2}(\cos \mu x + \cos \nu x).$$

Its integral is

$y = A \cos mx + B \sin mx + A' \cos nx + B' \sin nx$

$\qquad + \tfrac{1}{2} \dfrac{\cos \mu x}{(m^2 - \mu^2)(n^2 - \mu^2)} + \tfrac{1}{2} \dfrac{\cos \nu x}{(n^2 - \nu^2)(m^2 - \nu^2)}.$

But this assumes an indeterminate form (or rather the last two terms become infinite,) when $\mu = m$ and $\nu = n$.

The integral then assumes the form

$y = A \cos mx + B \sin mx + A' \cos nx + B' \sin nx$

$\qquad - \dfrac{x \sin mx}{4m} - \dfrac{x \sin nx}{4n}.$

The given equations may be written

$$\left(\frac{d}{dt} - a\right)x - by - c = 0,$$

$$-hx + \left(\frac{d}{dt} - b\right)y - e = 0,$$

whence, eliminating y, we get

$$\left\{\left(\frac{d}{dt} - a\right)\left(\frac{d}{dt} - b\right) - h^2\right\}x + bc - he = 0.$$

Hence, putting $a + b = \mu_1 + \mu_2$, $ab - h^2 = \mu_1\mu_2$,

$$x = P_1 \epsilon^{\mu_1 t} + P_2 \epsilon^{\mu_2 t} - \frac{bc - he}{\mu_1 \mu_2},$$

P_1, P_2 being arbitrary constants.

To determine them we have, when $t = 0$,

$$x = \alpha, \quad \frac{dx}{dt} = ax + by + c = a\alpha + h\beta + c,$$

therefore $\quad \alpha = P_1 + P_2 - \dfrac{bc - he}{\mu_1 \mu_2},$

$$a\alpha + b\beta + c = \mu_1 P_1 + \mu_2 P_2,$$

therefore $\quad P_1 = \dfrac{(a - \mu_2)\alpha + h\beta + c + \dfrac{bc - he}{\mu_1}}{\mu_1 - \mu_2}.$

Hence $\quad x = \dfrac{(a - \mu_2)\alpha + h\beta + c + \dfrac{bc - he}{\mu_1}}{\mu_1 - \mu_2} \epsilon^{\mu_1 t}$

$$+ \dfrac{(a - \mu_1)\alpha + h\beta + c + \dfrac{bc - he}{\mu_2}}{\mu_2 - \mu_1} \epsilon^{\mu_2 t} - \dfrac{bc - he}{\mu_1 \mu_2}.$$

Similarly $\quad y = \dfrac{(b - \mu_2)\beta + h\alpha + e + \dfrac{ae - hc}{\mu_1}}{\mu_1 - \mu_2} \epsilon^{\mu_1 t}$

$$+ \dfrac{(a - \mu_1)\beta + h\alpha + e + \dfrac{ae - hc}{\mu_2}}{\mu_2 - \mu_1} \epsilon^{\mu_2 t} - \dfrac{ae - hc}{\mu_1 \mu_2}.$$

5. Prove that, when a system is in equilibrium under gravity, the centre of gravity of the system is at a maximum depth in positions of stable equilibrium, and at a minimum depth in positions of unstable equilibrium.

A cylinder, the cross section of which is a spiral of Archimedes, is placed inside a fixed cylinder, of which the cross section is a parabola whose axis is horizontal, so that the pole of the spiral is in the axis of the parabola. Prove that, if no slipping takes place and the centre of gravity of the first cylinder is at the pole of the spiral, the cylinder will be in neutral equilibrium for finite displacements.

Let $r = a\theta$ be the equation of the spiral of Archimedes: then the polar subnormal (fig. 54) $SG = \dfrac{dr}{d\theta} = a$, and is therefore equal to the subnormal of the parabola AP of latus rectum $2a$.

Consequently the pole of the spiral, if properly placed, will describe the axis of the parabola, and therefore if the axis of the parabola be horizontal the equilibrium of the spiral will be neutral if the centre of gravity be at S, provided no slipping takes place.

6. State and prove the principle of conservation of energy in the case of a material system moving in two dimensions under gravity.

If l be the length of the simple equivalent circular pendulum of the motion of a wagon rolling under gravity inside a fixed horizontal circular cylinder of radius a, the radii of the wheels being c; and if l', l'' be the lengths of the equivalent pendulums when the body of the wagon is slung so as to move in the same way as in the cylinder (1) when the wheels are free to revolve, (2) when the wheels are fixed; find l, l', l'', and prove that

$$c^2 l + (a-c)^2 l' = c^2 l' + (a-c)^2 l''.$$

In the case of a conservative material system, moving under gravity, the increase or diminution of kinetic energy is equal to the weight of the system multiplied into the depth or height of the centre of gravity of the system below or above a certain plane.

Let M be the mass of the body of the wagon, m of the wheels, h the distance of the centre of gravity of the body of the wagon from the axis of the cylinder, k the radius of gyration of the body of the wagon about a parallel axis through its centre of gravity, κ the radius of gyration of the wheels about their axles.

Then, if θ denote the inclination to the vertical of the plane through the axis of the cylinder and the centre of gravity of the wagon, $\dot\theta$ being the angular velocity of the wagon,

(1) when the wagon rolls, $\dfrac{a-c}{c}\dot\theta$ will be the angular velocity of the wheels, and therefore the kinetic energy of the system

$$= \tfrac{1}{2} M(h^2 + k^2)\dot\theta^2 + \tfrac{1}{2} m(a-c)\dot\theta^2 + \tfrac{1}{2} m\left(\dfrac{a-c}{c}\right)^2 \kappa^2 \dot\theta^2,$$

$$= H + \{Mh + m(a-c)\} g \cos\theta,$$

by the principle of the conservation of energy; and therefore

$$l = \frac{M(h^2 + k^2) + m(a-c)^2\left(1 + \frac{\kappa^2}{c^2}\right)}{Mh + m(a-c)}.$$

(2) When the wagon is slung and the wheels are free, since the wheels do not revolve, the kinetic energy

$$= \tfrac{1}{2} M(h^2 + k^2)\dot\theta^2 + \tfrac{1}{2} m(a-c)^2 \dot\theta^2,$$
$$= H + \{Mh + m(a-c)\} g \cos\theta,$$

by the principle of the conservation of energy; and therefore

$$l' = \frac{M(h^2 + k^2) + m(a-c)^2}{Mh + m(a-c)}.$$

(3) When the wagon is slung and the wheels are fixed, then $\dot\theta$ is the angular velocity of the wheels, and therefore the kinetic energy

$$= \tfrac{1}{2} M(h^2 + k^2)\dot\theta^2 + \tfrac{1}{2} m(a-c)^2 \dot\theta^2 + \tfrac{1}{2} m\kappa^2 \dot\theta^2,$$
$$= H + \{Mh + m(a-c)\} g \cos\theta,$$

by the principle of the conservation of energy; and therefore

$$l'' = \frac{M(h^2 + k^2) + m(a-c)^2 + m\kappa^2}{Mh + m(a-c)}.$$

Therefore

$$l - l' = \frac{m(a-c)^2 \frac{\kappa^2}{c^2}}{Mh + m(a-c)}.$$

$$l'' - l' = \frac{m\kappa^2}{Mh + m(a-c)},$$

and therefore

$$c^2(l - l') = (a-c)^2 (l'' - l'),$$

or, $\quad c^2 l + (a-c)^2 l' = c^2 l' + (a-c)^2 l''.$

7. Prove that, if $\theta_1, \theta_2, \theta_3$ be the component angular velocities of a system of rectangular axes Ox, Oy, Oz considered as a rigid system moving about the origin O, and h_1, h_2, h_3 be the component angular momenta of any material system about the axes Ox, Oy, Oz, then

$$\frac{dh_1}{dt} - h_2 \theta_3 + h_3 \theta_2$$

with two similar expressions are the rates of change of h_1, h_2, h_3 about axes fixed in space, with which Ox, Oy, Oz are coincident at the instant considered.

Deduce the equations of motion of a rigid body moving about a fixed point referred to three rectangular axes fixed in the body.

Prove that, if Watt's governor be constrained to revolve round a vertical axis with constant angular velocity, and if the inclination θ of the arms be included between α and β, then $\left(\dfrac{d\theta}{dt}\right)^2$ varies as $(\cos\alpha - \cos\theta)(\cos\theta - \cos\beta)$, and that, if $\theta = \gamma$ in the position of relative equilibrium, $\cos\alpha + \cos\beta = 2\cos\gamma$.

Verify that, at any time t, $\tan\tfrac{1}{2}\theta = \tan\tfrac{1}{2}\beta\,\mathrm{dn}\left(K\dfrac{t}{T},\,k\right)$, where
$$k' = \tan\tfrac{1}{2}\alpha\cot\tfrac{1}{2}\beta.$$

Considering the motion of either ball, and denoting by A, C, the moments of inertia about the axes OA, OC (fig. 55), then $-A\omega\sin\theta$, $C\omega\cos\theta$ are the components of angular momentum of the system about the principal axes OA, OC; and therefore

$$h_1 = -A\dot\theta, \quad h_2 = (C-A)\,\omega\sin\theta\cos\theta, \quad h_3 = (C\cos^2\theta + A\sin^2\theta)\,\omega\,;$$

also $\qquad\qquad \theta_1 = 0, \quad \theta_2 = 0, \quad \theta_3 = \omega\,;$

and $\qquad\qquad \dfrac{dh_1}{dt} - h_2\theta_3 + h_3\theta_2 = Mgh\sin\theta,$

therefore $\qquad -A\ddot\theta + (A-C)\,\omega^2\sin\theta\cos\theta = Mgh\sin\theta\,;$

and integrating,
$$\tfrac{1}{2}A\dot\theta^2 = H + Mgh\cos\theta - \tfrac{1}{2}(A-C)\,\omega^2\cos^2\theta,$$

or $\qquad\qquad \dot\theta^2 = \dfrac{A-C}{A}\,\omega^2(\cos\alpha - \cos\theta)(\cos\theta - \cos\beta),$

if $\dot\theta = 0$ when $\theta = \alpha$ and $\theta = \beta$.

In the position of equilibrium, $\ddot\theta = 0$; and therefore γ is given by
$$\cos\gamma = \dfrac{Mgh}{(A-C)\,\omega^2} = \tfrac{1}{2}(\cos\alpha + \cos\beta).$$

Again, since
$$\dot\theta^2 = \dfrac{A-C}{A}\,\omega^2(\cos\alpha - \cos\theta)(\cos\theta - \cos\beta)$$
$$= \dfrac{A-C}{A}\,\omega^2\,\dfrac{(\tan^2\tfrac{1}{2}\theta - \tan^2\tfrac{1}{2}\alpha)(\tan^2\tfrac{1}{2}\beta - \tan^2\tfrac{1}{2}\theta)}{(1+\tan^2\tfrac{1}{2}\theta)^2(1+\tan^2\tfrac{1}{2}\alpha)(1+\tan^2\tfrac{1}{2}\beta)},$$

therefore
$$\sec^4\tfrac{1}{2}\theta\,\dot\theta^2 = \dfrac{A-C}{A}\,\omega^2\cos^2\tfrac{1}{2}\alpha\cos^2\tfrac{1}{2}\beta\,(\tan^2\tfrac{1}{2}\theta - \tan^2\tfrac{1}{2}\alpha)(\tan^2\tfrac{1}{2}\beta - \tan^2\tfrac{1}{2}\theta),$$

or
$$\left(\dfrac{d\tan\tfrac{1}{2}\theta}{dt}\right)^2 = 4\,\dfrac{A-C}{A}\,\omega^2\cos^2\tfrac{1}{2}\alpha\cos^2\tfrac{1}{2}\beta\,(\tan^2\tfrac{1}{2}\theta - \tan^2\tfrac{1}{2}\alpha)(\tan^2\tfrac{1}{2}\beta - \tan^2\tfrac{1}{2}\theta).$$

Now from the definition
$$\operatorname{dn}^2 x = 1 - k^2 \operatorname{sn}^2 x,$$
and therefore
$$k^2 \operatorname{sn}^2 x = 1 - \operatorname{dn}^2 x, \quad k^2 \operatorname{cn}^2 x = \operatorname{dn}^2 x - k'^2;$$
also
$$\frac{d}{dx} \operatorname{sn} x = \operatorname{cn} x \operatorname{dn} x,$$
$$\frac{d}{dx} \operatorname{dn} x = - k^2 \operatorname{sn} x \operatorname{cn} x,$$
$$= - \sqrt{(1 - \operatorname{dn}^2 x)} \sqrt{(\operatorname{dn}^2 x - k'^2)}.$$

Therefore, if $\tan \tfrac{1}{2}\theta = \tan \tfrac{1}{2}\beta \operatorname{dn} K \tfrac{t}{T}$, $k' = \tan \tfrac{1}{2}a \tan \tfrac{1}{2}\beta$
$$\left(\frac{d \tan \tfrac{1}{2}\theta}{dt} \right)^2 = \frac{K^2}{T^2} \tan^2 \tfrac{1}{2}\beta \left(1 - \operatorname{dn}^2 K \tfrac{t}{T} \right) \left(\operatorname{dn}^2 K \tfrac{t}{T} - k'^2 \right)$$
$$= \frac{K^2}{T^2} \cot^2 \tfrac{1}{2}\beta (\tan^2 \tfrac{1}{2}\beta - \tan^2 \tfrac{1}{2}\theta)(\tan^2 \tfrac{1}{2}\theta - \tan^2 \tfrac{1}{2}a),$$
and therefore
$$\frac{K^2}{T^2} = 4 \frac{A - C}{A} \omega^2 \cos^2 \tfrac{1}{2}a \sin^2 \tfrac{1}{2}\beta.$$

viii. An infinite mass of homogeneous gravitating liquid rotates with constant angular velocity ω about the axis of z. Prove that a possible form of the free surface for relative equilibrium is the elliptic cylinder
$$\frac{x^2}{a^2} + \frac{y^2}{b^2} = 1, \text{ where } \omega^2 = 4\pi\rho \frac{ab}{(a+b)^2}.$$
ρ being the density of the liquid.

If V be the potential of the infinite homogeneous elliptic cylinder $\frac{x^2}{a^2} + \frac{y^2}{b^2} = 1$, at any point of its mass, we have
$$V = 2\pi\rho ab \int_0^\infty \left(1 - \frac{x^2}{a^2 + \psi} - \frac{y^2}{b^2 + \psi} \right) \frac{d\psi}{\sqrt{a^2 + \psi} \cdot \overline{b^2 + \psi}}.$$

The evaluation of this definite integral would introduce an infinite constant. But we get rid of this by observing that
$$\frac{dV}{dx} = - 4\pi\rho ab \int_0^\infty \frac{x \, d\psi}{\sqrt{(a^2 + \psi)^3 (b^2 + \psi)}}$$
$$= - \frac{4\pi\rho b x}{a + b},$$
$$\frac{dV}{dy} = - \frac{4\pi\rho a y}{a + b}.$$

And, if p be the pressure at any point, we have
$$dp = \left(\frac{dV}{dx} + \omega^2 x\right) dx + \left(\frac{dV}{dy} + \omega^2 y\right) dy.$$
Hence, the form of the free surface is given by the equation
$$\left(\frac{\omega^2}{2} - \frac{2\pi\rho b}{a+b}\right) x^2 + \left(\frac{\omega^2}{2} - \frac{2\pi\rho a}{a+b}\right) y^2 = \text{const.}$$
If this coincide with the surface of the cylinder $\frac{x^2}{a^2} + \frac{y^2}{b^2} = 1$, we have
$$a^2 \left(\frac{\omega^2}{2} - \frac{2\pi\rho b}{a+b}\right) = b^2 \left(\frac{\omega^2}{2} - \frac{2\pi\rho a}{a+b}\right),$$
therefore
$$\frac{a^2 - b^2}{2} \omega^2 = 2\pi\rho \frac{ab(a-b)}{a+b},$$
therefore
$$\omega^2 = 4\pi\rho \frac{ab}{(a+b)^2}.$$

ix. Find the precession of a given star in right ascension and declination.

Prove that all stars, whose precession in right ascension is equal to a given quantity, lie on the surface of a cone of the second degree, one of whose axes is the line of equinoxes.

Let P (fig. 56) be the pole of the equator, Π of the ecliptic, S the star, S' the position to which, in a given time, it is displaced relatively to P, in consequence of precession. Then $S\Pi S' = \delta l$, which is the same for all stars, and $SPS' = \delta a$. Hence
$$\delta a = \frac{\delta l}{\sin S\Pi} \sin SP \cos \Pi SP.$$
And if ω be the obliquity of the ecliptic,
$$\cos \Pi SP = \frac{\cos \omega - \cos SP \cos S\Pi}{\sin SP . \sin S\Pi};$$
therefore
$$\delta a = \delta l \frac{\cos \omega - \cos SP \cos S\Pi}{\sin^2 S\Pi}.$$

Now, taking the line of the equinoxes as the axis of y, and the earth's axis as the axis of z, and r as the radius of the celestial sphere,
$$\cos SP = \frac{z}{r}, \quad \cos S\Pi = \frac{z \cos \omega + x \sin \omega}{r}, \quad \sin SP = \frac{x^2 + y^2}{r^2},$$
therefore
$$\delta a = \delta l \frac{\cos \omega (x^2 + y^2 + z^2) - z(z \cos \omega + x \sin \omega)}{x^2 + y^2},$$
or
$$(\delta l \cos \omega - \delta a)(x^2 + y^2) - \delta l \sin \omega \, zx = 0,$$
shewing that all stars, for which δa is equal to a given quantity, lie in a cone of the second degree, one of whose axes is the axis of y, i.e. the line of equinoxes.

WEDNESDAY, *January* 16, 1878. 9 to 12.

Mr Prior.

1. THE locus of the foci of rectangular hyperbolas which have a given diameter is a lemniscate.

Let QCP (fig. 57) be the given diameter; S, H the foci of any one of the hyperbolas.

Then, since $CP = CQ$, $CS = CH$, and $\angle PCS = \angle QCH$, therefore
$$SP = HQ.$$

But rect. $SQ \cdot QH =$ sq. on semi-diameter conjugate to $CQ = CQ^2$, therefore
$$PS \cdot QS = CQ^2 = CP^2;$$
therefore the locus of S is a lemniscate with foci P, Q.

Or thus: let
$$CP = CQ = a, \quad CS = r, \quad \angle SCP = \theta.$$
Then, since P lies on a rectangular hyperbola of which S is a focus and C the centre, $a^2 \cos 2\theta = r^2$, for this is the polar equation of that hyperbola, a, θ being the polar co-ordinates; therefore $r^2 = a^2 \cos 2\theta$ is the polar equation of the locus of S, r, θ being its polar co-ordinates: and this is the polar equation of a lemniscate.

2. If the sides of a triangle ABC meet two given straight lines in a_1, a_2; b_1, b_2; c_1, c_2 respectively; and if round the quadrilaterals $b_1b_2c_1c_2$, $c_1c_2a_1a_2$, $a_1a_2b_1b_2$ conics be described; the three other common chords of these conics will each pass through an angular point of ABC, and will all meet in one point.

Let $x = 0$, $y = 0$, $z = 0$ be the equations of the sides BC, CA, AB of the triangle; and let $u \equiv lx + my + nz = 0$, $u' \equiv l'x + m'y + n'z = 0$ be the equations of the two given lines.

Then the equations of the three conics are
$$uu' + k_1 yz = 0 \quad \ldots\ldots\ldots\ldots\ldots\ldots\ldots (1),$$
$$uu' + k_2 zx = 0 \quad \ldots\ldots\ldots\ldots\ldots\ldots\ldots (2),$$
$$uu' + k_3 xy = 0 \quad \ldots\ldots\ldots\ldots\ldots\ldots\ldots (3).$$

Of these (2) and (3) have common chords whose equation is
$$k_2 zx - k_3 xy = 0;$$
i.e. $x = 0$ and $k_2 z - k_3 y = 0$ are the equations of their common chords.

Thus $k_2 z - k_3 y = 0$, $k_3 x - k_1 z = 0$, $k_1 y - k_2 x = 0$ are the equations of the common chords of the problem, and each of these clearly passes through an angular point of ABC, while they all meet in the point whose co-ordinates are given by
$$\frac{x}{k_1} = \frac{y}{k_2} = \frac{z}{k_3}.$$

3. If a chord of an ellipse be drawn to cut the evolute of the ellipse at right angles, three times the difference between its segments intercepted between the evolute and the ellipse is equal to the diameter of curvature of the evolute at the point of intersection.

Let O (fig. 58) be any point of the evolute, P the corresponding point of the ellipse, centre C. Q_1OQ_2 the chord through O, perpendicular to OP which is a tangent to the evolute.

Since OP is the normal at P, Q_1Q_2 is parallel to the tangent at P; therefore PC produced bisects Q_1Q_2, say in V:

therefore $\qquad OQ_1 - OQ_2 = 2OV = 2OP \tan VPO$.

Let ρ be the radius of curvature of the evolute at O, σ the distance of O from a cusp measured along the evolute, ψ the angle between PO and the major axis of the ellipse; and let $PO = r$. Then $\sigma = r$, and $\rho = \dfrac{d\sigma}{d\psi} = \dfrac{dr}{d\psi}$.

Now let CA be the semi-major axis of the ellipse, and let the semi-axes be a, b; let $\angle PCA = \theta$, and let p be the perpendicular from C on the tangent at P.

Then
$$\tan VPO = \tan(\psi - \theta) = \frac{\tan\psi - \tan\theta}{1 + \tan\psi\tan\theta} = \frac{\tan\psi - \dfrac{b^2}{a^2}\tan\psi}{1 + \dfrac{b^2}{a^2}\tan^2\psi}$$

$$= \frac{(a^2 - b^2)\sin\psi\cos\psi}{a^2\cos^2\psi + b^2\sin^2\psi}.$$

Again $\qquad r = \dfrac{a^2b^2}{p^3} = \dfrac{a^2b^2}{(a^2\cos^2\psi + b^2\sin^2\psi)^{\frac{3}{2}}}$,

therefore
$$\frac{dr}{d\psi} = \frac{3a^2b^2(a^2-b^2)\sin\psi\cos\psi}{(a^2\cos^2\psi + b^2\sin^2\psi)^{\frac{5}{2}}} = 3r\frac{(a^2-b^2)\sin\psi\cos\psi}{a^2\cos^2\psi + b^2\sin^2\psi} = 3r\tan VPO;$$

therefore $\qquad 3(OQ_1 - OQ_2) = 6r\tan VPO = 2\rho$.

4. If ABC be a triangle circumscribing a parabola whose focus is S, and if SA, SB, SC meet BC, CA, AB in A', B', C' respectively, shew that the lines drawn through A, B, C perpendicular respectively to the other tangents through A', B', C' meet in a point.

This may be deduced from the reciprocal of the following:

If abc (fig. 59) be a triangle, and al, bm, cn its perpendiculars meet the circumscribing circle in a', b', c'; and if s be any point on the circle: then sa', sb', sc' meet bc, ca, ab in points on a straight line which passes through o the orthocentre of abc.

For, let sa', sb', sc' meet bc, ca, ab in f, g, h; and join fo, go, ca', cb'.

Then $\angle foc = \angle fa'c$ for the triangles foc, $fa'c$ are similar.

Similarly, $\angle goc = \angle gb'c$.

Therefore $\angle foc + \angle goc = \angle fa'c + \angle gb'c = 2$ right angles;

therefore fog is a straight line, and similarly h lies upon it.

Now, if we reciprocate with respect to a circle round S as centre, the circle and inscribed triangle become a parabola (fig. 60) and circumscribed triangle ABC. The focus is at S, the point s becoming the line at infinity. The line al becomes a point on BC which with A subtends a right angle at S, i.e. A''. Then the point a' becomes the second tangent $A''P$ through A''; sa' becomes a point at infinity on this tangent; and f a line drawn through A parallel to $A''P$. Hence the reciprocal theorem is, that this line and those drawn like it through B and C meet in a point.

Now, let SA meet BC in A' and let $A'P$ the other tangent from A' meet $A''P$ in P. Then the circle through $A'A''S$ passes through P; and $A'SA''$ being a right angle, so is $A'PA''$. Therefore the line through A parallel to $A''P$ is perpendicular to $A'P$, and it has been shewn that this line and those drawn like it through B and C meet in a point.

5. $ABPCDQ$ is a twisted polygon all whose angles are right angles; AB, CD lying on fixed straight lines.

Shew (1) that if A, B, C, D be any points on their respective lines the locus of P or Q is an hyperboloid of one sheet; and (2) that if A, B, C, D be so taken that P, Q are equidistant from the greater real and imaginary axes of the hyperboloid, and if the sides of the polygon represent forces, these forces have no moment about the lesser real axis of the hyperboloid.

Let FG, of length $2c$, be the shortest distance between AB and CD, F lying on AB. Take the origin at its middle point, and let OF be the axis of z. If $2a$ be the angle between AB and CD, their equations may be written

$$\left. \begin{array}{l} y = x \tan a \\ z = c \end{array} \right\} \text{ for } AB, \qquad \left. \begin{array}{l} y = -x \tan a \\ z = -c \end{array} \right\} \text{ for } CD.$$

Let x, y, z be the co-ordinates of P, and let $FB = h$, $GC = k$.

Then the co-ordinates of B are $h \cos a$, $h \sin a$, c; and those of C are $k \cos a$, $-k \sin a$, $-c$.

Then because the angles FBP, GCP, BPC are right angles, we have

$(x - h \cos a) \cos a + (y - h \sin a) \sin a = 0$,

$(x - k \cos a) \cos a - (y + k \sin a) \sin a = 0$,

$(x - h \cos a)(x - k \cos a) + (y - h \sin a)(y + k \sin a) + (z - c)(z + c) = 0$.

The two former equations give
$$h = x \cos a + y \sin a,$$
$$k = x \cos a - y \sin a,$$
as is evident also by projection.

Substituting these values in the third equation, we obtain
$$(x \sin^2 a - y \sin a \cos a)(x \sin^2 a + y \sin a \cos a)$$
$$+ (y \cos^2 a - x \sin a \cos a)(y \cos^2 a + x \sin a \cos a) + z^2 - c^2 = 0,$$
or
$$(\sin^2 a - \cos^2 a)(x^2 \sin^2 a - y^2 \cos^2 a) + z^2 - c^2 = 0,$$
or
$$-\cos 2a \sin^2 a \cdot \frac{x^2}{c^2} + \cos 2a \cos^2 a \cdot \frac{y^2}{c^2} + \frac{z^2}{c^2} = 1,$$
which shews that P and therefore Q lie on an hyperboloid of one sheet, of which FG is the lesser real axis, the other real axis lying in Ox or Oy according as $2a >$ or $< \pi$.

Let x_1, y_1, z_1 be the co-ordinates of P, x_2, y_2, z_2 those of Q. Then the components along the axes of the forces passing through P are
$$x_1 - (x_1 \cos a + y_1 \sin a) \cos a, \quad y_1 - (x_1 \cos a + y_1 \sin a) \sin a, \quad z_1 - c;$$
and
$$(x_1 \cos a - y_1 \sin a) \cos a - x_1, \quad -(x_1 \cos a - y_1 \sin a) \sin a - y_1, \quad -c - z_1 :$$
the sum of which may be written
$$-2y_1 \sin a \cos a, \quad -2x_1 \sin a \cos a, \quad -2c.$$

Similarly the sum of the components of the forces passing through Q is
$$2y_2 \sin a \cos a, \quad 2x_2 \sin a \cos a, \quad 2c.$$

Hence the moment of the forces round FG is
$$x_1(-2x_1 \sin a \cos a) - y_1(-2y_1 \sin a \cos a)$$
$$+ x_2(2x_2 \sin a \cos a) - y_2(2y_2 \sin a \cos a)$$
$$= 2 \sin a \cos a (-x_1^2 + y_1^2 + x_2^2 - y_2^2)$$
$$= 2 \sin a \cos a \{(y_1^2 + z_1^2) - (y_2^2 + z_2^2) - (z_1^2 + x_1^2) + (z_2^2 + x_2^2)\},$$
and therefore vanishes if
$$y_1^2 + z_1^2 = y_2^2 + z_2^2,$$
$$z_1^2 + x_1^2 = z_2^2 + x_2^2,$$
i.e. if P, Q are equidistant from the greater real and imaginary axes of the hyperboloid.

6. A rough rod AB, of length $2b$, whose centre of gravity is at its middle point C, rests upon the ends of a diameter LM of a fixed horizontal circular hoop of radius a, C lying between M and O the centre of the hoop. The rod is pulled by a horizontal force at B perpendicular to it, which is gradually increased till the rod begins to move. If k be the radius of gyration of the rod about C, and

$OC = c$; then if $a^2 - c^2 < bc$, the rod will turn about M; and if $a^2 - c^2 = bc$, the rod will turn about a point P between L and C, where $PC = \dfrac{k^2}{b}$.

If $a^2 - c^2 > bc$, what will be the initial motion of the rod?

Let W be the weight of the rod. Then the pressures at L, M are $\dfrac{a-c}{2a} W$ and $\dfrac{a+c}{2a} W$. Let F be the horizontal force at B, and G and H the consequent horizontal forces at L and M. Let μ be the coefficient of friction between the rod and hoop. If then $G < \dfrac{a-c}{2a} \mu W$, the rod will not move at L; and if $H < \dfrac{a+c}{2a} \mu W$, the rod will not move at M. If then the rod be about to move, one at least of these inequalities must be on the point of becoming an equality.

So long as the rod is at rest, G and H are found by taking moments about M and L respectively. Thus

$$G = \dfrac{b+c-a}{2a} F, \quad H = \dfrac{b+c+a}{2a} F.$$

(1) Let $a^2 - c^2 < bc$. Now the rod must be on the point of motion at L, as soon as

$$\dfrac{b+c-a}{2a} F = \dfrac{a-c}{2a} \cdot \mu W, \text{ or } F = \dfrac{a-c}{b+c-a} \cdot \mu W;$$

and, when F has this value, then

$$H = \dfrac{b+c+a}{b+c-a} \cdot \dfrac{a-c}{2a} \cdot \mu W;$$

and this is $< \dfrac{a+c}{2a} \cdot \mu W$, if

$$(b+c+a)(a-c) < (b+c-a)(a+c),$$
or $\qquad\qquad a^2 < (b+c)c,$
or $\qquad\qquad a^2 - c^2 < bc,$ which is the case.

In this case, then, the rod will not move nor be on the point of motion at M; but is on the point of motion at L. Hence we infer that, in this case, if F be just $> \dfrac{a-c}{b+c-a} \cdot \mu W$, the rod will turn about M.

(2) If $a^2 - c^2 = bc$, the values of G and H in terms of F become

$$G = \dfrac{a-c}{2c} F, \quad H = \dfrac{a+c}{2c} F.$$

Hence if $F = \dfrac{c}{a} \cdot \mu W$, the rod is on the point of moving both at L and at M. The actual motion must therefore be investigated in this case, as a kinetic question, and we shall find about what point the rod will begin to turn.

Let u' be the initial acceleration of C, ω' the initial angular acceleration of the rod about C; and let m be the mass of the rod.

Since the rod will move at L and M, if $F > \dfrac{c}{a} \cdot \mu W$, then

$$G = \frac{a-c}{2a} \cdot \mu W, \quad H = \frac{a+c}{2a} \cdot \mu W,$$

and the equations of motion will be

$$mu' = F + G - H = F - \frac{c}{a} \cdot \mu W,$$

$$mk^2 \omega' = Fb - G(a+c) - H(a-c)$$

$$= Fb - \frac{a^2 - c^2}{a} \cdot \mu W$$

$$= b \left\{ F - \frac{c}{a} \cdot \mu W \right\}, \text{ for } a^2 - c^2 = bc;$$

therefore $\qquad u' - \dfrac{k^2}{b} \omega' = 0,$

therefore the point P in LC, such that $CP = \dfrac{k^2}{b}$, will be initially at rest; i.e. the rod will begin to turn about P.

(3) If $a^2 - c^2 > bc$, a similar argument to that in (1) would shew that the rod will begin to turn about L.

(4) In (1) the assumption is made that as soon as $G = \dfrac{a-c}{2a} \mu W$ the rod will begin to move at L: this assumption would be correct were the portion of the rod at L to be an independent particle. As, however, this portion is part of a rigid rod, the objection might be raised that it is not necessary for it to move as soon as G becomes $= \dfrac{a-c}{2a} \mu W$. A similar remark will apply to the argument spoken of in (3). In each of these cases, therefore, the result may not be correct; for each case, being a case of motion, is a kinetic question; we shall however find, on investigating them kinetically, that these results are correct.

In both cases, if the rod initially turn about a point Q in LM, we have the same equations as in (2):

$$mu' = F - \frac{c}{a} \mu W,$$

$$mk^2 \omega' = Fb - \frac{a^2 - c^2}{a} \mu W,$$

and the cases to be considered are those in which $F < =$ or $> \dfrac{c}{a} \mu W$.

(α) If $F < \dfrac{c}{a}\mu W$, u' is negative, i.e. Q lies in CM. If $CQ = y$, $u' + y\omega' = 0$; hence

$$k^2\left\{F - \frac{c}{a}\mu W\right\} + y\left\{Fb - \frac{a^2 - c^2}{a}\mu W\right\} = 0,$$

or
$$F = \frac{c}{a}\mu W \frac{k^2 + \dfrac{a^2 - c^2}{c}y}{k^2 + by}.$$

Since F is always $< \dfrac{c}{a}\mu W$, and $k^2 + by$ is positive, we must have $a^2 - c^2 < bc$, which shews that we are now considering case (1).

Now the position of Q is given by that value of y which makes F a mimimum.

Putting F in the form $\dfrac{c}{a}\mu W\left\{\dfrac{a^2 - c^2}{bc} + \dfrac{k^2}{bc}\dfrac{bc - a^2 + c^2}{k^2 + by}\right\}$, we see that F diminishes as y increases; i.e. F is a minimum when $y = a - c$ its greatest possible value: i.e. Q is at M; the same result as in (1).

(β) If $F = \dfrac{c}{a}\mu W$, $u' = 0$, i.e. C is at rest: the rod will then turn about C if ω' be positive, i.e. if $Fb > \dfrac{a^2 - c^2}{a}\mu W$, or $\dfrac{bc}{a}\mu W > \dfrac{a^2 - c^2}{a}\mu W$, or $bc > a^2 - c^2$. But if this be the case, the rod will already have turned about M, as has been proved in (α).

(γ) If $F > \dfrac{c}{a}\mu W$, u' is positive, i.e. Q lies in LC. If $CQ = y$, $u' - y\omega' = 0$; hence

$$k^2\left\{F - \frac{c}{a}\mu W\right\} - y\left\{Fb - \frac{a^2 - c^2}{a}\mu W\right\} = 0,$$

or
$$F = \frac{c}{a}\mu W \frac{k^2 - \dfrac{a^2 - c^2}{c}y}{k^2 - by}.$$

Since F is always $> \dfrac{c}{a}\mu W$, $\dfrac{k^2 - \dfrac{a^2 - c^2}{c}y}{k^2 - by} > 1$; and we have again to distinguish between three cases:

(i) $k^2 - by > 0$; then $k^2 - \dfrac{a^2 - c^2}{c}y > k^2 - by$, or $a^2 - c^2 < bc$, and the rod, as proved in (α), will already have turned about M.

(ii) $k^2 - by = 0$, in which case the value found just above for F is inapplicable, and we must return to the preceding equation, from which we learn that $a^2 - c^2 = bc$; i.e. we are now considering case (2), the result of which is thus confirmed.

(iii) $k^2 - by < 0$; then $\dfrac{a^2 - c^2}{c} y - k^2 > by - k^2$, or $a^2 - c^2 > bc$: i.e. we are now considering case (3).

The position of Q is given by that value of y which makes F a minimum. Putting F in the form

$$\frac{c}{a} \mu W \left\{ \frac{a^2 - c^2}{bc} + \frac{k^2}{bc} \frac{a^2 - c^2 - bc}{by - k^2} \right\},$$

we see that F diminishes as y increases: i.e. F is a minimum when $y = a + c$, its greatest possible value: i.e. Q is at L; the same result as in (3).

[The results of (ii) and (iii) have been obtained on the hypothesis that $b(a + c) > k^2$. This, though presupposed in the question, is not necessarily the case. If $b(a + c) = k^2$, there need be no change in the results. If $b(a + c) < k^2$, we must take into account the portion of the rod outside the hoop beyond L, as Q, the point round which the rod will turn, might be in that portion. If so, the equations of motion become

$$mu' = F - G - H = F - \mu W,$$
$$mk^2 \omega' = Fb + G(a + c) - H(a - c) = Fb.$$

Now $u' - y\omega' = 0$, therefore

$$k^2 (F - \mu W) - Fby = 0,$$

or
$$F = \frac{k^2 \mu W}{k^2 - by};$$

which shows that y must be $< \dfrac{k^2}{b}$, and F is a minimum when y is least, i.e. when $y = a + c$; which confirms the result of (iii), but shows that the result of (ii) or of (2) is only true when $b(a + c) > k^2$. Accordingly if $b(a + c) < k^2$, and if also $a^2 - c^2 = bc$, the rod will turn about L and not about P; or, in other words, the rod will not turn about P unless P be a point in LC.]

7. Water is revolving with angular velocity ω in a smooth fine circular tube of radius a which it completely fills, and which rests on a horizontal plane. If the tube be made to revolve with uniform angular velocity ω' about a pivot O in its plane, shew that the absolute angular velocity of the water round the centre C of the tube is not altered. Also if ϖ be the average pressure of the water throughout the tube, shew that the mean pressure in the water for a section through any point P of the tube is

$$\varpi + \mu a c \omega'^2 \cos \theta,$$

and that the resultant pressure on the tube at P per unit length is $\dfrac{m\varpi}{\mu a} + ma\omega^2 + 2mc\omega'^2 \cos \theta$, where θ is the angle between CP and OC produced, $c = OC$, m is the mass of water which would fill an unit length of the tube, and μ that of an unit volume of water.

At any time t the velocity of every element of the water relatively to the tube is the same; i.e. the ring of water is moving as a rigid ring.

Now all the pressures of the tube upon this ring are normal, and therefore pass through its centre C. Hence there is no force to change the absolute angular velocity of the ring round C, which therefore remains unaltered.

The accelerations of the element at P are compounded of those of C and those of P relatively to C.

The acceleration of C is $c\omega'^2$ along CO; that of P relatively to C is $a\omega^2$ along PC.

Let p be the pressure of the water at P, R that on the tube there.

Resolving along the tangent to the tube at P we obtain

$$A\mu a c\omega'^2 \sin\theta = -A\frac{dp}{d\theta},$$

A being the area of a cross-section of the tube;

therefore $\qquad p = C + \mu a c\omega'^2 \cos\theta,$

C being a constant.

But the average value of $\cos\theta$ throughout the tube is zero, therefore $C = \varpi$, therefore $p = \varpi + \mu a c\omega'^2 \cos\theta$.

Resolving along the normal to the tube at P, we obtain

$$m(a\omega^2 + c\omega'^2 \cos\theta) = R - \frac{Ap}{a}$$

$$= R - \frac{m}{\mu a}(\varpi + \mu a c\omega'^2 \cos\theta),$$

for $\qquad m = \mu A;$

therefore $\qquad R = \frac{m\varpi}{\mu a} + ma\omega^2 + 2mc\omega'^2 \cos\theta.$

8. A cylinder of small radius a, which will submit to flexure but not to torsion, has one end fixed in a horizontal plane, so that that end of its axis is vertical. The axis is now slightly bent and made to describe a surface of revolution, so that the cross section through any point P on the cylinder always makes a small angle α with the horizon. If Q be the point at which this cross section meets the bent axis, shew that the path of P relatively to Q is given by the equations

$$\left. \begin{array}{l} (x + a\cos^2 \tfrac{1}{2}\alpha)^2 + y^2 = a^2 \sin^4 \tfrac{1}{2}\alpha \\ z^2 = 2a\cos^2 \tfrac{1}{2}\alpha (x + a) \end{array} \right\},$$

x, y, z being the co-ordinates of P referred to axes fixed in direction.

Hence shew that, if the motion of the axis be so slow as to be imperceptible to the eye, the cylinder will present the appearance of rotation.

Let the axes of x, y be horizontal, that of z vertical; and in any position of the axis, let θ be the angle between the plane xz and that through the axis and the vertical. When $\theta = 0$, let P be in the plane xz, its co-ordinates relative to Q being then $-a\cos a$, 0, and $a\sin a$.

In the position $\theta = \theta$, the projections of QP on the line in the vertical plane through the axis which makes an angle $\dfrac{\pi}{2} - a$ with QZ and on a perpendicular to this line in the cross section, which latter line is the intersection of the cross section and the horizontal plane through Q, are $a\cos\theta$ and $a\sin\theta$. This is seen most easily by supposing the axis first straightened from the position $\theta = 0$ and then bent into the position $\theta = \theta$.

Hence the new co-ordinates of P are
$$x = -a\cos\theta\cos a\cos\theta - a\sin\theta\sin\theta, \quad y = -a\cos\theta\cos a\sin\theta + a\sin\theta\cos\theta,$$
$$z = a\cos\theta\sin a.$$

Therefore
$$x = -a\cos a\cos^2\theta - a\sin^2\theta = -\tfrac{1}{2}a\cos a(1+\cos 2\theta) - \tfrac{1}{2}a(1-\cos 2\theta)$$
$$= -\tfrac{1}{2}a(1+\cos a) + \tfrac{1}{2}a(1-\cos a)\cos 2\theta$$
$$= -a\cos^2\tfrac{1}{2}a + a\sin^2\tfrac{1}{2}a\cos 2\theta,$$
$$y = a(1-\cos a)\sin\theta\cos\theta = a\sin^2\tfrac{1}{2}a\sin 2\theta,$$
$$z = a\sin a\cos\theta;$$

therefore
$$(x + a\cos^2\tfrac{1}{2}a)^2 + y^2 = a^2\sin^4\tfrac{1}{2}a\cos^2 2\theta + a^2\sin^4\tfrac{1}{2}a\sin^2 2\theta = a^2\sin^4\tfrac{1}{2}a,$$

and $\quad z^2 = a^2\sin^2 a\cos^2\theta = a^2\sin^2 a\,\dfrac{x+a}{a(1-\cos a)} = 2a\cos^2\tfrac{1}{2}a\cdot(x+a).$

If the motion of the axis be very slow, the eye will follow the lines in which a vertical plane through the axis cuts the cylinder and will suppose any point on either of these lines to be a fixed point on the cylinder. As these lines revolve, the point will seem to travel round the axis and the cylinder will seem to be twisting.

9. A roll of cloth of the small thickness ϵ, lying at rest upon a perfectly rough horizontal table, is propelled with initial angular velocity Ω so that the cloth unrolls. Apply the principle of Energy to shew that the radius of the roll will diminish from a to r (so long as r is not small in comparison with a) in the time
$$\frac{2\pi}{\epsilon}\sqrt{\frac{1}{3g}}\{(c^3 - r^3)^{\frac{1}{2}} - (c^3 - a^3)^{\frac{1}{2}}\},$$

where $\quad 4(c^3 - a^3)g = 3\Omega^2 a^4.$

Is the application of the principle of Energy to this problem correct?

At the time t let the length of cloth unrolled be x, and let its radius be r, and its angular velocity ω. Then

$$\epsilon \delta x = \pi \{r^2 - (r + \delta r)^2\}$$
$$= -2\pi r \delta r\,;$$

therefore $\dfrac{dx}{dt} = -\dfrac{2\pi}{\epsilon} r \dfrac{dr}{dt}$; and it also $= r\omega$.

The equation of Energy gives

$$\tfrac{1}{2} \pi r^2 \left\{\left(\dfrac{dx}{dt}\right)^2 + \dfrac{r^2}{2}\omega^2\right\} = \tfrac{1}{2}\pi a^2 \left\{a^2 \Omega^2 + \dfrac{a^2}{2}\cdot \Omega^2\right\} + \pi g a^2 \cdot a - \pi g r^2 \cdot r.$$

Therefore $\quad r^2 \dfrac{4\pi^2}{\epsilon^2} \cdot \tfrac{3}{2} r^2 \left(\dfrac{dr}{dt}\right)^2 = \tfrac{3}{2} a^4 \Omega^2 + 2g(a^3 - r^3),$

or $\quad\dfrac{4\pi^2}{\epsilon^2}\left(3 r^4 \dfrac{dr}{dt}\right)^2 = 9a^4 \Omega^2 + 12g(a^3 - r^3)$

$$= 12g(c^3 - r^3),$$

or $\quad \dfrac{\pi}{\epsilon}\cdot\dfrac{d}{dt}(r^3) = -\sqrt{3g(c^3 - r^3)}.$

Hence $\quad \dfrac{2\pi}{\epsilon}\left[\sqrt{c^3 - r^3}\right]_a^r = \sqrt{3g}\cdot t,$

or $\quad t = \dfrac{2\pi}{\epsilon}\sqrt{\dfrac{1}{3g}}\left\{(c^3 - r^3)^{\frac{1}{2}} - (c^3 - a^3)^{\frac{1}{2}}\right\}.$

If the cloth be the ideal mathematical cloth, all the forces except that of gravity pass through the instantaneous axis, and, since the motion is one of rolling, no work is done by or against them; hence the principle of Energy is applicable. If, however, the cloth be supposed cohesive, so that each fold coheres to the rest; or again, if the cloth be not perfectly flexible and elastic forces are called into play; the principle is not applicable.

10. The umbilical geodesics at the extremities of the mean axes of a system of confocal ellipsoids all touch one or other of two planes.

In the ellipsoid $\dfrac{x^2}{a^2} + \dfrac{y^2}{b^2} + \dfrac{z^2}{c^2} = 1$, we know that along any geodesic $pd = $ const.

But at an umbilicus $pb^2 = abc$, therefore $p = \dfrac{ac}{b}$, and $d = b$; therefore, for umbilical geodesics, $pd = ac$. Hence d at the extremity of the mean axis for an umbilical geodesic is given by $bd = ac$; therefore $d = \dfrac{ac}{b}.$

If then θ be the angle between this geodesic at the extremity of the mean axis and the plane through the two greater axes, we have

$$\frac{b^2}{a^2 c^2} = \frac{\cos^2\theta}{a^2} + \frac{\sin^2\theta}{c^2},$$

or
$$b^2 = c^2 \cos^2\theta + a^2 \sin^2\theta;$$

whence
$$\tan^2\theta = \frac{b^2 - c^2}{a^2 - b^2},$$

in which equation the right-hand side remains the same for all confocals to the above ellipsoid.

Therefore the planes which pass through the mean axis and are inclined at an angle θ to the plane through the two greater axes are touched by the umbilical geodesics at the extremities of the mean axes of all the confocals.

11. The polar equation of a nearly spherical surface is $r = a + bP_n$, where P_n is a zonal harmonic of the nth degree, and b is a small quantity whose powers above the second may be neglected. Shew that the area of the surface exceeds the area of a sphere of radius a by $2\pi b^2 \dfrac{n^2 + n + 2}{2n + 1}$.

The area of an elementary annulus of the surface enclosed between two conical surfaces, whose common axis is the axis of the system of harmonics, and whose semi-vertical angles are θ and $\theta + \delta\theta$, is

$$2\pi r \sin\theta \cdot \left\{\left(\frac{dr}{d\theta}\right)^2 + r^2\right\}^{\frac{1}{2}} \delta\theta$$

$$= -2\pi(a + bP_n)\left\{a^2 + 2abP_n + b^2\left(P_n^2 + (1-\mu^2)\left(\frac{dP_n}{d\mu}\right)^2\right)\right\}^{\frac{1}{2}} \delta\mu$$

$(\mu = \cos\theta)$

$$= -2\pi a^2 \left\{1 + \frac{b}{a}P_n\right\}\left\{1 + \frac{b}{a}P_n + \tfrac{1}{2}\frac{b^2}{a^2}(1-\mu^2)\left(\frac{dP_n}{d\mu}\right)^2\right\} \delta\mu$$

(neglecting powers of b above b^2)

$$= -2\pi a^2\left\{1 + 2\frac{b}{a}P_n + \frac{b^2}{a^2}P_n^2 + \tfrac{1}{2}\frac{b^2}{a^2}(1-\mu^2)\left(\frac{dP_n}{d\mu}\right)^2\right\} \delta\mu.$$

Now the integration is to extend all over the sphere, i.e. from $\theta = 0$ to $\theta = \pi$, i.e. from $\mu = 1$ to $\mu = -1$.

Also we have

$$\int_{-1}^{+1} P_n\, d\mu = 0; \quad \int_{-1}^{+1} P_n^2\, d\mu = \frac{2}{2n+1};$$

$$\int_{-1}^{+1}(1-\mu^2)\left(\frac{dP_n}{d\mu}\right)^2 d\mu = \int_{-1}^{+1}(1-\mu^2)\frac{dP_n}{d\mu}\, dP_n$$

$$= \left[(1-\mu^2)\frac{dP_n}{d\mu}\right]_{-1}^{+1} - \int_{-1}^{+1} P_n \frac{d}{d\mu}\left\{(1-\mu^2)\frac{dP_n}{d\mu}\right\} d\mu$$

$$= n(n+1) \int_{-1}^{+1} P_n^2 \, d\mu, \text{ for } \frac{d}{d\mu}\left\{(1-\mu^2)\frac{dP_n}{d\mu}\right\} + n(n+1) P_n = 0$$

$$= \frac{2n(n+1)}{2n+1}.$$

Therefore the area of the given surface

$$= 4\pi a^2 + 2\pi b^2 \left\{\frac{2}{2n+1} + \frac{n(n+1)}{2n+1}\right\}$$

$$= \text{area of a sphere of radius } a + 2\pi b^2 \frac{n^2+n+2}{2n+1}.$$

12. A uniform circular tube containing masses m_1, m_2 of two gases, which are separated by two adiathermanous pistons, is placed in a hot fluid. Assuming the flow of heat across the substance of the tube into the gases to be, at each instant, the same for every point, find the temperatures of the gases when they fill given portions of the tube.

Prove that the absolute temperatures t_1, t_2 of the two gases are constantly connected by the relation

$$\left(\frac{t_1}{T_1}\right)^{k_1(k_2-c_2)} = \left(\frac{t_2}{T_2}\right)^{k_2(k_1-c_1)},$$

where T_1, T_2 are their initial temperatures, k_1, c_1 and k_2, c_2 their specific heats under constant pressure and volume.

Let θ_1, θ_2 be the angles subtended at the centre of the tube by the gases when at temperatures t_1, t_2; and let $2\pi A$ be the volume of the tube. Also let $2\pi \delta q$ be the mechanical equivalent of the amount of heat that flows into the tube in any unit of time, and let p be the pressure of the gases at that time, being the same for each. Then, since the flow of heat across the substance of the tube is assumed to be at each instant the same for every point, we have by Carnot's Theorem or by Joule's result that in a gas no internal work is done except in raising its temperature,

$$\theta_1 \delta q = m_1 c_1 \delta t_1 + Ap \delta \theta_1,$$

$$\theta_2 \delta q = m_2 c_2 \delta t_2 + Ap \delta \theta_2.$$

Dividing these equations by θ_1, θ_2 and subtracting one from the other, we obtain

$$0 = \frac{m_1 c_1 \delta t_1}{\theta_1} - \frac{m_2 c_2 \delta t_2}{\theta_2} + Ap\left(\frac{\delta \theta_1}{\theta_1} - \frac{\delta \theta_2}{\theta_2}\right).$$

But by Gay Lussac's law, combined with Clausius' and Rankine's Theorem,

$$p\theta_1 = \frac{m_1}{A}(k_1 - c_1) t_1, \quad p\theta_2 = \frac{m_2}{A}(k_2 - c_2) t_2.$$

Substituting these values for θ_1, θ_2, we have

$$0 = \frac{c_1}{k_1 - c_1} \cdot \frac{\delta t_1}{t_1} - \frac{c_2}{k_2 - c_2} \frac{\delta t_2}{t_2} + \frac{\delta \theta_1}{\theta_1} - \frac{\delta \theta_2}{\theta_2}.$$

Also, by taking the logarithmic differentials of Gay Lussac's equations and subtracting one from the other, we obtain

$$0 = \frac{\delta t_1}{t_1} - \frac{\delta t_2}{t_2} - \frac{\delta \theta_1}{\theta_1} + \frac{\delta \theta_2}{\theta_2};$$

and, multiplying this equation by $\dfrac{c_2}{k_2 - c_2}$ and subtracting it from the last, we have

$$0 = \left(\frac{c_1}{k_1 - c_1} - \frac{c_2}{k_2 - c_2}\right) \frac{\delta t_1}{t_1} + \frac{k_2}{k_2 - c_2}\left(\frac{\delta \theta_1}{\theta_1} - \frac{\delta \theta_2}{\theta_2}\right);$$

and, since $\theta_1 + \theta_2 = 2\pi$, and consequently $\delta\theta_1 + \delta\theta_2 = 0$, this reduces to

$$0 = \left(\frac{c_1}{k_1 - c_1} - \frac{c_2}{k_2 - c_2}\right) \frac{\delta t_1}{t_1} + \frac{k_2}{k_2 - c_2} \cdot \frac{2\pi \delta\theta_1}{\theta_1 (2\pi - \theta_1)}.$$

Hence, integrating and writing a_1, a_2 for the initial values of θ_1, θ_2, we have

$$0 = \left(\frac{c_1}{k_1 - c_1} - \frac{c_2}{k_2 - c_2}\right) \log\left(\frac{t_1}{T_1}\right) + \frac{k_2}{k_2 - c_2} \log\left(\frac{\theta_1}{a_1} \cdot \frac{2\pi - a_1}{2\pi - \theta_1}\right);$$

whence

$$\frac{t_1}{T_1} = \left\{\frac{a_1 \theta_2}{a_2 \theta_1}\right\}^{\frac{k_2}{k_2 - c_2} \Big/ \frac{c_1}{k_1 - c_1} - \frac{c_2}{k_2 - c_2}}.$$

Similarly

$$\frac{t_2}{T_2} = \left\{\frac{a_2 \theta_1}{a_1 \theta_2}\right\}^{\frac{k_1}{k_1 - c_1} \Big/ \frac{c_2}{k_2 - c_2} - \frac{c_1}{k_1 - c_1}}.$$

These equations give the temperatures of the gases when they fill given portions of the tube. They also prove that

$$\left(\frac{t_1}{T_1}\right)^{k_1(k_2 - c_2)} = \left(\frac{t_2}{T_2}\right)^{k_2(k_1 - c_1)}.$$

13. In the case of steady rolling motion of two perfectly rough spheres of which one of radius a and mass A moves on a perfectly rough horizontal plane and supports the other of radius b and mass B, so that the line joining their centres makes an angle α with the vertical; shew that the radius of the circle described by the centre of the lower sphere will be

$$\frac{5B \sin\alpha \{c(1 + \cos\alpha)\lambda^2 + g\}}{\{7A + 5B(1 + \cos\alpha)\}\lambda^2},$$

where $c = a + b$, and λ is the angular velocity in this circle, being given by the equation

$$\lambda^2 c \cos a \{49A + 10B(1+\cos a)^2\}$$
$$- 2\lambda (\nu b + na \cos a)\{\ 7A + \ 5B(1+\cos a)\}$$
$$+ 5g\{\ 7A + \ \ B(5+2\cos^2 a)\} = 0,$$

n, ν being the angular velocities of the lower and upper spheres about a vertical and the line joining their centres respectively.

Let O be the centre of the circle described by the centre of the lower sphere, and let r be its radius. Let OZ be the vertical through O. Let P, Q be the centres of the lower and upper spheres at any time. Since the motion is steady, Q also describes a circle round OZ, and the vertical plane through P and Q makes a constant angle with the plane POZ. Let this angle be γ. Now let the axes at any time be OP, a line through O parallel to the direction of motion of P at the time, and OZ. Then the angular velocities of these axes about each other are $0, 0, \lambda$. Also let the forces exerted on this sphere by the plane at the point of contact be X, Y, Z in the direction of these axes.

Let R be the point of contact of the two spheres, and let the forces exerted on the upper sphere by the lower be F, G, H in the direction of the axes.

The co-ordinates of P at any time are r, 0, 0; therefore its velocities are 0, $r\lambda$, 0; and its accelerations $-r\lambda^2$, 0, 0.

Similarly the co-ordinates of Q are

$$r - c \sin a \cos \gamma, \quad c \sin a \sin \gamma, \quad c \cos a;$$

therefore its velocities are

$$-c \sin a \sin \gamma . \lambda, \quad (r - c \sin a \cos \gamma)\lambda, \quad 0;$$

and its accelerations

$$-(r - c \sin a \cos \gamma)\lambda^2, \quad -c \sin a \sin \gamma . \lambda^2, \quad 0.$$

Then for the motion of P and Q we have, omitting unnecessary equations,

$$A(-r\lambda^2) = X - F, \quad B\{-(r - c \sin a \cos \gamma)\lambda^2\} = F,$$
$$0 = Y - G, \qquad\qquad\qquad 0 = G,$$

and
$$0 = H - Bg;$$

which give

$$X = -\lambda^2 \{Ar + B(r - c \sin a \cos \gamma)\}, \quad Y = 0;$$
$$F = -\lambda^2 . B(r - c \sin a \cos \gamma), \quad G = 0, \quad H = Bg.$$

Now, let a_1, a_2, a_3 be the angular velocities of the lower sphere; β_1, β_2, β_3 those of the upper sphere about axes parallel to Ox, Oy, Oz through P and Q respectively. Then, since the point of contact between the plane and the lower sphere is momentarily at rest, and its co-ordinates referred to the axes of this sphere are 0, 0, $-a$, we have

$$-aa_2 = 0, \quad r\lambda + aa_1 = 0; \text{ while } a_3 = n.$$

Also, since the motion of the two points of contact on the lower and upper spheres is momentarily the same, and its co-ordinates referred to the axes of the lower sphere are $-a\sin a \cos\gamma$, $a\sin a \sin\gamma$, $a\cos a$; and referred to the axes of the upper sphere are $b\sin a\cos\gamma$, $-b\sin a\sin\gamma$, $-b\cos a$, we have

$$-a\sin a \sin\gamma . a_3 + a\cos a . a_2 = -c\sin a \sin\gamma . \lambda + b\sin a \sin\gamma . \beta_3 \\ -b\cos a . \beta_2,$$

$$r\lambda - a\cos a . a_1 - a\sin a \cos\gamma . a_3 = (r - c\sin a \cos\gamma)\lambda + b\cos a . \beta_1 \\ + b\sin a \cos\gamma . \beta_3,$$

$$a\sin a \cos\gamma . a_2 + a\sin a \sin\gamma . a_1 = -b\sin a \cos\gamma . \beta_2 - b\sin a \sin\gamma . \beta_1;$$

also $\qquad -\sin a \cos\gamma . \beta_1 + \sin a \sin\gamma . \beta_2 + \cos a . \beta_3 = \nu.$

If we write in these $aa_1 = -r\lambda$, $a_2 = 0$, $a_3 = n$, the three first equations transposed become

$$b\sin a \sin\gamma . \beta_3 - b\cos a . \beta_2 = c\sin a \sin\gamma . \lambda - a\sin a \sin\gamma . n,$$
$$b\cos a . \beta_1 + b\sin a \cos\gamma . \beta_3 = (r\cos a + c\sin a \cos\gamma)\lambda - a\sin a \cos\gamma . n,$$
$$b\sin a \cos\gamma . \beta_2 + b\sin a \sin\gamma . \beta_1 = r\sin a \sin\gamma . \lambda\,;$$

the fourth equation remaining unchanged.

We might solve these equations for β_1, β_2, β_3 in terms of ν; but the work will be simplified if we first take into account the dynamical equations of angular momentum.

Accordingly, taking moments about the axes through P, we have firstly, since the motion is steady,

$$\tfrac{2}{5} A a^2 \{-a_2\lambda\} = aY - a\sin a \sin\gamma H + a\cos a\, G\,;$$

which, combined with previous results, shew that $\sin\gamma = 0$; i.e. $\gamma = 0$, for if $\gamma = \pi$ the upper sphere would fall off the lower.

Secondly, using this result, we have

$$\tfrac{2}{5} A a^2 \{a_1\lambda\} = -aX - a\cos a\, F - a\sin aH,$$

which, combined with previous results, becomes

$$-\tfrac{2}{5} A ar\lambda^2 = a\lambda^2\{Ar + B(r - c\sin a)\} + a\cos a . \lambda^2 B(r - c\sin a) \\ - a\sin a\, By\,;$$

hence $\qquad r\{\tfrac{7}{5}A + B(1+\cos a)\}\lambda^2 = Bc\sin a\,(1+\cos a)\lambda^2 + Bg\sin a,$

or $\qquad r = \dfrac{5B\sin a\{c(1+\cos a)\lambda^2 + g\}}{\{7A + 5B(1+\cos a)\}\lambda^2};$

the first result given.

The third equation for the lower sphere is not needed, but if formed will be found to be consistent with previous results.

Again, taking moments about the axes through Q, and using previous results, we have firstly

$$\tfrac{2}{5} B b^2 \{-\beta_2\lambda\} = b\cos aG = 0\,; \text{ hence } \beta_2 = 0.$$

Secondly, we have

$$\tfrac{2}{b}Bb^2\{\beta_1\lambda\} = -b\cos a\, F - b\sin a\, H = b\cos a \,.\, \lambda^2 B\,(r - c\sin a) - b\sin a Bg\,;$$

hence $\qquad 2b\beta_1\lambda = 5\lambda^2 \cos a\,(r - c\sin a) - 5g\sin a.$

We must now substitute these values in the geometrical equations already found for $\beta_1, \beta_2, \beta_3$. Since $\beta_2 = 0$, the first and third equations give no result, because $\gamma = 0$. The second and fourth become

$$\cos a\,\{5\lambda^2 \cos a\,(r - c\sin a) - 5g\sin a\} + 2\sin a\,.\,b\beta_3\lambda$$
$$= 2\,(r\cos a + c\sin a)\,\lambda^2 - 2\sin a\,.\,an\lambda,$$

and $\quad -\sin a\,\{5\lambda^2 \cos a\,(r - c\sin a) - 5g\sin a\} + 2\cos a\,.\,b\beta_3\lambda = 2bv\lambda.$

Multiplying the first of these by $\cos a$ and the second by $\sin a$ and subtracting, we obtain

$$5\lambda^2 \cos a\,(r - c\sin a) - 5g\sin a = 2\lambda^2 \cos a\,(r\cos a + c\sin a)$$
$$- 2\lambda \sin a\,(vb + na\cos a)\,;$$

hence $\qquad r = \dfrac{\{7\lambda^2 c\cos a - 2\lambda\,(vb + na\cos a) + 5g\}\sin a}{\lambda^2 \cos a\,(5 - 2\cos a)}.$

Now equating this value of r to that already obtained, we have

$$\dfrac{5B\{\lambda^2 c\,(1 + \cos a) + g\}}{7A + 5B\,(1 + \cos a)} = \dfrac{7\lambda^2 c\cos a - 2\lambda\,(vb + na\cos a) + 5g}{\cos a\,(5 - 2\cos a)}\,;$$

therefore

$$\lambda^2 c\cos a\,\{49A + 5B\,(1 + \cos a)\,(7 - 5 + 2\cos a)\}$$
$$- 2\lambda\,(vb + na\cos a)\,\{7A + 5B\,(1 + \cos a)\}$$
$$+ 5g\,\{7A + 5B\,(1 + \cos a) - B\cos a\,(5 - 2\cos a)\} = 0,$$

or

$$\lambda^2 c\cos a\,\{49A + 10B\,(1 + \cos a)^2\} - 2\lambda\,(vb + na\cos a)\,\{7A + 5B\,(1 + \cos a)\}$$
$$+ 5g\,\{7A + B\,(5 + 2\cos^2 a)\} = 0\,;$$

the second result given.

14. A string of natural length $2l$, and of equal elasticity for compression and extension, hanging in equilibrium under gravity over a small smooth pulley, is cut through at a point whose unstretched distance from the nearer end is $\tfrac{1}{2}l$. Shew that during the time $\dfrac{l}{a}$ (where a is the wave-velocity) the velocity of separation of the two *new* ends thus severed is $\dfrac{gl}{a}$, and at the end of that time suddenly doubles. Shew also that the pressure on the pulley during the second half of this time is half its initial value.

(1) Let us first consider the portion of string that falls freely. Let its higher end be A and its lower end B. '

Take the origin at the equilibrium position of A, and the axis of x vertically downwards. Let P be any cross section of the string, whose unstretched distance from A is x, and let ξ be its abscissa at time t.

Then the equation of motion for the element of string at P is

$$\frac{d^2\xi}{dt^2} = a^2 \frac{d^2\xi}{dx^2} + g;$$

and its solution may be written

$$\xi = \tfrac{1}{2} g t^2 + f(x - at) + F(x + at).$$

Hence the velocity of the element at P is

$$v = \frac{d\xi}{dt} = gt + a\left[-f'(x-at) + F'(x+at)\right] \ldots\ldots\ldots(1),$$

and the stress at P is

$$X = E\left(\frac{d\xi}{dx} - 1\right) = E\left[f'(x-at) + F'(x+at) - 1\right]\ldots\ldots(2),$$

where E is the coefficient of Elasticity or Restitution.

The terminal conditions are: when $x = 0$ and when $x = \tfrac{1}{2}l$, $X = 0$ always: therefore

$$f'(-at) + F'(at) = 1 \ldots\ldots\ldots\ldots\ldots\ldots(3),$$

$$f'(\tfrac{1}{2}l - at) + F'(\tfrac{1}{2}l + at) = 1 \ldots\ldots\ldots\ldots(4).$$

The initial conditions are:

(1) when $t = 0$, $v = 0$ for all values of x from 0 to $\tfrac{1}{2}l$; therefore

$$-f'(x) + F'(x) = 0, \quad x = 0 \text{ to } \tfrac{1}{2}l \ldots\ldots\ldots\ldots(5);$$

(2) when $t = 0$, $X = mg(\tfrac{1}{2}l - x)$ for all values of x from 0 to $\tfrac{1}{2}l$, where $E = ma^2$; therefore

$$f'(x) + F'(x) - 1 = \frac{g}{a^2}(\tfrac{1}{2}l - x), \quad x = 0 \text{ to } \tfrac{1}{2}l \ldots\ldots\ldots(6).$$

These equations and conditions enable us to find the values of $f(z)$ and $F(z)$ for all values of z, a typical variable.

Thus, from $z = 0$ to $\tfrac{1}{2}l$, we learn from (5) and (6) that

$$f'(z) = F'(z) = \tfrac{1}{2}\left\{1 + \frac{g}{a^2}(\tfrac{1}{2}l - z)\right\}.$$

Then (3) shews that, from $z = 0$ to $-\tfrac{1}{2}l$,

$$f'(z) = 1 - \tfrac{1}{2}\left\{1 + \frac{g}{a^2}(\tfrac{1}{2}l + z)\right\} = \tfrac{1}{2}\left\{1 - \frac{g}{a^2}(\tfrac{1}{2}l + z)\right\};$$

and then (4) shews that, from $z = \tfrac{1}{2}l$ to l,

$$F'(z) = 1 - \tfrac{1}{2}\left\{1 + \frac{g}{a^2}(\tfrac{1}{2}l - l + z)\right\} = \tfrac{1}{2}\left\{1 + \frac{g}{a^2}(\tfrac{1}{2}l - z)\right\};$$

and, from $z = l$ to $\tfrac{3}{2}l$,

$$F'(z) = 1 - \tfrac{1}{2}\left\{1 - \tfrac{g}{a^2}(\tfrac{1}{2}l + l - z)\right\} = \tfrac{1}{2}\left\{1 + \tfrac{g}{a^2}(\tfrac{3}{2}l - z)\right\}.$$

Then (3), used once more with these two last results, shews that, from $z = -\tfrac{1}{2}l$ to $-l$,

$$f'(z) = 1 - \tfrac{1}{2}\left\{1 + \tfrac{g}{a^2}(\tfrac{1}{2}l + z)\right\} = \tfrac{1}{2}\left\{1 - \tfrac{g}{a^2}(\tfrac{1}{2}l + z)\right\};$$

and, from $z = -l$ to $-\tfrac{3}{2}l$,

$$f'(z) = 1 - \tfrac{1}{2}\left\{1 + \tfrac{g}{a^2}(\tfrac{3}{2}l + z)\right\} = \tfrac{1}{2}\left\{1 - \tfrac{g}{a^2}(\tfrac{3}{2}l + z)\right\}.$$

These results suffice to give the motion of A from $t = 0$ to $\dfrac{3l}{2a}$.

Thus, from $t = 0$ to $\dfrac{l}{a}$,

$$v_A = gt + a\left[-\tfrac{1}{2}\left\{1 - \tfrac{g}{a^2}(\tfrac{1}{2}l - at)\right\} + \tfrac{1}{2}\left\{1 + \tfrac{g}{a^2}(\tfrac{1}{2}l - at)\right\}\right] = \dfrac{gl}{2a};$$

and, from $t = \dfrac{l}{a}$ to $\dfrac{3l}{2a}$,

$$v_A = gt + a\left[-\tfrac{1}{2}\left\{1 - \tfrac{g}{a^2}(\tfrac{3}{2}l - at)\right\} + \tfrac{1}{2}\left\{1 + \tfrac{g}{a^2}(\tfrac{3}{2}l - at)\right\}\right] = \dfrac{3gl}{2a},$$

i.e. at the end of the time $\dfrac{l}{a}$ the velocity of A is suddenly trebled.

(2) Let us next consider the portion of string that passes over the pulley. Let its end that was attached to A be C and its other end D, and let the cross-section that is passing over the pulley at time t be denoted by E.

Take the equilibrium position of C as origin, and the axis of x along the string CE, and suppose ED to be a continuation of CE so far as measuring distances from C is concerned. Let the unstretched length of CE be y. Then the equations similar to (1) and (2) are in this case as follows, unaccented letters referring to CE and accented letters to ED.

For values of x between 0 and y, we have at time t

$$v = -gt + a\left[-\phi'(x - at) + \Phi'(x + at)\right],$$
$$X = E\left[\phi'(x - at) + \Phi'(x + at) - 1\right],$$

and for values of x' between y and $\tfrac{3}{2}l$, we have at time t

$$v' = gt + a\left[-\psi'(x' - at) + \Psi'(x' + at)\right],$$
$$X' = E\left[\psi'(x' - at) + \Psi'(x' + at) - 1\right].$$

The terminal condition at C is that when $x = 0$, $X = 0$ always; therefore

$$\phi'(-at) + \Phi'(at) = 1 \dots\dots\dots\dots\dots\dots\dots(7).$$

That at E is, that when $x = y$, $x' = y$, $v = v'$, $X = X'$ always; therefore
$$-gt + a\left[-\phi'(y-at) + \Phi'(y+at)\right] = gt + a\left[-\psi'(y-at) + \Psi'(y+at)\right],$$
$$\phi'(y-at) + \Phi'(y+at) = \psi'(y-at) + \Psi'(y+at);$$
from which we obtain
$$\Phi'(y+at) = \Psi'(y+at) + \frac{gt}{a} \quad\quad\quad\quad\quad\quad (8),$$
$$\phi'(y-at) = \psi'(y-at) - \frac{gt}{a} \quad\quad\quad\quad\quad\quad (9).$$

The terminal condition at D need not be introduced, as it would be found not to interfere with the motion during the limited time in question.

The initial conditions are:

(1) When $t=0$, $v=0$ for all values of x from 0 to $\frac{1}{2}l$, therefore
$$-\phi'(x) + \Phi'(x) = 0, \quad x = 0 \text{ to } \tfrac{1}{2}l \quad\quad\quad (10);$$

(2) When $t=0$, $v'=0$ for all values of x' from $\frac{1}{2}l$ to $\frac{3}{2}l$, therefore
$$-\psi'(x') + \Psi'(x') = 0, \quad x' = \tfrac{1}{2}l \text{ to } \tfrac{3}{2}l \quad\quad (11);$$

(3) When $t=0$, $X = mg(\frac{1}{2}l + x)$ for all values of x from 0 to $\frac{1}{2}l$, therefore
$$\phi'(x) + \Phi'(x) - 1 = \frac{g}{a^2}(\tfrac{1}{2}l + x), \quad x = 0 \text{ to } \tfrac{1}{2}l \quad\quad (12);$$

(4) When $t=0$, $X' = mg(\frac{3}{2}l - x')$ for all values of x' from $\frac{1}{2}l$ to $\frac{3}{2}l$, therefore
$$\psi'(x') + \Psi'(x') - 1 = \frac{g}{a^2}(\tfrac{3}{2}l - x'), \quad x' = \tfrac{1}{2}l \text{ to } \tfrac{3}{2}l \quad\quad (13).$$

From (10) and (12) we learn that, from $z = 0$ to $\frac{1}{2}l$,
$$\phi'(z) = \Phi'(z) = \tfrac{1}{2}\left\{1 + \frac{g}{a^2}(\tfrac{1}{2}l + z)\right\} \quad\quad\quad (14),$$
and from (11) and (13) we learn that, from $z = \frac{1}{2}l$ to $\frac{3}{2}l$,
$$\psi'(z) = \Psi'(z) = \tfrac{1}{2}\left\{1 + \frac{g}{a^2}(\tfrac{3}{2}l - z)\right\} \quad\quad\quad (15).$$

Then (7) shews that, from $z = 0$ to $-\frac{1}{2}l$,
$$\phi'(z) = 1 - \tfrac{1}{2}\left\{1 + \frac{g}{a^2}(\tfrac{1}{2}l - z)\right\} = \tfrac{1}{2}\left\{1 - \frac{g}{a^2}(\tfrac{1}{2}l - z)\right\} \quad\quad (16).$$

Equations (14) and (16) suffice to give the motion of C from $t = 0$ to $\dfrac{l}{2a}$; for during this time
$$v_c = -gt + a\left[-\tfrac{1}{2}\left\{1 - \frac{g}{a^2}(\tfrac{1}{2}l + at)\right\} + \tfrac{1}{2}\left\{1 + \frac{g}{a^2}(\tfrac{1}{2}l + at)\right\}\right] = \frac{gl}{2a};$$

therefore during this time the velocity of separation of the two *new* ends A and $C = v_A + v_C = \dfrac{gl}{a}$.

Now, initially $y = \tfrac{1}{2} l$, and, by the principle of unique solution, $\dot{y}$ will continue to be $\tfrac{1}{2} l$, so long as this value will make the equation

$$v = 0 = -gt + a\left[-\phi'\left(\tfrac{1}{2} l - at\right) + \Phi'\left(\tfrac{1}{2} l + at\right)\right]$$

consistent with (8), (14) and (15).

Equations (8) and (15) give, till $t = \dfrac{l}{a}$,

$$\Phi'\left(\tfrac{1}{2} l + at\right) = \tfrac{1}{2}\left\{1 + \frac{g}{a^2}\left(\tfrac{3}{2} l - \tfrac{1}{2} l - at\right)\right\} + \frac{gt}{a}$$

$$= \tfrac{1}{2}\left\{1 + \frac{g}{a^2}(l + at)\right\} \dotfill (17);$$

and (14) gives, till $t = \dfrac{l}{2a}$,

$$-\phi'\left(\tfrac{1}{2} l - at\right) = -\tfrac{1}{2}\left\{1 + \frac{g}{a^2}\left(\tfrac{1}{2} l + \tfrac{1}{2} l - at\right)\right\} = -\tfrac{1}{2}\left\{1 + \frac{g}{a^2}(l - at)\right\};$$

therefore $\quad -\phi'\left(\tfrac{1}{2} l - at\right) + \Phi'\left(\tfrac{1}{2} l + at\right) = \dfrac{gt}{a}$,

which is consistent with the above, making $v_E = 0$ till $t = \dfrac{l}{2a}$.

Now equations (7) and (17) will give the motion of C from $t = \dfrac{l}{2a}$ to $\dfrac{3l}{2a}$; for we have

$$v_C = -gt + a\left[-\phi'(at) + \Phi'(at)\right]$$

$$= -gt + a\left[-1 + 2\Phi'(at)\right] \text{ from } (7)$$

$$= -gt + a\left[-1 + 1 + \frac{g}{a^2}(\tfrac{1}{2} l + at)\right] \text{ for this period, from } (17)$$

$$= \frac{gl}{2a};$$

Now, from $t = \dfrac{l}{2a}$ to $\dfrac{l}{a}$, $v_A = \dfrac{gl}{2a}$; and from $t = \dfrac{l}{a}$ to $\dfrac{3l}{2a}$ $v_A = \dfrac{3gl}{2a}$.

Therefore from $t = \dfrac{l}{2a}$ to $\dfrac{l}{a}$ the velocity of separation $= \dfrac{gl}{a}$, the same as during the first period $t = 0$ to $\dfrac{l}{2a}$, and from $t = \dfrac{l}{a}$ to $\dfrac{3l}{2a}$, the velocity of separation $= \dfrac{3gl}{2a} + \dfrac{gl}{2a} = \dfrac{2gl}{a}$; i.e. at the end of the time $\dfrac{l}{a}$ the velocity of separation is suddenly doubled.

The initial value of X at the pulley is clearly $mgl = E\dfrac{gl}{a^2}$; as appears also from (14), which equation shews further that this continues to be the value of X there till $t = \dfrac{l}{2a}$. When $t = \dfrac{l}{2a}$ we have at the pulley

$X = E\left[\phi'(0) + \Phi'(l) - 1\right]$

$= E\left[\tfrac{1}{2}\left\{1 - \dfrac{g}{a^2}(\tfrac{1}{2}l)\right\} + \tfrac{1}{2}\left\{1 + \dfrac{g}{a^2}\left(l + \dfrac{l}{2}\right)\right\} - 1\right]$ from (16) and (17)

$= E\left\{\dfrac{gl}{2a^2}\right\};$

and so also till $t = \dfrac{l}{a}$ we have

$X = E\left[\phi'(\tfrac{1}{2}l - at) + \Phi'(\tfrac{1}{2}l + at) - 1\right]$

$= E\left[\tfrac{1}{2}\left\{1 - \dfrac{g}{a^2}(\tfrac{1}{2}l - \tfrac{1}{2}l + at)\right\} + \tfrac{1}{2}\left\{1 + \dfrac{g}{a^2}(l + at)\right\} - 1\right]$

from (16) and (17)

$= E\left\{\dfrac{gl}{2a^2}\right\};$

i.e. the stress at the pulley, and therefore the pressure on it during the time $\dfrac{l}{2a}$ to $\dfrac{l}{a}$ is half its initial value.

A more concise proof from general reasoning would run thus:

Equations (1), (2), (3), (5) and (6) shew at once that the initial velocity of A and of each successive cross-section of the string is $\dfrac{gl}{2a}$, i.e. that a wave travels down the string with velocity a, giving to each cross-section the velocity $\dfrac{gl}{2a}$, and so leaving the parts over which it has passed at rest relatively to each other. Then equation (4) shews how this wave is reflected at B at time $2a$, being the only wave generated in the string, and travels back with the same velocity, but doubling the downward velocity of each cross-section it passes over. Being reflected again at A at the time $\dfrac{l}{a}$, it imparts an additional velocity $\dfrac{gl}{2a}$ to each cross-section as it passes over it. Thus at time $\dfrac{l}{a}$, A begins to move with velocity $\dfrac{3gl}{2a}$, having previously been moving with velocity $\dfrac{gl}{2a}$.

Now the string at C is clearly in the same state of extension as that at A; hence the cross-section there begins to move with velocity $\dfrac{gl}{2a}$, and so does each cross-section of CD over which the wave passes. Till the wave passes over a cross-section it is at rest; i.e. D remains at rest till the time $\dfrac{3l}{2a}$, and during this time C is moving with an upward velocity $\dfrac{gl}{2a}$. Hence at time $\dfrac{l}{a}$ the velocity of separation of A and C is doubled.

Again, during the time which precedes the arrival of the upward wave at the pulley, the state of strain there is unaltered, i.e. the pulley has to support the whole string. Directly the wave passes the pulley, the string begins and continues for a time exceeding $\dfrac{2l}{a}$ to move over the pulley with velocity $\dfrac{gl}{2a}$: hence the pressure on the pulley is the same as if it were supporting a length $\tfrac{1}{2}l$ of the string on each side of it; i.e. at the time $\dfrac{l}{2a}$, the pressure on the pulley is suddenly diminished by one half, and continues thus for at least the second half of the time $\dfrac{l}{a}$.

[For a different discussion of this question see Mr Niven's paper "On a case of Wave Motion," *Messenger of Mathematics*, Vol. VIII. pp. 75—80 (September, 1878).]

15. In the midst of an infinite mass of homogeneous incompressible liquid at rest is a spherical surface of radius a, which is suddenly strained into an equal spheroid of small ellipticity. Find the kinetic energy due to the motion of the liquid contained between the given surface and an imaginary concentric spherical surface of radius c; and shew that if this imaginary surface were a real bounding surface which could not be deformed, the kinetic energy in this case would be to that in the former case in the ratio

$$c^5(3a^5 + 2c^5) : 2(c^5 - a^5)^2.$$

Let $r = a(1 + \epsilon P_2)$ be the equation of the spheroid of small ellipticity ϵ; P_2 being a zonal harmonic of the second degree. Then the displacement of any point is given by $a(1 + \epsilon P_2) - a = a\epsilon P_2$.

Let ϕ be the velocity-potential in the liquid when its outer boundary is a fixed spherical surface of radius c.

Then, since only harmonics of the second degree appear in the displacements, we may assume

$$\phi = \left(A_2 r^2 + \dfrac{B_2}{r^3}\right) P_2.$$

And when $r = a$, $\dfrac{d\phi}{dr} = \lambda a\epsilon P_2$, λ being a constant; when $r = c$, $\dfrac{d\phi}{dr} = 0$;

therefore $\lambda a\epsilon = 2A_2 a - \dfrac{3B_2}{a^4}$,

$$0 = 2A_2 c - \dfrac{3B_2}{c^4};$$

therefore
$$A_2 = \frac{-\lambda a^5 \epsilon}{2(c^5 - a^5)},$$

$$B_2 = \frac{-\lambda a^5 c^5 \epsilon}{3(c^5 - a^5)}.$$

Now the kinetic energy $= \frac{1}{2} \iiint \left\{ \left(\frac{d\phi}{dx}\right)^2 + \left(\frac{d\phi}{dy}\right)^2 + \left(\frac{d\phi}{dz}\right)^2 \right\} dx\,dy\,dz$

$$= \frac{1}{2} \iint \phi \frac{d\phi}{dn} dS,$$

the integrations extending over the spherical surfaces.

But over the outer surface $\frac{d\phi}{dn} = 0$: and over the inner surface
$$\frac{d\phi}{dn} = -\frac{d\phi}{dr} = -\lambda a \epsilon P_2.$$

Therefore the kinetic energy
$$= -\frac{1}{2} \lambda a \epsilon \left(A_2 a^2 + \frac{B_2}{a^3}\right) \iint P_2^2 dS$$

$$= -\frac{2\pi}{5} \lambda a^3 \epsilon \left(A_2 a^2 + \frac{B_2}{a^3}\right)$$

$$= \frac{2\pi}{5} \lambda a^3 \epsilon \left\{ \frac{\lambda a^5 \epsilon}{c^5 - a^5} \left(\frac{a^2}{2} + \frac{c^5}{3a^3}\right) \right\}$$

$$= \frac{\pi \lambda^2 a^5 \epsilon^2}{15} \cdot \frac{3a^5 + 2c^5}{c^5 - a^5}.$$

If now the bounding spherical surface of radius c be removed and the fluid extend to infinity, we have
$$\phi' = \frac{B_2'}{r^3} P_2,$$

where, since $\lambda a \epsilon = -\frac{3B_2'}{a^4}$, $B_2' = \frac{-\lambda a^5 \epsilon}{3}$.

Hence, over the spherical surface of radius a, $\frac{d\phi}{dn} = -\lambda a \epsilon P_2$, and over that of radius c, $\frac{d\phi}{dn} = \frac{-3B_2'}{c^4} P_2$.

Therefore the kinetic energy in this case
$$= -\frac{1}{2} \lambda a \epsilon \frac{B_2'}{a^3} \cdot \frac{4\pi a^2}{5} - \frac{1}{2} \frac{3B_2'}{c^4} \cdot \frac{B_2'}{c^3} \cdot \frac{4\pi c^2}{5}$$

$$= \frac{2\pi}{5} \cdot \left\{ \frac{\lambda^2 a^5 \epsilon^2}{3} - \frac{\lambda^2 a^{10} \epsilon^2}{3c^5} \right\}$$

$$= \frac{2\pi \lambda^2 a^5 \epsilon^2}{15} \cdot \frac{c^5 - a^5}{c^5}.$$

Hence the ratio of the kinetic energy in the first case to that in the second case is

$$\frac{\pi\lambda^2 a^3 \epsilon^2}{15} \cdot \frac{3a^5 + 2c^5}{c^5 - a^5} : \frac{2\pi\lambda^2 a^5 c^2}{15} \cdot \frac{c^5 - a^5}{c^5},$$

or
$$c^6 (3a^5 + 2c^5) : 2 (c^5 - a^5)^2.$$

WEDNESDAY, *January* 16, 1878. 1½ to 4.

Mr GREENHILL, Arabic numbers.
Mr NIVEN, Roman numbers.

1. DEFINE the terms invariant, covariant, and discriminant.

Prove that, if I be any invariant of the binary quantic $(a_0, a_1, a_2, \ldots a_n \gtrless x, y)^n$ of the order p in the coefficients, the weight of each term of I will be $\tfrac{1}{2}np$; and that I will satisfy the equations

$$a_0 \frac{dI}{da_1} + 2a_1 \frac{dI}{da_2} + 3a_2 \frac{dI}{da_3} + \ldots = 0,$$

and
$$na_1 \frac{dI}{da_0} + (n-1) a_2 \frac{dI}{da_1} + (n-2) a_3 \frac{dI}{da_2} + \ldots = 0.$$

Calculate the invariants of the quartic $(a, b, c, d, e \gtrless x, y)^4$ for which p is 2 and 3 respectively; and denoting them by S and T, prove that the discriminant is $S^3 - 27T^2$.

(Salmon, *Higher Algebra*, §§ 52, 56, 58, 137, 139, 203.)

2. Prove that

$$\frac{a + b - 2h \cos \omega}{c \sin^2 \omega} \quad \text{and} \quad \frac{ab - h^2}{c^2 \sin^2 \omega}$$

are invariants of the conic $ax^2 + 2hxy + by^2 + c = 0$, the angle between the axes being ω.

Prove that, if $u = 0$ be the rational equation of a conic in rectangular co-ordinates, the foci are given by

$$\frac{\left(\dfrac{du}{dx}\right)^2 - \left(\dfrac{du}{dy}\right)^2}{\dfrac{d^2u}{dx^2} - \dfrac{d^2u}{dy^2}} = \frac{\dfrac{du}{dx}\dfrac{du}{dy}}{\dfrac{d^2u}{dxdy}} = 2u.$$

Let
$$\frac{X - x}{l} = \frac{Y - y}{m} = r$$

be the equation of a straight line through a focus (xy).

At the intersection with the conic $u = 0$,

$$u + \left(l\frac{du}{dx} + m\frac{du}{dy}\right)r + \tfrac{1}{2}\left(l^2\frac{d^2u}{dx^2} + 2lm\frac{d^2u}{dxdy} + m^2\frac{d^2u}{dy^2}\right)r^2 = 0.$$

Now since the tangents to a conic through a focus pass through the circular points at infinity, we must have, putting $l = 1$, $m = \sqrt{-1}$, the equation

$$u + \left(\frac{du}{dx} + \sqrt{-1}\frac{du}{dy}\right)r + \tfrac{1}{2}\left(\frac{d^2u}{dx^2} + 2\sqrt{-1}\frac{d^2u}{dxdy} - \frac{d^2u}{dy^2}\right)r^2 = 0$$

a perfect square is r; and therefore

$$\left(\frac{du}{dx} + \sqrt{-1}\frac{du}{dy}\right)^2 = 2u\left(\frac{d^2u}{dx^2} - \frac{d^2u}{dy^2} + 2\sqrt{-1}\frac{d^2u}{dxdy}\right),$$

equivalent to

$$\frac{\left(\frac{du}{dx}\right)^2 - \left(\frac{du}{dy}\right)^2}{\frac{d^2u}{dx^2} - \frac{d^2u}{dy^2}} = \frac{\frac{du}{dx}\frac{du}{dy}}{\frac{d^2u}{dxdy}} = 2u,$$

the required equations of the foci.

3. Define the integral curvature, the horograph, and the average curvature of any portion of a surface, and the specific curvature at any point of a surface; and prove that the reciprocal of the product of the principal radii of curvature at any point of a surface measures the specific curvature.

Prove that the area of the surface, of which the specific curvature at any point is constant and equal to $-a^{-2}$, is $4\pi a^2$.

(Frost, *Solid Geometry*, §§ 604, 605.)

If dS denote an element of the surface, $d\sigma$ the corresponding element of the horograph; then

$$\frac{dS}{d\sigma} = \pm\rho\rho' = a^2,$$

therefore $\qquad S = \sigma a^2.$

And $\sigma = 4\pi$; therefore $S = 4\pi a^2$.

4. Find the velocity of the liquid at any point in an elliptic cylinder filled with liquid and rotating about the axis.

Prove that the stream lines of the liquid relative to the cylinder are similar ellipses for all axes of rotation parallel to the axis of the cylinder, and find the kinetic energy of the liquid.

A pendulum with an elliptic cylindrical cavity filled with liquid, the generating lines of the cylinder being parallel to the axis of suspension, performs finite oscillations under gravity. If l be the length of the equivalent pendulum, and l' the length of the equivalent pendulum when the liquid is solidified, find l and l', and prove that

$$l' - l = \frac{m}{M+m} \frac{a^2 b^2}{a^2 + b^2} \frac{1}{h},$$

where M is the mass of the pendulum, m of the liquid, h the distance of the centre of gravity of the whole mass from the axis of suspension, and a, b the semi-axes of the elliptic cylinder.

First suppose the cylinder to be revolving about its axis with angular velocity ω, and let O (fig. 61) represent the centre of a plane transverse section of the cylinder; $O\xi$, $O\eta$ fixed rectangular axes in the plane, and Ox, Oy axes coinciding with the axes of the elliptic section.

Then

$$\phi = \omega \frac{a^2 - b^2}{a^2 + b^2} (\xi \cos \theta + \eta \sin \theta)(-\xi \sin \theta + \eta \cos \theta)$$

$$= \omega \frac{a^2 - b^2}{a^2 + b^2} xy,$$

$$\psi = \tfrac{1}{2} \omega \frac{a^2 - b^2}{a^2 + b^2} (x^2 - y^2),$$

where ϕ and ψ are the velocity- and the current-functions of the liquid.

If χ denote the current-function of the liquid relative to the cylinder,

$$\chi = \psi - \tfrac{1}{2} \omega (x^2 + y^2)$$

$$= \tfrac{1}{2} \omega \frac{a^2 - b^2}{a^2 + b^2} (x^2 - y^2) - \tfrac{1}{2} \omega (x^2 + y^2)$$

$$= -\tfrac{1}{2} \omega \frac{b^2 x^2 + a^2 y^2}{a^2 + b^2} = -\tfrac{1}{2} \omega \frac{a^2 b^2}{a^2 + b^2} \left(\frac{x^2}{a^2} + \frac{y^2}{b^2} \right);$$

and therefore the relative stream lines are similar ellipses. (The motion of the liquid will therefore be the same if the cylinder be bounded internally by a similar, similarly situated, and co-axal elliptic cylinder.)

If the axis of revolution be parallel to the axis of the cylinder, then the motion of translation of the axis of the cylinder due to this motion will not produce any relative motion of the liquid, and the motion of rotation about the axis due to this motion will produce the same relative motion as before. Therefore the stream lines of the liquid relative to the cylinder are the same, that is, similar ellipses, for all axes of rotation parallel to the axis of the cylinder.

The kinetic energy of the liquid relative to the centre of mass of the liquid is

$$\tfrac{1}{2}\omega^2 \left(\frac{a^2-b^2}{a^2+b^2}\right) \iint \rho\,(x^2+y^2)\,dx\,dy$$

$$= \tfrac{1}{2}\omega^2 \left(\frac{a^2-b^2}{a^2+b^2}\right)^2 m\,\tfrac{1}{4}(a^2+b^2)$$

$$= \tfrac{1}{2} m \omega^2 \kappa^2,$$

where $\quad \kappa^2 = \tfrac{1}{4}(a^2+b^2)\left(\frac{a^2-b^2}{a^2+b^2}\right)^2;$

κ is therefore the effective radius of gyration of the liquid in the cylinder about the axis of the cylinder.

If K denote the radius of gyration of the mass M of the pendulum about the axis of suspension; if c denote the distance between the axis of suspension and the axis of the cylinder; and if θ denote the angle the plane through these axes makes with the vertical; then the kinetic energy of the pendulum and the liquid

$$= \tfrac{1}{2}MK^2\dot\theta^2 + \tfrac{1}{2}m\left\{c^2 + \tfrac{1}{4}(a^2+b^2)\left(\frac{a^2-b^2}{a^2+b^2}\right)^2\right\}\dot\theta^2$$

$$= H + (M+m)\,gh\cos\theta,$$

by the principle of energy; and therefore

$$l = \frac{MK^2 + m\left\{c^2 + \tfrac{1}{4}(a^2+b^2)\left(\frac{a^2-b^2}{a^2+b^2}\right)^2\right\}}{(M+m)h}.$$

If the liquid were solidified, the kinetic energy would be

$$= \tfrac{1}{2}MK^2\dot\theta^2 + \tfrac{1}{2}m\{c^2 + \tfrac{1}{4}(a^2+b^2)\}\dot\theta^2;$$

and therefore

$$l' = \frac{MK^2 + m\{c^2 + \tfrac{1}{4}(a^2+b^2)\}}{(M+m)h}.$$

Therefore

$$l' - l = \frac{m}{M+m}\frac{a^2+b^2}{4h}\left\{1 - \left(\frac{a^2-b^2}{a^2+b^2}\right)^2\right\}$$

$$= \frac{m}{M+m}\frac{a^2 b^2}{a^2+b^2}\frac{1}{h}.$$

5. Prove that, if the space between two infinite coaxal circular conducting cylinders be occupied by a dielectric of specific inductive capacity K, the capacity of the inner cylinder per unit of length is $\tfrac{1}{2}\dfrac{K}{\log\dfrac{b}{a}}$, where a is the radius of the outer cylinder and b of the inner.

If a conducting circular cylinder of radius b be surrounded by an uninsulated coaxal cylindrical grating of radius a, formed of n thin wires, prove that the electrification at any point of the cylinder, of which the radius makes an angle θ with the vector of a wire, is
$$\frac{Q}{2\pi b} \cdot \frac{a^{2n} - b^{2n}}{a^{2n} - 2a^n b^n \cos n\theta + b^{2n}},$$
where Q is the quantity of electricity per unit length of the cylinder.

Suppose the potential of a single wire at a distance ρ to be $\lambda \log \rho$; then if we take the n negative images of the wires in the cylinder (Maxwell, *Electricity*, § 189), the potential of the wires and their images at a point whose co-ordinates are r, θ will be
$$V = \lambda \log \frac{\rho_1 \rho_2 \cdots \rho_n}{\rho_1' \rho_2' \cdots \rho_n'},$$
$$= \tfrac{1}{2} \lambda \log \frac{r^{2n} - 2a^n r^n \cos n\theta + a^{2n}}{r^{2n} - 2\dfrac{b^{2n}}{a^n} r^n \cos n\theta + \dfrac{b^{4n}}{a^{2n}}},$$
by De Moivre's property of the circle.

If we put $r = b$, then
$$V = n\lambda \log \frac{a}{b},$$
a constant; and therefore if the cylinder $r = b$ be electrified with superficial density
$$-\frac{1}{4\pi} \frac{dV}{dr},$$
the potential of the external wires and this electrification will be constant in the interior of the cylinder; and therefore this will be the electrification of the cylinder when insulated and surrounded by the grating of n thin wires.

Now
$$-\frac{1}{4\pi} \frac{dV}{dr}(r = b)$$
$$= -\frac{n\lambda}{4\pi} \frac{b^{2n-1} - a^n b^{n-1} \cos n\theta}{b^{2n} - 2a^n b^n \cos n\theta + a^{2n}} + \frac{n\lambda}{4\pi} \frac{b^{2n-1} - \dfrac{b^{3n-1}}{a^n} \cos n\theta}{b^{2n} - 2\dfrac{b^{3n}}{a^n} \cos n\theta + \dfrac{b^{4n}}{a^{2n}}}$$
$$= \frac{n\lambda}{4\pi b} \frac{a^{2n} - b^{2n}}{a^{2n} - 2a^n b^n \cos n\theta + b^{2n}}.$$

Also
$$Q = \frac{n\lambda}{4\pi b} \int_0^{2\pi} \frac{a^{2n} - b^{2n}}{a^{2n} - 2a^n b^n \cos n\theta + b^{2n}} d\theta$$
$$= \tfrac{1}{2} n\lambda;$$

therefore the electrification

$$= \frac{Q}{2\pi b} \frac{a^{2n} - b^{2n}}{a^{2n} - 2a^n b^n \cos n\theta + b^{2n}}.$$

[This rider and the result were obtained as a generalization of § 189 of Maxwell's *Electricity*, but objections have been urged against the accuracy of the result.]

vi. Find the expressions for the stresses at any point of an isotropic elastic solid in terms of the strains at that point, and deduce the value of Young's modulus in terms of the coefficients of rigidity and the elasticity of volume.

A spherical shell of isotropic material and finite thickness expands under the influence of a gas of given pressure contained inside it; prove that, if a thin shell whose unstrained radii are r, $r + \delta r$ be strained into a shell whose inner radius is $r + u$, the work required to produce the strain in this part is

$$\tfrac{1}{2}(k - \tfrac{2}{3}n)\left(\frac{du}{dr} + \frac{2u}{r}\right)^2 + n\left\{\left(\frac{du}{dr}\right)^2 + \frac{2u^2}{r^2}\right\}$$

per unit volume, where n is the rigidity and k is the elasticity of volume, and deduce from this result the strains and stresses inside the shell.

How can the principal stresses at right angles to the radius be found?

One of the easiest methods of discussing the general problem of elasticity of solid bodies is the comprehensive method of Green.

The geometrical elements of the strain in the neighbourhood of any point are completely expressed by means of the six strains. If uvw be the displacements of a point whose co-ordinates are xyz, and if the strain be small, its components may be denoted by

$$e = \frac{du}{dx}, \qquad f = \frac{dv}{dy}, \qquad g = \frac{dw}{dz}$$

$$a = \frac{dv}{dz} + \frac{dw}{dy}, \quad b = \frac{dw}{dx} + \frac{du}{dz}, \quad c = \frac{du}{dy} + \frac{dv}{dx}.$$

Of which the three former are called normal, and the three latter the tangential, strains. The energy, W per unit volume, required to produce the state of strain of the element $dxdydz$ is, for an isotropic substance, a function of the invariants of the above system of magnitudes which is of the second degree in $e, f \ldots c$, and is therefore of the form

$$2W = m(e + f + g)^2 + n(e^2 + f^2 + g^2 - 2fg - 2ge - 2ef + a^2 + b^2 + c^2)$$

(see Thomson and Tait's *Natural Philosophy*, Appendix C).

n is the rigidity of the substance, and m is connected with the elasticity of volume by means of the equation

$$m - \tfrac{1}{3} n = k.$$

The value of W may be put into a somewhat more convenient form thus,

$$2W = (k - \tfrac{2}{3} n)(e + f + g)^2 + n(2e^2 + 2f^2 + 2g^2 + a^2 + b^2 + c^2).$$

To obtain the components of the stresses and the general equations of equilibrium, we observe that if XYZ be the components of the stress on an element dS of the surface of any portion of the body,

$$\int (X\delta u + Y\delta v + Z\delta w)\, dS - \int \delta W . \, dx\, dy\, dz = 0,$$

no impressed forces being supposed to act on the particles of the body, and X, Y, Z being expressed in the usual manner in terms of the elastic stresses. When we substitute for W in terms of $e, f \ldots$ and integrate by parts, we may equate to zero the coefficients of δu, δv, δw in the different parts of the surface integrals and volume integral, we obtain the general formulæ for the stresses and the equations of equilibrium.

In the case of a spherical shell symmetrically expanded by a gas inside it, these formulæ are greatly simplified, for there are no tangential stresses, and the normal stresses are reduced to a stress R in the direction of the radius, and another S at right angles to it.

Let a be the outer and b the inner radius, and let P be the pressure of the gas inside, P_0 that of the medium surrounding it; in ordinary cases P_0 will be the atmospheric pressure, and may be neglected: we shall however, for the sake of generality, include it.

When the shell is strained, let the radius r become $r + u$; the work done by the elastic forces in producing a small arbitrary strain of a shell, whose outer and inner radii are r and r_1, is

$$4\pi (Rr^2 \delta u - R_1 r_1^2 \delta u_1),$$

R being reckoned as a traction, in the usual manner.

Let us now consider any rectangular element of an indefinitely thin shell whose edges are dr, $r\alpha$, $r\beta$, α and β being two indefinitely small angles.

It strains into a rectangular element whose edges are

$$dr\left(1 + \frac{du}{dr}\right),\ r\alpha\left(1 + \frac{u}{r}\right),\ r\beta\left(1 + \frac{u}{r}\right);$$

and the three tangential strains are now zero; that is to say,

$$a = 0,\quad b = 0,\quad c = 0,$$

and

$$e = \frac{du}{dr},\ f = \frac{u}{r},\ g = \frac{u}{r};$$

the work done in straining the shell is therefore

$$W = \tfrac{1}{2}(k - \tfrac{2}{3}n)\left(\frac{du}{dr} + \frac{2u}{r}\right)^2 + n\left\{\left(\frac{du}{dr}\right)^2 + \frac{2u^2}{r^2}\right\}, \quad\ldots\ldots\ldots(6)$$

per unit volume.

The work done in straining the shell (r, r_1) is

$$4\pi \int_{r_1}^{r} r^2 W dr\,;$$

the general equation of equilibrium is, therefore,

$$r^2 R \delta u - R_1 r_1^2 \delta u_1 = \int_{r_1}^{r} r^2 \delta W . dr.$$

Now $\quad \tfrac{1}{2}\int r^2 \delta\left(\dfrac{du}{dr} + \dfrac{2u}{r}\right)^2 . dr = \int\left(r\dfrac{du}{dr} + 2u\right)\left(r\dfrac{d\delta u}{dr} + 2\delta u\right)dr$

$$= r^2 \theta\, \delta u - \int r^2 \frac{d\theta}{dr}\, \delta u\,.\, dr,$$

where $\qquad\qquad\qquad \theta = \dfrac{du}{dr} + \dfrac{2u}{r},$

and

$$\int\left\{r^2 \delta\left(\frac{du}{dr}\right)^2 + 2\delta\,.\,u^2\right\}dr = 2r^2\frac{du}{dr}\delta u - 2\int r^2 \frac{d\theta}{dr}\,.\,\delta u\,.\,dr.$$

We see from these results that the condition of equilibrium is

$$\frac{d\theta}{dr} = 0,$$

and that

$$R = (k - \tfrac{2}{3}n)\,\theta + 2n\frac{du}{dr}.$$

The solution of the former equation is

$$\theta = 2A,$$

$$u = A + \frac{B}{r^3},$$

and hence $\qquad\qquad R = (K - \tfrac{2}{3}n)A - \dfrac{4nB}{r^3}.$

To find A and B we observe that, when $r = a$, $R = P$, and when $r = b$, $R = P_0$; thus,

$$P = (k - \tfrac{2}{3}n)A - \frac{4nB}{a^3},$$

$$P_0 = (k - \tfrac{2}{3}n)A - \frac{4nB}{b^3}.$$

To find the other stress S, consider the equilibrium of a hemisphere of shell whose outer and inner radii are r, $r + dr$; it is acted on by a traction perpendicular to the edge equal to

$$2\pi r dr \cdot S,$$

while the resultant of the stresses perpendicular to its curved surface is

$$\frac{d}{dr}(2\pi r^2 R),$$

hence
$$rS = \frac{d}{dr}(r^2 R);$$

and thus,
$$S = 2\left(k - \tfrac{2}{3} n\right) Ar + \frac{4nB}{r^3}.$$

vii. Describe and explain the appearances presented, with divergent light, by a plate of a uniaxal crystal cut perpendicular to the axis, placed between a polarizer and an analyzer.

Describe the appearances presented when the plate is cut parallel to the axis.

If n equal and similar plates of a crystal be laid upon each other with their principal directions arranged like the steps of a uniform spiral staircase, and a polarised ray pass normally through them; prove that the component vibrations of the emergent ordinary and extraordinary rays have each the form

$$X \cos \frac{2\pi t}{T} + Y \sin \frac{2\pi t}{T},$$

where X and Y are each of the form

$$A \cos n\gamma + B \sin n\gamma, \quad \text{where } \cos \gamma = \cos \delta \cos \alpha;$$

α being the angle between the principal directions of two consecutive plates, and 2δ the difference of phase between the ordinary and extraordinary ray in passing through one plate. Determine also the condition that a ray originally plane polarised may emerge plane polarised.

For the form of the lines seen with a plate of uniaxal crystal cut parallel to its axes, see Verdet's *Optique Physique*, Art. 219, Vol. II.

To solve the second problem, let us first consider the relation between the components of the ordinary and extraordinary ray for the first two plates.

If the component vibrations along the two principal sections of the first plate be

$$x = a \cos \phi + b \sin \phi,$$
$$y = c \cos \phi + d \sin \phi,$$

ϕ being the phase of the ray.

After transmission through the plate, these become
$$x' = a \cos(\phi' - \delta) + b \sin(\phi' - \delta),$$
$$y' = c \cos(\phi' + \delta) + d \sin(\phi' + \delta),$$
2δ being the difference of phase established between the two rays by their passage through the plate.

Resolving along the axes of the second plate, we find the components to be
$$x' \cos a + y' \sin a,$$
$$y' \cos a - x' \sin a.$$
If these be written $a' \cos \phi' + b' \sin \phi',\ c' \cos \phi' + d' \sin \phi',$
$$a' = a \cos \delta \cos a - b \sin \delta \cos a + c \cos \delta \sin a + d \sin \delta \sin a$$
$$b' = a \sin \delta \cos a + b \cos \delta \cos a - c \sin \delta \sin a + d \cos \delta \sin a$$
$$c' = -a \cos \delta \sin a + b \sin \delta \sin a + c \cos \delta \cos a + d \sin \delta \cos a$$
$$d' = -a \sin \delta \sin a - b \cos \delta \sin a - c \sin \delta \cos a + d \cos \delta \cos a.$$
It follows from this that, if we put
$$l = \cos \delta \cos a,\quad m = \sin \delta \cos a,\quad p = \cos \delta \sin a,\quad q = \sin \delta \sin a,$$
the relations between the components of two consecutive systems of rays which are given by
$$x_n \cos \phi + y_n \sin \phi,\quad u_n \cos \phi + v_n \sin \phi,$$
are
$$\left.\begin{aligned}x_{n+1} &= lx_n - my_n + pu_n + qv_n \\ y_{n+1} &= mx_n + ly_n - qu_n + pv_n \\ u_{n+1} &= -px_n + qy_n + lu_n + mv_n \\ v_{n+1} &= -qx_n - py_n - mu_n + lv_n\end{aligned}\right\}\ \ldots\ldots\ldots\ldots(a).$$

To solve these, let
$$x_n = X\theta^n,\ y_n = Y\theta^n,\ u_n = U\theta^n,\ v_n = V\theta^n.$$
On substituting, we find
$$(-\theta + l)X\quad -mY\quad +pU\quad +qV = 0\ \ldots(1),$$
$$mX + (-\theta + l)Y\quad -qU\quad +pV = 0\ \ldots(2),$$
$$-pX\quad +qY + (-\theta + l)U\quad +mV = 0\ \ldots(3),$$
$$-qX\quad -pY\quad -mU + (-\theta + l)V = 0\ \ldots(4).$$
If $x = -\theta + l,$ we find from (1) and (2)
$$(p^2 + q^2)U + x(pX - qY) - m(pY + qX) = 0\ \ldots\ldots(5),$$
$$(p^2 + q^2)V + m(pX - qY) + x(pY + qX) = 0\ \ldots\ldots(6).$$
If we substitute these values in (3) or (4), we find that they are both satisfied by
$$x^2 + m^2 + p^2 + q^2 = 0.$$

From which it results that
$$x^2 = -(1-l^2) = -\sin^2\gamma,$$
$$\theta = l - x = \cos\gamma \pm \sqrt{-1}\sin\gamma.$$

x_n will therefore be of the form
$$A_1 e^{n\gamma\sqrt{-1}} + A_2 e^{-n\gamma\sqrt{-1}},$$

and we may put
$$A_1 e^{n\gamma\sqrt{-1}} + A_2 e^{-n\gamma\sqrt{-1}} = C\cos n\gamma + D\sin n\gamma,$$

and, at the same time,
$$\sqrt{-1}\,(A_1 e^{n\gamma\sqrt{-1}} - A_2 e^{-n\gamma\sqrt{-1}}) = -C\sin n\gamma + D\cos n\gamma.$$

In a similar manner we may take
$$y_n = B_1 e^{n\gamma\sqrt{-1}} + B_2 e^{-n\gamma\sqrt{-1}} = E\cos n\gamma + F\sin n\gamma.$$

On substituting in (5) and (6), we shall obtain for U and V two complex imaginary expressions of the form
$$U_1 = H + K\sqrt{-1},\quad U_2 = H - K\sqrt{-1}.$$

The corresponding value of u_n is therefore presented in the form
$$u_n = H\cos n\gamma + K\sin n\gamma.$$

This value may also be deduced from the equations (a), the first two of which may be solved for u_n and v_n.

We may also employ these equations to find the values of the constants C, D...

For, put $\quad u = 0,\ C = a,\ E = b,\ H = c$...

and
$$x_1 = C\cos\gamma + D\sin\gamma = la - mb + pc + qd,$$
$$y_1 = E\cos\gamma + F\sin\gamma = ma + lb - qc + pd,$$
$$u_1 = H\cos\gamma + K\sin\gamma = \text{etc.}$$
$$v_1 = \text{etc.}$$

The final expressions for the components are, therefore,
$$\left.\begin{array}{l} x_n = a\cos n\gamma + (-mb + pc + qd)\dfrac{\sin n\gamma}{\sin\gamma} \\[4pt] y_n = b\cos n\gamma + (+ma - qc + pd)\dfrac{\sin n\gamma}{\sin\gamma} \\[4pt] u_n = c\cos n\gamma + (-pa + qb + md)\dfrac{\sin n\gamma}{\sin\gamma} \\[4pt] v_n = d\cos n\gamma + (-qa - pb - mc)\dfrac{\sin n\gamma}{\sin\gamma} \end{array}\right\}\ \ldots\ldots\ldots(\beta).$$

The general conditions that a ray may be plane polarised can be easily found, for the two components are of the form

$$P\cos(\phi - A), \quad Q\cos(\phi - A);$$

the condition, therefore, plainly is

$$x_n v_n - y_n u_n = 0 \ldots\ldots\ldots\ldots\ldots\ldots\ldots\ldots(7).$$

In the present case, if we suppose a ray to enter plane polarised, we may take $\quad a = \cos\beta, \quad b = 0, \quad c = \sin\beta, \quad d = 0.$

Upon substituting the values of $x_n, y_n \ldots$ so found in (7), we shall find on reduction that

$$\tan n\gamma = \frac{\tan(2\beta + a)\sin\gamma}{\cos\delta \sin a}.$$

This is the condition that, after passing through n plates, the ray may be again plane polarised.

viii. Prove that the complete solution of a partial differential equation of the first order containing two independent variables is afforded by the system consisting of a single complete primitive with its accompanying general integrals and singular solution.

Find a complete primitive of the equation

$$\left(\frac{dz}{dx}\right)^2 + \left(\frac{dz}{dy}\right)^2 = x^2 + xy + y^2.$$

Present the complete integral of the equation

$$\frac{1}{a^2}\frac{d^2u}{dt^2} = \frac{d^2u}{dr^2} + \frac{2}{r}\frac{du}{dr} - \frac{n(n+1)u}{r^2}$$

in the form $\quad u = r^n \left(\frac{1}{r}\frac{d}{dr}\right)^n \frac{\phi(r+at) + \psi(r-at)}{r}.$

To find a complete primitive of the equation

$$\left(\frac{dz}{dx}\right)^2 + \left(\frac{dz}{dy}\right)^2 = x^2 + xy + y^2.$$

Consider x and y as the co-ordinates of a point, and turn the axes round through half a right angle; that is to say, take

$$x = \frac{\xi + y}{\sqrt{2}}, \quad y = \frac{\xi - y}{\sqrt{2}}.$$

By this transformation the equation will become

$$\left(\frac{dz}{d\xi}\right)^2 + \left(\frac{dz}{d\eta}\right)^2 = \xi^2 + \eta^2 + \tfrac{1}{2}(\xi^2 - \eta^2),$$

to find a complete primitive of which, put

$$\sqrt{2} \cdot \frac{dz}{d\xi} = \sqrt{(3\xi^2 - a^2)},$$

$$\sqrt{2} \cdot \frac{dz}{d\eta} = \sqrt{(a^2 + \eta^2)},$$

where a is an arbitrary constant;

therefore $\quad \sqrt{2}z = \int \sqrt{(3\xi^2 - a^2)}\, d\xi + \int \sqrt{(a^2 + \eta^2)}\, d\eta + b,$

b being another arbitrary constant.

These integrals belong to known forms, and may be readily found.

To present the complete integral of the equation

$$\frac{1}{a^2} \frac{d^2u}{dt^2} = \frac{d^2u}{dr^2} + \frac{2}{r}\frac{du}{dr} - \frac{n(n+1)}{r^2} u \dots\dots\dots\dots(1)$$

in the form

$$u = r^n \left(\frac{1}{r}\frac{d}{dr}\right)^n \cdot \frac{\phi(r+at) + \psi(r-at)}{r} \dots\dots\dots(2).$$

Since the form given contains two arbitrary functions, it must be the complete integral if it satisfy the equation at all. This is analogous to the general principle that any solution of an ordinary equation which contains the proper number of independent arbitrary constants is the complete solution. We have therefore only to shew that u satisfies the equation.

Put $\quad u = r^n v_n, \quad \dfrac{du}{dr} = r^n \dfrac{dv_n}{dr} + nr^{n-1} v_n,$

$$\frac{d^2u}{dr^2} = r^n \frac{d^2v_n}{dr^2} + 2nr^{n-1}\frac{dv_n}{dr} + n(n-1) r^{n-2} v_n.$$

On substituting, and throwing away the factor r^n,

$$\frac{1}{a^2}\frac{d^2v_n}{dt^2} = \frac{d^2v_n}{dr^2} + \frac{2(n+1)}{r}\frac{dv_n}{dr} \dots\dots\dots\dots(3).$$

Operate with $\dfrac{1}{r}\dfrac{d}{dr}$, and let $\dfrac{1}{r}\dfrac{dv_n}{dr} = w$;

$$\frac{1}{a^2}\frac{d^2w}{dt^2} = \frac{1}{r}\frac{d^2}{dr^2}(rw) + \frac{2(n+1)}{r}\frac{dw}{dr}$$

$$= \frac{d^2w}{dr^2} + \frac{2(n+2)}{r}\frac{dw}{dr}.$$

If therefore v_n satisfy (3), $\dfrac{1}{r}\dfrac{dv_n}{dr}$ will satisfy the same equation when $n+1$ is put for n.

But, when $n = 0$, equation (3) becomes

$$\frac{1}{a^2}\frac{d^2v_0}{dt^2} = \frac{d^2v_0}{dr^2} + \frac{2}{r}\frac{dv_0}{dr},$$

the solution of which is

$$v_0 = \frac{\phi(r+at) + \psi(r-at)}{r}.$$

The solution of (3) is therefore

$$v_n = \left(\frac{1}{r}\frac{d}{dr}\right)^n \cdot \frac{\phi(r+at) + \psi(r-at)}{r},$$

and, therefore, that of (1) is given by the expression (2).

See also Mr Glaisher's paper "On a differential equation allied to Riccati's," *Quarterly Journal*, Vol. XII. pp. 129—137 (1872).

ix. Determine the general conditions to be satisfied in any problem of magnetic induction.

Find the magnetisation of an infinite elliptic cylinder of soft iron placed in a uniform field of force.

This problem may be solved in a manner analogous to that given in Maxwell's *Treatise on Electricity and Magnetism*, Vol. II., Art. 437, for an ellipsoid.

Let the equation of the cylinder be

$$\frac{x^2}{a^2} + \frac{y^2}{b^2} = 1,$$

and let the components of the external magnetic force be X, Y, Z, and K the coefficient of induction for soft iron.

It may be shewn that all the conditions of the problem will be satisfied by supposing the cylinder magnetised uniformly.

Let us assume that this is so, and that the components of the magnetisation are L, M, N; then, since the potential of a uniform elliptic cylinder of unit density is

$$V = -2\pi\frac{bx^2 + ay^2}{a+b} + \text{const.}$$

the potential, due to uniform magnetisation LMN, will be

$$\Omega = \frac{4\pi}{a+b}(bLx + aMy).$$

The total magnetising force will therefore have for components

$$X - \frac{4\pi bL}{a+b}, \quad Y - \frac{4\pi aM}{a+b}, \quad Z,$$

and L, M, N are given by the equations

$$L = K\left(X - \frac{4\pi bL}{a+b}\right),$$

$$M = K\left(Y - \frac{4\pi aM}{a+b}\right),$$

$$N = KZ,$$

whence we obtain

$$L = \frac{K}{1 + \frac{4\pi bK}{a+b}} X, \quad M = \frac{K}{1 + \frac{4\pi aK}{a+b}} Y, \quad N = KZ.$$

These expressions, as well as the potential of the cylinder, may also be derived from the results given in the article referred to above, by putting

$$c = \infty, \quad K_1 = K_2 = K_3 = K$$

and $K_1' = K_2' = K_3' = 0.$

THURSDAY, *January* 17, 1878.   9 to 12.

Mr GLAISHER,   Arabic numbers.
Mr FERRERS,   Roman numbers.

1. DEFINE Bernoulli's numbers, and calculate the values of the first two.

Shew that, when n is very great, the nth Bernoullian number is very nearly equal to
$$4\pi^{-2n+\frac{1}{2}} e^{-2n} n^{2n+\frac{1}{2}}.$$

Obtain the development of $\dfrac{\sin 3x}{\sin x \sin 2x}$ in ascending powers of x, the coefficients being expressed in Bernoullian numbers.

(i) B_n denoting the nth Bernoullian number,

$$B_n = \frac{2(2n)!}{(2\pi)^{2n}}\left(1 + \frac{1}{2^{2n}} + \frac{1}{3^{2n}} + \&c.\right)$$

and n being large, $(2n)! = \sqrt{(2\pi \cdot 2n)} \cdot (2n)^{2n} e^{-2n}$

whence $B_n = 2 \cdot 2^{2n+1} \pi^{\frac{1}{2}} e^{-2n} \cdot n^{2n+\frac{1}{2}} \cdot 2^{-2n} \pi^{-2n} = 4\pi^{-2n+\frac{1}{2}} e^{-2n} n^{2n+\frac{1}{2}}$

when n is large.

(ii)
$$\frac{\sin 3x}{\sin x \sin 2x} = \cot x + \cot 2x$$

and
$$\cot x = \frac{1}{x} - \frac{2^2 B_1}{2!}x - \frac{2^4 B_2}{4!}x^3 - \frac{2^6 B_3}{6!}x^5 - \&c.$$

2. Write down the formulæ giving
$$\operatorname{sn}(u+v), \quad \operatorname{cn}(u+v), \quad \operatorname{dn}(u+v)$$
in terms of $\operatorname{sn} u, \operatorname{cn} u, \operatorname{dn} u, \operatorname{sn} v, \operatorname{cn} v, \operatorname{dn} v$.

Prove that
$$\frac{\operatorname{sn} u}{u} = \frac{\operatorname{cn}\tfrac{1}{2}u\,\operatorname{dn}\tfrac{1}{2}u \cdot \operatorname{cn}\tfrac{1}{4}u\,\operatorname{dn}\tfrac{1}{4}u \cdot \operatorname{cn}\tfrac{1}{8}u\,\operatorname{dn}\tfrac{1}{8}u \ldots}{(1-k^2\operatorname{sn}^4\tfrac{1}{2}u)(1-k^2\operatorname{sn}^4\tfrac{1}{4}u)(1-k^2\operatorname{sn}^4\tfrac{1}{8}u)\ldots},$$
and that
$$\frac{1-\operatorname{sn} u}{1+\operatorname{sn} u} = \frac{1}{k'^2} \frac{\operatorname{cn}^2 \tfrac{1}{2}(u+K)\,\operatorname{dn}^2 \tfrac{1}{2}(u+K)}{\operatorname{sn}^2 \tfrac{1}{2}(u+K)}.$$

Assuming the q-series for $\Theta\left(\dfrac{2Ku}{\pi}\right)$ and $H\left(\dfrac{2Ku}{\pi}\right)$, prove the relation
$$Hu = \frac{1}{i}\sqrt[4]{q}\, e^{\frac{\pi i u}{2K}}\,\Theta(u+iK').$$

(i) The equation is obtained by repeated use of the formula
$$\operatorname{cn} u = \frac{2\operatorname{sn}\tfrac{1}{2}u\,\operatorname{cn}\tfrac{1}{2}u\,\operatorname{dn}\tfrac{1}{2}u}{1-k^2\operatorname{sn}^4\tfrac{1}{2}u},$$
observing that, when $n = \infty$,
$$2^n \operatorname{sn}\frac{u}{2^n}, \quad \operatorname{cn}\frac{u}{2^n}, \quad \operatorname{dn}\frac{u}{2^n} = u,\ 1,\ 1$$
in the same manner as Euler's formula $\dfrac{\sin x}{x} = \cos\tfrac{1}{2}x \cos\tfrac{1}{4}x \ldots$ is obtained in Trigonometry.

(ii) Writing x for $\operatorname{sn} u$, we have (Cayley's *Elliptic Functions*, N°. 100, p. 72)
$$\operatorname{cn} 2u = \frac{1-2x^2+k^2x^4}{1-k^2x^4},\quad \operatorname{dn} 2u = \frac{1-2k^2x^2+k^2x^4}{1-k^2x^4},$$
whence
$$\frac{\operatorname{dn} 2u + \operatorname{cn} 2u}{\operatorname{dn} 2u - \operatorname{cn} 2u} = \frac{1-x^2-k^2x^2+k^2x^4}{k'^2 x^2} = \frac{1}{k'^2}\frac{\operatorname{cn}^2 u\,\operatorname{dn}^2 u}{\operatorname{sn}^2 u},$$
and the result in the question follows at once on substituting $\tfrac{1}{2}(u+K)$ for u, since
$$\operatorname{dn}(u+K) = \frac{k'}{\operatorname{dn} u},\quad \operatorname{cn}(u+K) = -k'\frac{\operatorname{sn} u}{\operatorname{dn} u}.$$

(iii) Put $\dfrac{2Ku}{\pi} = x$, then

$$\Theta x = 1 - 2q \cos 2u + 2q^4 \cos 4u - 2q^9 \cos 6u + \&c.$$
$$= 1 - q(e^{2iu} + e^{-2iu}) + q^4(e^{4iu} + e^{-4iu}) - q^9(e^{6iu} + e^{-6iu}) + \&c.$$

Change x into $x + iK'$, then u becomes $u + \dfrac{i\pi K'}{2K}$ and e^{iu} becomes $e^{iu - \frac{\pi K'}{2K}}$, viz. $q^{\frac{1}{2}}e^{iu}$. We thus have

$$\Theta(x + iK') = 1 - q(qe^{2iu} + q^{-1}e^{-2iu}) + q^4(q^2e^{4iu} + q^{-2}e^{-4iu}) - \&c.,$$

viz. $q^{\frac{1}{4}}e^{iu} \Theta(x + iK') = q^{\frac{1}{4}}(e^{iu} - e^{-iu}) - q^{\frac{9}{4}}(e^{3iu} - e^{-3iu}) + \&c. = i\mathrm{H}x,$

which is the theorem in the question.

3. Assuming the law of facility to be $\dfrac{h}{\sqrt{\pi}} e^{-h^2 x^2}$, determine how n direct, and presumably equally good, observations of the same thing are to be combined so as to afford the most probable result.

A, B, C, D are four places in order in the same straight line, AB is measured α times, BC β times, CD γ times, AC δ times, BD ϵ times, and AD ζ times; and the respective means of the measures are, for AB, a; for BC, b; for CD, c; for AC, d; for BD, e; for AD, f. Find the most probable value of BC; and, in the case of $\alpha = \beta = \ldots = \zeta$, find its probable error.

It will be useful to give here a brief statement of the process of the solution of equations by the method of least squares, and then to work out the above question as an example.

Suppose that we are given m equations connecting the μ unknown quantities $x, y, z, \ldots t$, viz.

$$\left. \begin{array}{l} a_1 x + b_1 y + c_1 z \ldots + k_1 t = n_1 \\ a_2 x + b_2 y + c_2 z \ldots + k_2 t = n_2 \\ \ldots\ldots\ldots\ldots\ldots\ldots\ldots\ldots\ldots\ldots \\ a_m x + b_m y + c_m z \ldots + k_m t = n_m \end{array} \right\} \quad \ldots\ldots\ldots\ldots (1),$$

wherein the coefficients $a_1, b_1, \ldots k_1, a_2, b_2, \ldots k_m$ are supposed to be known accurately by theoretical considerations or otherwise, and $n_1, n_2, \ldots n_m$ are m quantities which are obtained by observation (either directly or indirectly) and are therefore liable to error. If m, the number of equations, were equal to μ the number of unknowns, these equations would determine uniquely the values of the unknowns $x, y, z, \ldots t$; but the case contemplated in the method of least squares is when m is greater than μ, and in general much greater. The object is to obtain from the given system of equations (1), called the *equations of condition*, the values of $x, y, z, \ldots t$ that are to be adopted as the 'most probable' values of these quantities. The process is as follows. Form the system of μ equations called the *normal equations*,

$$\left.\begin{array}{l}[aa]\,x+[ab]\,y+[ac]\,z\,\ldots+[ak]\,t=[an]\\ [ba]\,x+[bb]\,y+[bc]\,z\,\ldots+[bk]\,t=[bn]\\ \cdots\cdots\cdots\cdots\cdots\cdots\cdots\cdots\cdots\cdots\cdots\cdots\\ [ka]\,x+[kb]\,y+[kc]\,z\,\ldots+[kk]\,t=[kn]\end{array}\right\}\ldots\ldots\ldots(2),$$

where $[aa]$ denotes $a_1^2+a_2^2\ldots+a_m^2$, $[ab]$ denotes $a_1b_1+a_2b_2\ldots+a_mb_m$, &c., so that $[pq]=[qp]$. The solution of these equations gives the most probable values of $x, y, z \ldots t$.

The normal equations are derived from the equations of condition by multiplying each equation by the coefficient of x in it, and adding all the equations so formed; we thus have the first normal equation (the x-equation): similarly multiplying each equation by the coefficient of y in it and adding we form the y-equation, and so on. Practically however when m does not much exceed μ and both are small, it is often convenient to obtain the normal equations by differentiating the expression

$$(a_1x+b_1y\ldots+k_1t-n_1)^2+(a_2x+b_2y\ldots+k_2t-n_2)^2\ldots+(a_mx+b_my\ldots+k_mt-n_m)^2$$

with respect to x for the x-equation, with respect to y for the y-equation, &c. The method derives its name from the fact that the most probable values of $x, y, z, \ldots t$ are the values that render this expression a minimum.

The next step is to form $[vv]$, the sum of the squares of the residuals. Substitute $x_0, y_0, z_0, \ldots t_0$ the most probable values of the unknowns found by solving the normal equations, in the equations of condition, and let

$$a_1x_0+b_1y_0+c_1z_0\ldots+k_1t_0-n_1=v_1,$$
$$a_2x_0+b_2y_0+c_2z_0\ldots+k_2t_0-n_2=v_2,$$
$$\cdots\cdots\cdots\cdots\cdots\cdots\cdots\cdots\cdots\cdots$$
$$a_mx_0+b_my_0+c_mz_0\ldots+k_mt_0-n_m=v_m,$$

then $[vv]=v_1^2+v_2^2\ldots+v_m^2$.

Now let ϵ be the mean error of an observation (i.e. of $n_1, n_2, \ldots$ or n_m), $\epsilon_x, \epsilon_y, \ldots$ the mean errors of the values of $x, y, \ldots$ found from the normal equations (i.e. of $x_0, y_0, \ldots$), and $X, Y, \ldots$ the weights of $x_0, y_0, \ldots$

then $\epsilon=\sqrt{\left(\dfrac{[vv]}{m-\mu}\right)}$ and $\epsilon_x=\dfrac{\epsilon}{\sqrt{X}}$, $\epsilon_y=\dfrac{\epsilon}{\sqrt{Y}}$, &c.

The weight X is the reciprocal of the value of x obtained by solving the system of equations

$$[aa]\,x+[ab]\,y+[ac]\,z\,\ldots+[ak]\,t=1,$$
$$[ba]\,x+[bb]\,y+[bc]\,z\,\ldots+[bk]\,t=0,$$
$$\cdots\cdots\cdots\cdots\cdots\cdots\cdots\cdots\cdots\cdots$$
$$[ka]\,x+[kb]\,y+[kc]\,z\,\ldots+[kk]\,t=0,$$

viz. these are the normal equations except that in the x-equation the right-hand member is unity, and in the other equations zero. Similarly Y is the reciprocal of the value of y obtained from a similar system of equations, the right-hand member in the y-equation being unity and in the other equations zero; and so on.

The probable error of any quantity is derived from the mean error by multiplying it by the constant $\cdot 674489\ldots$, this being the value of $f\sqrt{2}$, where f is given by the equation $\int_0^f e^{-t^2} dt = \tfrac{1}{4}\sqrt{\pi}$.

It has been hitherto assumed that all the equations of condition are of the same weight (unity). If the weight of the first equation be p_1, of the second, p_2, &c., then the process is exactly as above, except that the equations of condition are to be taken to be

$$\left.\begin{array}{l} p_1^{\frac{1}{2}} a_1 x + p_1^{\frac{1}{2}} b_1 y \ldots + p_1^{\frac{1}{2}} k_1 t = p_1^{\frac{1}{2}} n_1 \\ p_2^{\frac{1}{2}} a_2 x + p_2^{\frac{1}{2}} b_2 y \ldots + p_2^{\frac{1}{2}} k_1 t = p_2^{\frac{1}{2}} n_2 \\ \ldots\ldots\ldots\ldots\ldots\ldots\ldots\ldots\ldots\ldots\ldots\ldots\ldots \\ p_m^{\frac{1}{2}} a_m x + p_m^{\frac{1}{2}} b_m y \ldots p_m^{\frac{1}{2}} k_m t = p_m^{\frac{1}{2}} n_m \end{array}\right\} \ldots\ldots\ldots (3).$$

The square roots disappear from the normal equations, as for example the coefficient of y in the x-equation is $[p^{\frac{1}{2}} a \cdot p^{\frac{1}{2}} b] = [pab]$. We may also obtain the normal equations by differentiating with respect to $x, y, \ldots$ the expression

$$p_1 (a_1 x + b_1 y \ldots + k_1 t - n_1)^2 + p_2 (a_2 x + b_2 y \ldots + k_2 t - n_2)^2 \\ \ldots + p_m (a_m x + b_m y \ldots + k_m t - n_m)^2 \ldots\ldots (4),$$

and the sum of the squares of the residuals by substituting the most probable values of $x, y, z, \ldots t$ in this expression. It may be observed that, although in finding the values of $x, y, z, \ldots t$ we may replace an equation $u = n$ of weight p, by p identical equations[1] each of which is $u = n$, the probable error will not be the same in the two cases, as in the former case the denominator of the value of ϵ is $\sqrt{(m - \mu)}$, and in the latter $\sqrt{(p_1 + p_2 \ldots + p_m - \mu)}$.

If $x, y, z, \ldots t$ are known to be connected by one or more relations which must be exactly satisfied (*e.g.* if x, y, z are the angles of a triangle so that $x + y + z = 360°$), then the most probable values of $x, y, z, \ldots t$ are the values that render (4) a minimum subject to these conditions, and the rest of the process is as above.

It is also to be observed that if ρp stand either for the mean error of p or the probable error of p, then

$$\rho\phi(x_1, x_2, x_3, \ldots) = \sqrt{\left\{\left(\frac{d\phi}{dx_1}\right)^2 (\rho x_1)^2 + \left(\frac{d\phi}{dx_2}\right)^2 (\rho x_2)^2 + \left(\frac{d\phi}{dx_3}\right)^2 (\rho x_3)^2 + \&c.\right\}}.$$

As an example,

$$\rho \frac{x_1 + x_2 \ldots + x_n}{n} = \sqrt{\left(\frac{1}{n^2} + \frac{1}{n^2} \ldots + \frac{1}{n^2}\right)} \rho x_1 = \frac{\rho x_1}{\sqrt{n}}, \text{ if } \rho x_1 = \rho x_2 \ldots = \rho x_n.$$

An observation has a weight p if its mean (or probable) error is equal to the mean (or probable) error of a result derived from the combination of p standard observations, *i.e.* of the arithmetic mean of the p observations. Thus the weight of an observation varies inversely as the square of the mean (or probable) error.

---

[1] We can assume $p_1, p_2, \ldots p_m$ to be integers, as we may multiply the system of equations of condition by any the same arbitrary quantity throughout.

Applying the method to the example in the question, let
$$AB = x, \quad BC = y, \quad CD = z,$$
then the equations of condition multiplied by the square roots of their weights are

$$a^{\frac{1}{2}}x = a^{\frac{1}{2}}a,$$
$$\beta^{\frac{1}{2}}y = \beta^{\frac{1}{2}}b,$$
$$\gamma^{\frac{1}{2}}z = \gamma^{\frac{1}{2}}c,$$
$$\delta^{\frac{1}{2}}x + \delta^{\frac{1}{2}}y = \delta^{\frac{1}{2}}d,$$
$$\epsilon^{\frac{1}{2}}y + \epsilon^{\frac{1}{2}}z = \epsilon^{\frac{1}{2}}e,$$
$$\zeta^{\frac{1}{2}}x + \zeta^{\frac{1}{2}}y + \zeta^{\frac{1}{2}}z = \zeta^{\frac{1}{2}}f.$$

From these, or by differentiating the expression
$$a(x-a)^2 + \beta(y-b)^2 + \gamma(z-c)^2 + \delta(x+y-d)^2 + \epsilon(y+z-e)^2 + \zeta(x+y+z-f)^2,$$
we deduce the normal equations
$$(a + \delta + \zeta)x + (\delta + \zeta)y + \zeta z = aa + \delta d + \zeta f$$
$$(\delta + \zeta)x + (\beta + \delta + \epsilon + \zeta)y + (\epsilon + \zeta)z = \beta b + \delta d + \epsilon e + \zeta f$$
$$\zeta x + (\zeta + \epsilon)y + (\gamma + \epsilon + \zeta)z = \gamma c + \epsilon e + \zeta f,$$

whence, working out the two determinants, we have $x = \dfrac{P}{Q}$, where

$$P = aa(\beta\gamma + \beta\epsilon + \beta\zeta + \gamma\delta + \gamma\epsilon + \gamma\zeta + \delta\epsilon + \delta\zeta) - b\beta(\gamma\delta + \gamma\zeta + \delta\epsilon + \delta\zeta)$$
$$+ c\gamma(\delta\epsilon - \beta\zeta) + d\delta(\beta\gamma + \beta\epsilon + \beta\zeta + \gamma\epsilon)$$
$$- e\epsilon(\beta\zeta + \gamma\delta + \gamma\zeta + \delta\zeta) + f\zeta(\beta\gamma + \beta\epsilon + \gamma\epsilon + \delta\epsilon),$$
$$Q = a\beta\gamma + a\beta\epsilon + a\beta\zeta + a\gamma\delta + a\gamma\epsilon + a\gamma\zeta + a\delta\epsilon + a\delta\zeta$$
$$+ \beta\gamma\delta + \beta\gamma\zeta + \beta\delta\epsilon + \beta\delta\zeta + \beta\epsilon\zeta + \gamma\delta\epsilon + \gamma\epsilon\zeta + \delta\epsilon\zeta.$$

When $a = \beta = \gamma = \delta = \epsilon = \zeta$, the factor $a^{\frac{1}{2}}$, which is common to all the equations of condition, may be thrown out, and the normal equations are
$$3x + 2y + z = a + d + f,$$
$$2x + 4y + 2z = b + d + e + f,$$
$$x + 2y + 3z = c + e + f,$$

whence
$$x = \tfrac{1}{4}(2a - b + d - e + f),$$
$$y = \tfrac{1}{4}(-a + 2b - c + d + e),$$
$$z = \tfrac{1}{4}(-b + 2c - d + e + f).$$

Therefore
$$x - a = \tfrac{1}{4}(-2a - b + d - e + f),$$
$$y - b = \tfrac{1}{4}(-a - 2b - c + d + e),$$
$$z - c = \tfrac{1}{4}(-b - 2c - d + e + f),$$
$$x + y - d = \tfrac{1}{4}(a + b - c - 2d + f),$$
$$y + z - e = \tfrac{1}{4}(-a + b + c - 2e + f),$$
$$x + y + z - f = \tfrac{1}{4}(a + c + d + e - 2f),$$

and adding the squares of these six expressions we find
$$[vv] = \tfrac{1}{2}(a^2+b^2+c^2+d^2+e^2+f^2 + ab - ad + ae - af + bc - bd$$
$$- be + cd - ce - cf - df - ef)$$
$$= \tfrac{1}{2} Q \text{ say.}$$

The equations giving x', the reciprocal of X the weight of x, are
$$\left.\begin{array}{r}3x' + 2y + z = 1\\ 2x' + 4y + 2z = 0\\ x' + 2y + 3z = 0\end{array}\right\} \quad \ldots\ldots\ldots\ldots\ldots\ldots\ldots\ldots (5),$$
from which $X = 2$, and therefore the mean error of x
$$= \surd(\tfrac{1}{2}) \cdot \sqrt{\left(\frac{Q}{2(6-3)}\right)} = \tfrac{1}{2}\surd(\tfrac{1}{3}Q).$$
and the probable error is found by multiplying this quantity by ·674489... viz. it = ·674489... $\tfrac{1}{2} \surd(\tfrac{1}{3}Q)$.

Whenever we have, as in the above example, the most probable values of $x, y, \ldots$ given in terms of letters representing the results of the observations, it is unnecessary to write down and solve the systems of equations such as (5) in order to obtain the weights of $x, y, \ldots$ for we can write down at once the probable error of x in terms of the probable errors of the observed quantities by means of the formula for
$$\rho f(x_1, x_2, x_3, \ldots x_3, \ldots).$$
Thus in the present case we have, from the value of x,
$$\rho x = \surd\{\tfrac{1}{16}(4+1+1+1+1)\} \rho a = \surd(\tfrac{1}{2}) \rho a,$$
and therefore probable error of x
$$= \cdot 674489 \ldots \surd(\tfrac{1}{2}) \cdot \sqrt{\left(\frac{Q}{2(6-3)}\right)}$$
as before.

The method of least squares (including under this term all the processes described above) is due to Gauss, and has retained the form and in all essential respects the notation in which it was enunciated by him. Gauss's description of the method is given in the *Theoria Motus*, §§ 182—186 (*Werke*, Vol. VII. pp. 237—241), the *Theoria Combinationis Observationum* and the *Supplementum* to it (*Werke*, Vol. IV.), and the *Disquisitio de Elementis Ellipticis Palladis* (Comm. Soc. Gott., Vol. I. 1801—1811) in which his characteristic notation and algorithm first appeared. The most complete and systematic account of the mode of solution of equations by means of the method was published by Encke in the *Berliner Astronomisches Jahrbuch* for 1835. An abridgement of Encke's paper is given in Chauvenet's *Astronomy*, Vol. II. pp. 469—558, and to this work the reader is referred for further information upon the subject. In the present account the notation employed in these works has been very closely adhered to, the chief difference being that the signs of $n_1, n_2, \ldots n_m$ are changed so that the equations are written $a_1 x \ldots + k_1 t = n_1$, &c., instead of $a_1 x \ldots + k_1 t + n_1 = 0$, &c. For practical applications of the method the reader is referred to Merriman's *Elements of the Method of Least Squares*. It may be observed that it is usual to employ probable errors and not mean errors in the statement of results. The probable error conveys a definite idea to the mind, viz. it is the quantity such that it is an even chance that the error falls short of or exceeds it; also, there is a risk of confusion between the mean error and the mean of the errors (see Chauvenet, pp. 490, 491).

The method of least squares presupposes that the law of facility of error is $\frac{h}{\sqrt{\pi}} e^{-h^2 x^2}$, viz. that the probability of an error lying between x and $x + dx$ is $\frac{h}{\sqrt{\pi}} e^{-h^2 x^2} dx$. Thus the law of error is assumed to be always of this form, but h is a disposable constant which is larger the better the observations. The parameter h is called the measure of precision, and might be used in place of the mean or probable error to express the degree of excellence of the observations, results, &c.: the connexion between these quantities is mean error $= \frac{1}{h\sqrt{2}}$, probable error $= \frac{f}{h}$, (f being as above). If we suppose a standard observation to be one for which the law of facility is $\frac{h}{\sqrt{\pi}} e^{-h^2 x^2}$, then an observation of weight p is one for which the law is $\frac{h\sqrt{p}}{\sqrt{\pi}} e^{-ph^2 x^2}$. Gauss does not prove that the law of facility is of the form $\frac{h}{\sqrt{\pi}} e^{-h^2 x^2}$; his reasoning seems to have been of the following kind. We know that if we have n direct and presumably equally good observations of any quantity, we obtain a very good result and one that has been generally adopted, by taking the arithmetic mean of these quantities as the most probable value of the quantity observed, and it is required to extend this principle so as to obtain corresponding values of $x, y, \ldots$ when given by a system of linear equations such as (1). To effect this extension, assume that the arithmetic mean is really the most probable value of the quantity observed in the case of one unknown, and determine the law of facility which this implies; this law is found to be $\frac{h}{\sqrt{\pi}} e^{-h^2 x^2}$. Assuming now this to be the law of facility, determine the most probable values of $x, y \ldots$ from the system (1): this gives the method of least squares, which may thus be considered the generalisation of the method of the arithmetic mean. The analysis by which the extension is made is very simple. Let $x_1, x_2, \ldots x_n$ be n observed values of a certain quantity; we assume that the most probable value of the quantity is $(x_1 + x_2 \ldots + x_n) \div n$. Let a be the true value of the quantity, then $x_1 - a, x_2 - a, \ldots x_n - a$ are the errors, and if $\phi(x)$ be the law of facility the *à priori* probability of these errors is proportional to $\phi(x_1 - a) \phi(x_2 - a) \ldots \phi(x_n - a)$; whence it follows that, after the observations have been made, the probability that a was the true value is proportional to this same expression; which, therefore, in order to find the most probable value of a, must be made a maximum. Differentiating with regard to a we have

$$\frac{\phi'(x_1-a)}{\phi(x_1-a)} + \frac{\phi'(x_2-a)}{\phi(x_2-a)} \ldots + \frac{\phi'(x_n-a)}{\phi(x_n-a)} = 0,$$

or, say, $\psi(x_1-a) + \psi(x_2-a) \ldots + \psi(x_n-a) = 0$, which by hypothesis is to be satisfied by $a = (x_1 + x_2 \ldots + x_n) \div n$ for all integer values of n. Putting $x_2 = x_3 = \ldots = x_n = x_1 - na$ we have $a = x_1 - (n-1)a$, and therefore $\psi\{(n-1)a\} + (n-1)\psi(-a) = 0$, viz.

$$\frac{\psi\{(n-1)a\}}{(n-1)a} = \frac{\psi(-a)}{-a} \text{ for all values of } a;$$

therefore $\psi(x) \div x$ is constant and $\phi(x) = Ae^{\pm mx^2}$. Clearly m must be negative, $= -2h^2$ say, and since the integral of $\phi(x)\,dx$ between the limits $-\infty$ and ∞ is unity (for the error must lie between $-\infty$ and ∞), we find $A = h \div \sqrt{\pi}$, and thus obtain Gauss's function.

Assuming this to be the law of facility of the observed quantities $n_1, n_2, \ldots$ in the system of equations (1), we see that the most probable values of $x, y, \ldots$ are those which render

$$e^{-h^2(a_1x \ldots + k_1t - n_1)^2 - h^2(a_2x \ldots + k_2t - n_2)^2 \ldots - h^2(a_mx \ldots + k_mt - n_m)^2},$$

a maximum, that is which render

$$(a_1x \ldots + k_1t - n_1)^2 + (a_2x \ldots + k_2t - n_2)^2 \ldots + (a_mx \ldots + k_mt - n_m)^2$$

a minimum.

Various ineffectual attempts have been made to prove the 'principle of the arithmetic mean' without reference to how the errors are supposed to arise, and the principle has even been regarded as an axiom. If the principle of the arithmetic mean could be proved, it would be proved at the same time that the values of $x, y \ldots$ given by the method of least squares are really the most probable values.

It follows from Laplace's analysis in the *Théorie des Probabilités*, that if an actual error be supposed to be made up by the addition of a great number n of small errors $\epsilon_1, \epsilon_2, \ldots \epsilon_n$, then whatever be the laws of facility of $\epsilon_1, \epsilon_2 \ldots$ (viz. if the law of ϵ_1 be $\phi_1(x)$, of ϵ_2 be $\phi_2(x)$, &c.) the law of facility of $\epsilon_1 = \epsilon_1 + \epsilon_2 \ldots + \epsilon_n$, will be of Gauss's form if n be very great. The analytical statement of this is that the value of the integral $\iiint \ldots \phi_1(\epsilon_1)\phi_2(\epsilon_2) \ldots \phi_n(\epsilon_n)\,d\epsilon_1\,d\epsilon_2 \ldots d\epsilon_n$ subject to the condition that $\mu_1\epsilon_1 + \mu_2\epsilon_2 \ldots + \mu_n\epsilon_n$ lies between ϵ and $\epsilon + d\epsilon$ is of the form $Ae^{-h^2\epsilon^2}d\epsilon$, when n is very great, viz. this is the limiting form towards which the integral approaches as n is increased, whatever be the functions $\phi_1, \phi_2, \ldots \phi_n$. Considering now the manner in which an actual error is in reality formed, it appears that it is probably due to the combined action of a great many small causes, which may be regarded as independent and each of which produces separately a small error of varying amount; so that we thus have an *à priori* reason why the law of facility should be represented by Gauss's function.

Although Laplace's analysis admits of the application that has been just mentioned, this is not the use that he makes of it himself. In order to solve the system of equations (1), Laplace multiplies them by $\mu_1, \mu_2 \ldots \mu_m$ and adds them; his object being to find the values of $\mu_1, \mu_2 \ldots \mu_m$ which give the most advantageous values for $x, y, \ldots$ the laws of facilities of $n_1, n_2, \ldots$ being unknown functions $\phi_1(x), \phi_2(x), \ldots$. When m the number of the equations is very great, we obtain the method of least squares; but it is to be observed that it is assumed that the equations are to be combined linearly. It is readily seen that the analytical investigation is almost identical whether we combine linearly a number of observations $n_1, n_2, \ldots$ subject to arbitrary laws of facility, or regard the error in each observation as having arisen from the addition of a number of smaller errors. Laplace's investigation is very condensed and difficult; and the reader who wishes to study it will derive great assistance from Leslie Ellis's paper *On the method of least squares* in Vol. VIII. of the *Transactions of the Cambridge Philosophical Society* (reprinted in his *Writings*, pp. 12—37) and Todhunter's *History of the Theory of Probability* (1865), Chapter XX. pp. 560—588. The article on *Probabilities* in the *Encyclopædia Metropolitana* contains a close reproduction of Laplace's work with comments by De Morgan; and the different investigations of the law of facility are discussed in the *Memoirs of the Royal Astronomical Society*, Vol. XXXIX. pp. 75—124. A very valuable and complete bibliography of the subject is contained in Mr Mansfield Merriman's paper, "A list of writings relating to the method of Least Squares, with historical and critical notes" (*Transactions of the Connecticut Academy*, Vol. IV. 1877).

iv. Prove that, along a geodesic line on an ellipsoid, pd is constant, p being the perpendicular on the tangent plane, and d the semi-diameter, parallel to the tangent line to the geodesic.

Prove that, if λ, μ be the elliptic co-ordinates of any point on the surface of the ellipsoid $\dfrac{x^2}{a^2}+\dfrac{y^2}{b^2}+\dfrac{z^2}{c^2}=1$, the geodesic line for which $pd = \dfrac{abc}{f}$ is represented by the equation

$$\frac{\lambda (d\lambda)^2}{(a^2+\lambda)(b^2+\lambda)(c^2+\lambda)(f^2+\lambda)} = \frac{\mu (d\mu)^2}{(a^2+\mu)(b^2+\mu)(c^2+\mu)(f^2+\mu)}.$$

If x, y, z, be the co-ordinates of a point on the geodesic line, X, Y, Z those of an extremity of a parallel diameter, whose length is $2R$, we have

$$\frac{dx}{X} = \frac{dy}{Y} = \frac{dz}{Z} = \frac{ds}{R},$$

$$R^2 \left\{ \frac{1}{a^2}\left(\frac{dx}{ds}\right)^2 + \frac{1}{b^2}\left(\frac{dy}{ds}\right)^2 + \frac{1}{c^2}\left(\frac{dz}{ds}\right)^2 \right\} = 1.$$

And, since
$$\frac{x^2}{a^2}+\frac{y^2}{b^2}+\frac{z^2}{c^2}=1,$$

$$\frac{x^2}{a^2+\lambda}+\frac{y^2}{b^2+\lambda}+\frac{z^2}{c^2+\lambda}=1,$$

$$\frac{x^2}{a^2+\mu}+\frac{y^2}{b^2+\mu}+\frac{z^2}{c^2+\mu}=1,$$

we obtain
$$x^2=\frac{a^2(a^2+\lambda)(a^2+\mu)}{(a^2-b^2)(a^2-c^2)},$$

whence
$$\frac{dx}{x}=\tfrac{1}{2}\left(\frac{d\lambda}{a^2+\lambda}+\frac{d\mu}{b^2+\mu}\right);$$

therefore $dx^2 = \tfrac{1}{4}\dfrac{a^2}{(a^2-b^2)(a^2-c^2)}(a^2+\lambda)(a^2+\mu)\left(\dfrac{d\lambda}{a^2+\lambda}+\dfrac{d\mu}{a^2+\mu}\right)^2;$

therefore
$$\left(\frac{dx}{a}\right)^2+\left(\frac{dy}{b}\right)^2+\left(\frac{dz}{c}\right)^2$$

$$=\tfrac{1}{4}\frac{(c^2-b^2)(a^2+\lambda)(a^2+\mu)\left(\dfrac{d\lambda}{a^2+\lambda}+\dfrac{d\mu}{a^2+\mu}\right)^2+\ldots}{(b^2-c^2)(c^2-a^2)(a^2-b^2)}$$

$$=\tfrac{1}{4}\frac{\left\{(c^2-b^2)\dfrac{a^2+\mu}{a^2+\lambda}+(a^2-c^2)\dfrac{b^2+\mu}{b^2+\lambda}+(b^2-a^2)\dfrac{c^2+\mu}{c^2+\lambda}\right\}d\lambda^2+\ldots}{(b^2-c^2)(c^2-a^2)(a^2-b^2)}.$$

Now $(c^2-b^2)\dfrac{a^2+\mu}{a^2+\lambda}+(a^2-c^2)\dfrac{b^2+\mu}{b^2+\lambda}+(b^2-c^2)\dfrac{c^2+\mu}{c^2+\lambda}$

$$=(\mu-\lambda)\left(\frac{c^2-b^2}{a^2+\lambda}+\frac{a^2-c^2}{b^2+\lambda}+\frac{b^2-c^2}{c^2+\lambda}\right)$$

$$=(\mu-\lambda)\frac{(b^2-c^2)(c^2-a^2)(a^2-b^2)}{(a^2+\lambda)(b^2+\lambda)(c^2+\lambda)}.$$

Hence
$$\left(\frac{dx}{a}\right)^2+\left(\frac{dy}{b}\right)^2+\left(\frac{dz}{c}\right)^2$$

$$=\tfrac{1}{4}(\mu-\lambda)\left\{\frac{d\lambda^2}{(a^2+\lambda)(b^2+\lambda)(c^2+\lambda)}-\frac{d\mu^2}{(a^2+\mu)(b^2+\mu)(c^2+\mu)}\right\}.$$

Also $dx^2+dy^2+dz^2$

$$\tfrac{1}{4}\left\{a^2\frac{(c^2-b^2)(a^2+\mu)}{a^2+\lambda}\ldots\right\}\frac{d\lambda^2}{(b^2-c^2)(c^2-a^2)(a^2-b^2)}-\ldots$$

$$=\tfrac{1}{4}\left\{\frac{a^2(c^2-b^2)}{a^2+\lambda}+\frac{b^2(a^2-c^2)}{b^2+\lambda}+\frac{c^2(a^2-b^2)}{c^2+\lambda}\right\}(\mu-\lambda)\frac{d\lambda^2}{(b^2-c^2)(c^2-a^2)(a^2-b^2)}-\ldots$$

$$=\tfrac{1}{4}\frac{a^2(c^4-b^4)+b^2(a^4-c^4)+c^2(b^4-a^4)}{(b^2-c^2)(c^2-a^2)(a^2-b^2)}\lambda\frac{(\mu-\lambda)d\lambda^2}{(a^2+\lambda)(b^2+\lambda)(c^2+\lambda)}$$

$$=\tfrac{1}{4}\frac{(\lambda-\mu)(\lambda\cdot d\lambda^2-\mu\cdot d\mu^2)}{(a^2+\lambda)(b^2+\lambda)(c^2+\lambda)}.$$

Hence since
$$R^2 = \frac{dx^2 + dy^2 + dz^2}{\left(\dfrac{dx}{a}\right)^2 + \left(\dfrac{dy}{b}\right)^2 + \left(\dfrac{dz}{c}\right)^2},$$
we obtain
$$R^2 = -\frac{\dfrac{\lambda d\lambda^2}{(a^2+\lambda)(b^2+\lambda)(c^2+\lambda)} - \dfrac{\mu d\mu^2}{(a^2+\mu)(b^2+\mu)(c^2+\mu)}}{\dfrac{d\lambda^2}{(a^2+\lambda)(b^2+\lambda)(c^2+\lambda)} - \dfrac{d\mu^2}{(a^2+\mu)(b^2+\mu)(c^2+\mu)}}.$$

Also $p^2 = \dfrac{a^2 b^2 c^2}{\lambda \mu}$.

And, along a geodesic, $pR = \dfrac{abc}{f}$, hence

$$\frac{a^2 b^2 c^2}{\lambda\mu}\left\{\frac{\lambda\, d\lambda^2}{(a^2+\lambda)(b^2+\lambda)(c^2+\lambda)} - \frac{\mu\, d\mu^2}{(a^2+\mu)(b^2+\mu)(c^2+\mu)}\right\}$$
$$+ \frac{a^2 b^2 c^2}{f^2}\left\{\frac{d\lambda^2}{(a^2+\lambda)(b^2+\lambda)(c^2+\lambda)} - \frac{d\mu^2}{(a^2+\mu)(b^2+\mu)(c^2+\mu)}\right\} = 0,$$

or $\dfrac{d\lambda^2}{(a^2+\lambda)(b^2+\lambda)(c^2+\lambda)}\left(\dfrac{1}{\mu}+\dfrac{1}{f^2}\right) - \dfrac{d\mu^2}{(a^2+\mu)(b^2+\mu)(c^2+\mu)}\left(\dfrac{1}{\lambda}+\dfrac{1}{f^2}\right) = 0;$

therefore
$$\frac{\lambda\, d\lambda^2}{(a^2+\lambda)(b^2+\lambda)(c^2+\lambda)(f^2+\lambda)} - \frac{\mu\, d\mu^2}{(a^2+\mu)(b^2+\mu)(c^2+\mu)(f^2+\mu)} = 0.$$

5. Integrate:
$$\frac{d^2 u}{d\theta^2} + u = A\cos(\theta - \varpi),$$
and explain why, in the lunar theory, Clairaut substituted $c\theta$ for θ.

If QQ' be a small arc of an orbit described under a central force P tending to O and a perpendicular force T, and if $Q'N$ be drawn parallel to OQ and intersecting the tangent at Q, at N, and NR be the perpendicular on OQ produced, then in the limiting position.
$$\frac{Q'N}{RN^2} = \frac{P + T\tan\chi}{2u^2\left(h^2 + 2\int\dfrac{T}{u^3}\,d\theta\right)},$$
χ being the angle between OQ and the normal at Q.

If $s = \gamma \sin(v - \theta)$ satisfies the differential equation
$$\frac{d^2 s}{dv^2} + s = \gamma \sin(v - \theta),$$
in which γ and θ are functions of v, and $\dfrac{d\theta}{dv} = 1 - \dfrac{c}{\gamma^2}$, c being a constant, obtain the most general value of γ.

(i) Let QQ' (fig. 62) be described in time t, and let S be the position which the body would have occupied at the end of the time t, if the velocity and direction of motion had remained the same as at Q during the time t. Draw SV parallel to RN. Then $\angle QNR = \chi$ and

$$Q'N = Q'V + SV \tan \chi,$$

also
$$P = 2\frac{Q'V}{t^2}, \quad T = 2\frac{SV}{t^2};$$

therefore
$$\frac{Q'N}{RN^2} = \tfrac{1}{2}(P + T \tan \chi)\frac{t^2}{RN^2} \dots\dots\dots\dots\dots\dots(1).$$

Also
$$\frac{RN^2}{t^2} = \frac{H^2}{r^2} \text{ where } H^2 = h^2 + 2\int \frac{T}{u^2} d\theta \dots\dots\dots\dots\dots(2)$$

and the result follows at once from (1) and (2).

(ii) $\dfrac{ds}{dv} = \dfrac{d\gamma}{dv}\sin(v-\theta) + \gamma\cos(v-\theta)\left(1 - \dfrac{d\theta}{dv}\right) = \dfrac{d\gamma}{dv}\sin(v-\theta) + \dfrac{c}{\gamma}\cos(v-\theta),$

$\dfrac{d^2s}{dv^2} = \dfrac{d^2\gamma}{dv^2}\sin(v-\theta) + \dfrac{d\gamma}{dv}\cos(v-\theta) \cdot \dfrac{c}{\gamma^2} - \dfrac{c}{\gamma^2}\dfrac{d\gamma}{dv}\cos(v-\theta) - \dfrac{c}{\gamma}\sin(v-\theta) \cdot \dfrac{c}{\gamma^2} = 0;$

therefore $\dfrac{d^2\gamma}{dv^2} - \dfrac{c^2}{\gamma^3} = 0$, whence $v = a\sqrt{(\gamma^2 - a^2c^2)} + b$, a and b being arbitrary constants; and therefore $\gamma^2 = a^2c^2 + \left(\dfrac{v-b}{a}\right)^2$.

[On the conditions in order that $s = \gamma \sin(v - \theta)$ should be a solution of the differential equation

$$\frac{d^2s}{dv^2} + s + P\gamma \sin(v - \theta) = 0,$$

P and γ being functions of v, see Plana, *Théorie du mouvement de la lune*, t. I. pp. 230 et seq.]

6. Prove the equation

$$\frac{da}{dt} = \frac{2na^2}{\mu}\frac{dR}{de}.$$

If l be the mean anomaly, v the true anomaly, g the angular distance of the perihelion from the ascending node, h the longitude of the ascending node in the fixed plane of reference,

$$L = (\mu a)^{\frac{1}{2}}, \quad G = \{\mu a(1 - e^2)\}^{\frac{1}{2}}, \quad H = \{\mu a(1 - e^2)\}^{\frac{1}{2}}\cos i,$$

the other letters having their usual meanings, and if R denote the ordinary disturbing function + the term $\dfrac{\mu^2}{2L^2}$, prove that x, y, z, the co-ordinates of the planet, referred to the fixed plane as the plane of xy and to the line from which the longitudes are measured as the axis of x, are given by the equations

$$Gx = Gr \cos(v+g) \cos h - Hr \sin(v+g) \sin h,$$
$$Gy = Gr \cos(v+g) \sin h + Hr \sin(v+g) \cos h,$$
$$Gz = (G^2 - H^2)^{\frac{1}{2}} r \sin(v+g),$$

and, taking l, g, h, L, G, H, as the six elements, prove that

$$\frac{dL}{dt} = \frac{dR}{dl}, \quad \frac{dG}{dt} = \frac{dR}{dg}, \quad \frac{dH}{dt} = \frac{dR}{dh}.$$

We have $\dfrac{da}{dt} = \dfrac{2na^2}{\mu} \dfrac{dR}{d\epsilon}$, whence $\dfrac{1}{2} \dfrac{\mu^{\frac{1}{2}}}{a^{\frac{1}{2}}} \dfrac{da}{dt} = \dfrac{na^{\frac{3}{2}}}{\mu^{\frac{1}{2}}} \dfrac{dR}{d\epsilon}$.

Now $n^2 a^3 = \mu$, and since ϵ never occurs except through l, in the equation $l = nt + \epsilon$, $\dfrac{dR}{d\epsilon} = \dfrac{dR}{dl}$, and we thus obtain the first equation.

The projection of the radius vector upon the line of nodes is $r \cos(v+g)$, and on a line perpendicular to it in the plane of the orbit, is $r \sin(v+g)$; and projecting these on the axes of x, y, z,

$$x = r \cos(v+g) \cos h - r \sin(v+g) \cos i \sin h,$$
$$y = r \cos(v+g) \sin h + r \sin(v+g) \cos i \cos h,$$
$$z = r \sin(v+g) \sin i,$$

and substituting for i its value in terms of G, H these become the equations in the question.

The quantity H is double the areal velocity projected upon the plane of xy, therefore

$$\frac{dH}{dt} = x \frac{dR}{dy} - y \frac{dR}{dx} = \frac{dR}{dx} \frac{dx}{dh} + \frac{dR}{dy} \frac{dy}{dh} + \frac{dR}{dz} \frac{dz}{dh} = \frac{dR}{dh};$$

for, from the equations in the question for x, y, z, we have

$$\frac{dx}{dh} = -y, \quad \frac{dy}{dh} = x, \quad \frac{dz}{dh} = 0.$$

The quantity G is double the areal velocity, and therefore $\dfrac{dG}{dt} = \dfrac{dR}{dv}$ where R is supposed to be expressed in terms of r, v, G, H, g, h. Now g does not occur except in combination with v in the form $v + g$, so that $\dfrac{dR}{dv} = \dfrac{dR}{dg}$, and this equation is not affected when for r and v in R their values in terms of L, G, l are substituted. We thus obtain the third equation.

[The results in the question are three of Delaunay's equations, the other three being

$$\frac{dl}{dt} = -\frac{dR}{dL}, \quad \frac{dg}{dt} = -\frac{dR}{dG}, \quad \frac{dh}{dt} = -\frac{dR}{dH};$$

the term $\frac{\mu^2}{2L^2}$ is added to R in order that the first of these may hold good. The above proof is that given by Mr G. W. Hill in the *Analyst*, Vol. III. pp. 65—70 (1876), where the other three equations are also obtained in an elementary manner.]

vii. Prove that any function of a single independent variable may be expressed by a series of zonal harmonics.

Prove that the series

$$2P_1 + \Sigma_{i=1}^{i=\infty} (-1)^i (4i+1) \frac{1 \cdot 3 \cdot 5 \ldots (2i-3)}{2 \cdot 4 \cdot 6 \ldots (2i+2)} P_{2i}$$

is equal to $-\mu$ for all values of μ from -1 to 0, and to μ for all values of μ from 0 to 1.

Apply this formula to calculate the potential of a hemisphere, whose density varies as the distance from a diametral plane, at an external or internal point.

Let the required series be

$$C_0 + C_1 P_1 + \ldots + C_n P_n + \ldots$$

Multiply by P_n, and integrate from $\mu = -1$ to $\mu = +1$, then

$$\frac{2C_n}{2n+1} = \int_0^1 \mu P_n d\mu - \int_{-1}^0 \mu P_n d\mu.$$

Now, if n be odd, $\int_{-1}^0 \mu P_n d\mu = \int_0^1 \mu P_n d\mu$; and therefore $C_n = 0$.

But if n be even, $\int_{-1}^0 \mu P_n d\mu = -\int_0^1 \mu P_n d\mu$; hence writing $2i$ for n

$$C_{2i} = (4i+1) \int_0^1 \mu P_{2i} d\mu$$

$$= (4i+1) \int_0^1 \left(\frac{2i+1}{4i+1} P_{2i+1} + \frac{2i+1}{4i+1} P_{2i-1} \right) d\mu$$

$$= (2i+1) \int_0^1 P_{2i+1} d\mu + 2i \int_0^1 P_{2i-1} d\mu.$$

Again, $\frac{d}{d\mu}\left\{ (1-\mu^2) \frac{dP_{2i+1}}{d\mu} \right\} + (2i+1)(2i+2) P_{2i+1} = 0;$

therefore $(2i+1) \int P_{2i+1} d\mu = -\frac{1}{2i+2}(1-\mu^2) \frac{dP_{2i+1}}{d\mu};$

therefore $(2i+1) \int_0^1 P_{2i+1} d\mu = \frac{1}{2i+2} \frac{dP_{2i+1}}{d\mu}\bigg|_{\mu=0}.$

Similarly $2i \int_0^1 P_{2i-1} d\mu = \frac{1}{2i-1} \frac{dP_{2i-1}}{d\mu}\bigg|_{\mu=0}.$

And when $\mu = 0$

$$\frac{dP_{2i+1}}{d\mu} = (-1)^i \frac{3.5 \ldots (2i+1)}{2.4 \ldots 2i},$$

$$\frac{dP_{2i-1}}{d\mu} = (-1)^{i-1} \frac{3.5 \ldots (2i-1)}{2.4 \ldots (2i-2)};$$

therefore
$$C_{2i} = (-1)^i \left\{ \frac{3.5 \ldots (2i+1)}{2.4 \ldots 2i(2i+2)} - \frac{3.5 \ldots (2i-1)}{2.4 \ldots (2i-2)(2i-1)} \right\}$$

$$= (-1)^i \frac{3.5 \ldots (2i-3)}{2.4 \ldots (2i-2)} \left\{ \frac{(2i-1)(2i+1)}{2i(2i+2)} - 1 \right\}$$

$$= (-1)^i \frac{3.5 \ldots (2i-3)}{2.4 \ldots (2i-2)} \frac{(-4i-1)}{2i(2i+2)}$$

$$= (-1)^{i+1} (4i+1) \frac{3.5 \ldots (2i-3)}{2.4 \ldots (2i+2)}.$$

And, if $i = 0$, we have

$$C_0 = 4 \int_0^1 \mu\, d\mu = 2.$$

If $i=1$, $C_2 = 3\int_0^1 P_2\, d\mu + 2\int_0^1 P_1\, d\mu = \frac{5}{8}$.

Hence the required series is

$$2P_0 + \Sigma_{i=1}^{i=\infty} (-1)^{i+1}(4i+1) \frac{3.5 \ldots (2i-3)}{2.4 \ldots (2i+2)} P_{2i}.$$

Hence the potential of such a hemispherical shell (radius a) will be

$$4\pi a \left\{ 2P_0 + \Sigma_{i=1}^{i=\infty} (-1)^{i+1} \frac{3.5 \ldots (2i-3)}{2.4 \ldots (2i+2)} P_{2i} \left(\frac{r}{a}\right)^{2i+1} \ldots \right\}$$

for an internal point, and

$$4\pi a \left\{ 2P_0 \frac{a}{r} + \Sigma_{i=1}^{i=\infty} (-1)^{i+1} \frac{3.5 \ldots (2i-3)}{2.4 \ldots (2i+2)} P_{2i} \left(\frac{a}{r}\right)^{2i+1} \right\}$$

for an external point.

viii. Prove that the potential of an elliptic ring, cut out of a lamina of uniform thickness and density by two consecutive, similar, similarly situated and concentric ellipses, at a point whose co-ordinates, referred to the axes of the ring, are x, y, z is

$$\frac{1}{\pi} M \int_\mu^\infty \frac{d\psi}{\{(\psi-\mu)(\psi-\mu_1)(\psi-\mu_2)\}^{\frac{1}{2}}},$$

M being the mass of the ring, a, b its semiaxes, and μ the positive, μ_1, μ_2, the two negative, roots of the equation

$$\frac{x^2}{a^2+\mu} + \frac{y^2}{b^2+\mu} + \frac{z^2}{\mu} = 1.$$

If the point be situated on the hyperbola

$$y = 0, \quad \frac{x^2}{a^2 - b^2} - \frac{z^2}{b^2} = 1,$$

prove that the potential varies inversely as the mean axis of the ellipsoid, passing through the point, of which the elliptic ring is a focal conic.

The mass of an element of the ring being $M \dfrac{d\theta}{2\pi}$, the potential will be expressed by

$$M \int_0^{2\pi} \frac{d\theta}{\{(x - a\cos\theta)^2 + (y - b\sin\theta)^2 + z^2\}^{\frac{1}{2}}}.$$

We shall now change the co-ordinates, by taking the attracted point as origin, and the axes of the cone, of which the attracted point is the vertex, and the ring a section, as co-ordinate axes.

If ξ, η, ζ be the current co-ordinates of the new system, and if p, p_1, p_2, be the perpendiculars from the centre of the ring on the respective principal planes of the cone, the cosines of the angles between the old and new axes respectively will be expressed by the following scheme.

	x	y	z
ξ	$\dfrac{px}{a^2 + \mu}$	$\dfrac{py}{b^2 + \mu}$	$\dfrac{pz}{\mu}$
η	$\dfrac{p_1 x}{a^2 + \mu_1}$	$\dfrac{p_1 y}{b^2 + \mu_1}$	$\dfrac{p_1 z}{\mu_1}$
ζ	$\dfrac{p_2 x}{a^2 + \mu_2}$	$\dfrac{p_2 y}{b^2 + \mu_2}$	$\dfrac{p_2 z}{\mu_2}$

where

$$\frac{1}{p^2} = \frac{x^2}{(a^2 + \mu)^2} + \frac{y^2}{(b^2 + \mu)^2} + \frac{z^2}{\mu^2},$$

$$\frac{1}{p_1^2} = \frac{x^2}{(a^2 + \mu_1)^2} + \frac{y^2}{(b^2 + \mu_1)^2} + \frac{z^2}{\mu_1^2},$$

$$\frac{1}{p_2^2} = \frac{x^2}{(a^2 + \mu_2)^2} + \frac{y^2}{(b^2 + \mu_2)^2} + \frac{z^2}{\mu_2^2}.$$

Hence, the co-ordinates of the element, referred to the new system of axes, are

$$\xi = p - \frac{pa\cos\theta}{a^2+\mu}x - \frac{pb\sin\theta}{b^2+\mu}y,$$

$$\eta = p_1 - \frac{p_1 a\cos\theta}{a^2+\mu_1}x - \frac{p_1 b\sin\theta}{b^2+\mu_1}y,$$

$$\zeta = p_2 - \frac{p_2 a\cos\theta}{a^2+\mu_2}x - \frac{p_2 b\sin\theta}{b^2+\mu_2}y.$$

We shall next shew that $\dfrac{\xi^2}{\mu} + \dfrac{\eta^2}{\mu_1} + \dfrac{\zeta^2}{\mu_2} = 0$.

For, we have in the first place

$$\frac{p^2}{a^2+\mu} + \frac{p_1^2}{a^2+\mu_1} + \frac{p_2^2}{a^2+\mu_2} = 1,$$

$$\frac{p^2}{b^2+\mu} + \frac{p_1^2}{b^2+\mu_1} + \frac{p_2^2}{b^2+\mu_2} = 1 \dots\dots\dots\dots\dots(A),$$

$$\frac{p^2}{\mu} + \frac{p_1^2}{\mu_1} + \frac{p_2^2}{\mu_2} = 1.$$

Hence, k being any line whatever,

$$\frac{p^2}{k^2+\mu} + \frac{p_1^2}{k^2+\mu_1} + \frac{p_2^2}{k^2+\mu_2} = 1 - \frac{(k^2-a^2)(k^2-b^2)k^2}{(k^2+\mu)(k^2+\mu_1)(k^2+\mu_2)};$$

therefore

$$\frac{p^2}{\mu(k^2+\mu)} + \frac{p_1^2}{\mu_1(k^2+\mu_1)} + \frac{p_2^2}{\mu_2(k^2+\mu_2)} = \frac{(k^2-a^2)(k^2-b^2)}{(k^2+\mu)(k^2+\mu_1)(k^2+\mu_2)};$$

whence, differentiating with respect to k^2, and then putting $k^2 = a^2$, we get

$$\frac{p^2}{\mu(a^2+\mu)^2} + \frac{p_1^2}{\mu_1(a^2+\mu_1)^2} + \frac{p_2^2}{\mu_2(a^2+\mu_2)^2} = -\frac{a^2-b^2}{(a^2+\mu)(a^2+\mu_1)(a^2+\mu_2)}.$$

Now, from the equations,

$$\frac{x^2}{a^2+\mu} + \frac{y^2}{b^2+\mu} + \frac{z^2}{\mu} = 1,$$

$$\frac{x^2}{a^2+\mu_1} + \frac{y^2}{b^2+\mu_1} + \frac{z^2}{\mu_1} = 1,$$

$$\frac{x^2}{a^2+\mu_2} + \frac{y^2}{b^2+\mu_2} + \frac{z^2}{\mu_2} = 1,$$

it follows that, θ being any quantity whatever,

$$(b^2+\theta)\theta x^2 + \theta(a^2+\theta)y^2 + (a^2+\theta)(b^2+\theta)z^2 = (a^2+\theta)(b^2+\theta)\theta - (\theta-\mu)(\theta-\mu_1)(\theta-\mu_2);$$

S.-H. P.

whence, putting $\theta = -a^2$,

$$(a^2 - b^2) a^2 x^2 = (a^2 + \mu)(a^2 + \mu_1)(a^2 + \mu_2);$$

therefore
$$\frac{p^2}{\mu(a^2+\mu)^2} + \frac{p_1^2}{\mu_1(a^2+\mu_1)^2} + \frac{p_2^2}{\mu_2(a^2+\mu_2)^2} = -\frac{1}{a^2 x^2}.$$

Similarly

$$\frac{p^2}{\mu(b^2+\mu)^2} + \frac{p_1^2}{\mu_1(b^2+\mu_1)^2} + \frac{p_2^2}{\mu_2(b^2+\mu_2)^2} = -\frac{1}{b^2 y^2}.$$

Hence, when the expression $\dfrac{\xi^2}{\mu} + \dfrac{\eta^2}{\mu_1} + \dfrac{\zeta^2}{\mu_2}$ is formed, it follows that the coefficients of $\cos^2\theta$ and $\sin^2\theta$ are each equal to -1, and that the term independent of θ is unity. Hence, the sum of these three terms is 0.

Again the coefficient of $\cos\theta \sin\theta$ will be 0, as may be seen by multiplying the equations (A) in order, by $b_1^2 - a_1^2$ and $a^2 - b^2$, and adding.

And the coefficients of $\cos\theta$ and $\sin\theta$ are separately 0.

Hence
$$\frac{\xi^2}{\mu} + \frac{\eta^2}{\mu_1} + \frac{\zeta^2}{\mu_2} = 0.$$

We may therefore write $\eta^2 = -\mu_1 \dfrac{\xi^2}{\mu}\cos^2 T$, $\zeta^2 = -\mu_2 \dfrac{\xi^2}{\mu}\sin^2 T$.

Hence the potential becomes

$$\frac{M}{2\pi}\int_0^{2\pi} \frac{d\theta \sqrt{\mu}}{\xi(\mu - \mu_1 \cos^2 T - \mu_2 \sin^2 T)^{\frac{1}{2}}},$$

where
$$\xi = p - \frac{pa\cos\theta}{a^2+\mu}x - \frac{pb\sin\theta}{b^2+\mu}y.$$

Now, since

$$p\left(1 - \frac{a\cos\theta}{a^2+\mu}x - \frac{b\sin\theta}{b^2+\mu}y\right)\cos T = \left(-\frac{\mu}{\mu_1}\right)^{\frac{1}{2}} p_1\left(1 - \frac{a\cos\theta}{a^2+\mu_1}x - \frac{b\sin\theta}{b^2+\mu_1}y\right)$$

and

$$p\left(1 - \frac{a\cos\theta}{a^2+\mu}x - \frac{b\sin\theta}{b^2+\mu}y\right)\sin T = \left(-\frac{\mu}{\mu_2}\right)^{\frac{1}{2}} p_2\left(1 - \frac{a\cos\theta}{a^2+\mu_2}x - \frac{b\sin\theta}{b^2+\mu_2}y\right),$$

we obtain, differentiating these equations, and squaring and adding,

$$p^2\left(1 - \frac{a\cos\theta}{a^2+\mu}x - \frac{b\sin\theta}{b^2+\mu}y\right)^2 dT^2$$

$$+ p^2\left(\frac{a\sin\theta}{a^2+\mu}x - \frac{b\cos\theta}{b^2+\mu}y\right)^2 d\theta^2$$

$$= -\mu \left\{ \frac{p_1^2}{\mu_1} \left(\frac{a \sin \theta}{a^2 + \mu_1} x - \frac{b \cos \theta}{b^2 + \mu_1} y \right)^2 \right.$$
$$\left. + \frac{p_2^2}{\mu_2} \left(\frac{a \sin \theta}{a^2 + \mu_2} x - \frac{b \cos \theta}{b^2 + \mu_2} y \right)^2 \right\} d\theta^2,$$
$$\frac{p^2}{\mu} \left(1 - \frac{a \cos \theta}{a^2 + \mu} x - \frac{b \sin \theta}{b^2 + \mu} y \right)^2 dT^2$$
$$= - \left\{ \frac{p^2}{\mu} \left(\frac{a \sin \theta}{a^2 + \mu} x - \frac{b \cos \theta}{a^2 + \mu} y \right)^2 \right.$$
$$+ \frac{p_1^2}{\mu_1} \left(\frac{a \sin \theta}{a^2 + \mu_1} x - \frac{b \cos \theta}{b^2 + \mu_1} y \right)^2$$
$$\left. + \frac{p_2^2}{\mu_2} \left(\frac{a \sin \theta}{a^2 + \mu_2} x - \frac{b \cos \theta}{b^2 + \mu_2} y \right)^2 \right\} d\theta^2.$$

On the right-hand side of this equation, it will be seen as before, that the coefficient of $(\sin \theta)^2$ is

$$-\left\{ \frac{p^2}{\mu(a^2+\mu)^2} + \frac{p_1^2}{\mu_1(a^2+\mu_1)^2} + \frac{p_2^2}{\mu_2(a^2+\mu_2)^2} \right\} a^2 x^2 = 1.$$

Similarly, that of $(\cos \theta)^2$ is 1, and that of $\cos \theta \sin \theta$ is 0.

Hence,
$$\frac{p^2}{\mu} \left(1 - \frac{a \cos \theta}{a^2 + \mu} x - \frac{b \sin \theta}{b^2 + \mu} y \right)^2 dT^2 = d\theta^2 ;$$

therefore
$$\frac{d\theta}{p - \frac{pa \cos \theta}{a^2 + \mu} x - \frac{pb \sin \theta}{b^2 + \mu} y} = \frac{dT}{\sqrt{\mu}} ;$$

therefore the potential is $\dfrac{M}{2\pi} \displaystyle\int_0^{2\pi} \dfrac{dT}{(\mu - \mu_1 \cos^2 T - \mu_2 \sin^2 T)^{\frac{1}{2}}}$

$$= \frac{2M}{\pi} \int_0^{\frac{\pi}{2}} \frac{dT}{(\mu - \mu_1 \cos^2 T - \mu_2 \sin^2 T)^{\frac{1}{2}}}.$$

Now, putting $\tan T = \left(\dfrac{\mu - \mu_1}{\psi - \mu} \right)^{\frac{1}{2}},$

the limits of ψ will be μ and ∞; also

$$\cos^2 T = \frac{\psi - \mu}{\psi - \mu_1}, \qquad \sin^2 T = \frac{\mu - \mu_1}{\psi - \mu_1};$$

therefore
$$\mu - \mu_1 \cos^2 T - \mu_2 \sin^2 T = \frac{\mu(\psi - \mu_1) - \mu_1(\psi - \mu) - \mu_2(\mu - \mu_1)}{\psi - \mu_1}$$
$$= \frac{(\mu - \mu_1)(\psi - \mu_2)}{(\psi - \mu_1)},$$

and
$$\sin T \cos T \, dT = -\tfrac{1}{2} \frac{\mu - \mu_1}{(\psi - \mu_1)^2} d\psi;$$
therefore
$$\frac{(\mu - \mu_1)(\psi - \mu)}{(\psi - \mu_1)^2} dT^2 = \tfrac{1}{4} \frac{(\mu - \mu_1)^2}{(\psi - \mu_1)^2} d\psi;$$
therefore
$$dT^2 = \tfrac{1}{4} \frac{\mu - \mu_1}{(\psi - \mu_1)^2} \frac{d\psi}{\psi - \mu};$$
therefore
$$\frac{dT^2}{\mu - \mu_1 \cos^2 T - \mu_2 \sin^2 T} = \tfrac{1}{4} \frac{d\psi}{(\psi - \mu)(\psi - \mu_1)(\psi - \mu_2)}.$$

Hence the potential is reduced to the form
$$\frac{M}{\pi} \int_\mu^\infty \frac{d\psi}{\{(\psi - \mu)(\psi - \mu_1)(\psi - \mu_2)\}^{\frac{1}{2}}}.$$

Now, for any point on the hyperbola
$$y = 0, \quad \frac{x^2}{a^2 - b^2} - \frac{z^2}{b^2} = b,$$
we have
$$\mu_1 = \mu_2 = -b^2.$$

And the potential is
$$\frac{M}{\pi} \int_\mu^\infty \frac{d\psi}{\{(\psi - \mu)(\psi + b^2)^2\}^{\frac{1}{2}}},$$
or, putting $\psi = \mu + v^2$, the potential becomes
$$\frac{2M}{\pi} \int_0^\infty \frac{dv}{v^2 + \mu + b^2}$$
$$= \frac{2M}{\pi} \frac{1}{\sqrt{\mu + b^2}} \cdot \frac{\pi}{2}$$
$$= \frac{M}{\sqrt{\mu + b^2}},$$

i.e. varies inversely as the mean axis of the ellipsoid
$$\frac{x^2}{a^2 + \mu} + \frac{y^2}{b^2 + \mu} + \frac{z^2}{\mu} = 1.$$

If in the result of question viii. we put $\psi - \mu = \chi$, it becomes
$$\frac{1}{\pi} M \int_0^\infty \frac{d\chi}{\{\chi(\chi + \mu - \mu_1)(\chi + \mu - \mu_2)\}^{\frac{1}{2}}}.$$

Now, the potential of an ellipsoidal shell, whose mass is M, whose least semiaxis is 0, and whose other two semiaxes are $\sqrt{\mu - \mu_1}$, $\sqrt{\mu - \mu_2}$, at any point on its surface, is
$$\frac{M}{2} \int_0^\infty \frac{d\chi}{\{\chi(\chi + \mu - \mu_1)(\chi + \mu - \mu_2)\}^{\frac{1}{2}}}.$$

Hence, the potential of the ring mentioned in the question is to the potential of such an ellipsoidal shell in the ratio of 2 to π^1.

In connexion with the subject of this question, Gauss' *Determinatio attractionis* (Gauss, *Werke*, Band III. p. 351) should be referred to.

[Putting
$$\psi = \frac{\mu - \mu_1 \sin^2\phi}{\cos^2\phi},$$
we shall find the potential to be
$$\frac{2MK}{\pi\sqrt{\mu - \mu_2}},$$
where
$$K = \int_0^{\frac{1}{2}\pi} \frac{d\phi}{\sqrt{(1 - k^2 \sin^2\phi)}}, \qquad k^2 = \frac{\mu_1 - \mu_2}{\mu - \mu_2}.$$

At a point on the focal hyperbola, $\mu_1 = \mu_2 = -b^2$; and therefore $k^2 = 0$, $K = \frac{1}{2}\pi$, and the potential is
$$\frac{M}{\sqrt{\mu + b^2}}.]$$

ix. If a cylindrical surface filled with water revolve with angular velocity ω about a fixed line parallel to its generating lines, prove that the component velocities parallel to the axes of x and y respectively of any particle of the water will be $\dfrac{d\psi}{dy}$, $-\dfrac{d\psi}{dx}$, where ψ is a function of x and y, satisfying the equation $\dfrac{d^2\psi}{dx^2} + \dfrac{d^2\psi}{dy^2} = 0$, and whose value at every point of the cylindrical surface is
$$\tfrac{1}{2}\omega(x^2 + y^2),$$
the fixed line being taken as axis of z.

If the cylindrical surface be the sector bounded by the right circular cylinder $r = a$, and the planes $\theta = \alpha$, $\theta = -\alpha$, prove that
$$\psi = \tfrac{1}{2}\omega r^2 \frac{\cos 2\theta}{\cos 2\alpha}$$
$$+ 32\omega^2 a^2 \Sigma_{i=0}^{i=\infty} (-1)^{i+1} \frac{\left(\dfrac{r}{a}\right)^{(2i+1)\frac{\pi}{2\alpha}} \cos(2i+1)\dfrac{\pi\theta}{2\alpha}}{\{(2i+1)\pi - 4\alpha\}\{(2i+1)\pi\}\{(2i+1)\pi + 4\alpha\}}.$$

Adopting polar co-ordinates, we have to find a function ψ which satisfies the equation
$$\left(r\frac{d}{dr}\right)^2 \psi + \frac{d^2\psi}{d\theta^2} = 0,$$

[1] For another solution of this question, see *Quarterly Journal of Mathematics*, Vol. XIV. p. 21 (December, 1875).

and which is equal to $\frac{1}{2}\omega r^2$, when $\theta = \pm a$ and r is less than a, and also when $r = a$, and θ lies between a and $-a$. It also must not become infinite for any value of r less than a.

Now, putting $\psi - \frac{1}{2}\omega r^2 = \chi$, we see that χ must be $= 0$, at every point of the boundary of the sector. Also we shall have

$$\frac{d^2\chi}{dx^2} + \frac{d^2\chi}{dy^2} = -2\omega.$$

Hence if we conceive a sector of uniform density $\dfrac{\omega}{2\pi}$, surrounded by a film of repelling matter which will make the potential at the boundary everywhere zero, the potential of this sector will be the required value of χ.

Now, the density of such a sector is expressed by

$$\frac{4}{\pi} \cdot \frac{\omega}{2\pi}\left\{\cos\frac{\pi}{2}\frac{\theta}{a} - \frac{1}{3}\cos\frac{3\pi}{2}\frac{\theta}{a} + \ldots + (-1)^i\frac{1}{2i+1}\cos\frac{(2i+1)\pi}{2}\frac{\theta}{a} - \ldots\right\},$$

or
$$\frac{2\omega}{\pi^2}\Sigma(-1)^i\frac{1}{2i+1}\cos\frac{(2i+1)\pi}{2}\frac{\theta}{a}.$$

Now, the potential of such a sector as this is

$$-\frac{8\omega}{\pi}r^2\Sigma(-1)^i\frac{\dfrac{1}{2i+1}\cos\dfrac{(2i+1)\pi}{2}\dfrac{\theta}{a}}{4 - \left\{\dfrac{(2i+1)\pi}{2a}\right\}^2}.$$

For this satisfies the equation

$$\frac{1}{r^2}\left\{\left(r\frac{d}{dr}\right)^2\psi + \frac{d^2\psi}{d\theta^2}\right\} = -4\pi \cdot \frac{\omega}{2\pi},$$

and is also $= 0$ when $\theta = \pm a$.

We have now to add a series of terms which shall make this equal to 0 when $r = a$, and shall themselves satisfy the condition

$$\left(r\frac{d}{dr}\right)^2 + \frac{d^2}{d\theta^2} = 0.$$

These will be

$$\frac{8\omega}{\pi}a^2\Sigma(-1)^i\left(\frac{r}{a}\right)^{\frac{(2i+1)\pi}{2a}}\frac{\dfrac{1}{2i+1}\cos\dfrac{(2i+1)\pi}{2}\dfrac{\theta}{a}}{4 - \left\{\dfrac{(2i+1)\pi}{2a}\right\}^2}.$$

Hence, the required value of χ may be expressed as

$$\frac{8\omega}{\pi}\Sigma(-1)^i\left\{a^2\left(\frac{r}{a}\right)^{\frac{2i+1}{2}\frac{\pi}{a}} - r^2\right\}\frac{\dfrac{1}{2i+1}\cos\dfrac{(2i+1)\pi}{2}\dfrac{\theta}{a}}{4 - \left(\dfrac{2i+1}{2}\cdot\dfrac{\pi}{a}\right)},$$

or $32\omega a^2 a^2 \Sigma (-1)^{i+1}$

$$\times \left\{ \left(\frac{r}{a}\right)^{\frac{2i+1}{2}\frac{\pi}{a}} - \left(\frac{r}{a}\right)^2 \right\} \frac{\cos \frac{2i+1}{2} \frac{\pi\theta}{a}}{\{(2i+1)\pi - 4a\}(2i+1)\pi\{(2i+1)\pi + 4a\}},$$

or $32\omega a^2 a^2 \Sigma (-1)^{i+1}$

$$\times \left\{ \left(\frac{r}{a}\right)^{\frac{2i+1}{2}\frac{\pi}{a}} - \left(\frac{r}{a}\right)^2 \right\} \frac{\cos \frac{2i+1}{2} \frac{\pi\theta}{a}}{\{(2i+1)\pi - 4a\}(2i+1)\pi\{(2i+1)\pi + 4a\}} \quad \ldots\ldots(1).$$

The coefficient of $\left(\frac{r}{a}\right)^2$ may be summed. For, putting

$$\Sigma (-1)^i \frac{\cos \frac{2i+1}{2} \frac{\pi\theta}{a}}{\{(2i+1)\pi - 4a\}(2i+1)\pi\{(2i+1)\pi + 4a\}} = u,$$

we get

$$\frac{d^2u}{d\theta^2} + 4u$$

$$= -\Sigma \frac{4 - \left(\frac{2i+1}{2}\frac{\pi}{a}\right)^2}{\{(2i+1)\pi - 4a\}(2i+1)\pi\{(2i+1)\pi + 4a\}} (-1)^i \cos \frac{2i+1}{2}\frac{\pi\theta}{a}$$

$$= -\frac{1}{4a^2} \Sigma (-1)^i \frac{\cos(2i+1)\frac{\pi}{2}\frac{\theta}{a}}{(2i+1)\pi}$$

$$= -\frac{1}{4a^2\pi} \cdot \frac{\pi}{4}, \text{ for values of } \theta \text{ between } -a \text{ and } a,$$

$$= -\frac{1}{16a^2};$$

therefore $\quad u = -\frac{1}{64a^2} + A \cos 2\theta + B \sin 2\theta,$

A and B being arbitrary constants.

Now $B = 0$, since the value of u is unchanged by a change in the sign of θ.

Also $u = 0$ when $\theta = \pm a$;

therefore $\quad 0 = -\frac{1}{64a^2} + A \cos 2a;$

therefore $\quad u = -\frac{1}{64a^2}\left(1 - \frac{\cos 2\theta}{\cos 2a}\right);$

or

$$\chi = 32\omega a^2 a^2 \Sigma (-1)^{i+1} \left(\frac{r}{a}\right)^{\frac{2i+1}{2}\frac{\pi}{a}} \frac{\cos \frac{2i+1}{2}\frac{\pi\theta}{a}}{\{(2i+1)\pi - 4a\}(2i+1)\pi\{(2i+1)\pi + 4a\}}$$

$$- \tfrac{1}{2}\omega r^2 \left(1 - \frac{\cos 2\theta}{\cos 2a}\right).$$

Hence, since $\psi = \chi + \tfrac{1}{2}\omega r^2$,
we obtain

$$\psi = \tfrac{1}{2}\omega r^2 \frac{\cos 2\theta}{\cos 2a}$$

$$+ 32\omega a^2 a^2 \Sigma_{i=0}^{i=\infty} (-1)^{i+1} \frac{\left(\dfrac{r}{a}\right)^{\frac{(2i+1)\pi}{2a}} \cos \dfrac{2i+1}{2}\dfrac{\pi\theta}{a}}{\{(2i+1)\pi - 4a\}(2i+1)\pi\{(2i+1)\pi + 4a\}}.$$

[In a quadrantal sector $a = \tfrac{1}{4}\pi$, and the first two terms in the value of ψ assume the indeterminate form $\infty - \infty$, and must be evaluated, by putting $a = \tfrac{1}{4}\pi - \phi$, expanding on the supposition that ϕ is so small that its square may be neglected, and finally putting $\phi = 0$. Or, we may take the first term of the expression (1) for χ which assumes the form $\dfrac{0}{0}$, and evaluate it as an indeterminate fraction.

It will be found that the remaining terms of the series for ψ can be summed, and we shall find finally that for a quadrantal sector

$$\psi = -\frac{2\omega}{\pi} r^2 \cos 2\theta \log \frac{r}{a} + \frac{2\omega}{\pi} r^2 \sin 2\theta \cdot \theta$$

$$+ \tfrac{1}{4}\frac{\omega a^2}{\pi}\left(\frac{r^2}{a^2} - \frac{a^2}{r^2}\right) \cos 2\theta \log\left(1 + 2\frac{r^4}{a^4}\cos 4\theta + \frac{r^8}{a^8}\right)$$

$$- \tfrac{1}{2}\frac{\omega a^2}{\pi}\left(\frac{r^2}{a^2} + \frac{a^2}{r^2}\right) \sin 2\theta \tan^{-1}\frac{r^4 \sin 4\theta}{a^4 + r^4 \cos 4\theta} + \frac{\omega a^2}{\pi}\tan^{-1}\frac{2a^2 r^2 \cos 2\theta}{a^4 - r^4}.]$$

x. If v_1, v_2 be the velocities of propagation through a biaxal crystal, of the two waves corresponding to a plane front whose direction-cosines are l, m, n, prove that

$$l^2 = \frac{(a^2 - v_1^2)(a^2 - v_2^2)}{(a^2 - b^2)(a^2 - c^2)}, \quad m^2 = \frac{(b^2 - v_1^2)(b^2 - v_2^2)}{(b^2 - c^2)(b^2 - a^2)},$$

$$n^2 = \frac{(c^2 - v_1^2)(c^2 - v_2^2)}{(c^2 - a^2)(c^2 - b^2)}.$$

If a plane be drawn, parallel to the axis of y, intersecting the planes of xy and yz in straight lines, each of which joins two imaginary conical points of the wave-surface, prove that this plane will touch the wave-surface along a circle.

Any one of the four planes, mentioned in the question, meets the wave-surface in a curve of the fourth degree with four double points, which must therefore break up into two curves of the second degree. It remains to consider the nature of the intersection of these curves with the line at infinity in their own plane.

Now any one of these four planes is represented by the equation

$$(a^2 - c^2)^{\frac{1}{2}} b \pm (b^2 - c^2)^{\frac{1}{2}} z \pm (a^2 - b^2)^{\frac{1}{2}} x = 0,$$

and therefore the four planes together are represented by

$$(a^2-c^2)^2 b^4 + (b^2-c^2)^2 z^4 + (a^2-b^2)^2 x^4$$
$$-2(b^2-c^2)(a^2-b^2)z^2x^2 - 2(a^2-b^2)(a^2-c^2)b^2x^2 - 2(a^2-c^2)(b^2-c^2)b^2z^2 = 0\ldots(1).$$

The planes parallel to them through the axis of y are therefore represented by

$$(b^2-c^2)^2 z^4 + (a^2-b^2)^2 x^4 - 2(b^2-c^2)(a^2-b^2) z^2x^2 = 0,$$

or
$$\{(b^2-c^2)z^2 - (a^2-b^2)x^2\}^2 = 0 \ldots\ldots\ldots\ldots\ldots\ldots(2),$$

and these, of course, intersect the plane at infinity in the same lines as those above mentioned. But since the left-hand member of (2) is a square, these four lines become two double lines, and therefore each of the planes (1) meets the wave-surface in a curve which has two double points at infinity.

Therefore the curve of the fourth degree has *six* double points, and must therefore degenerate into a double curve of the second degree, i.e. each of the four planes *touches* the surface, along a curve of the second degree. But this curve meets the wave-surface, at infinity, in the points determined by the equations

$$a^2x^2 + b^2y^2 + c^2z^2 = 0, \quad x^2 + y^2 + z^2 = 0,$$

from the latter of which it appears that the curve is a circle.

THURSDAY, *January* 17, 1878. 1½ to 4.

Mr FERRERS,   Arabic numbers.
Mr NIVEN,   Roman numbers.

1. IF a curve of the fourth degree have three double points, prove that it will have four double tangents, whose points of contact lie on a conic section.

If the curve be represented by the equation

$$(A, B, C, A', B', C' \S yz, zx, xy)^2 = 0,$$

prove that the equation of the conic will be

$$BCx^2 + CAy^2 + ABz^2 - (A'x + B'y + C'z)^2 = 0.$$

Hence deduce the equation of the four double tangents.

Write, for shortness,

$$\Sigma = (A, B, C, A', B', C', \S yz, zx, xy)^2,$$
$$S = BCx^2 + CAy^2 + ABz^2 - (A'x + B'y + C'z)^2,$$
$$\sqrt{BC}x = \xi,\ \sqrt{CA}y = \eta,\ \sqrt{AB}z = \zeta,\ A'x + B'y + C'z = \omega.$$

Then $S^2 - 4ABC\Sigma$
$$= (\xi^2 + \eta^2 + \zeta^2 - \omega^2)^2 - 4\eta^2\zeta^2 - 4\zeta^2\xi^2 - 4\xi^2\eta^2 - 8\xi\eta\zeta\omega.$$

Now this vanishes if $\omega = \xi + \eta + \zeta$, for it then becomes
$$(2\eta\zeta + 2\zeta\xi + 2\xi\eta)^2 - 4(\eta^2\zeta^2 + \zeta^2\xi^2 + \xi^2\eta^2) - 8\xi\eta\zeta(\xi + \eta + \zeta)$$
$$= 8\xi^2\eta\zeta + 8\eta^2\zeta\xi + 8\zeta^2\xi\eta - 8\xi\eta\zeta(\xi + \eta + \zeta) = 0.$$

Hence $\xi + \eta + \zeta - \omega$ is a factor of $S^2 - 4ABC\Sigma$.

And the expression $S^2 - 4ABC\Sigma$ involves ξ, η, ζ, ω, symmetrically.

And the coefficient of ξ^4 is unity.

Hence
$$S^2 - 4ABC\Sigma = -(-\xi + \eta + \zeta + \omega)(\xi - \eta + \zeta + \omega)(\xi + \eta - \zeta + \omega)(\xi + \eta + \zeta - \omega)$$
identically.

Therefore, where any one of the four straight lines
$$-\xi + \eta + \zeta + \omega = 0, \quad \xi - \eta + \zeta + \omega = 0, \quad \xi + \eta - \zeta + \omega = 0, \quad \xi + \eta + \zeta - \omega = 0,$$
meets the quartic $\Sigma = 0$, it also meets the conic $S = 0$. That is, it meets the quartic in two points only, and therefore is a double tangent.

2. Integrate the following differential equations:

(i) $\quad z = px + qy - sxy,$

(ii) $\quad z = \dfrac{pqs}{rt - s^2},$

(iii) $\quad q^2(z - px - qy) + (qs - pt)zx = 0.$

(i) $\quad z = px + qy - sxy.$

Differentiating with respect to x, we get
$$p = p + rx + sy - sy - \frac{ds}{dx}xy,$$
or $\quad 0 = rx - \dfrac{ds}{dx} \cdot xy;$

therefore $\quad y\dfrac{ds}{dx} - r = 0,$ i.e. $y\dfrac{dr}{dy} - r = 0;$

therefore $\quad \dfrac{r}{y} = f''(x),$ or $\dfrac{dp}{dx} = yf''(x);$

therefore $\quad p = yf'(x) + \phi(y).$

Similarly, $\quad q = x\phi'(y) + f(x);$

whence $\quad s = f'(x) + \phi'(y);$

therefore $z = px + qy - sxy$
$= x\{yf'(x) + \phi(y)\} + y\{x\phi'(y) + f(x)\}$
$\qquad - xy\{f'(x) + \phi'(y)\}$
$= x\phi(y) + yf(x).$

(ii) $\qquad z = \dfrac{pqs}{rt - s^2}.$

Putting $\qquad p = X, \quad q = Y, \quad px + qy - z = Z,$
we obtain (see Boole's *Differential Equations*),

$$r = \frac{\dfrac{d^2Z}{dY^2}}{\dfrac{d^2Z}{dX^2}\dfrac{d^2Z}{dY^2} - \left(\dfrac{d^2Z}{dXdY}\right)^2}, \ldots$$

whence the equation is reduced to

$$Z = X\frac{dZ}{dx} + Y\frac{dZ}{dy} - XY\frac{d^2Z}{dXdY},$$

which is of the same form as (i).

(iii) $\qquad q^2(z - px - qy) + (qs - pt)zx = 0.$

Adding and subtracting $yzqt$, this becomes

$$q^2(z - px - qy) + z\{q(xs + yt) - t(px + qy)\} = 0,$$

or $\qquad qz(xs + yt + q) - (px + qy)(q^2 + zt) = 0;$

therefore $\qquad qz\dfrac{d}{dy}(px + qy) - (px + qy)\dfrac{d}{dy}(qz) = 0;$

therefore $\qquad \dfrac{px + qy}{qz} = $ a function of x, $\phi(x)$ suppose;

therefore $\qquad x\dfrac{dz}{dx} + \{y - z\phi(x)\}\dfrac{dz}{dy} = 0,$

or, changing the dependent variable from z to y,

$$x\frac{dy}{dx} - y + z\phi(x) = 0,$$

or $\qquad \dfrac{d}{dx}\left(\dfrac{y}{x}\right) = -\dfrac{z\phi(x)}{x^2};$

therefore $\qquad \dfrac{y}{x} = -z\int\dfrac{\phi(x)}{x^2}dx + f(z);$

therefore writing $\qquad -x\int\dfrac{\phi(x)}{x^2}dx = \psi(x),$

$$y = z\psi(x) + xf(z).$$

iii. State and prove Lagrange's Equations for the motion of a dynamical system.

Shew that the kinetic energy of a system of mutually attracting masses $m_1, m_2, \ldots$ is

$$\tfrac{1}{2} M (u^2 + v^2 + w^2) + \tfrac{1}{2} \cdot \frac{\Sigma m_r m_s V_{rs}^2}{M},$$

where u, v, w are the velocities of the centre of inertia of the system, M its total mass, and V_{rs} is the relative velocity of the particles m_r, m_s.

Thence obtain the general equations for the relative motions of the system.

Let the masses of a system of particles be $m_1, m_2, m_3 \ldots$, and their co-ordinates $x_1, y_1, z_1 \ldots$, the kinetic energy of their motions is

$$\tfrac{1}{2} \Sigma m (\dot{x}^2 + \dot{y}^2 + \dot{z}^2).$$

But, on expansion, it will be seen that

$$(m_1 + m_2 + m_3 + \ldots)(m_1 \dot{x}_1^2 + m_2 \dot{x}_2^2 + \ldots)$$
$$= (m_1 \dot{x}_1 + m_2 \dot{x}_2 + \ldots)^2 + m_1 m_2 (\dot{x}_1 - \dot{x}_2)^2 + m_1 m_3 (\dot{x}_1 - \dot{x}_3)^2 + \ldots$$

If therefore u, v, w, V_{rs} have the values stated in question,

$$M = m_1 + m_2 + m_3 + \ldots,$$
$$Mu = m_1 \dot{x}_1 + m_2 \dot{x}_2 + \ldots,$$
$$V_{12}^2 = (\dot{x}_1 - \dot{x}_2)^2 + (\dot{y}_1 - \dot{y}_2)^2 + (\dot{z}_1 - \dot{z}_2)^2,$$

and the kinetic energy

$$= \tfrac{1}{2} M (u^2 + v^2 + w^2) + \tfrac{1}{2} \cdot \frac{\Sigma m_r m_s V_{rs}^2}{M}.$$

If there be n masses, the $3n$ co-ordinates of the system may be represented by the three co-ordinates of the centre of gravity and $3n - 3$ other generalized co-ordinates $\theta, \phi, \psi \ldots$ expressing the relative motion; the kinetic energy due to the relative motion is that given in the second member of the equation; let us call it T.

The equations of relative motion are then of the form

$$\frac{d}{dt} \cdot \frac{dT_1}{d\dot{\theta}} - \frac{dT_1}{d\theta} = -\frac{dV}{d\theta}.$$

iv. Prove that the vibrations of any dynamical system moving under conservative forces about a configuration of stable equilibrium may be resolved into a system of normal types, whose periods are real.

Investigate the effect on the normal vibrations of introducing (1) small variations in the constants which determine the constitution of the system, and (2) small frictional forces on the particles of the system proportional to their velocities.

If a system primitively free be restricted by constraints to r degrees of freedom, prove that the periods of the constrained system are all intermediate between the greatest and least periods of the free system, and that the sums of the products s together of the squares of the new periods lie between the greatest and least values of similar functions of the original periods, s being any number less than r.

The effect of a small alteration in the constitution of a conservative system has been analysed by Lord Rayleigh (*Theory of Sound*, § 190). To trace the effect of introducing small frictional forces.

Let the generalized co-ordinates of the system be $x_1, x_2,...$, and let the kinetic and potential energies be reduced to the normal forms; that is to say,
$$T = \tfrac{1}{2}(a_1 \dot{x}_1^2 + a_2 \dot{x}_2^2 + ...),$$
$$V = \tfrac{1}{2}(c_1 x_1^2 + c_2 x_2^2 + ...).$$

When the frictional forces which act on the particles of the system are proportional to their velocities, there exists a dissipative function,
$$F = \tfrac{1}{2}(b_{11} \dot{x}_1^2 + b_{22} \dot{x}_2^2 + 2b_{12} \dot{x}_1 \dot{x}_2 + ...).$$

The general equations of motion are of the type
$$\frac{d}{dt} \cdot \frac{dT}{d\dot{x}} + \frac{dF}{d\dot{x}} - \frac{dT}{dx} + \frac{dV}{dx} = 0.$$

For the case of small motions under contemplation, the equations are
$$a_1 \ddot{x}_1 + c_1 x_1 + (b_{11} \dot{x}_1 + b_{12} \dot{x}_2 + ...) = 0,$$
$$a_2 \ddot{x}_2 + c_2 x_2 + (b_{21} \dot{x}_1 + b_{22} \dot{x}_2 + ...) = 0.$$

When the frictional forces are altogether neglected, the motion consists of a series of normal types of which the periods are given by
$$a_1 p_1^2 = c_1, \quad a_2 p_2^2 = c_2, \quad ....$$

Let us consider the effect of friction on the type p_1, and put therefore
$$x_1 = A e^{(p_1 \sqrt{-1} + f_1)t}, \quad x_2 = A_2 e^{(p_1 \sqrt{-1} + f_1)t}, \quad ...$$

Where friction is neglected, $A_2, A_3, ...$ vanish, and therefore $A_2 ... f$ are of the order of the small coefficients (b).

Neglecting, therefore, squares and products of small quantities, we obtain
$$A a_1 \{(p_1 \sqrt{-1} + f_1)^2 + p_1^2\} + p_1 \sqrt{-1} \,(A b_{11} + A_2 b_{12} + ...) = 0$$
$$A_2 a_2 (-p_1^2 + p_2^2) \qquad + p_1 \sqrt{-1} \,.\, A b_{12} \qquad = 0$$
$$A_3 a_3 (-p_1^2 + p_3^2) \qquad + p_1 \sqrt{-1} \,.\, A b_{13} \qquad = 0;$$

from these we obtain

$$f_1 = -\frac{b_{11}}{a_1}, \quad A_2 = A \cdot \frac{p_1}{p_1^2 - p_2^2} \cdot \frac{b_{12}}{a_2}\sqrt{-1}, \text{ &c.}$$

The real system of vibrations which these indicate is

$$x_1 = A \cdot e^{-\frac{b_{11}}{a_1}t}\cos p_1 t, \quad x_2 = A \cdot \frac{p_1}{p_2^2 - p_1^2}\frac{b_{12}}{a_2}e^{-\frac{b_{11}}{a_1}t}\sin p_1 t, \text{ &c.}$$

Each normal vibration, therefore, gradually dies away, and is accompanied with other normal vibrations which are each a quarter of a phase in advance or rear of it, according as $p_2 >$ or $< p_1$.

To investigate the motions of a constrained conservative system, let $y_1, y_2, \ldots y_m$ be the new types in which the system can vibrate; then we must put

$$x_1 = A_1 y_1 + B_1 y_2 + \ldots$$
$$x_2 = A_2 y_1 + B_2 y_2 + \ldots$$

where A_1, B_1 are new constants.

The kinetic energy

$$T = \tfrac{1}{2}\{a_{11}\dot{y}_1^2 + 2a_{12}\dot{y}_1\dot{y}_2 + \ldots\},$$

and the potential energy

$$V = \tfrac{1}{2}\{\beta_{11} y_1^2 + 2\beta_{12} y_1 y_2 + \ldots\},$$

where

$$a_{11} = a_1 A_1^2 + a_2 A_2^2 + a_3 A_3^2 \ldots, \quad a_{12} = a_1 A_1 B_1 + a_2 A_2 B_2 + \ldots$$
$$\beta_{11} = c_1 A_1^2 + c_2 A_2^2 + c_3 A_3^2 \ldots, \quad \beta_{12} = c_1 A_1 B_1 + c_2 A_2 B_2 + \ldots.$$

The equations of motion are

$$a_{11}\ddot{y}_1 + a_{12}\ddot{y}_2 + \ldots + \beta_{11}y_1 + \beta_{12}y_2 + \ldots = 0,$$
$$a_{12}\ddot{y}_1 + a_{22}\ddot{y}_2 + \ldots + \beta_{12}y_1 + \beta_{22}y_2 + \ldots = 0,$$
$$\text{&c.} \qquad\qquad = 0.$$

To solve these, put

$$y_1 = Y_1^{\circ}\cos pt, \quad y_2 = Y_2^{\circ}\cos pt, \ldots$$

On substituting, and eliminating $Y_1^{\circ}, \ldots$, we obtain for p the following determinant, wherein $a_{11}, \beta_{11} \ldots$ are replaced by their proper values,

$$\begin{vmatrix} (-a_1 p^2 + c_1)A_1^2 + (-a_2 p^2 + c_2)A_2^2 + \ldots, & (-a_1 p^2 + c_1)A_1 B_1 + (-a_2 p^2 + c_2)A_2 B_2 + \ldots, & \text{&c.} \\ (-a_1 p^2 + c_1)A_1 B_1 + (-a_2 p^2 + c_2)A_2 B_2 + \ldots, & (-a_1 p^2 + c_1)B_1^2 + (-a_2 p^2 + c_2)B_2^2 + \ldots, & \text{&c.} \\ \text{&c.} & \text{&c.} & \text{&c.} \end{vmatrix}$$
$$= 0 \ldots\ldots\ldots\ldots(\text{I}).$$

This determinant may be split up by columns, and it will be observed that any one of the new determinants found by taking two corresponding parts out of any two of the columns must vanish. To see the law of decomposition let us take the 1st part of the 1st column, the 2nd part of the 2nd, and so on; and let us introduce the original periods for (c) by means of the equations $c_1 = a_1 p_1^2, \ldots$. The partial determinant required is

$$a_1 a_2 a_3 \ldots a_r (p_1^2 - p^2)(p_2^2 - p^2) \ldots (p_r^2 - p^2) \begin{vmatrix} A_1, & A_2 \ldots A_r \\ B_1, & B_2 \ldots B_r \\ \vdots & \vdots & \vdots \end{vmatrix} A_1 B_2 \ldots K_r.$$

But each constituent of the determinant Δ consists of n terms, and the determinant itself has r rows; and it is evident that the result of the decomposition is the following equation:

$$\Sigma \{a_1 a_2 \ldots a_r (p^2 - p_1^2)(p^2 - p_2^2) \ldots \times (A_1, B_2, \ldots K_r)^2 = 0 \ldots \ldots \ldots (\text{II}).$$

In this result $(A_1, B_2, \ldots K_r)$ represents the determinant on Sylvester's umbral notation, and the summation denoted by Σ is extended over combinations r together of the n symbols $1, 2, 3 \ldots n$.

From this form of the equation in p, it is obvious that no value of p can be greater than the greatest of the original periods $p_1 p_2 \ldots$ or less than the least of them, it being remembered that $a_1, a_2 \ldots$ are essentially positive.

Let the roots of the above equation be $\varpi_1^2, \varpi_2^2 \ldots$, and let $(\varpi^2)_s$ denote the sum of the products s together of these quantities, $(p^2)_{s,i}$ the sum of the products s together of the squares of any i of the original periods

$$(\varpi^2)_s = \frac{e_1 (p^2)_{s,1} + e_2 (p^2)_{s,2} + \ldots}{e_1 + e_2 + \ldots}$$

$e_1, e_2, \ldots$ being the coefficients of the equation for p in its form (II). As $e_1, e_2, \ldots$ are all positive, it follows from a known theorem in Algebra that $(\varpi^2)_s$ is intermediate between the greatest and least of the series

$$(p^2)_{s,1}, (p^2)_{s,2} \ldots$$

5. Assuming the following equations for the determination of the motion of the Earth about its centre of gravity, as affected by the action of the Sun,

$$A \frac{d}{dt}\left(\frac{d\psi}{dt} \sin \theta\right) - C n \frac{d\theta}{dt} = -3n'^2 (C-A) \cos n't \sin n't \sin \theta,$$

$$A \frac{d^2\theta}{dt^2} + C n \frac{d\psi}{dt} \sin \theta = -3n'^2 (C-A) \sin^2 n't \sin \theta \cos \theta,$$

prove that the pole of the earth, in consequence of solar nutation, describes an ellipse with an acceleration tending to its centre, the absolute acceleration being $4n'^2$, and the semi-axes being

$$\frac{3n'}{4n} \frac{C-A}{C} \sin \theta, \text{ and } \frac{3n'}{4n} \frac{C-A}{C} \cos \theta, \text{ respectively.}$$

vi. Investigate the conditions necessary that

$$\int_{x_0}^{x_1} \phi\left(x, y, \frac{dy}{dx}, \frac{d^2y}{dx^2} \ldots\right) dx$$

may be a maximum or minimum, discussing the conditions which may be imposed at the limits.

Uniform elastic wire is held bent by proper forces between two points A and B so that, the area between the wire and AB being given, the work expended in bending the wire may be the least possible. Shew that the curvature at any point varies as $r^2 - a^2$, where $AB = 2a$, and r is the distance of the point from the middle point of AB. Shew also that, if the wire be bent completely round to satisfy the same conditions, the form of the wire will be given by $r^3 = c^3 \cos 3\theta$.

The work W done in bending the wire will be

$$\tfrac{1}{2} \int a^2 \frac{1}{\rho^2} ds,$$

where ρ is the radius of curvature and

$$\frac{1}{\rho^2} = \left(\frac{d^2x}{ds^2}\right)^2 + \left(\frac{d^2y}{ds^2}\right)^2.$$

The area A enclosed between the curve and AB

$$= \int y\, dx = \int y \frac{dx}{ds}\, ds.$$

We have, therefore, according to Ohm's rule, to put

$$\delta W - \lambda \delta A = 0 \ldots\ldots\ldots\ldots\ldots\ldots\ldots (I).$$

Now

$$\delta W = a^2 \int \left(\frac{d^2x}{ds^2} \cdot \frac{d^2\delta x}{ds^2} + \frac{d^2y}{ds^2} \cdot \frac{d^2\delta y}{ds^2}\right) ds$$

$$= a^2 \left(\frac{d^2x}{ds^2} \cdot \delta \frac{dx}{ds} + \frac{d^2y}{ds^2} \delta \frac{dy}{ds}\right) - a^2 \int \left(\frac{d^3x}{ds^3} \frac{d\delta x}{ds} + \frac{d^3y}{ds^3} \frac{d\delta y}{ds}\right) ds;$$

and

$$\left(\frac{dx}{ds}\right)^2 + \left(\frac{dy}{ds}\right)^2 = 1;$$

therefore

$$\frac{dx}{ds} \frac{d\delta x}{ds} + \frac{dy}{ds} \frac{d\delta y}{ds} = 0.$$

The second term of the value of δW may therefore be put in the form

$$-a^2 \int \left(\frac{d^3y}{ds^3} - \frac{\frac{dy}{ds}}{\frac{dx}{ds}} \frac{d^3x}{ds^3}\right) \frac{d\delta y}{ds}\, ds$$

$$= -a^2\left(\frac{d^3y}{ds^3} - \frac{\frac{dy}{ds}}{\frac{dx}{ds}}\frac{d^3x}{ds^3}\right)\delta y + a^2\int\frac{d}{ds}\left(\frac{d^3y}{ds^3} - \frac{\frac{dy}{ds}}{\frac{dx}{ds}}\frac{d^3x}{ds^3}\right)\delta y\, ds.$$

$$\delta A = \int\frac{dx}{ds}\delta y\, ds + \int y\delta\frac{dx}{ds}\, ds$$

$$= \int\frac{dx}{ds}\delta y\, ds - y\frac{\frac{dy}{ds}}{\frac{dx}{ds}}\delta y + \int\frac{d}{ds}\left[y\frac{\frac{dy}{ds}}{\frac{dx}{ds}}\right]ds\,.\,\delta y.$$

Substituting in equation (I), and equating to zero the parts under the sign of integration,

$$a^2\frac{d}{ds}\left[\frac{\frac{dx}{ds}\cdot\frac{d^3y}{ds^3} - \frac{dy}{ds}\cdot\frac{d^3x}{ds^3}}{\frac{dx}{ds}}\right] - \lambda\frac{dx}{ds} - \lambda\frac{d}{ds}\left[y\frac{\frac{dy}{ds}}{\frac{dx}{ds}}\right] = 0.$$

Integrating and multiplying up by $\frac{dx}{ds}$,

$$\frac{dx}{ds}\frac{d^3y}{ds^3} - \frac{dy}{ds}\frac{d^3x}{ds^3} - \lambda\left(x\frac{dx}{ds} + y\frac{dy}{ds}\right) = c\frac{dx}{ds}.$$

Integrating again,

$$\frac{dx}{ds}\cdot\frac{d^2y}{ds^2} - \frac{dy}{ds}\frac{d^2x}{ds^2} - \tfrac{1}{2}\lambda(x^2 + y^2) = cx + c',$$

or
$$\frac{1}{\rho} - \frac{\lambda}{2}(x^2 + y^2) = cx + c'\ldots\ldots\ldots\ldots\ldots\ldots(II).$$

Let us return now to equation I; the terms outside the sign of integration are of the form

$$a^2\left(\frac{d^2x}{ds^2}\cdot\delta\frac{dx}{ds} + \frac{d^2y}{ds^2}\cdot\delta\frac{dy}{ds}\right)_A^B - (Q\delta y)_A^B,$$

where Q is the coefficient of δy, and the integration is taken between A and B.

This may also be written

$$a^2\cdot\left(\frac{1}{\rho}\,\delta\theta\right)_A^B - (Q\delta y)_A^B,$$

where θ is the angle which the tangent at any point makes with the axis of x.

Now $\delta y = 0$ at both limits, and $\delta\theta$ is perfectly arbitrary; therefore, at both limits, $\frac{1}{\rho} = 0$.

S.-H. P.

Let us introduce these conditions in equation II, and suppose $AB = 2a$, the origin being at A;

$$0 = c'$$

$$-\frac{\lambda}{2} 4a^2 = 2ca; \text{ therefore } c = -\lambda a.$$

Hence $\quad \dfrac{1}{\rho} = \tfrac{1}{2}\lambda\{(x-a)^2 + y^2 - a^2\} = \tfrac{1}{2}\lambda(r^2 - a^2)$,

as in the problem.

When $a = 0$, the wire is bent completely round, and we may put for $\dfrac{1}{\rho}$ its value $\dfrac{dp}{rdr}$,

therefore $\qquad \dfrac{dp}{dr} = \tfrac{1}{2}\lambda r^3$,

hence $\qquad p = \tfrac{1}{8}\lambda r^4$,

no constant being necessary because, when $r = 0$, $p = 0$.

Put $\tfrac{1}{8}\lambda = \dfrac{1}{c^3}$, and remember that

$$\frac{1}{p^2} = \frac{1}{r^2} + \frac{1}{r^4}\left(\frac{dr}{d\theta}\right)^2,$$

we thus find

$$\left(\frac{dr}{d\theta}\right)^2 = \frac{c^6}{r^4} - r^2,$$

$$3\theta = \int \frac{3r^2 dr}{\sqrt{(c^6 - r^6)}} = \sin^{-1}\left(\frac{r^3}{c^3}\right) + \text{const.}$$

and this may be put into the form

$$r^3 = c^3 \cos 3\theta.$$

vii. Determine the permanent temperature in a uniform plane plate which extends to infinity in one direction and is bounded by three straight edges two of which are parallel and at right angles to the third, the parallel edges being kept at temperature 0 and the remaining edge at temperature 1.

A plate extends to infinity in two directions and is bounded by two straight edges which meet at right angles in A. Both edges are at temperature 0 except a portion AB of one edge which is kept at temperature 1, prove that the temperature at any point P of the plate is given by

$$\frac{2}{\pi} \tan^{-1} \frac{a_2 b_2}{a_1 b_1}, \text{ and by } \frac{1}{\pi}(\angle APB - \angle APC),$$

where a_1, b_1 are the axes of the ellipse, and a_2, b_2 those of the hyperbola which can be drawn through the point having A as centre and B as focus, and where C lies in BA produced so that

$$AC = AB.$$

Fourier, in his *Théorie de la Chaleur* (p. 208), has given an expression for the permanent temperature at any point of a rectangular table infinite in length in one direction (that of x), of which the two parallel edges are kept at temperature 0, and the third edge at temperature 1.

If $2a$ be the distance between the two parallel edges, and one of the angles be taken as the origin, the temperature is

$$v = \frac{2}{\pi} \tan^{-1} \frac{2 \sin \frac{2\pi y}{a}}{e^{\frac{2\pi x}{a}} - e^{-\frac{2\pi x}{a}}}.$$

Let the edges of the plate be AX and AY, and let the confocal system be drawn of which B is one focus and A the centre (fig. 63). Let a, β be the thermometric parameters of any point in the plane.

Then the semi-axes of the ellipse and hyperbola which pass through any point are, respectively,

$$c \cosh a, \ c \sinh a; \ \text{and} \ c \cos \beta, \ c \sin \beta.$$

The temperature satisfies the equation

$$\frac{d^2 V}{da^2} + \frac{d^2 V}{d\beta^2} = 0,$$

and also the following conditions,

along AB $a = 0$, $V = 1$; at the infinite boundary $a = \infty$, $V = 0$;

along BX, $\beta = 0$ and $V = 0$; along AY, $\beta = \frac{\pi}{2}$ and $V = 0$.

The problem is therefore, analytically, the same as that of Fourier.

Therefore $\quad V = \frac{2}{\pi} \tan^{-1} \left(\frac{\cos \beta \sin \beta}{\cosh a \sinh a} \right) = \frac{2}{\pi} \tan^{-1} \left(\frac{a_2 b_2}{a_1 b_1} \right).$

The second form of the result may be thus derived.

Let XA be produced indefinitely to X', and take $AC = AB$, and suppose AC kept at temperature -1.

Then the expression,

$$V = \frac{1}{\pi} (\angle APB - \angle APC),$$

expresses the temperature in the infinite plate bounded by the edge XX'; for (1), the angle APB, being $= \angle PBX - \angle PAX$, satisfies the equation $\frac{d^2 V}{dx^2} + \frac{d^2 V}{dy^2} = 0$; (2) within AB, $\angle APB = \pi$ and $\angle APC = 0$, and therefore $V = 1$, (3) the temperature in AC is similarly $= -1$, and (4) in BX and CX', $V = 0$.

The above expression for V therefore expresses the temperature in the plate, and since $V = 0$ for all points in AY, the expression represents the temperature at any point of the plate bounded by AX and AY.

It is easy to prove, geometrically, that the two expressions are equivalent.

8. If V, α, β be three functions of x and y which satisfy the equations

$$\frac{d^2V}{dx^2} + \frac{d^2V}{dy^2} = 0, \quad \frac{d^2\alpha}{dx^2} + \frac{d^2\alpha}{dy^2} = 0, \quad \frac{d^2\beta}{dx^2} + \frac{d^2\beta}{dy^2} = 0,$$

and if

$$\frac{d\alpha}{dx}\frac{d\beta}{dx} + \frac{d\alpha}{dy}\frac{d\beta}{dy} = 0, \quad \left(\frac{d\alpha}{dx}\right)^2 + \left(\frac{d\alpha}{dy}\right)^2 = \left(\frac{d\beta}{dx}\right)^2 + \left(\frac{d\beta}{dy}\right)^2,$$

prove that

$$\frac{d^2V}{d\alpha^2} + \frac{d^2V}{d\beta^2} = 0.$$

A plane area is bounded by a semi-ellipse and its axis major. The elliptic boundary is maintained at the uniform temperature unity, and the axis major at the uniform temperature 0. Prove that the temperature at any point within the area is

$$\frac{4}{\pi} \left(\frac{\sinh \phi}{\sinh \lambda} \sin \theta + \frac{1}{3} \frac{\sinh 3\phi}{\sinh 3\lambda} \sin 3\theta + \ldots \right),$$

where $c \cosh \phi$, $c \sinh \phi$; $c \cos \theta$, $c \sin \theta$, are respectively the semi-axes of the ellipse and hyperbola passing through the given point, and confocal with the elliptic boundary, and λ is the value of ϕ at that boundary.

We have first to shew that ϕ and θ satisfy the equations

$$\frac{d^2\phi}{dx^2} + \frac{d^2\phi}{dy^2} = 0, \quad \frac{d^2\theta}{dx^2} + \frac{d^2\theta}{dy^2} = 0.$$

Now, $x = c \cosh \phi \cos \theta$, $y = c \sinh \phi \sin \theta$,

therefore $x + \sqrt{-1}\, y = \frac{c}{2} (\epsilon^\phi \epsilon^{\sqrt{-1}\theta} + \epsilon^{-\phi} \epsilon^{-\sqrt{-1}\theta})$,

$$= c \cosh (\phi + \sqrt{-1}\, \theta).$$

Similarly $x - \sqrt{-1}\, y = c \cosh (\phi - \sqrt{-1}\, \theta);$

therefore $\phi = \frac{1}{2} \left\{ (\cosh)^{-1} \frac{x + \sqrt{-1}\, y}{c} + (\cosh)^{-1} \frac{x - \sqrt{-1}\, y}{c} \right\};$

and therefore satisfies the condition $\dfrac{d^2\phi}{dx^2} + \dfrac{d^2\phi}{dy^2} = 0$;

similarly $\theta = \dfrac{1}{2\sqrt{-1}}\left\{(\cosh)^{-1}\dfrac{x+\sqrt{-1}\,y}{c} - (\cosh)^{-1}\dfrac{x-\sqrt{-1}\,y}{c}\right\}$,

and therefore also satisfies this condition

$$\dfrac{d^2\theta}{dx^2} + \dfrac{d^2\theta}{dy^2} = 0.$$

Now, if V be the temperature at any point, we require that

$$\dfrac{d^2 V}{d\theta^2} + \dfrac{d^2 V}{d\phi^2} = 0 \quad\dotfill\quad (1),$$

also V must be equal to 1 throughout the elliptic boundary and $= 0$ throughout the axis major.

Now, consider the series

$$\dfrac{4}{\pi}\left(\dfrac{\sinh\phi}{\sinh\lambda}\sin\theta + \dfrac{1}{3}\dfrac{\sinh 3\phi}{\sinh 3\lambda}\sin 3\theta + \dots\right).$$

This evidently satisfies the condition (1) for every term separately does so.

Also, throughout the elliptic boundary, $\phi = \lambda$, and the above expression therefore becomes

$$\dfrac{4}{\pi}(\sin\theta + \tfrac{1}{3}\sin 3\theta + \tfrac{1}{5}\sin 5\theta + \dots),$$

which is equal to unity.

With regard to the axis major, we must consider separately the portion included between the foci, and the two portions between the respective foci and vertices.

For the former of these, $\phi = 0$, and therefore every term of the above expression vanishes separately.

For the latter, $\theta = 0$, or $\theta = \pi$, and therefore also every term vanishes separately.

Hence, all the boundary conditions are satisfied.

[The series for the temperature expressed by elliptic functions is

$$\dfrac{2}{\pi}\tan^{-1}\left\{k\operatorname{sn}\left(\dfrac{2K}{\pi}\theta, k\right)\operatorname{tn}\left(\dfrac{K'}{\lambda}\phi, k'\right)\right\},$$

where $\dfrac{K}{K'} = \dfrac{\pi}{2\lambda}.$

It can be readily verified that this expression satisfies all the required conditions.

The expression for the temperature is also the expression for the current function of electricity flowing in the semi-elliptic area, the electrodes being at the vertices of the major axis of the ellipse, and the strength of the current being unity.]

ix. A mass of fluid of variable density revolves uniformly round an axis under the influence of its own attractive forces; assuming the layers of equal density to be surfaces of revolution, investigate the equation which determines their form.

What external phenomena, due to the earth's attraction, are independent of its internal constitution?

If the earth consisted of a nearly spherical mass of fluid of density σ, and mean radius b, surrounded by a mass of fluid of density ρ, and mean thickness $a-b$, shew that, on the equilibrium theory, the tides of the two fluids, due to a distant body situated in the equator, would have constantly the same ratio at two places in the same radius, and that that ratio is

$$c(5s + 2 + 3c^3) : 5s + 5c^3, \text{ where } s = \frac{\rho}{\sigma - \rho}, \text{ and } c = \frac{b}{a}.$$

Let the axis of z coincide with the axis of rotation, and the axis of x pass through the moon, whose distance suppose to be D, and mass M.

Let $\quad x^2 + y^2 + z^2 = r^2$, and $\lambda = \frac{x}{r}$, $\mu = \frac{z}{r}$; and let

$$S_2 = \tfrac{1}{3} - \mu^2, \quad S_2' = \tfrac{1}{3} - \lambda^2.$$

These are the two spherical harmonics upon which the forms of the outer surface of the earth and its fluid core will depend.

For the potential at any point due to rotation

$$= \frac{\omega^2}{2}(x^2 + y^2) = \frac{\omega^2 r^2}{2}(\tfrac{2}{3} + S_2),$$

and the potential due to the moon is

$$\frac{M}{\sqrt{(D-x)^2 + y^2 + z^2}} = \frac{M}{D}\left(1 + \frac{x}{D} - \frac{3r^2}{2D^2} \cdot S_2' + \ldots\right).$$

The first two terms of the latter expression will not affect the form of the earth, but merely the position of its centre of gravity; we shall, therefore, neglect them, and consider only the third term $-\frac{3Mr^2}{2D^3} S_2'$.

Let the form of the outer surface be given by $r = a(1 + Y_2)$,
and that of the fluid by $r = b(1 + Z_2)$, $\quad \ldots(1)$,

Y_2 and Z_2 being two surface harmonics of the second degree.

If we put $\delta = \sigma - \rho$, we may consider the attraction of the earth as due to two solid masses of densities ρ, δ.

The potential at any point of the outer surface consists of two parts V_1, V_2, due to the outer and inner spheroids

$$V_1 = \frac{4\pi a^2 \rho}{3r} + \frac{4\pi a^3}{5r^3} Y_2, \quad V_2 = \frac{4\pi b^3 \delta}{3r} + \frac{4\pi b^5}{3r^3} Z_2.$$

Putting, in the first terms,
$$r^{-1} = a^{-1}(1 - Y_2),$$
we find for the potential at the outer surface,
$$V = \frac{4\pi}{3a}(a^3\rho + b^3\delta)(1 - Y_2) + \frac{4\pi}{5a^2}(a^5\rho Y_2 + b^5\delta Z_2)$$
$$= \text{const.} + 4\pi a^2 (AZ_2 - BY_2),$$
where
$$A = \frac{b^5\delta}{5a^2}, \quad B = \frac{2a^3\rho + 5b^3\delta}{15} \quad \ldots\ldots\ldots\ldots\ldots (2).$$

The equation of equilibrium of the outer surface is
$$4\pi a^2 (AZ_2 - BY_2) + \frac{\omega^2 a^2}{2} S_2 - \frac{3Ma^2}{2D^3} S_2' = 0,$$
or
$$AZ_2 - BY_2 + \frac{\omega^2}{8\pi} S_2 - \frac{3M}{8\pi D^3} S_2' = 0 \ldots\ldots\ldots\ldots\ldots (3).$$

The potential at the inner surface will also consist of two parts V_1 and V_2, where
$$V_1 = \text{const.} - \tfrac{2}{3}\pi\rho r^2 + \tfrac{4}{5}\pi\rho r a\, Y_2,$$
$$V_2 = \frac{4\pi b^3 \delta}{3r} + \frac{4\pi b^5 \delta}{5r^3} \cdot Z_2.$$

Putting now $r = b(1 + Z_2)$, we obtain for the complete potential at the inner surface
$$V = \text{const.} + 4\pi b^2 (B'Y_2 - A'Z_2),$$
where
$$A' = \tfrac{1}{15}(2\delta + 5\rho), \quad B' = \tfrac{1}{5}\rho,$$
and the equation of equilibrium of the inner surface is
$$B'Y_2 - A'Z_2 + \frac{\omega^2}{8\pi} S_2 - \frac{3M}{8\pi D^3} \cdot S_2' = 0 \ldots\ldots\ldots\ldots (4).$$

If we solve (3) and (4), we see that Y_2 and Z_2 are each the sum of multiples of S_2 and S_2'. The former of these terms express the forms of the surfaces when the moon's action is altogether neglected: the latter give the tidal effect of that action.

Considering only these, we find the parts of Y_2 and Z_2 due to them to be given by
$$(AB' - A'B) Y_2' = \frac{3M}{8\pi D^3}(B + B'),$$
$$(AB' - A'B) Z_2' = \frac{3M}{8\pi D^3}(A + A').$$

It is clear, from these results, that the two tides have constantly the same ratio at points in the same radius, and that that ratio is

$$b(A + A') : a(B + B').$$

Now $\quad A + A' = \frac{1}{15}\left\{5\rho + \delta\left(2 + 3\frac{b^5}{a^5}\right)\right\},$

and $\quad B + B' = \frac{1}{15}\left(5\rho + 5\delta \cdot \frac{b^3}{a^3}\right).$

If, therefore, $\quad c = \dfrac{b}{a}$, and $s = \dfrac{\rho}{\delta} = \dfrac{\rho}{\sigma - \rho},$

the ratio becomes $\quad c(5s + 2 + 3c^5) : 5s + 5c^2.$

FRIDAY, *January* 18, 1878.   9 to 12.

Mr FERRERS,   Arabic numbers.
Mr GREENHILL,   Roman numbers.
Mr NIVEN,   Greek numbers.

1. ENUNCIATE Sturm's Theorem.

Prove that, if α, β, γ... be the roots of the given equation, the successive functions are of the form

$$\Sigma (\alpha - \beta)^2 \frac{f(x)}{(x - \alpha)(x - \beta)} \ldots,$$

$$\Sigma (\alpha - \beta)^2 (\alpha - \gamma)^2 (\beta - \gamma)^2 \frac{f(x)}{(x - \alpha)(x - \beta)(x - \gamma)} \ldots,$$

each with a constant multiplier.

(See Salmon's *Modern Higher Algebra*, Arts. 47 and 48, p. 45.)

ii. Define the elliptic functions sn x, cn x, and dn x, and solve completely the differential equations

(i) $\dfrac{d^2u}{dt^2} + n^2u + \alpha u^2 = 0$;   (ii) $\dfrac{d^2u}{dt^2} + n^2u + \beta u^3 = 0.$

Prove that, if a uniform chain fixed at two points rotate in relative equilibrium with constant angular velocity about an axis in the same plane with the line joining the two points, the form of the curve assumed by the chain will be given by

$$y = b \operatorname{sn} K \frac{x}{a},$$

the axis of rotation being the axis of x.

If
$$x = \int_0^\phi \frac{d\phi}{\sqrt{(1-k^2\sin^2\phi)}},$$

then ϕ is called the amplitude of x, the modulus being k, and is denoted by $\operatorname{am}(x, k)$, and $\sin \phi$ is the sine of the amplitude of x and is denoted by $\operatorname{sn} x$; $\cos \phi$ is denoted by $\operatorname{cn} x$, and $\sqrt{(1-k^2\sin^2\phi)}$ by $\operatorname{dn} x$.

Consequently if $y = \operatorname{sn} x$, then
$$x = \int_0^y \frac{dy}{\sqrt{\{(1-y^2)(1-k^2 y^2)\}}};$$

if $y = \operatorname{cn} x$, then
$$x = \int_y^1 \frac{dy}{\sqrt{\{(1-y^2)(1-k^2+k^2 y^2)\}}};$$

and if $y = \operatorname{dn} x$, then
$$x = \int_y^1 \frac{k^2 dy}{\sqrt{\{(1-y^2)(y^2-1+k^2)\}}}.$$

(i) If
$$\frac{d^2 u}{dt^2} + n^2 u + au^2 = 0,$$

multiplying by $\frac{du}{dt}$ and integrating,
$$\tfrac{1}{2}\left(\frac{du}{dt}\right)^2 + \tfrac{1}{2} n^2 u^2 + \tfrac{1}{3} au^3 = C,$$

or
$$\tfrac{1}{2}\left(\frac{du}{dt}\right)^2 = C - \tfrac{1}{2} n^2 u^2 - \tfrac{1}{3} au^3.$$

I. If C is negative or greater than $\dfrac{n^6}{6a^2}$, the right-hand side has only one real linear factor, and we must put
$$\tfrac{1}{2}\left(\frac{du}{dt}\right)^2 = \tfrac{1}{3} a(a-u)\{(u-m)^2 + n'^2\},$$

where a is greater than $\dfrac{n^2}{2a}$ if C is greater than $\dfrac{n^6}{6a^2}$, and is less than $-\dfrac{3n^2}{2a}$ if C is negative.

We must now put
$$a - u = b\,\frac{1-\cos\phi}{1+\cos\phi},$$

and therefore
$$(u-m)^2 + n'^2 = \left(a - m - b\,\frac{1-\cos\phi}{1+\cos\phi}\right)^2 + n'^2$$
$$= (a-m)^2 + n'^2 - 2b(a-m)\frac{1-\cos\phi}{1+\cos\phi} + b^2\left(\frac{1-\cos\phi}{1+\cos\phi}\right)^2$$
$$= 4b^2\,\frac{1-k^2\sin^2\phi}{(1+\cos\phi)^2},$$

if $\quad b^2 = (a-m)^2 + n^2, \quad k^2 = \tfrac{1}{2}\left(1 + \dfrac{a-m}{b}\right).$

Also $\quad \dfrac{du}{d\phi} = -\dfrac{2b\sin\phi}{(1+\cos\phi)^2};$

therefore $\left(\dfrac{d\phi}{dt}\right)^2 = \tfrac{2}{3}ab(1 - k^2\sin^2\phi),$

and therefore $\phi = \operatorname{am}\left\{\dfrac{K}{T}(t-\tau), k\right\},$ where $\dfrac{K^2}{T^2} = \tfrac{2}{3}ab:$

and therefore $\quad u = a - b\,\dfrac{1 - \operatorname{cn}\dfrac{K}{T}(t-\tau)}{1 + \operatorname{cn}\dfrac{K}{T}(t-\tau)}.$

II. If C lies between 0 and $\dfrac{n^2}{6a^2}$, the right-hand side of the equation will break up into three real linear factors, and we must put

$$\tfrac{1}{2}\left(\dfrac{du}{dt}\right)^2 = \tfrac{1}{3}a(u+a)(u+b)(c-u),$$

and the limits of u are therefore either $-\infty$ and $-a$, or $-b$ and c.

First suppose u to lie between $-\infty$ and $-a$; we must put

and then
$$u + a = -(a-b)\tan^2\phi,$$
$$u + b = -(a-b)\sec^2\phi,$$

$$c - u = (a+c)\dfrac{1 - k^2\sin^2\phi}{\cos^2\phi}, \quad k^2 = \dfrac{b+c}{a+c}.$$

Also $\quad \dfrac{du}{d\phi} = -2(a-b)\dfrac{\sin\phi}{\cos^3\phi};$

therefore $\left(\dfrac{d\phi}{dt}\right)^2 = \tfrac{1}{6}a(a+c)(1 - k^2\sin^2\phi),$

and therefore $\phi = \operatorname{am}\left\{\dfrac{K}{T}(t-\tau), k\right\},$ where $\dfrac{K^2}{T^2} = \tfrac{1}{6}a(a+c);$

therefore $\quad u = -a - (a-b)\operatorname{tn}^2\dfrac{K}{T}(t-\tau).$

Secondly, suppose u to lie between $-b$ and c; we must put
$$u = c\cos^2\phi - b\sin^2\phi, \text{ and then } u + a = (a+c)(1 - k^2\sin^2\phi);$$
$$u + b = (b+c)\cos^2\phi, \quad c - u = (b+c)\sin^2\phi;$$

where $\quad k^2 = \dfrac{a+b}{a+c},$

and then
$$\left(\frac{d\phi}{dt}\right)^2 = \tfrac{1}{6}a(a+c)(1-k^2\sin^2\phi),$$

and therefore $\phi = \operatorname{am}\left\{\dfrac{K}{T}(t-\tau),\, k\right\}$, where $\dfrac{K^2}{T^2} = \tfrac{1}{6}a(a+c)$:

and therefore
$$u = c\,\operatorname{cn}^2\frac{K}{T}(t-\tau) - b\,\operatorname{sn}^2\frac{K}{T}(t-\tau).$$

(ii) If
$$\frac{d^2u}{dt^2} + n^2u + \beta u^3 = 0,$$

multiplying by $\dfrac{du}{dt}$ and integrating,
$$\tfrac{1}{2}\left(\frac{du}{dt}\right)^2 + \tfrac{1}{2}n^2u^2 + \tfrac{1}{4}\beta u^4 = C,$$

or
$$\left(\frac{du}{dt}\right)^2 = 2C - n^2u^2 - \tfrac{1}{2}\beta u^4.$$

C must therefore be positive, and the right-hand side of the equation will split up into two factors, so that we may put
$$\left(\frac{du}{dt}\right)^2 = \tfrac{1}{2}\beta(a^2 - u^2)(u^2 + b^2),$$

and therefore
$$u = a\,\operatorname{cn}\frac{K}{T}(t-\tau),$$

where
$$k^2 = \frac{a^2}{a^2+b^2},\qquad \frac{K^2}{T^2} = \tfrac{1}{2}\beta(a^2+b^2).$$

[The approximate solution of these differential equations when u is small is considered in Lord Rayleigh's *Sound*, § 67.]

Suppose the chain to be revolving with angular velocity ω, and let m be the mass per unit of length of the chain, t the tension at any point.

Then the equations of relative equilibrium are
$$\frac{d}{ds}\left(t\frac{dx}{ds}\right) = 0,\qquad \frac{d}{ds}\left(t\frac{dy}{dt}\right) = -m\omega^2 y.$$

Therefore $t\dfrac{dx}{ds} = T$, a constant, and
$$\frac{d}{ds}\left(\frac{dy}{dx}\right) = -\frac{m\omega^2}{T}y,\quad \text{or}\quad \frac{d^2s}{dx^2} = -\frac{m\omega^2}{T}y\frac{dy}{dx}.$$

Therefore, integrating,
$$\frac{ds}{dx} = 1 + \frac{m\omega^2}{2T}(b^2 - y^2),\quad \text{since } \frac{ds}{dx} = 1,\text{ when } y = b.$$

Therefore $\left(\dfrac{dy}{dx}\right)^2 = \dfrac{m\omega^2}{T}(b^2-y^2)\left\{1+\dfrac{m\omega^2}{4T}(b^2-y^2)\right\}$,

and therefore $y = b\,\mathrm{sn}\,K\dfrac{x}{a}$,

where $k^2 = \dfrac{m\omega^2 b^2}{4T+m\omega^2 b^2}$, and $\dfrac{K^2}{a^2}=\dfrac{m\omega^2}{T}\left(1+\dfrac{m\omega^2 b^2}{4T}\right)$,

or $\dfrac{m\omega^2 ab}{2T} = Kk.$

iii. State and prove Green's theorem, and deduce with the usual notation that

$$\iiint (V\nabla^2 U - U\nabla^2 V)\,dx\,dy\,dz = \iint \left(V\dfrac{dU}{dn} - U\dfrac{dV}{dn}\right) dS.$$

Hence prove by putting $U=\dfrac{1}{r}$, that if an equipotential surface be coated with matter so that at each point the surface-density is $\dfrac{R}{4\pi}$, where R is the resultant force due to the original matter acting outwards from that point of the surface; then the potential of the coated surface at any point of the outside of the surface will be equal to the potential at the same point due to that part of the original matter which was on the inside of the surface; and the potential due to the coated surface at any point of the inside added to that due to the part of the original matter on the outside will be equal to C, the potential at the surface.

Putting $U=\dfrac{1}{r}$, where r is the distance of any point xyz from a fixed point O, and first supposing O outside the equipotential surface; then $\nabla^2 U = 0$ inside the surface, and over the surface

$$\iint V\dfrac{dU}{dn}\,dS = C\iint \dfrac{dU}{dn}\,dS = 0.$$

Also $\nabla^2 V = -4\pi\rho$, and $\dfrac{dV}{dn} = -R$;

therefore Green's theorem becomes

$$\iiint \dfrac{4\pi\rho}{r}\,dx\,dy\,dz = \iint \dfrac{R}{r}\,dS,$$

or $\iiint \dfrac{\rho}{r}\,dx\,dy\,dz = \iint \dfrac{R}{4\pi r}\,dS,$

which proves the first part.

Secondly, supposing O inside the surface, then $\nabla^2 U = 0$ inside the surface except at the point O, and $\iiint V\nabla^2 U\,dx\,dy\,dz = -4\pi V_0$, where V_0

is the value of V at the point O; also

$$\iint V\frac{dU}{dn}dS = C\iint \frac{dU}{dn}dS = -4\pi C.$$

Therefore Green's theorem becomes

$$-4\pi V_0 + \iiint \frac{4\pi\rho}{r}dxdydz = -4\pi C + \iint \frac{R}{r}dS,$$

or
$$\iint \frac{R}{4\pi r}dS + V_0 - \iiint \frac{\rho}{r}dxdydz = C,$$

which proves the second part.

4. A material system in stable equilibrium, under the action of a conservative system of forces, is subjected to a given displacement. The kinetic energy of the actual motion will be less than that of any other geometrically possible motion by the energy of the motion which must be compounded with the actual motion to produce the other motion.

(See Thomson and Tait's *Natural Philosophy*, Art. 317, p. 225.)

v. Prove that the velocity U of propagation of waves of small displacement of length λ in water of depth h is given by

$$U^2 = \frac{g\lambda}{2\pi}\tanh\frac{2\pi h}{\lambda}.$$

If liquids of densities ρ and ρ' and depths h and h' be contained between two fixed horizontal planes at a distance $h + h'$, prove that the velocity U of propagation of waves of small displacement of length λ at the common surface is given by

$$(U - V\cos\alpha)^2 \rho \coth\frac{2\pi h}{\lambda}$$
$$+ (U - V'\cos\alpha')^2 \rho' \coth\frac{2\pi h'}{\lambda} - \frac{g\lambda}{2\pi}(\rho - \rho') = 0,$$

where V and V' are the mean velocities of the currents in the liquids, and α and α' the angles the currents make with the direction of propagation of the waves, the currents slipping over each other.

Reducing the motion to plane steady motion by applying at every point of the liquids the reversed velocity of the cross currents and the reversed velocity of the wave propagation, and supposing the equation of the surface of separation to be $y = b\sin mx$; then if ψ, ψ' denote the current functions of the liquids,

$$\psi = (U - V\cos\alpha)\left\{y - b\frac{\sinh m(h+y)}{\sinh mh}\sin mx\right\},$$

$$\psi' = (U - V'\cos\alpha')\left\{y - b\frac{\sinh m(h'-y)}{\sinh mh'}\sin mx\right\}.$$

For ψ and ψ' satisfy the equation of continuity and the conditions that $v = \dfrac{d\psi}{dx} = 0$ when $y = -h$, and $v = \dfrac{d\psi'}{dx} = 0$ when $y = h$; also when $y = 0$ in the coefficient of b, that ψ and ψ' both denote the same stream line

$$y = b \sin mx.$$

The dynamical equations are

$$\frac{p}{\rho} + gy + \tfrac{1}{2}\rho q^2 = H,$$

$$\frac{p'}{\rho'} + gy + \tfrac{1}{2}\rho' q'^2 = H',$$

where q, q' denote the velocities in the liquid, and H, H' are constants.

Neglecting b^2,

$$q^2 = \left(\frac{d\psi}{dy}\right)^2 = (U - V\cos\alpha)^2 \left\{1 - 2mb\,\frac{\cosh m(h+y)}{\sinh mh}\sin mx\right\},$$

$$q'^2 = \left(\frac{d\psi'}{dy}\right)^2 = (U - V'\cos\alpha')^2 \left\{1 + 2mb\,\frac{\cosh m(h'-y)}{\sinh mh'}\sin mx\right\}.$$

At the common surface of the liquids $p = p'$,

or $\qquad \tfrac{1}{2}(\rho' q'^2 - \rho q^2) - g(\rho - \rho')y = \rho H - \rho' H',$

or, putting $y = 0$ in the coefficients of b,

$\tfrac{1}{2}\rho'(U - V'\cos\alpha')^2 - \tfrac{1}{2}\rho(U - V\cos\alpha)^2$
$+ m\{(U - V'\cos\alpha')^2 \rho' \coth mh' + (U - V\cos\alpha)^2 \rho \coth mh\} b \sin mx$
$- g(\rho - \rho') b \sin mx = \rho H - \rho' H';$

and equating to zero the coefficient of $b \sin mx$,

$$m\{(U - V'\cos\alpha')^2 \rho' \coth mh' + (U - V\cos\alpha)^2 \rho \coth mh\} - g(\rho - \rho') = 0,$$

and $\qquad m = \dfrac{2\pi}{\lambda},$

giving the required result

$$(U - V\cos\alpha)^2 \rho \coth \frac{2\pi h}{\lambda} + (U - V'\cos\alpha')^2 \rho' \coth \frac{2\pi h'}{\lambda} - \frac{g\lambda}{2\pi}(\rho - \rho') = 0.$$

If we put $\rho' = 0$, $V = 0$, $V' = 0$, we obtain

$$U^2 = \frac{g\lambda}{2\pi} \tan \frac{2\pi h}{\lambda},$$

the result of the book-work.

Suppose however the motion not to be reduced to plane steady motion; but denote by ϕ, ϕ' the velocity functions of the actual motion of the liquids; then if

$\phi = V\cos\alpha \cdot x + V\sin\alpha \cdot z + A \cosh m(h+y) \cos(mx - nt),$

$\phi' = V'\cos\alpha' \cdot x + V'\sin\alpha' \cdot z + A' \cosh m(h'-y) \cos(mx - nt);$

then ϕ and ϕ' satisfy the equation of continuity and the conditions that $\dfrac{d\phi}{dy} = 0$ when $y = -h$, and $\dfrac{d\phi'}{dy} = 0$ when $y = h'$.

At the surface of separation the direction of motion of the liquid relative to the moving surface of separation $y = b \sin(mx - nt)$ must be a tangent to the surface, and therefore

$$\frac{\dfrac{d\phi}{dy}}{\dfrac{d\phi}{dx} - U} = \frac{\dfrac{d\phi'}{dy}}{\dfrac{d\phi'}{dx} - U} = \frac{dy}{dx};$$

or, neglecting A^2 and A'^2,

$$\frac{mA \sinh mh \cos(mx - nt)}{V \cos \alpha - U} = \frac{-mA' \sinh mh' \cos(mx - nt)}{V' \cos \alpha' - U}$$

$$= mb \cos(mx - nt),$$

or $\qquad \dfrac{A \sinh mh}{V \cos \alpha - U} = \dfrac{-A' \sinh mh'}{V' \cos \alpha' - U} = b;$

and therefore

$$\phi = V \cos \alpha \cdot x + V \sin \alpha \cdot z + (V \cos \alpha - U) b \frac{\cosh m(h + y)}{\sinh mh} \cos(mx - nt),$$

$$\phi' = V' \cos \alpha' \cdot x + V' \sin \alpha' \cdot z - (V' \cos \alpha' - U) b \frac{\cosh m(h' - y)}{\sinh mh'} \cos(mx - nt).$$

The dynamical equations are

$$\frac{p}{\rho} + gy + \frac{d\phi}{dt} + \tfrac{1}{2} q^2 = \Pi,$$

$$\frac{p'}{\rho'} + gy + \frac{d\phi'}{dt} + \tfrac{1}{2} q'^2 = \Pi';$$

and at the surface of separation $p = p'$,

or $\qquad \tfrac{1}{2}(\rho' q'^2 - \rho q^2) + \rho' \dfrac{d\phi'}{dt} - \rho \dfrac{d\phi}{dt} - g(\rho - \rho')y = \rho' \Pi' - \rho \Pi.$

Also at the surface of separation, neglecting b^2,

$$q^2 = V^2 - 2V \cos \alpha (V \cos \alpha - U) mb \coth mh \sin(mx - nt),$$

$$q'^2 = V'^2 + 2V' \cos \alpha' (V' \cos \alpha' - U) mb \coth mh' \sin(mx - nt);$$

and therefore

$\tfrac{1}{2} \rho' V'^2 - \tfrac{1}{2} \rho V^2$
$+ \{V' \cos \alpha'(V' \cos \alpha' - U)\rho' \coth mh' + V \cos \alpha (V \cos \alpha - U)\rho \coth mh\} mb \sin(mx - nt)$
$- \{(V' \cos \alpha' - U)\rho' \coth mh' + (V \cos \alpha - U)\rho \coth mh\} nb \sin(mx - nt)$
$- g(\rho - \rho') b \sin(mx - nt) = \rho' \Pi' - \rho \Pi;$

and equating to zero the coefficient of $\sin(mx - nt)$,

$\{V'\cos a'(V'\cos a' - U)\rho'\coth mh' + V\cos a(V\cos a - U)\rho\coth mh\}m$
$- \{(V'\cos a' - U)\rho'\coth mh' + (V\cos a - U)\rho\coth mh\}n$
$- g(\rho - \rho') = 0$,

and $m = \dfrac{2\pi}{\lambda}$, $n = \dfrac{2\pi U}{\lambda}$: leading to the same result as before.

6. If a uniform horizontal bar, both of whose ends are fixed, be so displaced longitudinally that, initially, one-half is uniformly extended, the other uniformly compressed, prove that the displacement (y) of any particle (x) at the time t will be

$$\frac{8nl}{\pi^2} \Sigma \frac{1}{(2i+1)^2} \cos(2i+1)\frac{\pi}{2}\frac{at}{l} \cos(2i+1)\frac{\pi}{2}\frac{x}{l},$$

$2l$ being the length of the bar, the middle point being origin, and nl the initial displacement of the middle point.

The value of y must be such as to satisfy the equation

$$\frac{d^2y}{dt^2} = a^2 \frac{d^2y}{dx^2} \quad\quad\quad\quad\quad\quad\quad\quad\quad\quad (1).$$

It must also, for all values of t, be equal to zero when $x = \pm l$.

And we require that, initially, y shall be equal to $nl\dfrac{l-x}{l}$, for all values of x between 0 and l, and to $nl\dfrac{l+x}{l}$ for all values of x between $-l$ and 0.

Now it is known that the expression

$$\sin\frac{\pi}{2}\frac{x}{l} + \frac{1}{3}\sin\frac{3\pi}{2}\frac{x}{l} + \ldots + \frac{1}{2i+1}\sin\frac{(2i+1)\pi}{2}\frac{x}{l} + \ldots$$

is equal to $\dfrac{\pi}{4}$ from $x = 0$ to $x = l$, and to $-\dfrac{\pi}{4}$ from $x = -l$ to $x = 0$.

Hence, integrating with respect to x, we see that

$$\frac{2l}{\pi}\left\{\cos\frac{\pi}{2}\frac{x}{l} + \frac{1}{3^2}\cos\frac{3\pi}{2}\frac{x}{l} + \ldots + \frac{1}{(2i+1)^2}\cos\frac{(2i+1)\pi}{2}\frac{x}{l} + \ldots\right\}$$

is equal to $\dfrac{\pi}{4}(l-x)$ from $x = 0$ to $x = l$, and to $\dfrac{\pi}{4}(l+x)$ from $x = -l$ to $x = 0$,—the arbitrary constant being determined by the fact that the series vanishes when $x = \pm l$.

Hence, multiplying by $\dfrac{4}{\pi}\dfrac{nl}{l}$ we obtain, for the initial value of y

$$\frac{8}{\pi^2}nl \sum_{i=0}^{i=\infty} \frac{1}{(2i+1)^2}\cos\frac{(2i+1)\pi}{2}\frac{x}{l},$$

and therefore, for the general value

$$\frac{8}{\pi^2} nl \sum_{i=0}^{i=\infty} \frac{1}{(2i+1)^2} \cos\frac{(2i+1)\pi}{2}\frac{at}{l}\cos\frac{(2i+1)\pi}{2}\frac{x}{l},$$

since this satisfies the differential equation (1).

ζ. Describe and explain the phenomenon of external conical refraction.

If one of the directions of vibration in a plane wave inside a crystal make angles α, β with the optic axes, and the other make angles γ, δ, prove that

$$\cos\alpha\cos\delta + \cos\beta\cos\gamma = 0.$$

Prove also that, if a ray be incident on the face of a crystal in a plane passing through one of the optic axes, the directions of vibration inside the crystal will be either perpendicular to this axis, or will lie on the surface of a cone of the second degree.

Imagine a unit sphere drawn with centre at the origin O, and let the mean axis of the ellipsoid of elasticity be chosen as the axis of z, and let its two circular sections be denoted by

$$y = -x\tan A, \quad y = +x\tan A.$$

Suppose, also, that any third central section DCD' (fig. 64) meets the first circle in D, D' and the second in C. Let V_1, V_2 be the middle points of CD, CD' then OV_1, and OV_2 are the two directions of vibration in the wave.

Let $ZC = \theta_1$, $ZD = \theta_2$, $ZD' = \pi - \theta_2$, $CD = \psi$.

The co-ordinates of C are $\sin\theta_1\cos A$, $\sin\theta_1\sin A$, $\cos\theta_1$,
................D ... $\sin\theta_2\cos A$, $-\sin\theta_2\sin A$, $\cos\theta_2$,
................D' ... $-\sin\theta_2\cos A$, $\sin\theta_2\sin A$, $-\cos\theta_2$.

Those of V_1 (l_1, m_1, n_1) by

$$\left.\begin{array}{l}2l_1\cos\tfrac{1}{2}\psi = (\sin\theta_1 + \sin\theta_2)\cos A,\\ 2m_1\cos\tfrac{1}{2}\psi = (\sin\theta_1 - \sin\theta_2)\sin A,\\ 2n_1\cos\tfrac{1}{2}\psi = \cos\theta_1 + \cos\theta_2\end{array}\right\}\ldots\ldots\ldots(1).$$

Those of V_2 (l_2, m_2, n_2) by

$$2l_2\sin\tfrac{1}{2}\psi = (\sin\theta_1 - \sin\theta_2)\cos A,$$
$$2m_2\sin\tfrac{1}{2}\psi = (\sin\theta_1 + \sin\theta_2)\sin A,$$
$$2n_2\sin\tfrac{1}{2}\psi = \cos\theta_1 - \cos\theta_2.$$

The optic axis O_1, perpendicular to ZC is given by $\sin A$, $-\cos A$, 0
.... O_2, ... ZD .... $\sin A$, $\cos A$, 0 $\Big\}(2).$

It is obvious from these equations that

$$\cos \widehat{V_1 O_1} \cos \widehat{V_2 O_2} + \cos \widehat{V_1 O_2} \cos \widehat{V_2 O_1} = 0 \quad \ldots\ldots\ldots\ldots (a).$$

Let λ, μ, ν be the direction-cosines of the normal to the wave; then, since it is at right angles to OC and OD,

$$\lambda \cos A \sin \theta_1 + \mu \sin A \sin \theta_1 + \nu \cos \theta_1 = 0,$$
$$\lambda \cos A \sin \theta_2 - \mu \sin A \sin \theta_2 + \nu \cos \theta_2 = 0.$$

From these equations we obtain

$$\left. \begin{array}{l} 2\lambda \cos A \sin \theta_1 \sin \theta_2 + \nu \sin (\theta_1 + \theta_2) = 0 \\ 2\mu \sin A \sin \theta_1 \sin \theta_2 + \nu \sin (\theta_2 - \theta_1) = 0 \end{array} \right\} \ldots\ldots\ldots (3).$$

But, turning to equation (1), we see that

$$\left. \begin{array}{l} \tan \tfrac{1}{2} (\theta_1 + \theta_2) = \dfrac{l}{n \cos A} ; \\[4pt] \text{therefore } \sin (\theta_1 + \theta_2) = \dfrac{2ln \cos A}{l^2 + n^2 \cos^2 A}, \quad \cos (\theta_1 + \theta_2) = \dfrac{n^2 \cos^2 A - l^2}{n^2 \cos^2 A + l^2}, \\[4pt] \tan \tfrac{1}{2} (\theta_1 - \theta_2) = \dfrac{m}{n \sin A} ; \\[4pt] \text{therefore } \sin (\theta_1 - \theta_2) = \dfrac{2mn \sin A}{m^2 + n^2 \sin^2 A}, \quad \cos (\theta_1 - \theta_2) = \dfrac{n^2 \sin^2 A - m^2}{n^2 \sin^2 A + m^2}; \end{array} \right\} (4).$$

From these we also derive

$$2 \sin \theta_1 \sin \theta_2 (n^2 \cos^2 A + l^2)(n^2 \sin^2 A + m^2) = 2n^2(l^2 \sin^2 A - m^2 \cos^2 A)\ldots(5).$$

Suppose now the normal to a wave, incident upon a given face of a crystal, to lie in a given plane; the normal to the refracted wave will also lie in the same plane; suppose, therefore, that we have

$$a\lambda + \beta\mu + \gamma\nu = 0 \ldots\ldots\ldots\ldots\ldots\ldots\ldots (6),$$

where a, β, γ are the direction-cosines of the plane of incidence; the above equations (3), (4), (5) enable us to determine the conditions thereby imposed upon the directions of vibration.

We obtain, on substitution,

$$aln (m^2 + n^2 \sin^2 A) - \beta mn (l^2 + n^2 \sin^2 A)$$
$$- \gamma n^2 (l^2 \sin^2 A - m^2 \cos^2 A) = 0 \ldots\ldots\ldots (7).$$

Rejecting the factor n from this equation, we see that, when the normal to the incident wave lies in a given plane, the directions of vibration lie on the surface of a cone of the third degree.

Let the given plane contain the optic axis O_1,

then $\quad a \sin A - \beta \cos A = 0;$

we may therefore take $\quad a = c . \cos A,$

$$\beta = c . \sin A.$$

The cone (7) now takes the form
$$clm\,(m\cos A - l\sin A) - cn^2 \sin A \cos A\,(m\cos A - l\sin A)$$
$$+ \gamma n\,(m^2 \cos^2 A - l^2 \sin^2 A) = 0,$$
which breaks up into the plane
$$l\sin A - m\cos A = 0,$$
and the cone
$$c\,(lm - n^2 \sin A \cos A) + \gamma n\,(l\sin A + m\cos A) = 0.$$
The plane is evidently at right angles to the optic axis O_1.

η. Obtain the general equations of equilibrium of an elastic plate of small thickness, under given forces.

A thin uniform spherical shell of isotropic material, whose weight may be neglected, is made to perform vibrations in the direction of the radius, symmetrical about a diameter. Shew how they may be found.

Prove that they are given by
$$\delta r = a \sin nt\, P_i(\mu),$$
where $\qquad n^2 = (i-1)(i+2)\{A\,(i-1)(i+2) - B\},$

A and B being constants depending on the radius, thickness and substance of the shell, and i a positive integer, and the other symbols having their usual meanings.

In the case of a strained plate, which was originally plane, the work done to produce the state of strain is (see Lord Rayleigh, *Theory of Sound*, Art. 214) of the form
$$\tfrac{1}{2}A_1\left(\frac{1}{\rho_1^2} + \frac{1}{\rho_2^2}\right) + \tfrac{1}{2}B_1\,\frac{1}{\rho_1\rho_2} \quad \text{per unit of area;}$$
or, as we might write it,
$$\tfrac{1}{2}A\left(\frac{1}{\rho_1} + \frac{1}{\rho_2}\right)^2 + \tfrac{1}{2}B\,\frac{1}{\rho_1\rho_2}\,,$$
ρ_1 and ρ_2 being the principal radii of curvature of the surface.

It is an obvious extension of this result that, if the plate were originally spherical and of radius a, the work necessary to strain it is of the form
$$W = \iint \left\{ \frac{A}{2}\left(\frac{1}{\sigma_1} + \frac{1}{\sigma_2}\right)^2 + B\cdot\frac{1}{\sigma_1\sigma_2} \right\} dS \quad \ldots\ldots\ldots\ldots\ldots(1),$$
where
$$\frac{1}{\sigma_1} = \frac{1}{\rho_1} - \frac{1}{a}, \quad \frac{1}{\sigma_2} = \frac{1}{\rho_2} - \frac{1}{a}.$$

Here $\dfrac{1}{\sigma_1}$ and $\dfrac{1}{\sigma_2}$ are the changes of curvature at any point of the plate.

The kinetic energy of the plate for transversal vibrations will be

$$\tfrac{1}{2} \int \rho \dot{r}^2 \, dS,$$

ρ being the surface-density.

The equation giving the transversal motions will be

$$\int \rho \ddot{r} \, \delta r \, dS + \delta W = 0 \dots\dots\dots\dots\dots\dots(2),$$

and we may suppose ρ to be incorporated with A, B, and so to be put $= 1$.

We have now to find σ_1 and σ_2 in the case where the sphere is deformed into a surface of revolution.

Let ρ_1 be the radius of curvature of a meridional section, $\rho_2 = $ the normal PG (fig. 65), and let the equation of the surface be

$$r = a(1+u) \dots\dots\dots\dots\dots\dots(3),$$

$$\tan SPG = \frac{1}{r}\frac{dr}{d\theta} = \frac{du}{d\theta},$$

treating u as a small quantity of the first order, and neglecting its square.

To the same order of approximation,

$$\sin SPG = \frac{du}{d\theta}, \quad \cos SPG = 1, \quad \text{and} \quad ds = a(1+u)\,d\theta.$$

If $\phi = PGS$, $\sin\phi = \sin\theta - \cos\theta \dfrac{du}{d\theta}$, $\cos\phi = \cos\theta + \sin\theta \dfrac{du}{d\theta}$,

$$\rho_2 = a(1+u)\sin\theta \div \sin\phi = a\left(1 + u + \cot\theta \frac{du}{d\theta}\right).$$

If we put $\mu = \cos\theta$,

$$\frac{a}{\sigma_2} = \mu \frac{du}{d\mu} - u \dots\dots\dots\dots\dots\dots(4).$$

Moreover,

$$\frac{1}{\rho} = \frac{r^2 - r\dfrac{d^2r}{d\theta} + 2\left(\dfrac{dr}{d\theta}\right)^2}{\left\{r^2 + \left(\dfrac{dr}{d\theta}\right)^2\right\}^{\frac{3}{2}}}$$

$$= \frac{1}{a}\left\{1 - u - \frac{d^2u}{d\theta^2}\right\};$$

therefore

$$-\frac{a}{\sigma_1} = (1-\mu^2)\frac{d^2u}{d\mu^2} - \mu\frac{du}{d\mu} + u \dots\dots\dots\dots(5).$$

We have now to substitute these values in (1); and, before proceeding to take the variation of W, we shall integrate as far as possible, because any variation of the terms which appear outside the sign of integration will not affect the equation upon which the vibratory motion depends.

Now
$$dS = -2\pi a^2 d\mu,$$
and the constant part of this expression will disappear from equation (2); so we may neglect it.

If we put
$$\mu \frac{du}{d\mu} - u = \omega, \quad \mu \frac{d^2u}{d\mu^2} = \frac{d\omega}{d\mu}.$$

Hence
$$-\int \frac{a^2}{\sigma_1 \sigma_2} d\mu = \int \left\{ \left(\mu \frac{du}{d\mu} - u\right) \frac{d^2u}{d\mu^2} - \mu\omega \frac{d\omega}{d\mu} - \omega^2 \right\} d\mu.$$

But
$$\int \mu \frac{du}{d\mu} \frac{d^2u}{d\mu^2} d\mu = \frac{\mu}{2} \left(\frac{du}{d\mu}\right)^2 - \tfrac{1}{2} \int \left(\frac{du}{d\mu}\right)^2 d\mu,$$

and
$$\int u \frac{d^2u}{d\mu^2} d\mu = u \frac{du}{d\mu} - \int \left(\frac{du}{d\mu}\right)^2 d\mu,$$

and
$$\int \mu\omega\, d\omega = \mu \frac{\omega^2}{2} - \tfrac{1}{2} \int \omega^2 d\mu.$$

Hence
$$-\int \frac{a^2}{\sigma_1 \sigma_2} d\mu - \frac{\mu}{2}\left(\frac{du}{d\mu}\right)^2 - u \frac{du}{d\mu} - \tfrac{1}{2}\mu\omega^2 + \tfrac{1}{2} \int \left\{ \left(\frac{du}{d\mu}\right)^2 - \omega^2 \right\} d\mu.$$

We observe, further, that the term under the integral contains a term
$$\int 2\mu u \frac{du}{d\mu} d\mu,$$
which may be written
$$\mu u^2 - \int u^2 d\mu,$$

hence
$$-a^2 \int \frac{1}{\sigma_1 \sigma_2} d\mu = [\ldots] + \tfrac{1}{2} \int \left\{ (1-\mu^2)\left(\frac{du}{d\mu}\right)^2 - 2u^2 \right\} d\mu,$$

hence
$$-a^2 \delta . \int \frac{1}{\sigma_1 \sigma_2} d\mu = \int \left\{ (1-\mu^2) \frac{du}{d\mu} \frac{d\delta u}{d\mu} - 2u\,\delta u \right\} d\mu + [\ldots]$$

$$= -\int \left[\frac{d}{d\mu} \left\{ (1-\mu^2) \frac{du}{d\mu} \right\} + 2u \right] \delta u . d\mu + [\ldots] \ldots (6),$$

the expressions $[\ldots]$ denoting terms outside the symbol of integration.

We have next to find the variation of
$$\frac{a^2}{2} \int \left(\frac{1}{\sigma_1} + \frac{1}{\sigma_2}\right)^2 d\mu$$

$$-a\left(\frac{1}{\sigma_1}+\frac{1}{\sigma_2}\right)=(1-\mu^2)\frac{d^2u}{d\mu^2}-2\mu\frac{du}{d\mu}+2u$$

$$=\frac{d}{d\mu}\left(\overline{1-\mu^2}\frac{du}{d\mu}\right)+2u=P \text{ say}.$$

Hence,

$$a^2\delta.\tfrac{1}{2}\int\left(\frac{1}{\sigma_1}+\frac{1}{\sigma_2}\right)^2 d\mu=\int P\delta P$$

$$=\int P\left\{(1-\mu^2)\frac{d^2\delta u}{d\mu^2}-2\mu\frac{d\delta u}{d\mu}+2\delta u\right\}$$

$$=\int\left[\frac{d^2}{d\mu^2}\{(1-\mu^2)P\}+2\frac{d}{d\mu}.\mu P+2P\right]\delta u\,.\,d\mu+[\ldots]$$

$$=\int\left\{(1-\mu^2)\frac{d^2P}{d\mu^2}-2\mu\frac{dP}{d\mu}+2P\right\}\delta u\,.\,d\mu+[\ldots]$$

$$=\int\left[\frac{d}{d\mu}\left\{(1-\mu^2)\frac{d}{d\mu}\right\}+2\right]^2 u\,.\,\delta u\,.\,d\mu+[\ldots]\ldots(7).$$

On substituting these expressions for the variation of δW in equation (2), we may evidently write the equation of vibrating motion

where
$$\left.\begin{array}{l}\dfrac{d^2u}{dt^2}+(A\Delta^2+B\Delta)\,u=0,\\[6pt] \Delta=\dfrac{d}{d\mu}\left\{(1-\mu^2)\dfrac{d}{d\mu}\right\}+2\end{array}\right\}\quad\ldots\ldots\ldots\ldots\ldots(8).$$

We may satisfy this equation by putting

$$u=P_i(\mu)\sin nt,$$

for $\quad\Delta P_i=-(i^2+i-2)P_i=-(i-1)(i+2)P_i,$

and hence

$$n^2=(i-1)(i+2)\{A(i-1)(i+2)-B\}.$$

ix. Define the potential function ϕ and the current function ψ of electricity moving in a uniform conducting plate; and prove that, if the specific resistance of the plate be taken as unity, they are conjugate functions and satisfy the same differential equation of the second order.

Verify that, if the electrodes of a current C be placed at opposite corners of a uniform conducting rectangle,

$$\phi=\frac{RC}{\pi}\log\frac{1-\operatorname{cn}^2\left(K\frac{x}{a},\ k\right)\operatorname{cn}^2\left(K'\frac{y}{b},\ k'\right)}{k^2\operatorname{cn}^2\left(K\frac{x}{a},\ k\right)+k'^2\operatorname{cn}^2\left(K'\frac{y}{b},\ k'\right)}$$

$$\psi = \frac{2C}{\pi} \tan^{-1} \frac{\operatorname{sn}\left(K'\frac{y}{b},\ k'\right) \operatorname{dn}\left(K'\frac{y}{b},\ k'\right) \operatorname{cn}\left(K\frac{x}{a},\ k'\right)}{\operatorname{sn}\left(K\frac{x}{a},\ k\right) \operatorname{dn}\left(K\frac{x}{a},\ k\right) \operatorname{cn}\left(K'\frac{y}{b},\ k'\right)},$$

where $\frac{K}{K'} = \frac{a}{b}$; a, b being the sides of the rectangle, R the specific resistance of the plate, and the axes of co-ordinates being two adjacent sides of the rectangle meeting in an electrode.

To verify the theorem we must prove that

$$\frac{d\phi}{dx} = R\frac{d\psi}{dy},\qquad \frac{d\phi}{dy} = -R\frac{d\psi}{dx},$$

and that the value of ψ along the edges $x=0$ and $y=b$ must be constant and exceed the value of ψ along the edges $y=0$ and $x=a$ by c; the strength of the current.

Now, since $\quad \dfrac{d}{dx}\operatorname{sn} x = \operatorname{cn} x\, \operatorname{dn} x,$

putting $\quad \operatorname{sn} K\dfrac{x}{a} = a,\ \ \operatorname{sn} K'\dfrac{y}{b} = \beta,$

$$\phi = \frac{RC}{\pi} \log \frac{a^2 + \beta^2 - a^2\beta^2}{1 - k^2 a^2 - k'^2 \beta^2},$$

$$\psi = \frac{2C}{\pi} \tan^{-1} \frac{\beta\sqrt{(1-k'^2\beta^2)}\sqrt{(1-a^2)}}{a\sqrt{(1-k^2 a^2)}\sqrt{(1-\beta^2)}};$$

and therefore

$$\frac{d\phi}{dx} = \frac{RC}{\pi}\frac{K}{a}\left(\frac{2a - 2a\beta^2}{a^2+\beta^2-a^2\beta^2} + \frac{2k^2 a}{1-k^2 a^2 - k'^2\beta^2}\right)\sqrt{(1-a^2)}\sqrt{(1-k^2 a^2)}$$

$$= 2\frac{RC}{\pi}\frac{K}{a}\frac{1 - 2k'^2\beta^2 + k'^2\beta^2}{(a^2+\beta^2-a^2\beta^2)(1-k^2 a^2 - k'^2\beta^2)} a\sqrt{(1-a^2)}\sqrt{(1-k'^2 a^2)};$$

$$\frac{d\psi}{dy} = \frac{2C}{\pi}\frac{K'}{b}\frac{\dfrac{\sqrt{(1-k'^2\beta)}}{\sqrt{(1-\beta^2)}} - \dfrac{k^2\beta^2}{\sqrt{(1-\beta^2)}\sqrt{(1-k'^2\beta^2)}} + \dfrac{\beta^2\sqrt{(1-k'^2\beta^2)}}{(1-\beta^2)^3}}{1 + \dfrac{\beta^2(1-k'^2\beta^2)(1-a^2)}{a^2(1-k^2 a^2)(1-\beta^2)}}$$

$$\frac{\sqrt{(1-a^2)}}{a\sqrt{(1-k^2 a^2)}}\sqrt{(1-\beta^2)}\sqrt{(1-k'^2\beta^2)}$$

$$= \frac{2C}{\pi}\frac{K'}{b}\frac{(1-k'^2\beta^2)(1-\beta^2) - k'^2\beta^2(1-\beta^2) + \beta^2(1-k'^2\beta^2)}{a^2(1-k^2 a^2)(1-\beta^2) + \beta^2(1-k'^2\beta^2)(1-a^2)} a\sqrt{(1-a^2)}\sqrt{(1-k^2 a^2)}$$

$$= \frac{2C}{\pi}\frac{K'}{b}\frac{1 - 2k'^2\beta^2 + k'^2\beta^2}{(a^2+\beta^2-a^2\beta^2)(1-k^2 a^2 - k'^2\beta^2)} a\sqrt{(1-a^2)}\sqrt{(1-k'^2 a^2)};$$

and therefore
$$\frac{d\phi}{dx} = R\frac{d\psi}{dy}.$$

Similarly it may be found that
$$\frac{d\phi}{dy} = -R\frac{d\psi}{dx}.$$

Also when $y=0$ or $x=a$, $\psi = \frac{2C}{\pi}\tan^{-1} 0$;

and when $x=0$ or $y=b$, $\psi = \frac{2C}{\pi}\tan^{-1}\infty$:

and within the rectangle the numerator or denominator in the expression for ψ do not vanish; therefore, when $y=0$ or $x=a$, we may put $\psi=0$, and when $x=0$ or $y=b$, we may put $\psi=C$, and therefore C is the strength of the current crossing any line joining the sides $y=0$ or $x=a$ with the sides $x=0$ or $y=b$; and, since on the boundary ψ has a constant value, therefore ψ satisfies all the required conditions.

The values of ϕ and ψ can be found synthetically by supposing the plate to be infinite, and positive electrodes placed at the points $2ma$, $2m'b$; and negative electrodes at the points $(2m+1)a$, $(2m'+1)b$; when m and m' are any integers, taken between the values $-\infty$ and ∞.

Then at any point of the plate

$$\phi + iR\psi = \frac{2RC}{\pi}\log \prod_{m,\,m'=-\infty}^{m,\,m'=\infty} \frac{(x-2ma) + i(y-2m'b)}{\{x-(2m+1)a\} + i\{y-(2m'+1)b\}}$$

$$= \frac{2RC}{\pi}\log \frac{\mathrm{H}\left(K\frac{x}{a} + iK'\frac{y}{b}\right)}{\Theta_1\left(K\frac{x}{a} + iK'\frac{y}{b}\right)}$$

where $\frac{K}{K'} = \frac{a}{b}$ (Cayley, *Elliptic Functions*, § 39); and therefore, omitting constant terms,

$$\phi + iR\psi = \frac{2RC}{\pi}\log \frac{\operatorname{sn}\left(K\frac{x}{a} + iK'\frac{y}{b}\right)}{\operatorname{dn}\left(K\frac{x}{a} + iK'\frac{y}{b}\right)}$$

$$= \frac{2RC}{\pi}\log \frac{\operatorname{sn}\left(K\frac{x}{a} + iK'\frac{y}{b}\right)\operatorname{dn}\left(K\frac{x}{a} - iK'\frac{y}{b}\right)}{\operatorname{dn}\left(K\frac{x}{a} + iK'\frac{y}{b}\right)\operatorname{dn}\left(K\frac{x}{a} - iK'\frac{y}{b}\right)}$$

$$= \frac{2RC}{\pi} \log \frac{\operatorname{sn} K\frac{x}{a} \operatorname{dn} K\frac{x}{a} \operatorname{cn} iK'\frac{y}{b} + \operatorname{sn} iK'\frac{y}{b} \operatorname{dn} iK'\frac{y}{b} \operatorname{cn} K\frac{x}{a}}{\operatorname{dn}^2 K\frac{x}{a} + \operatorname{dn}^2 iK'\frac{y}{b} - 1 + k^2 \operatorname{sn}^2 K\frac{x}{a} \operatorname{sn}^2 iK'\frac{y}{b}}$$

$$= \frac{2RC}{\pi} \log U, \text{ where } U =$$

$$\frac{\operatorname{sn}\left(K\frac{x}{a},k\right)\operatorname{dn}\left(K\frac{x}{a},k\right)\operatorname{cn}\left(K'\frac{y}{b},k'\right) + i\operatorname{sn}\left(K'\frac{y}{b},k'\right)\operatorname{dn}\left(K'\frac{y}{b},k'\right)\operatorname{cn}\left(K\frac{x}{a},k\right)}{k^2 \operatorname{cn}^2\left(K\frac{x}{a},k\right) + k'^2 \operatorname{cn}^2\left(K'\frac{y}{b},k'\right)};$$

and therefore

$$\phi = \frac{RC}{\pi} \log \frac{\operatorname{sn}^2 K\frac{x}{a} \operatorname{dn}^2 K\frac{x}{a} \operatorname{cn}^2 K'\frac{y}{b} + \operatorname{sn}^2 K'\frac{y}{b} \operatorname{dn}^2 K'\frac{y}{b} \operatorname{cn}^2 K\frac{x}{a}}{\left(k^2 \operatorname{cn}^2 K\frac{x}{a} + k'^2 \operatorname{cn}^2 K'\frac{y}{b}\right)^2}$$

$$= \frac{RC}{\pi} \log \frac{1 - \operatorname{sn}^2 K\frac{x}{a} \operatorname{cn}^2 K'\frac{y}{b}}{k^2 \operatorname{cn}^2 K\frac{x}{a} + k'^2 \operatorname{cn}^2 K'\frac{y}{b}},$$

$$\psi = \frac{2C}{\pi} \tan^{-1} \frac{\operatorname{sn} K'\frac{y}{b} \operatorname{dn} K'\frac{y}{b} \operatorname{cn} K\frac{x}{a}}{\operatorname{sn} K\frac{x}{a} \operatorname{dn} K\frac{x}{a} \operatorname{cn} K'\frac{y}{b}}.$$

[If the sides of the rectangle $y = 0$ and $x = a$ be maintained at the temperature zero, and if the other sides $x = 0$ and $y = b$ be maintained at the temperature unity, then it is obvious that ψ denotes the permanent temperature at any point of the rectangle].

ι. Obtain the general equations of electromotive force in the electromagnetic field.

What modifications do they undergo when the axes of reference are moving in any manner?

If a circular plate oscillate normally in front of a magnetic pole A very near its centre C, prove that, if the mutual induction of the currents be neglected, these currents will be given by the equation

$$\frac{1}{PA} - \frac{fx}{a^2} = \text{const.},$$

where a is the radius of the disc, f the projection of CA upon it, x the abscissa of any point P of the disc measured along f.

If the pole of the magnet be in the centre of an induction coil, shew how to find the currents which will be induced in the coil, and shew that they are approximately of the same period as the vibrations of the plate.

The general equations of electromotive force are (see Maxwell, *Electricity and Magnetism*, Vol. II., Art. 598),

$$P = c\frac{dy}{dt} - b\frac{dz}{dt} - \frac{dF}{dt} - \frac{d\psi}{dx},$$

$$Q = a\frac{dz}{dt} - c\frac{dx}{dt} - \frac{dG}{dt} - \frac{d\psi}{dy},$$

$$R = b\frac{dx}{dt} - a\frac{dy}{dt} - \frac{dH}{dt} - \frac{d\psi}{dz}.$$

The first two terms on the right-hand side express the inductive effect due to the motion of the conductor across the lines of force, the third terms that are due to variation of the currents, and the last give the force due to the variation of electric potential. In our case, when we neglect the mutual induction of the currents, we may neglect the third terms and put for a, b, c the components

$$-\frac{d\Omega}{dx}, \quad -\frac{d\Omega}{dy}, \quad -\frac{d\Omega}{dz}$$

of force due to the external magnetism.

Let us choose the axis of z in the direction of the normal to the disc, and the axes of x and y as indicated in the question, and let the normal velocity of the disc at any time be

$$\frac{dz}{dt} = V = A \sin nt;$$

also $\quad\dfrac{dx}{dt} = 0, \quad \text{and} \quad \dfrac{dy}{dt} = 0.$

It is manifest that the currents are entirely in the plane of the disc, and we may therefore put

$$R = 0, \quad \frac{d\psi}{dz} = 0.$$

If ϕ be the current function,

$$P = \sigma u = \sigma \frac{d\phi}{dy},$$

$$Q = \sigma v = -\sigma \frac{d\phi}{dx},$$

and the equations of the currents become

$$\left.\begin{array}{l}\sigma\dfrac{d\phi}{dy}=V\dfrac{d\Omega}{dy}-\dfrac{d\psi}{dx}\text{ or }\dfrac{d}{dy}(\sigma\phi-V\Omega)=-\dfrac{d\psi}{dx}\\[6pt]-\sigma\dfrac{d\phi}{dx}=-V\dfrac{d\Omega}{dx}-\dfrac{d\psi}{dy}\text{ or }\dfrac{d}{dx}(\sigma\phi-V\Omega)=+\dfrac{d\psi}{dy}\end{array}\right\}\ldots\ldots(1).$$

We must also remember that, since there is no flow of electricity across the boundary,

$$x\dfrac{d\phi}{dy}-y\dfrac{d\phi}{dx}=\dfrac{d\phi}{d\theta}=0\text{ when }r=a\ldots\ldots\ldots\ldots(2),$$

where $\qquad x=r\cos\theta,\quad y=r\sin\theta.$

If we put $\qquad \chi=\sigma\phi-V\Omega,$

the conditions to be satisfied are

$$\left.\begin{array}{l}\dfrac{d^2\chi}{dx^2}+\dfrac{d^2\chi}{dy^2}=0,\\[6pt]\dfrac{d\chi}{d\theta}=-V\dfrac{d\Omega}{d\theta}\text{ when }r=a\end{array}\right\}\ldots\ldots\ldots\ldots\ldots(3).$$

But, if A be a pole of unit strength, at a distance h from the plate,

$$\Omega=\dfrac{1}{PA}=\dfrac{1}{\sqrt{(x-f)^2+y^2+h^2}}$$

$$=\dfrac{1}{r}\left(1+\dfrac{fx}{r^2}+\ldots\right),$$

for points not near the centre; and when $r=a$,

$$\dfrac{d\Omega}{d\theta}=\dfrac{-f\sin\theta}{a^2},\text{ very nearly.}$$

The general value of χ from equation (3) is

$$\chi=\Sigma r^i(A\cos i\theta+B\sin i\theta).$$

The solution to be chosen is, therefore,

$$\chi=Ar\cos\theta,$$

where $\qquad -Aa=\dfrac{f}{a}.$

The value of ϕ is, therefore,

$$\phi=V\left(\dfrac{1}{PA}-\dfrac{fx}{a^3}\right)\ldots\ldots\ldots\ldots\ldots(4).$$

If the magnetic pole be surrounded by a coil, the variation of strength of the currents in the plate will induce currents in the coil; but these currents, being of the first order of small quantities, will not induce sensible changes in the currents of the plate.

Let R be the resistance of the coil, L its coefficient of self-induction, M the coefficient of mutual induction between the coil and unit current established in the plate according to the geometrical law (4). Let the current in the coil be y_1, and that in the plate y_2, the equation of induction will be

$$Ry_1 + \frac{d}{dt}(Ly_1 + My_2) = 0.$$

But M may be treated as sensibly constant, and therefore this equation may be written

$$\left(L\frac{d}{dt} + R\right)y_1 + M\frac{dy_2}{dt} = 0.$$

And y_2 is of the form $A \sin nt$,

hence
$$y_1 = -\frac{1}{R + L\frac{d}{dt}} \cdot Mn A \cos nt$$

$$= -\frac{MnA}{R^2 + L^2 n^2} \cdot (R \cos nt + nL \sin nt).$$

If we neglect L, the currents in the coil are a quarter of a phase in advance of those in the disc.

FRIDAY, *January* 18, 1878. 1½ to 4.

Mr PRIOR, Arabic Numbers.
Mr NIVEN, Roman Numbers.

1. IF the orbit in which a body moves revolves round the centre of force with an angular velocity which always bears a fixed ratio to that of the body; prove, by Newton's method, that the body may be made to move in the revolving orbit in the same manner as in the orbit at rest by the action of a force tending to the same centre.

If the orbit at rest be an equiangular spiral, shew that the orbit in space of the body moving in the revolving orbit is also an equiangular spiral, such that if μ, μ' be the absolute forces of the centres, α, α' the angles of the spiral in the two cases,

$$\mu' \cos^2 \alpha' = \mu \cos^2 \alpha.$$

If in the case of the orbit at rest the particle be moving from rest at infinity in a smooth spiral tube, and if, when it is at distance a from the centre, the tube begin to revolve with a uniform velocity ω, shew that the orbit in space of the particle will be

$$\frac{r}{ae^{\theta\cot a}} = \left\{\frac{\omega r^2 + c^2 + \sqrt{\omega^2 r^4 + 2\omega c^2 r^2 + \mu}}{\omega a^2}\right\}^{i\cosec a}$$

where $\qquad 2c^2 = 2\sqrt{\mu}\sin a - \omega a^2 \cos^2 a.$

(1) At any time let r be the distance of the particle from the centre, v its velocity in the orbit at rest, λv the angular velocity of the orbit; also let v' be the actual velocity of the particle, and ϕ' the angle between the radius vector and its actual direction of motion in its orbit in space.

Then we have

$$\tan \phi' = \frac{v\sin a + \lambda v}{v \cos a} = \frac{\sin a + \lambda}{\cos a} = \text{const.};$$

hence we learn that the orbit in space is an equiangular spiral, and

$$\frac{\sin a + \lambda}{\cos a} = \tan a'.$$

Now, since each orbit is an equiangular spiral, the forces tending to the centres vary inversely as the cubes of the distances; hence, if ρ, ρ' be the radii of curvature in the two spirals, we have,

$$\frac{v^2}{\rho} = \frac{\mu}{r^3}\sin a, \qquad \frac{v'^2}{\rho'} = \frac{\mu'}{r^3}\sin a';$$

while $\qquad \rho = r\cosec a, \qquad \rho' = r\cosec a'.$

Therefore $\qquad \dfrac{v^2}{v'^2} = \dfrac{\mu}{\mu'}.$

But the radial velocity $= v\cos a$ and also $= v'\cos a'$;

therefore $\qquad \dfrac{v}{v'} = \dfrac{\cos a'}{\cos a};$

therefore $\qquad \dfrac{\cos^2 a'}{\cos^2 a} = \dfrac{\mu}{\mu'},$

or $\qquad \mu'\cos^2 a' = \mu\cos^2 a.$

(2) Since, as the particle moves from rest at infinity to the distance a from the centre, the pressure on the tube is zero, we have

$$\frac{v^2}{\rho} = \frac{\mu}{r^3}\sin a, \quad \text{and} \quad \rho = r\cosec a,$$

therefore $\qquad v^2 = \dfrac{\mu}{r^2};$

therefore at distance a $\qquad v^2 = \dfrac{\mu}{a^2}.$

At any subsequent time, let u be the inward velocity of the particle relatively to the tube, and r its distance from the centre; then the velocities of the particle in space are, along the tube outward

$$\omega r \sin a - u = w, \text{ say,}$$

and perpendicular to the tube in the direction of revolution,

$$\omega r \cos a.$$

Also, to find the motion relative to the tube, we may reduce the tube to rest by giving to every particle an acceleration $\omega^2 r$ along the radius, and a velocity ωr perpendicular to the radius in the direction opposite to that of revolution.

Accordingly we have for the moving particle,

$$u \frac{du}{ds} = -\frac{\mu}{r^2} \cos a + \omega^2 r \cos a,$$

or

$$u \frac{du}{dr} = -\frac{\mu}{r^2} + \omega^2 r,$$

therefore $\quad u^2 = \dfrac{\mu}{r} + \omega^2 r^2 + 2\omega c^2$, where c is a constant.

Therefore $\quad w = \omega r \sin a - \dfrac{1}{r} \sqrt{(\omega^2 r^4 + 2\omega c^2 r^2 + \mu)}.$

But when $r = a$, $w = -\dfrac{\sqrt{\mu}}{a}$, for the impulse upon the particle due to the starting of the tube is normal to the tube, and therefore makes no change in the velocity in space along the tangent to the tube:

therefore $\quad \sqrt{\mu} + \omega a^2 \sin a = \sqrt{(\omega^2 a^4 + 2\omega c^2 a^2 + \mu)},$

or $\quad 2c^2 = 2\sqrt{\mu} \sin a - \omega a^2 \cos^2 a.$

Now, if θ be the angular co-ordinate of the particle, we have

$$r \frac{d\theta}{dr} = \frac{w \sin a + \omega r \cos^2 a}{w \cos a - \omega r \cos a \sin a} = \frac{\omega r - u \sin a}{-u \cos a};$$

therefore $\quad \tan a - r \dfrac{d\theta}{dr} = \dfrac{\omega r}{u \cos a},$

or $\quad \dfrac{1}{r} - \cot a \dfrac{d\theta}{dr} = \dfrac{\omega}{u \sin a} = \dfrac{\omega r \operatorname{cosec} a}{\sqrt{(\omega^2 r^4 + 2\omega c^2 r^2 + \mu)}}.$

Therefore integrating

$$\frac{r}{ae^{\theta \cot a}} = \left\{ \frac{\omega r^2 + c^2 + \sqrt{(\omega^2 r^4 + 2\omega c^2 r^2 + \mu)}}{\omega a^2} \right\}^{\frac{\operatorname{cosec} a}{2}},$$

the constants being inserted in this form for consistency of dimensions.

2. Explain the nature of the superficial tension between fluid surfaces in contact; and find the height to which liquid rises in a capillary tube.

Shew that the potential energy of the liquid produced by the capillary action is (to a first approximation) independent of the size of the tube.

A drop of oil is at rest in the midst of a liquid of the same density; assuming the form of its surface to be a surface of revolution, prove that it will assume the form of a sphere if either end of the axis be free in the surrounding liquid; but that, if both ends be held, it may assume a tubular form: and reduce to integration the equation of the surface.

(1) Let Z be the vertical capillary force, exerted on an unit length of the edge of the liquid in contact with the interior of the tube supposed vertical: let r be the radius of the tube, h the height to which the liquid rises in it, and ρ the density of the liquid.

Then
$$2\pi r Z = \pi r^2 h \cdot g\rho,$$

or
$$h = \frac{2Z}{g\rho} \cdot \frac{1}{r}.$$

The potential energy thus produced is measured by $\pi r^2 h \cdot g\rho \cdot \frac{1}{2}h$, for the mass, as a whole, has been raised to the height of its centre of gravity; hence the potential energy

$$= \tfrac{1}{2}\pi r^2 g\rho \frac{4Z^2}{g^2\rho^2} \cdot \frac{1}{r^2} = \frac{2\pi Z^2}{g\rho},$$

which is independent of r.

(2) Let P be the pressure in the oil at a given level, P' that in the surrounding liquid at same level; then the pressures at a depth z below this level are respectively $P + g\rho z$ and $P' + g\rho z$, where ρ is the density of the oil and liquid. Hence the resultant pressure outwards on the surface, per unit area, $= P - P'$ everywhere. Also if T be the surface tension of the oil in the liquid, the component of the surface tension inwards, per unit area,

$$= T\left(\frac{1}{\rho} + \frac{1}{\rho'}\right);$$

ρ, ρ' being the principal radii of curvature. The form of the surface is therefore given by

$$\frac{1}{\rho} + \frac{1}{\rho'} = \frac{P - P'}{T} = \text{a constant} = K \text{ (say).}$$

Now let the axis of revolution of the surface be that of z; let x be the perpendicular distance from this axis of a point on the surface, ϕ the angle between the normal at the point and the horizon, and s the length of the meridian-arc measured from the highest point of the surface: then

$$\rho = x \sec \phi,$$

$$\rho' = -\frac{ds}{d\phi} = -\frac{ds}{dx} \cdot \frac{dx}{d\phi} = -\frac{1}{\sin \phi} \frac{dx}{d\phi}.$$

Hence the above equation of equilibrium becomes

$$\frac{c}{x} + \frac{dc}{dx} = K, \quad \text{where } c = \cos \phi;$$

therefore the equation of the surface is

$$cx = \tfrac{1}{2} K x^2 + \text{constant}.$$

Now, if it be possible to have $x = 0$, that is if the axis of revolution cut the surface, the constant $= 0$; then

$$c = \tfrac{1}{2} K x.$$

Hence
$$\frac{dz}{dx} = \frac{c}{\sqrt{(1-c^2)}} = \frac{x}{\sqrt{(k^2 - x^2)}},$$

where
$$k = \frac{2}{K};$$

therefore $z - a = -\sqrt{(k^2 - x^2)}$, or $(z-a)^2 + x^2 = k^2$;

therefore the surface is a sphere.

In general we may write the equation of the surface in the form

$$cx = \frac{x^2 + b^2}{k}, \quad \text{where } b^2 = \frac{2 \, \text{constant}}{K},$$

which may be really negative.

Then
$$\frac{dz}{ds} = \frac{x^2 + b^2}{xk},$$

$$\frac{dz}{dx} = \frac{x^2 + b^2}{\{x^2 k^2 - (x^2 + b^2)^2\}^{\frac{1}{2}}}.$$

This may be written

$$\frac{dz}{dx} = \frac{x^2 + a_1 a_2}{\{(x^2 - a_1^2)(a_2^2 - x^2)\}^{\frac{1}{2}}},$$

where
$$a_1 a_2 = b^2, \quad a_1^2 + a_2^2 = k^2 - 2b^2.$$

This shews that the generating curve lies between the lines

$$x = a_1, \quad x = a_2.$$

Further
$$\frac{d^2z}{dx^2} = \frac{(a_1 + a_2)^2 (a_1 a_2 - x^2) x}{\{(x^2 - a_1^2)(a_2^2 - x^2)\}^{\frac{3}{2}}},$$

which shews that there are points of inflexion on the line $x = \sqrt{a_1 a_2} = b$. Hence the generating curve is undulatory, and the surface generated by it may be called tubular, since it may be described by a horizontal circle whose centre moves vertically, and whose radius alternately expands and contracts between the values a_1 and a_2.

The integral of the above equation is

$$z = \int \frac{(x^2 + a_1 a_2)\, dx}{\{(x^2 - a_1^2)(a_2^2 - x^2)\}^{\frac{1}{2}}},$$

which reduces to

$$z = a_1 F(c, \phi) + a_2 E(c, \phi),$$

where F and E are the elliptic integrals of the first and second kind, $c^2 = \dfrac{a_2^2 - a_1^2}{a_2^2}$, and $x^2 = a_1^2 \sin^2 \phi + a_2^2 \cos^2 \phi$.

[It is clear that the pressures at a given level in the oil and the surrounding liquid must be different, otherwise no curved surface of equilibrium could be possible except one belonging to the series of surfaces

$$\frac{1}{\rho} + \frac{1}{\rho'} = 0,$$

which are essentially anticlastic everywhere.

For a full discussion of this question, see Beer's *Elasticität und Capillarität* (1869), pp. 161 ff.]

3. *The potential due to any attracting masses cannot have a maximum or minimum value at any point of space unoccupied by matter.*

If in the midst of any attracting masses a closed surface be drawn, in some parts cutting the masses, and in some parts free, and be covered with a surface density ρ: and if V be the potential due to the attracting masses and this surface density, and U a function having arbitrary values at all points of the surface: then in order that $V - U$ may have a constant value for occupied parts of the surface and not have a less value at any other part of the surface, shew that if the whole quantity of matter on the surface be constant, its distribution must be such as to give

$$\iint (V - 2U)\, \rho\, \delta\sigma \text{ a minimum value.}$$

Hence, or otherwise, shew that Green's imaginary distribution (ρ) may be defined as a solution of the equation

$$\iint \frac{(-\rho)\delta\sigma}{r} = \text{a maximum},$$

subject to the condition that $\iint \rho \delta\sigma + 1 = 0$.

(1) This is virtually a proposition due to Gauss, *Werke*, Band v. pp. 232—234. See also Thomson and Tait's *Natural Philosophy*, pp. 410, 411. Gauss' method of proof may be thus applied to the question as stated.

Let $W = V - U$, and let A be the constant value which W is to have at occupied parts of the surface, the value of W at unoccupied parts being not $< A$. Also let $\Omega = \iint (V - 2U)\rho d\sigma$, so that

$$\delta\Omega = \iint \delta V \rho d\sigma + \iint (V - 2U)\delta\rho d\sigma,$$

where δ refers to any arbitrary variation of ρ. Suppose the distribution such that Ω is a minimum, and if possible let there then be two points on the occupied parts of the surface at which W is not $= A$: viz. at one point P let $W < A$, and at the other point Q let $W > A$: then at P, $W - A$ is negative, and at Q, $W - A$ is positive. This supposition may be justified by observing that, unless $W = A$ at all points of the occupied parts of the surface, W must have a minimum value at some point which may be taken as P and a maximum value at some other point which may be taken as Q; A being then some value between these maximum and minimum values, or, it may be, coinciding with one or other of them. In this latter case $W - A$ may be 0 at P or at Q, but the following proof will remain valid.

Now let the operation δ mean, alter the distribution arbitrarily by taking a quantity of matter $\delta\rho$ from round Q and place it round P: then $\iint (W - A)\delta\rho d\sigma$ is negative, for $\delta\rho = 0$ at all points except P and Q.

Also $\qquad \iint A \delta\rho d\sigma = A \iint \delta\rho d\sigma = 0;$

therefore adding we learn that

$$\iint W \delta\rho d\sigma \text{ is negative}.$$

Further, we have

$$\iint \delta V \rho d\sigma = \iint \rho d\sigma \left\{ \frac{\delta\rho}{r_P} - \frac{\delta\rho}{r_Q} \right\},$$

where r_P, r_Q denote the distances of P and Q from the element $d\sigma$.

Also, remembering that $\delta\rho = 0$ except at P and Q, we have

$$\iint V \delta\rho d\sigma = \iint \left\{ \frac{\rho}{r_P} \delta\rho - \frac{\rho}{r_Q} \delta\rho \right\} d\sigma.$$

Therefore, $\qquad \iint \delta V \rho d\sigma = \iint V \delta\rho d\sigma.$

Hence $\delta\Omega = 2\iint(V-U)\delta\rho\, d\sigma = 2\iint W\delta\rho\, d\sigma = $ a negative quantity.

By this arbitrary change therefore we can diminish Ω, i.e. the supposed distribution is not such that Ω is a minimum unless $W = A$ at all occupied parts of the surface.

A similar proof will apply, if $\dot{P}$ be a point on the unoccupied parts.

(2) Let us now take the particular case in which $U = -\dfrac{1}{r}$, (r being measured from a point E not on the surface,) and V is due only to the mass distributed on the surface.

Then $W = V - U$ is the potential due to the mass on the surface and an unit mass at E. If then the distribution over the surface is to be such as to make it an equipotential surface for the potential W, W is to be constant, and therefore by the proposition, Ω is to be a minimum, i.e.

$$\iint\left(V + \frac{2}{r}\right)\rho\, d\sigma = \text{a minimum.}$$

Now Green's (ρ) (*Mathematical Papers of the late George Green*, p. 32) refers to the distribution over a surface joined to earth produced by an unit mass at E: therefore in his case $W = 0$ over the surface, i.e. $V = -\dfrac{1}{r}$ over the surface. This gives $\iint\dfrac{(\rho)\, d\sigma}{r} = $ a minimum, or $-\iint\dfrac{(\rho)\, d\sigma}{r} = $ a maximum, (ρ) being a negative quantity restricted by

$$\iint(\rho)\, d\sigma + 1 = 0.$$

iv. Investigate the expression for a tesseral surface harmonic; also find the integral of the square of a tesseral harmonic over the surface of the unit sphere.

If the general expression for a tesseral harmonic be of the form

$$A(1-\mu^2)^{\frac{m}{2}} \vartheta^{(m)}_n \cos m\phi,$$

where the coefficient of the highest power of μ in $\vartheta^{(m)}_n$ is unity, prove that

$$\vartheta^{(m)}_{n+1} = \mu\vartheta^{(m)}_n - \frac{n^2 - m^2}{4n^2 - 1}\vartheta^{(m)}_{n-1}.$$

In Todhunter's treatise on the functions of Laplace, Lamé and Bessel, Art. 150, we find the following expression for the part of the tesseral harmonic depending on μ,

$$(\mu^2 - 1)^{\frac{m}{2}} \vartheta^{(m)}_n = \frac{2^n}{\pi} \frac{(m+n)!\,(m-n)!}{(2n)!} \int_0^\pi \{\mu + \sqrt{(\mu^2-1)}\cos\psi\}^n \cos m\psi\, d\psi.$$

Let us write $u_n = \int_0^\pi (\mu + \sqrt{(\mu^2-1)}\cos\psi)^n \cos m\psi\, d\psi$,

and put $M = \mu + \sqrt{(\mu^2-1)}\cos\psi$,

and let us find the relation between u_{n+1}, u_n, u_{n-1}. It is clear that this relation will lead to the corresponding one for (ϑ), since m is the same for all three.

$$u_{n+1} = \int_0^\pi M^{n+1} \cos m\psi\, d\psi,$$

and, integrating by parts,

$$= \frac{n+1}{m}\int_0^\pi M^n \sqrt{(\mu^2-1)} \sin\psi \sin m\psi\, d\psi,$$

and, integrating again by parts,

$$= \frac{n+1}{m^2}\int \cos m\psi \left\{ \sqrt{(\mu^2-1)} \cos\psi\, M^n - n(\mu^2-1)\sin^2\psi\, M^{n-1} \right\} d\psi.$$

Now $\sqrt{(\mu^2-1)}\cos\psi = M - \mu$,

$(\mu^2-1)\sin^2\psi = 2\mu M - M^2 - 1$.

Substituting these values, we obtain

$$u_{n+1} = \frac{(n+1)^2}{m^2} u_{n+1} - \frac{(2n+1)(n+1)}{m^2}\mu u_n + \frac{n(n+1)}{m^2} u_{n-1},$$

whence

$$(n+1+m)(n+1-m) u_{n+1} + (2n+1)(n+1)\mu u_n - n(n+1) u_{n-1} = 0.$$

Replacing $u_{n+1} \ldots$ by the corresponding expressions in (ϑ), and rejecting the common factor $(\mu^2-1)^{\frac{m}{2}}\pi$ and other common factors, we obtain the relation in the problem

$$\vartheta_{n+1}^{(m)} - \mu\, \vartheta_n^{(m)} + \frac{n^2-m^2}{4n^2-1} \vartheta_{n-1}^{(m)} = 0.$$

For the purpose of obtaining the relations of this sort, the expressions in terms of definite integrals are extremely convenient.

[The result may also be obtained by starting from the known equations

$$(n+1) P_{n+1} + n P_{n-1} = (2n+1)\mu P_n,$$

$$P_{n+1} - P_{n-1} = (2n+1)\int_0^\mu P_n\, d\mu.$$

Differentiating both of these m times and eliminating $\dfrac{d^{m-1}P_n}{d\mu^{m-1}}$, the result follows at once by means of the general relation

$$(1-\mu^2)^{\frac{1}{2}m}\cos m\phi \,\frac{d^m P_n}{d\mu^m} = \frac{2.4.6\ldots 2n}{2n(2n-1)\ldots(n-m+1)}\, S_n^{(m)}.]$$

V. Obtain the equations of motion of a vibrating string, and explain the reflection of a wave at a fixed end.

A string is stretched between two points, and, being displaced from equilibrium, is allowed to vibrate; prove that it will subsequently consist of three straight parts, of which the middle part preserves a constant direction, and the two end parts are constantly parallel to one or other of the initial directions of the string.

Find also how the points of intersection will run along the string.

The method of determining the vibrations of a plucked string AB is explained in Lord Rayleigh's Treatise on Sound, Art. 146. Two infinite trains of waves start to move along AB in opposite directions with velocities which are each equal to c, the velocity of transmission of sound along the string. The waves are initially coincident, and the displacement at right angles to AB in any point of either is initially half that in the string; and the lengths of the waves are each double AB. The initial position of either train is shewn in fig. (66). At any subsequent time, the form of the string will be found by adding the displacements in AB due to these two waves. The one which moves in the direction AB may be called the positive wave, the other the negative wave.

We shall consider the changes which take place in half a period, these being simply reflected in the other half; and shall divide this time into three intervals corresponding to the times when CD in the positive wave crosses B, and when CD in the negative wave crosses A. Let $AD = a$, $BD = b$, $CD = h$, and suppose $a > b$.

(1) In the first interval, the string will consist of three pieces, of which the first is formed by the superposition of two lines parallel to AC, and whose equation is therefore $y = \dfrac{2h}{a}x$; and similarly the last piece will be given by $y = \dfrac{2h}{b}(a+b-x)$. The middle piece will be the result of superposing a line parallel to AC and a line parallel to BC: its equation will therefore be of the form $y = h\left(\dfrac{1}{a} - \dfrac{1}{b}\right)x + $ function of t.

(2) In the second interval, that is from $t = \dfrac{b}{c}$ to $t = \dfrac{a}{c}$, both the end

pieces are evidently parallel to $y = \dfrac{2h}{a} x$; and the middle piece, being still compounded of two waves one of which is parallel to AC and the other to BC, will still have an equation of the form

$$y = h \left(\dfrac{1}{a} - \dfrac{1}{b} \right) x + \text{function of } t.$$

(3) From $t = \dfrac{a}{c}$ to $t = \dfrac{a+b}{c}$, the part $c_1 c_2$ of the positive wave is passing over A, and the part cc' of the negative wave is also passing over it; hence through this interval the form of the string at A is $y = \dfrac{-2h}{b} x$. The form of another portion through B, being derived from two waves parallel to AC, will have, for its equation, $y = 2\dfrac{h}{a}\{x - (a + b)\}$. The intermediate portion will be compounded of a line parallel to AC and a line parallel to BC, and its equation will therefore be still of the form $y = h \left(\dfrac{1}{a} - \dfrac{1}{b} \right) x + \text{function of } t$.

These results coincide with the statements in the first part of the question.

To solve the latter part, let (fig. 67) AEB be the initial position of the string, and let the parallelogram $AEBE'$ be completed.

Consider any position of the string $APQB$ in the first interval; in this interval, the middle portion of the string is made up of the lines

$$y = \dfrac{h}{a} (x - ct)$$

$$y = \dfrac{h}{b} \{a + b - (x + ct)\}.$$

Its equation is, therefore,

$$y = h \left\{ \dfrac{a+b}{b} + x \left(\dfrac{1}{a} - \dfrac{1}{b} \right) - ct \left(\dfrac{1}{a} + \dfrac{1}{b} \right) \right\},$$

and the intersections of this line with AE, EB are given, respectively, by

$$x_1 = b - ct, \quad x_2 = b + ct.$$

The velocities of P and Q are therefore uniform, and their components along AB are each $= c$.

The same result obviously holds during the second and third intervals.

P and Q therefore run round the parallelogram $AEBE'$, in opposite directions, with velocities whose components along AB are constantly equal, numerically, to c.

6. In the case of sound waves travelling along in a straight tube of finite length without change of type, prove that nodes and loops occur at equal intervals.

If the tube be of infinite length and adiathermanous and no conduction of heat take place through the air, prove that the equations of motion may be accurately satisfied by supposing a wave of condensation to travel along the tube with a velocity of transmission which at each point depends only on the condensation at that point, and which for a density ρ is

$$\sqrt{\frac{p_0 \gamma}{\rho_0}} \left[1 + \frac{\gamma+1}{\gamma-1} \left\{ \left(\frac{\rho}{\rho_0}\right)^{\frac{\gamma-1}{2}} - 1 \right\} \right],$$

where p_0, ρ_0 are the pressure and density at each end of the wave, and γ is the ratio of the specific heat of air at constant pressure to its specific heat at constant volume.

Explain the consequent tendency to a bore in the fore part of such a wave, and the gradual prolongation of its front.

This result and its explanation were given by the Rev. S. Earnshaw in the *Philosophical Transactions* for 1860, Vol. 150, pp. 137, 144 ff. See also Lord Rayleigh's *Sound*, Vol. II. Arts. 250—252.

The result may also be obtained as follows. Let the axis of the tube be taken as the axis of x and let u be the particle-velocity at time t at a point whose abscissa is x. Then by the equation of continuity,

$$\frac{d\rho}{dt} + \frac{d}{dx}(\rho u) = 0 \quad \ldots \ldots \ldots \ldots \ldots \ldots \ldots \ldots (1).$$

Also if $\phi'(\rho)$ be the velocity of transmission of the wave of condensation for a density ρ, which is the density of the *wave* of condensation which we are following, and which is occupying the place x at time t, we have, because this ρ remains unaltered,

$$0 = \delta\rho = \frac{d\rho}{dx}\delta x + \frac{d\rho}{dt}\delta t, \quad \text{and } \frac{dx}{dt} = \phi'(\rho),$$

therefore
$$\frac{d\rho}{dt} + \phi'(\rho)\frac{d\rho}{dx} = 0 \quad \ldots \ldots \ldots \ldots \ldots \ldots \ldots \ldots (2).$$

From (1) and (2) we obtain

$$\frac{d(\rho u)}{dx} = \phi'(\rho)\frac{d\rho}{dx},$$

therefore
$$\rho u = \phi(\rho), \quad u = \frac{\phi(\rho)}{\rho}.$$

Now the equation of variation of pressure is

$$\frac{1}{\rho}\frac{dp}{dx} = -\frac{du}{dt} - u\frac{du}{dx},$$

therefore $\dfrac{1}{\rho} \cdot \dfrac{dp}{d\rho} \cdot \dfrac{d\rho}{dx} = -\dfrac{du}{d\rho} \cdot \dfrac{d\rho}{dt} - u\dfrac{du}{d\rho} \cdot \dfrac{d\rho}{dx}$

$$= \frac{du}{d\rho} \cdot \frac{d(\rho u)}{d\rho} \cdot \frac{d\rho}{dx} - u\frac{du}{d\rho} \cdot \frac{d\rho}{dx} \text{ by (1)},$$

therefore $\dfrac{1}{\rho} \cdot \dfrac{dp}{d\rho} = \dfrac{du}{d\rho} \cdot \rho\dfrac{du}{d\rho}$, therefore $\dfrac{1}{\rho^2}\dfrac{dp}{d\rho} = \left(\dfrac{du}{d\rho}\right)^2$ ....(3).

Now $\dfrac{p}{p_0} = \left(\dfrac{\rho}{\rho_0}\right)^\gamma$, or $p = A\rho^\gamma$ where $A = \dfrac{p_0}{\rho_0^\gamma}$.

Hence (3) gives

$$A\gamma\rho^{\gamma-3} = \left(\frac{du}{d\rho}\right)^2,$$

therefore $u = \dfrac{2\sqrt{(A\gamma)}}{\gamma - 1}\{\rho^{\frac{\gamma-1}{2}} - \rho_0^{\frac{\gamma-1}{2}}\},$

therefore $\phi(\rho) = \dfrac{2\rho\sqrt{(A\gamma)}}{\gamma - 1}\{\rho^{\frac{\gamma-1}{2}} - \rho_0^{\frac{\gamma-1}{2}}\},$

therefore $\phi'(\rho) = \dfrac{2\sqrt{(A\gamma)}}{\gamma - 1}\left\{\dfrac{\gamma+1}{2}\rho^{\frac{\gamma-1}{2}} - \rho_0^{\frac{\gamma-1}{2}}\right\}$

$$= \sqrt{\left(\frac{p_0\gamma}{\rho_0}\right)} \cdot \left\{\frac{\gamma+1}{\gamma-1}\left(\frac{\rho}{\rho_0}\right)^{\frac{\gamma-1}{2}} - \frac{2}{\gamma-1}\right\}$$

$$= \sqrt{\left(\frac{p_0\gamma}{\rho_0}\right)} \cdot \left[1 + \frac{\gamma+1}{\gamma-1}\left\{\left(\frac{\rho}{\rho_0}\right)^{\frac{\gamma-1}{2}} - 1\right\}\right].$$

7. Define the tortuosity of a curve, and flexual rigidities of a wire. Prove that if one end of a wire originally straight and of equal flexibility in all directions be held fixed, and a couple G be applied at the other end round an axis inclined at an angle θ to its length, the wire assumes the form of a helix on a cylinder of radius $\dfrac{B \sin \theta}{G}$, where B is the rigidity of flexure of the wire.

If A be the rigidity of torsion of a wire originally straight, which is twisted and strained and then has its ends fastened together so that it assumes the form of an endless spiral round a tubular core: shew that the stress at every point of the spiral is always perpendicular to some one plane, and $= A\dfrac{T}{2Q}$, where T is the integral twist of the wire, and Q the area enclosed by its projection on this plane.

It appears from symmetry that the axis of the tubular core or ring round which the wire appears to be spirally coiled, lies more or less in one plane and is of a more or less circular form round a centre. Take this plane as that of xy and this centre, O, as the origin.

Then at any point x, y, z, the direction-cosines of the tangent are

$$\frac{dx}{ds}, \frac{dy}{ds}, \frac{dz}{ds};$$

and if ρ, τ be the radii of curvature and of torsion at this point, the direction-cosines of the normal to the osculating plane there will be

$$\rho\left\{\frac{dy}{ds}\cdot\frac{d^2z}{ds^2}-\frac{dz}{ds}\cdot\frac{d^2y}{ds^2}\right\}, \rho\left\{\frac{dz}{ds}\cdot\frac{d^2x}{ds^2}-\frac{dx}{ds}\cdot\frac{d^2z}{ds^2}\right\}, \rho\left\{\frac{dx}{ds}\cdot\frac{d^2y}{ds^2}-\frac{dy}{ds}\cdot\frac{d^2x}{ds^2}\right\},$$

which we shall denote by λ, μ, ν.

Let the components of the stress at the point be X, Y, Z.

Then, since no external forces act on the wire, the components of the couples round the axes due to the curvature, the twist and the stress at any point must be constant throughout the wire. Call these components L, M, N; and we have

$$L = \frac{B}{\rho}\lambda + A\tau\frac{dx}{ds} + yZ - zY,$$

$$M = \frac{B}{\rho}\mu + A\tau\frac{dy}{ds} + zX - xZ,$$

$$N = \frac{B}{\rho}\nu + A\tau\frac{dz}{ds} + xY - yX.$$

Let F, H be two points in which the wire cuts successively the plane xy, F being further from O than H, so that a point moving along FH would at first rise to the positive side of this plane, then for a moment move parallel to the plane at a point G, and afterwards drop towards the plane again till H: and throughout FGH the point will approach O.

Let the axis of x pass through F, and let $OF = a$, $OH = b$.

Then, at F, by symmetry, $\dfrac{dx}{ds} = 0$, $\dfrac{dy}{ds} = \cos\alpha$ (say), therefore

$$\frac{dz}{ds} = \sin\alpha, \quad \lambda = 0, \quad \mu = -\sin\alpha, \quad \nu = \cos\alpha.$$

Hence the above equations become at F, if suffixes be used to restrict the quantities to their values at F,

$$L = 0,$$

$$M = -\frac{B}{\rho_F}\sin\alpha + A\tau_F\cos\alpha - aZ_F,$$

$$N = \frac{B}{\rho_F}\cos\alpha + A\tau_F\sin\alpha + aY_F.$$

Now let F' be the point in which the wire after H next cuts the plane xy. Its co-ordinates are $a\cos\dfrac{2\pi}{n}$, $a\sin\dfrac{2\pi}{n}$, 0, if n be the total number of turns of the wire.

The direction-cosines of its tangent are

$$-\cos a \sin\frac{2\pi}{n}, \quad \cos a \cos\frac{2\pi}{n}, \quad \sin a;$$

and those of the normal to its osculating plane are

$$\sin a \sin\frac{2\pi}{n}, \quad -\sin a \cos\frac{2\pi}{n}, \quad \cos a.$$

Also the stress at F'' is, by symmetry, the same as that at F; hence at F'

$$X_{F'} = X_F \cos\frac{2\pi}{n} - Y_F \sin\frac{2\pi}{n},$$

$$Y_{F'} = X_F \sin\frac{2\pi}{n} + Y_F \cos\frac{2\pi}{n},$$

$$Z_{F'} = Z_F.$$

Thus the general equations become at F',

$$0 = \frac{B}{\rho_F} \sin a \sin\frac{2\pi}{n} - A\tau_F \cos a \sin\frac{2\pi}{n} + a\sin\frac{2\pi}{n} Z_F,$$

$$M = -\frac{B}{\rho_F} \sin a \cos\frac{2\pi}{n} + A\tau_F \cos a \cos\frac{2\pi}{n} - a\cos\frac{2\pi}{n} Z_F,$$

$$N = \frac{B}{\rho_F} \cos a + A\tau_F \sin a + aY_F:$$

and it is plain that similar equations hold when $\dfrac{4\pi}{n}$ or $\dfrac{6\pi}{n}$ &c. are written for $\dfrac{2\pi}{n}$.

The two first equations shew that

$$-\frac{B}{\rho_F} \sin a + A\tau_F \cos a = aZ_F, \quad M = 0.$$

But, considering the equilibrium of a length FP of the wire, and resolving along the axes, we obtain

$$X_P = X_F, \quad Y_P = Y_F, \quad Z_P = Z_F;$$

and, if we take P at P', and combine with these equations the values of $X_{P'}$ and $Y_{P'}$ in terms of X_P and Y_P written above, we find that $X_P = 0$, $Y_P = 0$; and therefore

$$X_P = 0, \quad Y_P = 0, \quad Z_P = -\frac{1}{a}\left\{\frac{B}{\rho_P}\sin a - A\tau_P \cos a\right\} = \text{constant},$$

which proves that the stress at every point of the spiral is always perpendicular to the plane xy.

Further, our original equations now become

$$0 = \frac{B}{\rho}\lambda + A\tau\frac{dx}{ds} + yZ,$$

$$0 = \frac{B}{\rho}\mu + A\tau\frac{dy}{ds} - xZ,$$

$$N = \frac{B}{\rho}\nu + A\tau\frac{dz}{ds}.$$

Multiplying by $\frac{dx}{ds}$, $\frac{dy}{ds}$, $\frac{dz}{ds}$, and adding, we have

$$N\frac{dz}{ds} = A\tau + Z\left(y\frac{dx}{ds} - x\frac{dy}{ds}\right).$$

Integrating round the spiral, we obtain

$$A\int \tau ds = N[z]_0^0 + Z\int\left(x\frac{dy}{ds} - y\frac{dx}{ds}\right),$$

or $\qquad AT = Z(2Q);$

therefore $\qquad Z = \dfrac{AT}{2Q}.$

viii. If a number of sets of elastic spheres be moving in any space under the action of a system of conservative forces, determine the conditions to be satisfied when the distribution has become permanent, and state any conclusions which can be drawn from the result.

If the containing vessel move uniformly along a screw, prove that a permanent distribution will also take place, and that the pressure in the fluid will be the same as if it were acted on by a centrifugal force from the axis of the screw in addition to the other forces of the system.

See review of Watson's *Kinetic Theory of Gases*, by Prof. Maxwell, in *Nature*, Vol. XVI., p. 244, (July 26, 1877.)

ix. Define the thermometric parameters (α, β, γ) of a confocal system, and prove that, if α be the parameter corresponding to an ellipsoid which lies in an electric field, the surface integral of electric induction over any portion of it is of the form

$$\iint \frac{dV}{d\alpha} \psi\,(\beta,\,\gamma)\,d\beta\,d\gamma,$$

where V is the potential at any point due to the electricity: and deduce from this result the transformation of Laplace's equation to ellipsoidal co-ordinates.

If δv be the conical volume which an element of the ellipsoid round any point P subtends at its centre, v the whole volume of the ellipsoid, prove that $\dfrac{\int V dv}{v}$ is the same for all confocal ellipsoids which enclose no electricity; and that the value of this expression for any ellipsoid (a, b, c) which encloses all the electricity is

$$\tfrac{1}{2} E \int_0^\infty \frac{d\lambda}{\sqrt{(a^2+\lambda)(b^2+\lambda)(c^2+\lambda)}},$$

where E is the total quantity of electricity in the field.

The result in the first part of the question is the same as that given in Maxwell's *Electricity and Magnetism*, Vol. I. Art. 148, wherein it is shewn that

$$R_1 ds_2 ds_3 = \frac{dV}{d\alpha} \cdot \frac{D_1^2}{c}\, d\beta\, d\gamma \quad\ldots\ldots\ldots\ldots\ldots\ldots (1),$$

the meaning of the symbols being there explained. We observe that the surface induction $= \iint R_1 ds_2 ds_3$, and that $D_1^2 = \lambda_2^2 - \lambda_3^2$, of which λ_2 is a function of β only and λ_3 of γ only.

To prove the second part of the question, we may also express the above result in the form

$$\iint R_1 ds_2 ds_3 = -\iint \frac{dV}{d\alpha} \frac{c}{D_2 D_3}\, dS \quad\ldots\ldots\ldots\ldots\ldots (2),$$

where dS is an element of the surface of the ellipsoid, and D_2, D_3 are the semiaxes of the central section parallel to dS, c is defined by the condition that the confocal system is

$$\frac{x^2}{\lambda^2} + \frac{y^2}{\lambda^2 - b^2} + \frac{z^2}{\lambda^2 - c^2} = 1,$$

and $c > b$.

It is obvious, from these two forms of the surface induction, that it may be also written in the third form

$$\iint R_1 ds_2 ds_3 = -\frac{d}{da}\left(\iint V \cdot \frac{c}{D_2 \overline{D_3}} dS\right) \quad \text{(3)}.$$

If p be the perpendicular on the tangent plane to the ellipsoid,

$$pD_2 D_3 = a'b'c', \quad \tfrac{1}{3}p\,dS = dv \text{ and } v = \tfrac{4}{3}\pi a'b'c',$$

where $a'b'c'$ are the semiaxes of the ellipsoid (a).

We may therefore transform (3) into

$$\iint R_1 ds_2 ds_3 = -4\pi c \frac{d}{da}\left(\frac{\iint V dv}{v}\right) \quad \text{(4)}.$$

If the ellipsoid enclose no attracting matter, $\iint R_1 ds_2 ds_3 = 0$,

therefore
$$\frac{\iint V dv}{v} = \text{const.} \quad \text{(A)}.$$

If the ellipsoid enclose all the attracting matter E,

$$\iint R_1 ds_2 ds_3 = -4\pi E,$$

hence
$$E a = c \cdot \frac{\iint V dv}{v} \quad \text{(5)},$$

where a is supposed to vanish when $\lambda = \infty$, and where therefore $V = 0$.

But
$$a = \int_{a'}^{\infty} \frac{c\,d\lambda}{\sqrt{\{(\lambda^2 - b^2)(\lambda^2 - c^2)\}}},$$

and
$$b'^2 = a'^2 - b^2, \quad c'^2 = a'^2 - c^2.$$

If, therefore, we put

$$\lambda^2 = \lambda_1 + a'^2, \quad \lambda^2 - b^2 = \lambda_1 + b'^2, \quad \lambda^2 - c^2 = \lambda_1 + c'^2,$$

and the above integral becomes

$$a = \frac{c}{2} \cdot \int_0^{\infty} \frac{d\lambda_1}{\sqrt{\{(a'^2 + \lambda_1)(b'^2 + \lambda_1)(c'^2 + \lambda_1)\}}},$$

and therefore

$$\int \frac{Vdv}{v} = \tfrac{1}{2} E \int_0^\infty \frac{d\lambda}{\sqrt{\{(a'^2+\lambda)(b'^2+\lambda)(c'^2+\lambda)\}}}, \quad \ldots\ldots\ldots\ldots\ldots\text{(B)},$$

$a'b'c'$ being the semiaxes of the ellipsoid.

By supposing the ellipsoid a sphere, we obtain Gauss' Theorem.

[The integral in the question may be reduced to the standard form

$$\frac{2}{\sqrt{(a^2-c^2)}} F\left\{\cos^{-1}\frac{c}{a},\ \sqrt{\left(\frac{a^2-b^2}{a^2-c^2}\right)}\right\},$$

as on p. 111.]

MATHEMATICAL WORKS.

BY PROF. BOOLE, D.C.L., F.R.S.

DIFFERENTIAL EQUATIONS. Third and Revised Edition. Edited by I. TODHUNTER. Crown 8vo. 14s. Supplementary Volume. Edited by I. TODHUNTER. 8s. 6d.

THE CALCULUS OF FINITE DIFFERENCES. Crown 8vo. 10s. 6d. New Edition, revised by J. F. MOULTON.

CAMBRIDGE SENATE-HOUSE PROBLEMS AND RIDERS WITH SOLUTIONS:—
1875—PROBLEMS AND RIDERS. By A. G. GREENHILL, M.A. Crown 8vo. 8s. 6d.

THE ELEMENTS OF DYNAMIC. An Introduction to the Study of Motion and Rest in Solid and Fluid Bodies. By W. K. CLIFFORD, F.R.S., Professor of Applied Mathematics and Mechanics at University College, London. PART I. KINETIC. Crown 8vo. 7s. 6d.

AN INTRODUCTION TO THE THEORY OF ELECTRICITY. By LINNÆUS CUMMING, M.A., one of the Masters of Rugby School. With Illustrations. Crown 8vo. 8s. 6d.

GEOMETRICAL TREATISE ON CONIC SECTIONS. By W. H. DREW, M.A., St John's College, Cambridge. New Edition, enlarged. Crown 8vo. 5s. Solutions, 4s. 6d.

BY THE REV. N. M. FERRERS, M.A.

AN ELEMENTARY TREATISE ON TRILINEAR CO-ORDINATES, the Method of Reciprocal Polars, and the Theory of Projectors. New Edition, revised. Crown 8vo. 6s. 6d.

AN ELEMENTARY TREATISE ON SPHERICAL HARMONICS, AND SUBJECTS CONNECTED WITH THEM. Crown 8vo. 7s. 6d.

ELEMENTS OF THE METHOD OF LEAST SQUARES. By MANSFIELD MERRIMAN, Ph.D., Professor of Civil and Mechanical Engineering, Lehigh University, Bethlehem, Penn. Crown 8vo. 7s. 6d.

ELEMENTS OF DESCRIPTIVE GEOMETRY. By J. B. MILLAR, C.E., Assistant Lecturer in Engineering in Owens College, Manchester. Crown 8vo. 6s.

BY S. PARKINSON, D.D., F.R.S.

AN ELEMENTARY TREATISE ON MECHANICS. With a Collection of Examples. New Edition, revised. Crown 8vo. 9s. 6d.

A TREATISE ON OPTICS. New Edition, revised and enlarged. Crown 8vo. 10s. 6d.

ELEMENTARY HYDROSTATICS. With numerous Examples. By J. B. PHEAR, M.A., Fellow and late Assistant Tutor of Clare College, Cambridge. New Edition. Crown 8vo. 5s. 6d.

MACMILLAN AND CO., LONDON.

MATHEMATICAL WORKS (*continued*).

LESSONS ON RIGID DYNAMICS. By the Rev. G. PIRIE, M.A., Fellow and Tutor of Queens' College, Cambridge. Crown 8vo. 6s.

AN ELEMENTARY TREATISE ON CONIC SECTIONS AND ALGEBRAIC GEOMETRY. By G. H. PUCKLE, M.A. New Edition, revised and enlarged. Crown 8vo. 7s. 6d.

BY E. J. ROUTH, M.A., F.R.S.

AN ELEMENTARY TREATISE ON THE DYNAMICS OF THE SYSTEM OF RIGID BODIES. With numerous Examples. Third and enlarged Edition. 8vo. 21s.

STABILITY OF A GIVEN STATE OF MOTION, PARTICULARLY STEADY MOTION. Adams Prize Essay for 1877. 8vo. 8s. 6d.

A TREATISE ON DYNAMICS OF A PARTICLE. With numerous Examples. By Professor TAIT and Mr STEELE. Fourth Edition, revised and enlarged. Crown 8vo. 12s.

BY I. TODHUNTER, M.A., F.R.S.

ALGEBRA. For the use of Colleges and Schools. New Edition. Crown 8vo. 7s. 6d. KEY. 10s. 6d.

AN ELEMENTARY TREATISE ON THE THEORY OF EQUATIONS. New Edition, revised. Crown 8vo. 7s. 6d.

PLANE TRIGONOMETRY. For Schools and Colleges. New Edition. Crown 8vo. 5s. KEY. 10s. 6d.

SPHERICAL TRIGONOMETRY. New Edition. Crown 8vo. 4s. 6d.

PLANE CO-ORDINATE GEOMETRY, as applied to the Straight Line and the Conic Sections. With numerous Examples. New Edition. Crown 8vo. 7s. 6d.

THE DIFFERENTIAL CALCULUS. With numerous Examples. New Edition. Crown 8vo. 10s. 6d.

THE INTEGRAL CALCULUS AND ITS APPLICATIONS. With numerous Examples. New Edition. Crown 8vo. 10s. 6d.

EXAMPLES OF ANALYTICAL GEOMETRY OF THREE DIMENSIONS. New Edition, revised. Crown 8vo. 4s.

ANALYTICAL STATICS. With numerous Examples. New Edition. Crown 8vo. 10s. 6d.

MATHEMATICAL PROBLEMS, on Subjects included in the First and Second Divisions of the Schedule of Subjects for the Cambridge Mathematical Tripos Examination. Devised and arranged by JOSEPH WOLSTENHOLME, late Fellow of Christ's College, sometime Fellow of St John's College, and Professor of Mathematics in the Royal Indian Engineering College. New Edition, greatly enlarged. 8vo. 18s.

MACMILLAN AND CO., LONDON.

www.ingramcontent.com/pod-product-compliance
Lightning Source LLC
Chambersburg PA
CBHW020804230426
43666CB00007B/841